THIS BUSINESS OF
URBAN MUSIC

A Practical Guide to Achieving Success in the Industry, from Gospel to Funk to R&B to Hip-Hop

JAMES L. WALKER, JR., ESQ.

BILLBOARD BOOKS

AN IMPRINT OF WATSON-GUPTILL PUBLICATIONS
NEW YORK

Executive Editor: Bob Nirkind
Project Editor: Ross Plotkin
Production Manager: Salvatore Destro
Series Interior Designer: Lorraine Patsco
Jacket Design by Timothy Hsu
The principal typefaces used in the composition of this book were Janson Text and Frutiger Condensed

First published in 2008 by Billboard Books,
An imprint of Watson-Guptill Publications,
Nielsen Business Media,
a division of The Nielsen Company,
770 Broadway, New York, NY 10003
www.watsonguptill.com

Library of Congress Control Number: 2007933753

ISBN-13: 978-0-8230-7758-8
ISBN-10: 0-8230-7758-6

Printed in the United States

First printing, 2008

1 2 3 4 5 6 7 8 9 / 16 15 14 13 12 11 10 09 08

CONTENTS

PART I

THE SIGNING OF AGREEMENTS AND BUILDING THE TEAM

CHAPTER 1

Introduction and Overview

"In the music industry, you come along and make your contribution; then it's someone else's turn."

—FORMER MOTOWN CHAIRMAN CLARENCE AVANT,
OWNER OF AVANT PUBLISHING AND CONSIDERED BY
MANY TO BE THE GODFATHER OF THE MUSIC INDUSTRY

In 2005, urban music accounted for over 25 percent of all record sales in the music industry. Artists like 50 Cent, Kirk Franklin, Ciara, Destiny's Child, Jay-Z, and Hezekiah Walker are selling millions of records. Encompassing gospel music, "black" music, R&B, and hip-hop, *urban music* has dominated the *Billboard* charts. However, even with the success of urban music, Shawn "Jay-Z" Carter recently told the *New York Times* that there are only ten guys in the rap game really making money. I remember speaking to gospel star Donnie McClurkin and informing him that the gospel industry probably did not even have five gospel artists who were millionaires. In essence, although the music is selling millions and grossing billions, the urban artist and his or her supporting role players—i.e., producers, managers, agents, publicists, and yes, attorneys—are not all financially reaping the benefits of this rapid growth. In this book, we set out to discuss the urban music scene and provide a comprehensive understanding of the business behind the genre.

Black artists are owning labels, running production companies, and signing long-term recording contracts. Hip-hop has become the pulse of America. Gospel music has been its inspirational cousin in *urban America*, simultaneously showing up in McDonald's ads, on movie soundtracks, and even on *Soul Train*. Labels have shifted their focus from solely niche marketing to announcing the creation of divisions like Sony's Urban Music. But, even with this growth, expansion, and branding into mainstream, as Carter so eloquently reminded us, the urban artist (whether hip-hop or gospel), is still struggling financially.

Several years ago, I had heard some of my own clients talking about the difficulties of being a major artist in the public eye, yet privately still financially struggling and not really understanding how the music business worked. I was surprised at how many clients had sold millions of records but never read a royalty statement. Most had either never read or never understood their own recording contract. Some had even executed songwriter publishing agreements that gave away an interest in their copyrights but had no idea what it really meant from a *business* standpoint as an urban artist.

It was at this time that I started pulling together my notes and thoughts for a book that would introduce these artists, producers, managers, and urban music industry enthusiasts to the "business" known as the music industry. After typing up a short outline, and months of drafts and redrafts with the help of my editors, this book is the final project of a long journey of outlines, research, and dozens of interviews.

These interviews took me back to when I started in the music industry in 1989, booking and promoting shows in the Washington, DC area. These shows featured Phyllis Hyman, Stephanie Mills, and later Yolanda Adams. I recall sitting with Phyllis Hyman at Blues Alley in Washington and having *her* tell *me* how important it was "for artists to get paid." "If you pay people and take care of people, you will be in this industry a long time," said the forty-something-year-old artist to the twenty-year-old pre-law Howard college kid. We sat for a while at a bar where she and her road manager, Larry Kendricks, shared with me how many artists were financially struggling and had to resort to gigging week-to-week to make ends meet and survive in the business.

Following the event with Hyman, I worked more and more in the industry. The longer I stayed in the game, the more enjoyable and exciting it became and the more I wanted to learn about it. Sadly, the more I learned about it, the more disappointed I became. I discovered that black artists had been exploited and taken advantage of for over fifty years, starting in the days of blues, jazz, and rock 'n' roll, and continuing to present-day R&B, gospel, and hip-hop.

For example, if ten rappers are making a decent living, or *living the life*, as they say in their bling-bling videos, I would estimate that only four to five gospel artists could say the same. Very few gospel artists could take two years off, go to Africa, and take care of themselves and their families from a financial standpoint. Even though it is a billion-dollar industry, the gospel industry still lags behind the overall urban community in terms of budgets, payment, and performance fees.

Practicing law for nearly fifteen years now, and being in the music industry for almost two decades, I've heard horror story after horror story of black artists signing away their publishing income (i.e., the royalties you make as a songwriter), turning over their recording masters to a label for little or no money, hiring bad management, or simply not understanding the importance of the word *business* in the term "music business." Thus, I wrote this book in the hopes of enlightening the next generation eagerly awaiting a career in the music industry; I also wrote it to wake up the uneducated artist who is already a member of this club.

With an eye toward the process of breaking into and surviving in this business of urban music, we've divided the book into four parts: Part I: The Signing of Agreements and Building the Team; Part II: Corporate Matters: Running the Label; Part III: The Song Copyrights: It's All about the Benjamins; and Part IV: Marketing and Other Helpful Tips.

First, as an attorney, I've always taught my clients and anyone else who would listen that empowerment was very important. By empowerment, I suggested clients own their songs, limit their album commitments, and definitely prepare for the future. Recording contracts are so critical to the artist first breaking into the business and later for his own empowerment; therefore, I start the book with a detailed chapter called Getting and Signing a Recording Contract and provide an understanding of the legal ramifications of such signing. This is a very technical chapter, but if you are an artist or plan to be an artist in the music industry, please read this chapter once, twice, and even a third time to understand the most critical document you might sign.

A few years ago, I watched Tavis Smiley conduct an informative and honest interview with Prince on BET. Prince had publicly blasted his label Warner Bros. for its restrictive contracts and Smiley wisely brought him on the network to explain his contracts. When Prince told millions of viewers that he had signed a bad contract and Warner Bros. had made millions from his album sales, but he was still not reaping the total financial benefits of his labor, it caused the music industry to sit up and take notice.

To think that an artist at the level of Prince could be locked into a bad, unprofitable, non-royalty-paying contract was just mind-boggling to everyone. Not long after that interview, word spread throughout the industry that gospel powerhouse Yolanda Adams was filing a lawsuit and demanding out of Verity, a label that grew to number one but continually had problems with gospel artists demanding payment of royalties. Yes, Verity is a *gospel label*, but gospel artists as well must realize that at the end of the day they are in business to make money, not disciples. If the opposite were true, would contracts even be necessary?

So, in Chapter Two, we start the first step of the journey in making the demo and signing a recording contract. Additionally, like Amy Goldson and Larkin Arnold, two of the finest entertainment lawyers ever to practice, I often tell clients and artists, "Understand what you're signing." Goldson would often tell me that "an artist is so excited about a deal, that they often won't read the contract." And Arnold, one of the top black execs in the pioneering days of the 1970s and 1980s, as well as the executive producer of *Thriller*, added, "It is important to read everything you sign as an artist, songwriter, or producer." My hope is that artists will at least read this book prior to rushing into a bad deal.

In Chapter Three, we'll explore the dos and don'ts of hiring a manager. In addition, we'll explore several other key areas of the industry involving musical groups and team building. A good recording contract means nothing without a good manager. Similarly, a good manager can only do so much without a solid recording contract for his client, the artist.

In Chapters Four and Five, we look at the difficulties of signing as a group as well as the key points of signing to an indie label. It is very important to know the distinctions of signing as a solo, a group, or a choir, as well as signing with a major label or strong indie, or even a mom-and-pop operation.

Because of the nature of my practice and the similarities of the gospel and R&B scenes on some fronts, I juggle tidbits of the gospel, hip-hop, and urban industries to best hammer home specific business tips. Hopefully, these examples can help you remember what to do in a similar business setting that may arise.

And, in Chapter Six, I zoom in on the entire construction of the artist's team and the role each member should play in support of the artist. It is critical that an artist understands very early on how important his team can be in developing his or her career. Using examples like manager Michael Elder, publicist Elisa Keys, business manager Bert Padell, and attorney Matthew Middleton, the chapter explores their firsthand input to guide you.

Likewise, for urban artists, producers, and managers to comfortably prepare for a career post-music, it is important to understand not just the music business but the corporate legalities in setting up a business and running a label. This includes, but not limited to the corporate issues, copyright and trademark issues and distribution issues. We discuss all in Chapters Eight through Thirteen of Part II. My dear law professor, Spencer Boyer, taught for more than forty years at Howard University School of Law, and he always stressed "teach the artist to become empowered, to protect themselves, and to have long careers." In our chapters on starting and maintaining a label as a corporation, it is my hope that you will gain some insight on the ups and downs of running a label; and, if you decide to open a label, run it like a true corporation with bylaws, minute books for meetings, and resolutions for actions taken by the company.

Also, many artists do not understand the accounting necessary to manage money and to establish a financially secure future. Some do not know how to build a team or how to quarterback their plans for the future. My hope is that they will read this book and hear about Vernon Brown, Laura Gordon, and other great players in the industry, so that they may openly learn about business management and how it works.

In Part III of the book, we spend several exhaustive chapters on publishing, copyrights, mechanical licenses, synchronization licenses, the Copyright Act, and self-publishing. These chapters are critical in understanding the bundle of rights associated with copyright protection. Keep in mind, I only provide a basic introduction to the laws of copyright. Be advised that this is not an exhaustive breakdown on copyright law but a summary of and an introduction to the world of copyright. The hope is that you will read up further on the law of copyrights before erroneously abandoning your songwriting publishing or hiring a law firm.

Copyright law plays such a significant role in the life of a songwriter that I almost wish every young writer would call the Library of Congress' Copyright Office and get a copy of the handouts on copyrights and the rights associated therein. Millions of songs are exploited, played, assigned, used, and distributed each day, and the urban songwriter, whether a gospel artist or hip-hop artist, has no idea how many millions he or she is losing for not grasping the rules of copyright.

While the urban music industry is a multibillion-dollar industry, many of the artists who made the music, as Prince explained to Tavis Smiley, struggle their entire careers and die penniless, all while corporate America is making billions from their talent. Many artists do not understand the importance of marketing, videos, touring, branding, attending key conferences, and using the Internet in the age of digital downloading. These are some of the topics I provide a general introduction to in the last chapters of this book under Part IV.

We use the stories of Rodney Jerkins, L. A. Reid, Sylvia Rhone, Benny Medina, Chamillionaire, Big John Platt, Vicki Mack-Lataillade, Muhammad Ali, Berry Gordy, and dozens of others throughout the book, for the sole purpose of getting you to understand how their examples apply to the substantive issue or point at stake in the chapter. Use the anecdotes of their careers, their ups and downs, to learn and find your own style and navigate your own way.

Also, note that I could share firsthand accounts, but too many books offer the *author's* suggestions and firsthand experiences as the only way. I wanted a book that would give real-world stories from the real people who hold the various titles and positions each day in the music industry. Rather than my sole interpretation, I wanted the artist's and manager's firsthand accounts of these stories to enlighten you. Take from them what you will.

For example, when we examine Benny Medina and his management team, Handprint Entertainment, it is for the sole purpose of highlighting the role of a manager. Please do not read the example as my endorsement or attempt to present anything more than an illustration of the success these artists or legends have brought to the music industry. Be mindful that there are dozens of others that we just could not fit into this book owing to space limitations. Lastly, in dissecting the illustrious career of Diane Warren as a self-publisher, it is my hope that you will remember Diane Warren for more than simply writing hit records for Toni Braxton, Celine Dion, and Debarge but also as the blueprint to being a self-publisher.

There are so many other things that I could have put in this book, but my goal was to walk an artist or producer through some of the major steps. I hope if you understand what you are signing, how to assemble a business team, how to retain your copyrights, and the ins and outs of marketing and merchandising your brand, you can survive for a long time in this industry.

Over the course of the next twenty years, we will see another Jay-Z, Kirk Franklin, 50 Cent, Usher, or Erykah Badu. And while the name has changed several times ("black music," "urban music," "new jack swing," etc.), the financial model will not, and the "black" or "urban" artists, producers, and managers, among other players, will not share in the financial *business* of the music they so dearly love, unless we share the knowledge. My hope is that these artists will come into this business more educated, empowered, and enlightened in the ways of the music industry.

If you read this book and understand how Michael Jackson could have made $50 million in artist royalties (see Chapter Sixteen), or how Beyoncé trademarked her name, or how Lauryn Hill and the Fugees licensed a song made classic by Roberta Flack (Chapter Twenty), or how Antonio "L. A." Reid ran LaFace and then Arista (Chapter Ten) and then Island Def Jam, then this book has served its purpose.

Phyllis Hyman did not live to see the full evolution of *urban music*. She died in 1995 alone in a New York hotel room just hours before she was scheduled to perform at the Apollo Theatre. On the night Luther Vandross died in 2005, I was promoting and booking a Patti LaBelle concert at Foxwoods and was happy to know that Vandross' business affairs were handled properly. Both of these great performers did not live to see the current evolution of the music they so deeply appreciated and an industry that reaped so much from their gifts. However, they both were well aware of the struggles of the black artist and wanted nothing more than to see the financial success of the urban artist. So in some ways I dedicate this book to them.

But, you are still here and eager to get in the industry or eager to learn the industry that you have already worked in for many years. If so, read this book and utilize what information you need to equip yourself for a career in the desired area that you choose.

Lastly, I must mention that Clarence Avant was the perfect choice for the many quotes that lead the chapters of this book, given his encouragement and strength for too many people to name. I concur with his findings and thoughts on social responsibility—that we must each take up our turn in doing something responsible for the best interest of the black music scene.

With this book, I strive to "take my turn" at doing something responsible and making my contribution as Avant suggests for the music industry that has blessed me so much.

CHAPTER 2

Getting and Signing a Recording Contract

> *"When I signed a recording contract, I did not realize I became a slave to a record company."* —PRINCE

These dramatic words from the Purple One, while painful, are truthful in describing the restrictive nature of a recording contract. Each day thousands of young musicians create demo tapes, contact record labels, and dream of signing an agreement that will result in their becoming music's next superstar. Most do not realize that the recording contract is a one-sided document that in many instances is designed to ensure that artists will never realize any substantial income from their hard work, no matter how talented they are. In the urban music scene, it is common to hear R&B and hip-hop stars romanticizing the glamour and allure of being part of that scene—P. Diddy boasting "I Know You Saw Me in the Video," Jay-Z talking about "A Hard Knock Life," Outkast screaming "Hey-Ya," and Luther Vandross proudly singing about "Dancing with My Father."

Rarely do we hear about the flip side of such success, horror stories of artists such as Melba Moore, TLC, and Toni Braxton, who signed contracts that left them strapped for cash and nearly bankrupt. But, there have been a lot of successful stories too. For example, former Columbia Records head Michael Mauldin was the first African American president of the label and was responsible for the signing of the Fugees, Nas, Maxwell, and Destiny's Child, among so many others. He is also credited with promoting the careers of artists from Alicia Keys to Bow Wow.

And, whenever you hear Mauldin speak, he will tell you that an artist must understand what he or she is signing and learn to understand the business. In this chapter you will read about the steps you need to take to secure a fair recording contract. But before you can get any contract—before you can get your foot in the door—very often, you must create a demo package. (If you have already made the demo, skip to the section ahead on signing a recording contract.) So the chapter first outlines making the demo. In this second part of this chapter, we zoom in and analyze the signing of the recording contract.

THE DEMONSTRATION PACKAGE

The first step for any artist who wants to launch a successful career in the music business is to create a demonstration package, or a "demo." A bare-bones demo consists of a brief biographical sketch (the "bio"), a CD, and a photograph.

The artist's main objective is to create a package that truly accentuates his or her look, style, sound, and story. Your chances of signing a recording contract in urban music are slim even with a good demo, but without one, most often you've got no chance at all. In putting together your package, there are dozens of things to consider. However, here are some main considerations:

- ◆ Audience and record label
- ◆ Song selection and length of songs
- ◆ Your photo
- ◆ Your biography
- ◆ How to record the demo
- ◆ Demo packaging and labeling
- ◆ The submission process
- ◆ Signing the demo recording agreement
- ◆ The right package for the right label

AUDIENCE AND RECORD LABEL

Before you begin creating your demo, make sure you have accurately identified your target audience. If you are an urban artist, don't send your demo to a record label that specializes in pop or heavy metal. Similarly, if you are a gospel artist, don't send your demo to a jazz or hip-hop label. Carefully consider both your audience and the label to make sure it handles your style of music. I have sat on numerous panels with marketing genius James "Jazzy" Jordan of the Jive-Zomba/Sony family and heard him advise numerous artists on the importance of understanding your market.

Longtime industry executive Michael Elder recalled, "I could not believe how many kids made demos and did not consider if our label was the right home for them as an artist." Elder, who manages and books dates for the likes of Atlantic Starr, Johnny Gill, and Dionne Warwick, added, "It's like they want a deal so bad that they make one demo tape and send it to the jazz, R&B, and pop departments of the label with no clue that label execs talk to each other." Finally, keep in mind that a demo that attempts to show an ability to do jazz, rock, pop, classical, and R&B is usually too broad and too encompassing to impress any label executive.

SONG SELECTION

Another critical step in creating a demo package is deciding what songs and how many of them to put on the demo itself. In the past it was common to put only three songs on a demo. Today, however, many artists record entire twelve-song CDs. Regardless of how many you include, the key is to make sure you select the right songs for your demo. One executive told me that within ten seconds of playing a demo she could assess whether the artist had selected the right material for it. Added former Malaco exec Kenny Taylor, "The songs are the key. No matter how great you sing, if you pick the wrong songs, the label may miss your talent and pass on signing you."

Your songs (no fewer than three and no more than twelve) should capture the essence of your talent and feature slow, mid-tempo, and fast songs that highlight your delivery, range, and vocal capabilities. A record label should be able to assess your potential for success by listening to your demo.

DURATION OF SONGS

The optimal length of a demo song is two-and-a-half to four minutes. On the gospel side, a common but unfortunate trend is to do what we call the "gospel remix" and have a song be too long. If the demo song is over five minutes long, that is often so because a two- to three-minute vamp or repeated hook has been appended to its end. The song thus becomes a marathon and loses both its essence and impact. Vamps are appropriate for performances or CDs, but not for demos.

YOUR PHOTO

A photograph is not necessarily essential for gospel or hip-hop artists. It is, however, important if the artist or group is more R&B–based and/or has potential for crossover success. For example, Arista label head Clive Davis took a look at Newark, New Jersey, schoolgirl Whitney Houston and reinvented her look to make her the girl next door. After 100,000,000 records sold, many other labels have attempted to do the same and have searched endlessly to find the next girl-next-door face.

When a record label receives a demo package, the photo is the only element that can be reviewed quickly. So, it is crucial to be certain that your photo is professional and truly reflects you as an artist. Do not send instant-camera photos or photos taken at a nightclub or in the parking lot of your church. Instead, hire a professional photographer and get a glossy, black-and-white 8 ½ × 11 photo. It should be a headshot, and you and your group should be dressed appropriately. Recently, two sisters sent me a photo scantily dressed that was considerably more than a headshot and made me wonder whether they were selling music or something else.

YOUR BIOGRAPHY

Once the label exec has listened to the CD and taken a casual look at the accompanying photo, and determined that both of those are *impressive* or *hot*, he or she will review the bio. The purpose of a bio is to provide the record company with a basic understanding of how an artist's career has unfolded to that point. The bio should focus on a few initial successes and the pattern established by those successes and indicate how signing with an urban label would benefit both the artist and the label. Keep in mind that labels are fully aware of how much floss and fluff there is likely to be in the average bio. I know of an artist who had merely introduced hip-hop legend Jay-Z at a show, but his bio read "opened for Jay-Z." If discovered, that sort of misrepresentation can hurt your chances of landing that record deal you are working toward.

RECORDING THE DEMO: SHOULD YOU DO IT YOURSELF?

In the past, the only option for aspiring artists who wanted to create a professional demo was to record in a studio, which would supply the necessary equipment, engineers, mixers, and even backup musicians. Today, an increasing number of musicians, especially in the world of hip-hop and gospel, are producing their own demos. Using equipment such as Pro Tools, CakeWalk, or Apple's Garage Band, artists who have the requisite technical abilities can record a high-quality demo for a minimal cost.

The alternative is to record in a professional studio. The costs of a studio-produced demo vary, depending on the number of songs and their length and the number of musicians, but they can run thousands of dollars. However, if neither you nor anyone on your team has sound-recording experience, you should hire professionals.

DEMO PACKAGING AND LABELING

The first rule of thumb is not to adorn your demo with a label boasting "the best CD you will ever hear," or "play song four." The label for your demo CD should be simple and basic: your name, the title of the songs, a copyright notice, and a phone number or email address where you or your designated representative can be contacted. For the most part, it is okay to take the basic TDK label and neatly write in the information with a ballpoint pen or indelible black marker. You can also use a typewriter or a computer and laser printer. A typical example might read: "John Smith Demo, 4 songs, 212-555-0107."

THE SUBMISSION PROCESS AND THE DEMO-RECORDING AGREEMENT

Now that your package is complete, there comes the chore of shopping it to record labels and industry executives. This can be an especially arduous and painful task if you are new to the industry.

It is very important to put in writing any agreement you may have with someone shopping your CD to labels. Do not assume because you are friends, "things will work out." When a label telephones a manager or your "friend" and says, "We want to sign this artist," the friend who was "helping" you out will very likely want a commission. (As we discuss later, a manager will expect 5 to 20 percent of any monies you receive if a label ultimately signs you on the basis of your demo.)

A carefully worded written agreement with a manager, friend, or, often, attorney that clearly sets forth the expectations of the parties involved can avoid any confusion. There are several simple steps involved in this process. First, you must reach an agreement on how many packages you will give your representative to shop. Next you will agree on which or what type of labels will be approached. Most important, you and your representative must agree on the fee or commission that he or she will receive if a deal is secured.

SIGNING A DEMO-RECORDING AGREEMENT

In certain cases—for example, when a label is impressed by a rough demo or when the label's execs think that an artist or group has star potential—a label will advance an artist enough cash to record a high-quality three- or four-song demo. The advance is made under the terms of what is known as a demo-recording agreement, and you should be very clear that demo deals are *not* guarantees that the label will enter into a full-length recording contract.

Where there is uncertainty about an artist's or group's long-term potential, signing a demo deal gives the label a chance to evaluate the artist's or group's musical direction and material before investing millions of dollars in a recording contract. It allows the artist or group to record a few high-quality tracks before a label pays for completing a full CD.

Obviously, the record label has more leverage when negotiating the terms of a demo-recording agreement. Generally, the artists making their first demo are not signed by anyone and have little bargaining power. The key terms of demo agreements include the following:

- The amount of money that will be advanced and whether the advance can be recouped from royalties earned by (1) the songs on the demo recording or (2) any songs placed with the label (or publisher)
- The right of first refusal—that is, the label's right to hold on to the demo (song *and* artist) for a certain period after the demo is completed before offering (or deciding not to offer) a full recording contract to the artist
- An agreement by the artist that if the label decides to sign the artist, he or she will negotiate the terms of the agreement "in good faith" (i.e., without being "difficult" and negotiating under reasonable industry standards).

Now that we have looked at a brief overview of the demo, we can talk about the most important contract the artist will sign.

SIGNING THE RECORDING CONTRACT

Over twenty years ago, Prince signed with Warner Bros., the still-powerful major label started in the late 1950s. With hits like "Purple Rain," "Little Red Corvette," "Kiss," and "When Doves Cry," Prince sold over 50 million records for the record label. As a result, Warner Bros. probably grossed over a half a billion dollars from his music. Uneducated about the music industry when he signed his first recording deal in the 1980s, Prince assumed he would rake in huge profits from his record sales. He was wrong.

Prince's story is a classic example of what happens to most artists: they sign a deal and do not realize the long-term effects! The contract Prince signed most likely gave the label ownership of his masters, which allowed the company to re-release his records at their discretion as well as to create greatest hits compilations without his approval.

While the worldwide publicity surrounding Prince's story was only mildly embarrassing to Warner Bros., it was a much needed wake-up call for urban artists. During the 1990s, Prince appeared several times on major media outlets with the word *slave* printed on his face, a symbol of how he regarded his relationship with Warner Bros. In 1996, he released a triple CD, *Emancipation*, the title of which referred to his freedom from the odious contract with the label. Prince made it a mission to educate young artists on the tragic realities of the music business by stressing the implications of signing a recording contract and the long-term effects of entering into a flawed agreement.

In the following section, we explore the key elements and conditions of a recording contract, citing examples where appropriate, to further explain the impact of a given clause.

KEY CLAUSES OF A STANDARD RECORDING CONTRACT

+ Exclusivity
+ Term and Length of Contract
+ Recording Funds and Recording Costs
+ Selection of Material
+ Artist Royalty Rate
+ Standard Deductions
+ Deductions in Foreign Countries
+ Royalties Not Paid
+ Marketing and Promotional Deductions
+ Unrecouped Expenses
+ Controlled Compositions and Mechanical Royalties
+ Music Publishing
+ Ownership and Reversion of Masters
+ Group Artists and Leaving Members
+ Sideman Rights
+ Bankruptcy

A couple of decades ago, Anita Baker was signed as an artist to Elektra. Over the course of a very successful career, countless sold out concerts and numerous awards from the Grammys, American Music Awards and NAACP, Ms. Baker created national news with complaints about her contract and eventually left the label. In knowing the standard terms of a recording contract, I wondered then if Ms. Baker, like dozens of successful artists, was every aware of the key clauses of a recording contract and the specific provisions needed to protect her in the long run after signing a contract. Was she aware of the exclusive nature and the long-term effects of a recording contract and the record label's right to establish release dates and marketing? Or was she like most new urban artists, initially so excited to have a major deal in hand that she didn't know what it meant legally! Thus, this chapter is very critical to understand particularly the intentions and legal interpretation of the common clauses detailed later.

The first matter to be aware of is the confidential and binding nature of this agreement you sign. For example, under the terms of a standard recording contract, an artist is signed to provide exclusive personal services to the record label. This is generally the requirement whether signing with a major label or an indie (independent label), as discussed later in the book. According to Andrew Merritt, president of Bajada Records in Detroit, "The label insists on exclusivity because it has no intention of spending hundreds of thousands (if not millions) of dollars in an artist's career only to share the profits deriving from that artist's success with another record company."

Sometimes the exclusivity requirement is found in the opening paragraph of the contract, which gives the date of the agreement and the signatories, and sometimes it is stated in a separate section. The language of contracts varies depending on the label and the artist, but all recording contracts specify, in addition to the exclusive nature of the relationship, the length (term) of the agreement, how many albums will be required (the recording commitment), how royalties will be calculated, and a litany of other clauses, all of which must be examined thoroughly by the artist's attorney and then hopefully read by the artist.

EXCLUSIVITY

Generally, a record company will not sign an artist to a recording contract unless the contract provides for that artist to record exclusively for that record company. In essence, the company is saying, "We are not going to invest thousands of dollars in you without being assured we have exclusive rights for your services as an artist, singer, songwriter, or performer."

An exclusivity clause is straightforward for the most part. The artist can only perform, sing, and record for the label he or she signed with, unless the label agrees to an appearance on an album released by another label. In addition, the label contractually retains all of the exclusive rights and interests to the artist's name, likeness, and image under this clause. Generally an exclusivity clause will read as follows:

SECTION 1. EXCLUSIVITY

Services. During the Term of this Agreement, including all renewals, extensions, and days of suspension and all periods added by amendments or by other agreements, I will not perform for the purpose of or myself engage in making records (other than permitted recordings) for anyone other than Record Label and I will not authorize the use of my name, likeness, or other identification for the purpose of distributing, selling, advertising, or exploiting records for anyone other than Record Label.

Nowhere is the emphasis of this clause better illustrated than in the case of gospel star Tonex. Tonex stormed onto the music scene in the late 1990s with his debut album, *Pronounced Toe-nay*, and garnered a blitz of media attention and interest as the new wunderkind of gospel. Ironically, he was described as the next Prince of gospel music, owing to his vocal prowess, writing ability, dance moves, and musicianship.

Because of the national attention, Tonex was allowed to perform at the Stellar Awards, gospel's top award show. At that time, it was reported that Tonex was finalizing a major deal with a record label. Shortly after the national buzz began, a controversy broke out as to who owned the exclusive rights to the artist. Specifically, the dispute had to do with whether Tommy Boy, Verity Records, or a small label in his hometown of San Diego owned the "exclusive" right to Tonex's services as a recording artist. Sadly, much of the buzz surrounding Tonex was diminished over time as his legal representatives and handlers diligently scrambled to determine who owned the exclusive rights. To this day, many feel he has never realized the potential he showed in 1999, but to date he has earned a Grammy nomination for his album *Out of the Box*. Nevertheless, one wonders if the question of exclusivity stood in the way of Tonex's ability to promptly deliver a record to the marketplace. (Years later, Tonex would sign exclusively to Verity and win several Stellar Awards.)

TERM AND LENGTH OF CONTRACT

After the recording contract indicates it will be exclusive, the next clause usually deals with the term. The length of a recording contract can be very difficult to understand. Some labels will offer an artist a contract that calls for a fixed commitment of five albums, with two options, for a total of seven albums. An option is a label's right to exercise a clause that requires an artist to record more albums. Some labels may request that an artist sign a contract with a commitment of lesser albums but more options. A record label will usually present the artist with a contract that requires a commitment of five to seven albums. Again, it might read as follows:

SECTION 2. TERM

Recording Commitment and Term. A) The Term of this Agreement will commence on the date hereof and continue, unless extended as provided for herein, for a first Contract Period (sometimes referred to as the "Initial Contract Period") ending nine (9) months after the date of completion of Artist's service for the first album recording hereunder. B) Additionally, you hereby grant Record Label six (6) separate options to extend the term of this Agreement for additional Contract Periods ("Option Periods") on the same terms and conditions applicable to the Initial Contract Period, unless the Agreement provides otherwise herein.

In essence, this sample clause requires the artist to record seven albums exclusively to satisfy the contract. As for cash, the artist is given an advance in return for which he or she is required to attend recording sessions, deliver commercially acceptable albums, and agree to aggressively promote those albums. In most cases, a new artist signed to J Records, such as *American Idol*'s Ruben Studdard, would follow label head Clive Davis's decision on selecting songs, producers, and structure for the album during the Initial Contract Period.

As you may be aware, the length, or "term," of a contract is difficult to measure in actual years owing to the unpredictable nature of when the artist records and releases his or her next project. The term is also affected by the success of a project and how long that project appears on the *Billboard* record charts. For example, the artist could sign a seven-album deal and record the first project in 2006. If his or her album soars like the recent Usher *Confessions* album, the artist could sit on the chart for two years with the same album. Like Usher, the artist's label would ride the wave of success as long as the cash register at music stores delivers profits.

As a result, the second album for this artist would probably hit stores in 2009. This, of course, creates a gap in the number of years between the two recordings. If we calculate the making of seven albums with this possible release between albums gap, it could take fifteen to twenty years to fulfill a contract, even though the agreement inferred one album per year for a total of seven years.

New York and California are two common states where many artists enter into contracts with major record labels. This is because the major companies (Jive-Zomba/Sony, Warner Bros., BMG, et cetera) are based in Los Angeles and New York City. In recent years, however, urban and gospel music have exploded in Tennessee and Georgia, and these regions have become nearly as popular for recording-contract terms. At the writing of this book, New York, Tennessee, and Georgia had not adopted any laws that limit the term of an artist's recording contract. However, California limits the term of any personal service contract, which would include a recording agreement, to a maximum of seven years. The California Labor Code, Section 2855 provides:

> A contract to render personal services . . . may not be enforced against the employee beyond seven years from the commencement of services under it. Any contract, otherwise valid, to perform or render services of a special, unique, unusual, extraordinary, or intellectual character, which gives it a peculiar value and the loss of which can not be reasonably or adequately compensated in damages in an action at law, may nevertheless be enforced against the person contracting to render such service, for a term not to exceed seven years from the commencement of service under it.

As a result of the law and cases filed under the statute, record labels wised up and revised their contracts to indicate what's known as a "contract period," and they avoid services being performed under California law. Alternately, if the contract falls under California law, the artist must renew the agreement. With this renewal, the seven-year period starts all over again.

This renewal could come after the first album is delivered, which means the contract period would begin from the date the album is delivered rather than with the passage of time. When the artist delivers his or her first album, whether in six months or sixteen months, the first contract period is completed. It can take an additional eighteen months or thirty-six months to deliver a second album. Upon delivery of the second album, the second contract period is fulfilled. It is critical for artists to understand the length, or term, of their contracts and to have their representatives thoroughly examine how long a contract actually runs.

Critical to this understanding is the failure in California courts to break a contract if the label has paid minimum cash advances to the artist. For example, California has two methods for determining what guaranteed compensation must be in order to seek injunctive relief. In one scenario, the money is guaranteed at the time of signing the contract as follows:

Year	Minimum Payment
Contract Period 1	$9,000
Contract Period 2	$12,000
Contract Period 3	$15,000
Contract Period 4	$15,000
Contract Period 5	$15,000
Contract Period 6	$15,000
Contract Period 7	$15,000

The other method under California law requires the record label to guarantee and retroactively pay higher minimums at a future date. This method is known as the "superstar insurance" method. Here a record company electing not to contractually guarantee minimum payments attempts to still hold a right to injunctive relief in court, if the label makes actual payments on a cumulative basis at least ten times the minimum rates established in the previous table. So, in this instance, the contract would normally read as follows:

Year	Payment
Contract Period 1	$90,000
Contract Period 2	$120,000
Contract Period 3	$150,000
Contract Period 4	$300,000
Contract Period 5	$300,000
Contract Period 6	$450,000
Contract Period 7	$450,000

No one totally understands what these grids mean, but there was a time when just about every record company placed one of the preceding charts or some cash variation in all of their agreements in an attempt to offset any future claim that it violated California law. Without the guaranteed minimum or retroactive payments, the label cannot obtain injunctive relief, having a court rule that an artist is prevented from recording for anyone else. Note also that the cumulative total for year one is the amount the artist receives for that year, while additional years would be a cumulative of that given year, plus the prior year or years. Thus, in contract period 7, the cumulative totals above would be $186,000 and $1,860,000. One well-known artist attempted to leave his label and the label secured an injunction from the California courts to prohibit him from leaving.

It is important to note that in some states a standard recording contract provides that an artist is paid no less than union scale established in agreements with the applicable union. In the entertainment industry, two of the important relevant unions are the American Federation of Television and Radio Artists (AFTRA) for vocalists and the American Federation of Musicians (AFM) for musicians and instrumentalists. Both unions work hard to protect the rights of singers and musicians by requiring labels to abide by set financial scales when paying an artist. Keep in mind that these scales are minimal. The AFM also urges artists not to sign a contract longer than five years. An artist signed to a long-term, seven-album deal with most major labels will take much longer than five years to complete the requirements of that contract. A good legal or financial representative will consider the various factors to ensure that the artist receives the appropriate pay, such as the marketplace or the artist's track record.

Years ago, Bad Boy Records' urban act 112 found out how restrictive and long term their contract was after they sold millions of records and then attempted to leave the label. After much negotiation and near legal action between the group and Bad Boy, the two parties resolved the matter when the group and the label agreed to modify the initial contract. After a brief stint with Def Jam/Def Soul, the group is currently scheduled to release a record on its own label (One Twelve Music) distributed through Irv Gott's The Inc. company.

RECORDING FUNDS AND RECORDING COSTS

Generally, a recording contract will indicate in the first few pages what the recording fund and budget will be for the albums to be recorded. The contract will also discuss recording costs. Recording costs are those expenses incurred by the record label in recording the masters and are generally recoupable from future royalties. This is critical to understand because it basically means that as the artist you pay for everything out of your future royalties. Typically, the contract will have language that states:

SECTION 3. RECORDING COSTS

Recording Costs. The words "recording costs" shall mean all costs incurred by Record Label for and with respect to the production of masters, as distinguished from manufacturing and distribution costs, including, without limitation, the cost to the Record Label of all instrumental musicians, vocalists, conductors, arrangers, orchestrators, copyists, etc., all studio, tape editing, mastering, and other similar costs in connection with the production of the final master, and all other costs and expenses incurred by the Record Label in producing masters hereunder, from time to time, and which are customarily recognized as recording costs in the phonograph record industry.

Music industry veteran Angelo Ellerbee, the president and CEO of the Double XXposure Agency, is a legend in the music industry. Ellerbee once told a packed audience at BMI's New York headquarters that "a record label or record company is just a bank that loans you money." Ellerbee explained, similar to the clause above, how he had to educate his artists that they would pay everything at the end of the day and to realize "nothing was free." Seeing a need to guide urban artists, Ellerbee created a "charm school" to train and manage such stars as Mary J. Blige, Dionne Warwick, DMX, Ginuwine, and dozens of others in dealing with the media and overall artistic presentation.

With over twenty years experience in the music business, Ellerbee was asked by our law firm and BMI to discuss his career and touch on the "dos and don'ts" of the music industry. Some members of the audience shook their head in disbelief at Ellerbee's suggestion to view a label as a bank, but his comments were accurate in many ways. A label essentially loans artists the money to pay recording costs, marketing costs, and any other unforeseen expenditures that arise during the term of the contract.

Similar to the Recording Costs clause, the initial pages of the contract will include a section focusing on the Recording Fund. Without a recording fund, you can't pay for the recording costs! Thus, a Recording Fund is a fixed amount of money determined by the label and the artist's representative and used to complete the project from beginning to end. At one point in the music industry, a recording fund for an

R&B artist making his first album at a major label could range from a low of $250,000 to a high of $500,000 or even a million or more, as discussed below, if top-notch producers are retained. Traditionally, in urban music, the label established certain minimums and maximum funds for the album. And, the recording contract clause with the fund might increase slightly for each album thereafter and read as follows:

SECTION 4. RECORDING FUND

Recording Fund. Conditioned upon Artist's full performance of all the material conditions hereof, Record Label shall pay to Artist the following aggregate recording advances (inclusive of all recording costs) for each album delivered to Record Label in satisfaction of the terms herein . . . the recording fund advance shall be an amount equal to twenty five (25%) percent of the aggregate royalties, less actual returns and credits (after provision for reasonable reserves for returns and credits) earned by Artist from sales of the prior two (2) albums delivered to company and released through normal retail channel hereunder (except as to the second album delivered to the Record Label hereunder, fifty (50%) percent of the aggregate royalties less actual returns and credits) . . . Notwithstanding the foregoing, each such advance for the Recording Fund, if there is any, payable pursuant to this Paragraph 4, shall not be less than, nor more than the following applicable amounts:

Album	Minimum Fund	Maximum Fund
#1	$200,000	$250,000
#2	$225,000	$275,000
#3	$250,000	$300,000
#4	$275,000	$325,000
#5	$300,000	$350,000
#6	$325,000	$375,000
#7	$350,000	$400,000

This Minimum and Maximum Fund, sometimes called a "Mini-Maxi" budget, is basically a way of ensuring that the artist will receive a certain minimum and capped maximum on subsequent examples. Thus, the formula above is basically one where the label is promising that the recording fund will be 25 percent of the aggregate net royalty earned from the two prior albums, except for the first album above, which is at the base rate of $200,000, and the second album which would be based on 50 percent of the Artist's first album net royalty. It is a little complicated, but it is a good idea to have it spelled out in your agreement, so you can have someway of knowing what the recording fund will be on future albums. These numbers above will vary from label to label, and you should not expect to see this grid in all contracts as each label has its own form contract.

It is also important to note that in gospel music, the budget might be half of these amounts, if that much, because of fewer record sales, unless you are the *gospel superstars* Donnie McClurkin, Yolanda Adams, or Kirk Franklin. (I italicized gospel superstars as it sounds like an oxymoron!)

Although recording costs should not exceed the established fund, this is often the case as the making of an album is full of surprise expenses and unforeseen costs. If an artist is expected to deliver a great album, the label is generally prepared to add more money. For example, if the label has the opportunity to bring in a super-hot writer-producer such as Diane Warren or Jermaine Dupri, it will increase the recording fund to secure top talent for the project.

Typically, many urban artists have struggled financially most of their lives. The thought of seeing anywhere from $500,000 to $1 million committed to their artistry is very enticing, but keep in mind that a recording fund is not provided as a blank check. The label releases funds on a week-to-week basis as the artist works with various producers and studios to record an album. Most often, payment is made directly to the studios, corporations, or other entities involved with the recording process.

In many cases, the artist will receive a 10 to 20 percent advance from the fund for living expenses or his own personal use. If an agreement is negotiated to include what is known as "overage," the artist can keep the remaining money if the entire budget or fund is not used. In most instances, however, a new artist will utilize the entire budget, so most artists are stuck with their advance as the only money they see for quite some time.

In addition to an advance, recording costs include everything imaginable, from studio time, engineers, musicians, background singers, and producers, to cutting demos, traveling, and living arrangements for the artist, as well as food and clothes. As stated above, the label will cut checks for each of these costs as they arise during the recording process. The label's goal is to record and produce an album that falls in line with the budget pre-established by the top executives. Like Ellerbee points out, it is important to understand that an advance and overall recording fund is just a loan from a bank. In this case the bank is called a *record label*.

Finally, under the standard recording contract, a copy of which is available at our website (www.thisbusinessofurbanmusic.com), the record company covers all of the associated costs with the recording session, as well as those costs associated with the recording's manufacture, marketing, promotions, and sales. As Prince and so many others have learned the hard way, these upfront expenditures can create a high six- or seven-figure debt that must be repaid. In the music industry, before the artist receives any profits, his or her record label will deduct the debt accrued making the album. The debt is deducted from the revenue derived from the CD sales, and this occurs before the artist sees a penny, despite profits made by the record label. This concept, prevalent in the recording industry, is known simply as a label "recouping" its expenses.

As a result, an artist may have to sell millions of records to recognize any profit from his or her album. For example, if an artist makes fifty cents a record and sells one million records, the artist would be due $500,000 from the record company's gross revenue. Here's the problem: The label takes the $500,000 that is due to the artist and deducts all costs, advances, and expenditures associated with making the album. It is only once all associated costs are paid off that the artist will see revenue from his or her album. It is an unbelievable accounting system and a strange way of doing things, but that is the music business. Clearly, we can now understand why Prince felt like a slave to his label. If you don't understand, don't worry, by necessity we discuss this in more detail later in this chapter and the book.

SELECTION OF MATERIAL

In the 1960s, Berry Gordy established Motown Records. He also established a lesser-known company called Jobete Publishing, named after his three children: Hazel Joy, Berry, and Terry. Although not as popular, Jobete became the vehicle through which he would administer hundreds of songs for many years to come. Gordy strategically owned both the label and the powerful publishing house while maintaining his involvement as a songwriter, producer, and arranger. From the Four Tops, the Temptations, and the Supremes to the Jackson Five, he co-wrote or co-owned songs for most of Motown's major artists and generally selected what material to include on the album. With this style, Gordy designed a process that for many years to come would be the way of life for the artist signing to an urban label.

During the process of negotiating a recording contract, an artist will often insist that he or she must have complete control over the songs selected, producer selected, and overall material on the album. However, a new artist is not in a position to make such a creative-control demand, and that request will rarely be granted. While a label will consider an artist's input, at the end of the day it is the label that makes the final decision and runs the show. Generally, a selection clause will read as follows:

SECTION 5. SELECTION OF MATERIAL

Selection of Material. Record Label shall have the sole right to select all material, songs, and producers that contribute to the album. Record Label, in good faith, will seek input from the artist in the selection of material and songs.

As indicated by this language, the record company may consider the artist's ideas, but it does not have to follow his or her suggestions and can make the final decision. This clause is very significant for several reasons, including the fact that many artists will feel they know their sound and will sometimes refuse to yield to suggestions from the label. It is also important because of the songwriting royalties due and payable when certain material makes the album by a given writer.

ARTIST ROYALTY RATE

When reading the recording contract, you will see the opening clauses establishing the Term, Exclusivity and Advances and Recording Funds, and ultimately, one of the most important, the Royalty Clause, which sets forth how much money the label has agreed to pay to the Artist as a royalty. Sometimes royalty figures are called "points" and this term means the same thing as percent. For example, if Anita Baker had a 10-point royalty, it is the same as a 10-percent royalty.

It is important to understand that if you are an artist signing a recording contract or an attorney reviewing a recording contract, first analyze whether the royalty rate is based upon a wholesale price, which is the price charged to the seller of the record, or a retail price, i.e., the price paid by the consumer who buys the record at Barnes & Noble, Strawberries, or Wal-Mart. Whatever you do, make sure you understand this and remember, the general rule for determining the basic royalty rate is simple: a royalty rate based on wholesale price should be approximately double a royalty rate based on the retail price. (I have provided a few examples at our website, www.thisbusinessofurbanmusic.com.)

For purposes of this chapter, a standard royalty clause provides for the artist to be paid a cash percentage of the profits earned on the recording. The royalty paid is a small percentage of the suggested retail list price, or SRLP (as the term is abbreviated in the contract). I generally advise my clients to seek an Adjusted Base Rate, which slides upwards as the album sales increase. Generally, the clause, in summary, might appear as follows:

SECTION 6. ROYALTIES

<u>Royalties.</u> Subject to the other provisions of this Agreement, in respect of sales by Record Label on its top popular label in the United States of any album consisting entire of masters through Normal Retail Channels in the United States ("USNRC Sales") the royalty payable hereunder for such sales (as determined in accordance with the Record Label's standard accounting procedures and as reflected on statements rendered hereunder) shall be as follows:

(b) Artist Royalties Rate Escalation on Album (1) Sales shall be:

Albums Sold	Rate
0 to 499,999	10%
500,000 to 999,999	11%
1 million or more	12%

(c) Artist Royalty Rate Escalation on Album (2) Sales shall be:

0 to 499,999	11%
500,000 to 999,999	12%
1 million or more	13%

(d) Artist Royalty Rate Escalation on Album (3) based on sales:

0 to 499,999	12%
500,000 to 999,999	13%
1 million or more	14%

This chart above basically establishes a royalty rate that starts at a different base of 10 percent on album #1, 11 percent on album #2, and 12 percent on album #3, thus assuring the artist is constantly improving his share of the profits by raising his base royalty rate and imposing certain royalty increases as the album becomes gold, platinum, or better.

After the contract sets forth the royalty rate for the artist, the Record Label will generally have a clause explaining the payment to producer. Specifically, most producers will ask for "points," as stated above, which will typically come from the artist royalty payments. A typical clause could read as follows:

SECTION 7. PRODUCER POINTS

Producer Points. Artist will be solely responsible for producer points of three percent (3%) or less. Any producer points above three percent (3%) to a maximum cap of five percent (5%) will be split equally fifty/fifty (50/50) between Artist and Record Label. Record Label will be responsible for any part of percentage of producer's points that exceed five percent (5%) or higher.

This above clause sets forth that the label will reduce the artist royalty to pay the producer up until a maximum of three points. In the event, the producer's points is higher, the label will split this cost with the artist. A top-notch producer can demand a full 5-percent royalty. There are tons of lawsuits involving producers suing artists for points.

On April 15, 2006, the Grammy-winning singer-producer Kenneth "Babyface" Edmonds filed a breach of contract lawsuit against Anita Baker, claiming she owed him more than a quarter of a million dollars. Specifically, in his lawsuit, Babyface alleged that Baker broke two oral agreements with him, as co-writer, co-producer, and a performer on the song "Like You Used to Do" on her 2004 album *My Everything*. The lawsuit alleged that Baker refused to pay Babyface producers royalties equaling at least $100,000 from an estimated more than 500,000 album sold. He also alleged that he and Baker had an agreement to perform four concerts together, but that she canceled two shows and refused to pay him $150,000 in damages for those dates.

Another good example is the Tupac story. When Tupac Shakur died in 1996, he did not have solid legal counsel. In fact, Dina LaPolt, who advises the late rapper's mother and estate explained in a recent interview that "When Tupac died, he never had a music lawyer." And LaPolt advised, "When you are a recording artist, every royalty payment that goes to producers and other third-party royalty participants, people that perform on your album, comes out of the artist's royalty." With Tupac's combination of writing teams and producers, she explained, if they write music with the artist, then the artist has to do agreements with them, like song split agreements, so these people share in the publishing money." But, "when Tupac died, nothing was papered on his behalf." And, sadly, LaPolt shared, "Under the terms of Tupac's recording agreement, the label was still allowed to release all his albums notwithstanding the fact that none of the paperwork was done, and they just didn't pay him."

In fact, according to LaPolt, the record label "just froze all the royalty streams and kept their profits . . . and there was literally over $13 million in frozen royalty payments that belonged to Tupac, his producers, all his co-writers." LaPolt, a brilliant attorney, and other attorneys spent quite some time untangling the legal issues, going "song by song and working out all the copyright splits" to pay all the songwriters and producers, whether it was Dr. Dre or the OutLawz, to make sure everyone was paid. So the moral of the story as an artist is to understand the business of music in signing that recording contract and make sure paperwork is done to pay the producers and everyone else.

STANDARD DEDUCTIONS

From the SRLP of $19.99 for each compact disc (CD) sold, the record label deducts the manufacturing costs, excise taxes, foreign duties, and other expenses it incurred to reduce the amount of profit payable to the artist. Longstanding gospel artist William Becton, whose hit "Be Encouraged" sold over a million copies, often tells me, "the record label will deduct everything possible, and it's very important for artists to realize this when they sign a recording contract." With all of these expenses deducted from the label's gross profits, the record company will then pay a new artist a royalty rate somewhere between 7 and 12 percent of the SRLP for each CD sold in the United States market. In the sample contract language above, the artist started at a 10-percent royalty rate, with built-in potentials for escalation depending on sales increases.

DEDUCTIONS IN FOREIGN COUNTRIES

It is important to note that there is a different rate paid for non-American record sales. For example, in Canada, the artist receives the same royalty that he receives in the United States. But, in other countries, such as Japan and Australia, there may be a 25-percent reduction in the royalty rate. If so, the artist receives a 10-percent royalty in the United States (per chart), that royalty rate would be 7.5 percent in these markets. As for the rest of the world, or ROW, as abbreviated in the contract, the artist receives a 50-percent reduction in the royalty rate unless his or her representatives can secure a higher percentage. These rates are general standards, but an artist is always free to negotiate a better deal and seek higher royalty rates across the board. Naturally, this is only possible with solid legal representation.

New Artist vs. Superstar. In our hypothetical example we used a 12-percent royalty rate. It is important to understand that the artist royalty rate is determined by the status of the artist and how well that artist's representatives negotiate the deal. To determine the artist royalty rate and the negotiation process for such clauses we place the artist in one of three categories: new artist, mid-level artist, and superstar artist. The royalty scale for these three categories is usually as follows:

ARTIST	ROYALTY RATE
a) New artist	7%–12%
b) Mid-level artist	13%–15%
c) Superstar artist	16%–20% or higher

For purposes of illustrating the grid above, we can look at three urban artists who fit these categories. In 2002, EMI Gospel signed urban gospel artist Smokey Norful. Norful had sent me his demo years prior, and when he soared to success right out of the gate, I was not surprised at all given the hot production work of Derrick "DOA" Allen, who made the hit album. But, as a new artist his royalty rate most likely fell into the lower new artist category above of 7 to 12 percent. Despite his debut album being certified "gold" by selling over 500,000 units, unless he had specific step-up language in his contract that increased his royalty percentage upon reaching certain thresholds or number of records sold, he most likely continued to receive the royalty rate typical for a new artist. Furthermore, unless he renegotiates the term of his recording contract, he will most likely see the same royalty rate on album number two, and like most artists will stay in debt to his label for thousands of dollars as he records his future albums.

Likewise, artist Brian McKnight, who has sold a combined total of over 16 million albums, would command a royalty rate in the mid-level range. A mid-level artist is an artist who has not reached Michael Jackson or Prince status but has sold consistently over the years and usually sells a couple million copies on each album release. McKnight, who has recorded for several labels, including Motown for several years and now Warner Bros., has built a solid consumer audience that places him in the mid-level range in negotiating his royalty rate. Keep in mind that his expenditures, budget, and marketing costs are most likely much higher than a new artist like Norful, so despite the record sales, he can still find himself in debt to the label after a top-selling album.

Major performers like Alicia Keys, Whitney Houston, and Aretha Franklin are artists who could demand a superstar royalty rate and most likely receive over a dollar per record. An artist can begin to generally demand a superstar royalty rate when his or her sales have exceeded 10 million copies for a prior record. When an artist sells 10 million records that album is considered to have reached the "diamond" plateau. There are only a few artists who fall into this category (Britney Spears, the Backstreet Boys, Nelly, and Usher are a few). Keep in mind that they have achieved this level by being enormously successful for many years. Keys has sold more than 20 million records, Houston has sold over 80 million records, and Franklin, an icon for more than forty years, has sold over 100 million records. Usher took his hit song "My Boo" and stormed to over 10 million records sold in one album.

ROYALTIES NOT PAID

Whether a new artist, a mid-level artist, or a superstar icon, the record label will generally attempt to only pay on 90 percent of records sold. Record companies maintain that approximately one out of ten records or CD shipped to stores are damaged, returned, or destroyed. This is a discrepancy that has existed betweens artists and labels for years and in recent years artists have successfully fought the labels on this issue.

Record companies also refuse to pay artists a royalty on "free goods" given away as promotional or marketing materials. For example, in the fall of 2004, Universal urban artist Nelly released two CDs that debuted at #1 and #2 on the *Billboard* Top 200 Chart. In an attempt to create some buzz and excitement, Universal executives most likely sent out thousands of promotional copies of the album at no charge to radio stations, music journalists, and other potential marketing outlets.

Unfortunately for Nelly, these promotional copies, or "free goods," will not render any financial royalties for the superstar rapper, who has sold more than 20 million albums in the last five years. However, because of Nelly's superstar status, his representatives can request (and will most likely receive) a cap on the number of free goods given away. If it is possible, an artist should limit the number of free goods to no more than 5 to 10 percent of records shipped. The recording contract will provide a clause that states:

SECTION 8. FREE GOODS

Free Goods. Royalties shall not be payable with respect to the following: Records given away, invoiced on a "no charge" basis, or furnished at a substantially reduced price to any customary recipient of free or discounted promotional records, including, but not limited to, Artist, a disc jockey, a program director, a record reviewer, a radio or television station or network, a motion picture company, a music publisher, Record Label's employees, an individual producer, any performer on the record, an educational institution, a library. . . .

This language is clear in setting forth what records will not produce any monies or royalties for the artist. The artist should negotiate his or her contract to specifically state what are free goods and a limitation on how many records are sent out as free goods.

A Sample Royalty Calculation

With all of the information above, it is important to see how it plays out for the artist. Let us examine a sample royalty calculation. Many agreements will state the following: "A new artist has a 12-percent 'all-in' royalty." An all-in royalty rate means that the artist must pay the producer a royalty out of the artist's 12 percent. The producer royalty is generally around 3 percent, unless the individual is a superstar producer who commands a higher 5-percent royalty rate. Assuming for purposes of this illustration that the artist hired an average producer who charges the 3 percent, this leaves a 9-percent net royalty for the artist, who initially received 12 percent. From this 9-percent royalty, the following deductions are made:

> 25 percent for packaging
> 25 percent for the record company's reserves
> 15 percent for "free goods"
> 15 percent CD (new technology) deduction for a CD
> 10 percent for damaged or destroyed goods

Thus, the 12-percent all-in royalty is in actuality a 3.29 percent royalty after all deductions: 12 percent minus 3 percent (for the producer royalty) × 0.75 (for packaging) × 0.90 (discounting damaged goods for 90 percent of sales) × 0.85 (for "free goods" given away) × 0.85 (CD rate) × 0.75 (for reserves kept by label). Unfortunately, at the end of the day, the artist will receive approximately $0.65 cents for each $19.99 CD sold instead of the deceiving $2.39 (12 percent of $19.99). (We get this figure by dividing $19.99 by 3.29%, equaling 0.65 cents). And, as stated, even if the artist sells 1,000,000 (one million) copies, at .65 cents a record, the label would only owe you about $650,000 (and of course, all expenses would come out of your royalty check before you see a dime as an artist).

MARKETING AND PROMOTIONAL DEDUCTIONS

Free goods are considered a form of marketing for the label, along with advertising. If a record company has more than one artist on its roster, each artist will pay his share in a joint marketing campaign. Specifically, the label will purchase an ad and charge each artist a proportionate share of the label's total marketing and promotions cost. As background it is important to understand how important marketing is and we discuss such in depth in a later chapter. However, for this section, one key marketing player who comes to mind is Jackie Rhinehart.

As former Vice President of Marketing at Universal Records, pioneer Rhinehart worked on top artists Rakim, Nelly, Murphy Lee, Boyz II Men, and Erykah Badu, to name just a few. She explained to me that marketing is the real key for breaking an artist and often her goal was to "motivate the purchase of records." "I want to make an artist's concept clear so people can see what the artist is all about." Sometimes Rhinehart would "send out promo copies (i.e., free goods) of the album and solicit feedback." This *feedback* was used to give Motown a clear picture of the target audience, according to Rhinehart, a graduate of USC, who also worked with Dionne Warwick and LaFace Records.

Most likely if Rhinehart created a marketing plan for Universal Motown's artists, the cost was shared. For example, Motown had artists India Arie, Boyz II Men, and Smokey Robinson under contract. If the label bought a print advertisement featuring photos of these three artists, the cost of this advertisement would be divided among the artists and go toward their unrecouped balances or outstanding debt as listed on their royalty statements. An unrecouped balance is simply outstanding debt for monies the label has spent in the past. Likewise, labels hire street teams and independent promoters, or "indies," to promote an artist's record and create "street buzz." Generally, the record company attempts to pass this cost off to the artist, and the artist sees a huge "unrecouped" debt on the next royalty statement.

UNRECOUPED EXPENSES

The term *unrecouped* is important for an artist to understand. In our example, the artist sold a million records but still remains unrecouped. Most likely, 99 percent of all urban and gospel artists find themselves unrecouped and still in debt to the record company. An artist should be aware that any money advanced by the record company is deemed unrecouped, whether the money was used for recording purposes or personal matters—e.g., an apartment, clothing, a haircut, a video, a new car, or just cash in hand to the artist for per diems. If the record company lays out the money, they want to fully recoup what they spend.

A classic example is the instance above where a label spends $2 million to make an album, the accompanying videos, and the marketing blitz. The artist then goes on to sell a million records and the record company grosses well over $10 million (assuming the label had the record on sale at an SRLP of $10, this would tally as $10 × 1,000,000 units sold = $10,000,000). Assume the royalty clause in that artist's contract promises approximately $.60 per record after those items listed in our chart above are deducted. On a platinum-selling record the company would owe the artist $600,000 in royalties out of the $10 million gross. However, the label deducts this $600,000 amount from the "unrecouped" $1.5 million it spent to make the album, produce the videos, pay for all of the artist's personal expenditures (apartment, limos, clothes, et cetera), as well as the layout funds for the recording's marketing. So the math would be $1,600,000 (expenses) minus $600,000 (royalty amount owed to artist) which results in negative $1,000,000 (the negative debt owed by the artist on a platinum album). As a result, the platinum-selling artist heads into the studio to record his or her second album with a $1 million unrecouped debt. The label still turns a profit, grosses $10 million, and fully recoups its initial investment. The label relies solely on the artist's royalties to pay the album's cost. It's as if they create two pots: one with their profits and the other with the artist's profits. Unfortunately, they only dip into the artist's pot to pay the costs.

Top-selling R&B legend Freddie Jackson once told me that despite selling over 10 million records and recording a dozen top-selling hit songs (including "You Are My Lady," "Rock Me Tonight," "Jam Tonight," and "Tasty Love") he never saw a substantial royalty check. Jackson shared countless stories of how his label would always say those infamous words: "Freddie, you are still unrecouped."

That recoupment will travel with the artist from album one to album two and so on until you are fully recouped. In essence, you record a second album but still have debt from album one on top of the second album costs.

CONTROLLED COMPOSITIONS AND MECHANICAL ROYALTIES

The artist as a songwriter has to scan carefully for what is called a "controlled composition" clause. This is very important because it addresses not only who will own the songs and pay mechanical royalties, but also whether the artist will get the full statutory rate of nearly ten cents per song and per copy. The controlled competition clause generally reads as follows:

SECTION 9. CONTROLLED COMPOSITIONS AND MECHANICAL ROYALTIES

Mechanical Royalties. a) All musical compositions or material recorded pursuant to this agreement which are written or composed, in whole or in part by Artist or any producer of the masters subject hereto, or which are owned or controlled, directly or indirectly, in whole or in part, by Artist or any producer of the masters subject thereto (herein called "Controlled Compositions") shall be and are hereby licensed to Record Label for the United States and Canada and each other country throughout the world, at seventy-five percent (75%) of the minimum applicable United States or Canadian statutory royalty rate or other corresponding rate (without regard to playing time) as of the date upon which the Masters are first recorded hereunder. Mechanical royalties shall only be payable on records for which royalties are payable hereunder. The license granted in this subparagraph a) includes the right, without additional compensation, to record, reproduce and perform the Controlled Compositions in synchronization with audiovisual recordings.

Notwithstanding the above paragraph, the maximum rate which Record Label or its Affiliates or their licensees shall be required to pay in respect of an album shall be equal to ten (10) times the Controlled Composition Rate, and the maximum rate in respect of any other record shall be equal to the number of compositions contained thereon (not to exceed three (3) times the Controlled Rate). If a 12-inch (12") Single released by Record Label or its Affiliates, or their licensees contains more than two (2) recordings of the same Controlled Composition, such releasing party shall not be obligated to pay more than two (2) times the above rate in respect of such Controlled Composition on such record. Without limiting any other rights hereunder, if the aggregate mechanical royalty rate for any record exceeds the rate provided for herein, a pro rata share of such excess may be deducted from any and all sums due you hereunder.

In this clause, the label makes it clear as to what they will pay for each song written. As we will fully discuss in Chapter Fourteen, under copyright law a songwriter is paid approximately ten cents per copy sold for having a song appear on an album. If the artist is the songwriter and wrote all ten or so songs on the album, he or she will receive about one dollar for the total number of songs on the album per copy sold.

Note in this sample language above that the label limits to ten the number of songs on which they will pay the mechanical license fee. The label also seeks a license from the artist as songwriter to use these songs and requires that the ten cents is reduced to 75 percent of this figure, or what is commonly called, "3/4ths stat." The label will seek to limit the amount it pays to only ten songs at most. As a result, if an artist records an album with twenty-two tracks, the label is only paying mechanical royalties on an amount equal to $.075 $\times$ (times) ten songs, or $0.75 in total. The twenty-two tracks would be prorated to approximately 0.037 cents a song, per CD sold. (See our publishing story about the LOX later to fully understand.)

It is important to understand publishing income versus artist royalty income. As discussed in later chapters, the label pays an artist a royalty rate of about fifty cents per copy sold. However, any songwriter royalty is paid to the copyright owner. Thus, on a platinum album where the artist is allowed to include some of his or her song material, that artist could see a few hundred thousand dollars in mechanical royalties. For instance, if Diana Ross owned "Baby Love" and "Stop! In the Name of Love," she would still be collecting publishing income today on the millions of recordings sold, licensed, and reproduced each year.

Motown artists learned the hard way that mechanical license and publishing income trickles in over many years. For many urban artists, this income is their livelihood when they no longer have a record on the *Billboard* charts. As a result, it is highly encouraged that an artist develop as a writer for longevity and financial reasons. For example, a hit song like Stevie Wonder's "I Just Called to Say (I Love You)" can be licensed many times over for jingles, movie soundtracks, samples, remakes, re-releases, or commercials. If administered professionally the revenue for the writer would easily exceed seven figures annually.

Artists are best served by hiring an advisor to interpret and fully explain music publishing. But, owing to their failure to understand this concept, most urban artists end up financially strapped.

MUSIC PUBLISHING

Several years ago, Berry Gordy sold Jobete Publishing for more than $100 million to EMI Music Publishing. According to Marty Bandier, the head of EMI, the catalog is "the greatest American body of music produced during the twentieth century, [with] a library containing 100 number-one records." The announcement of the EMI purchase of Jobete sent shockwaves through the music industry and the business sector worldwide as it reportedly took two decades to win over Gordy. Most people were unaware that Gordy owned a substantial portion of the Motown hits. As a label president, Gordy guided the careers of Diana Ross and the Supremes, the Four Tops, the Temptations, the Jackson Five, Marvin Gaye, and many others. While publicly guiding their careers, Gordy was privately guiding the development of a lucrative publishing catalog. Unfortunately, many of the top artists of the Motown era did not understand what music publishing, co-publishing, mechanical licenses, and cross-collateralization meant to their careers. Years later, many would publicly complain of struggling financially, while Gordy amassed a fortune in publishing income. We discuss this at great length in Part III (copyrights) on music publishing, but it is very relevant to negotiating the recording contract as well.

For each song written by an artist that is five minutes or less, that artist can expect to earn approximately ten cents for every CD sold. As a result, a platinum-selling CD would earn the artist almost $90,000 to $100,000 for the placement of one original song, five minutes or less, written by the artist as the copyright holder. (A later section addresses what occurs if the song is longer than five minutes.) If the record company refuses to select any original material authored by the artist as the songwriter, that artist loses a great potential earning opportunity. When the artist, as a songwriter, grants the record label or its related entity, a share in the publishing, the publishing clause generally reads as follows:

SECTION 10. PUBLISHING

Publishing. Artist hereby consents and agrees to share, assign and convert a 50% interest in all of his copyrights for songs written during the Term. Artist hereby agrees to execute the necessary documents for purposes of indicating the joint ownership, and in the event of failure to do such, Artist grants the record label the power of attorney to file the necessary legal paperwork to effectuate joint copyright ownership.

As was the case with Gordy in the 1960s, today's music moguls and executives (Diddy, Dr. Dre, Kirk Franklin) are writers or producers themselves. In addition, they have writers with whom they frequently do business for the artists signed to their roster. So when a new artist signs with a label, the label generally knows which writer or producer it hopes to use for the project. All of these factors play a key role in whether the artist is able to secure his or her own original work on the album.

As previously stated, Gordy made a fortune selecting songs for his artists that he "coincidentally" owned. He also reaped the profits of that same material for years to follow in publishing income. Like Gordy, Diddy followed this blueprint with his Bad Boy label and co-owned many of the songs recorded on his artists' releases. A number of other label owners, including super-hot urban producers Jermaine Dupri, Dallas Austin, and Babyface have all selected and co-owned the material that their artists perform on a given album. Despite this common trend, an artist should try to secure his or her own material on their recordings and profit from the future publishing income associated with those songs.

As a new artist, it is difficult to demand to keep your publishing rights, but where possible an artist should seek a clause like that above, which retains all of the artist's rights as a songwriter and publisher of his or her original music. If the label owns the publishing, the clause would indicate a 50/50 split.

OWNERSHIP AND REVERSION OF MASTERS

Several years ago, a New Orleans rapper named Percy Miller started selling records from the trunk of his car. Many in the music industry thought Miller and his unknown label were just another fad. Most thought of Miller as another gang-member-turned-label-executive who wouldn't be around long. Little did the industry know that Master P (as Miller was called) would dramatically change the landscape of rap and prove artists and their self-owned labels could control the use of their master recordings.

Simply put, a "master" is that final embodiment of the music and lyrics that the artist records at a studio or recording facility in the form of a reel, tape, CD, DAT, or computer file. Once the complete master is recorded, the label orders copies from the master in the printing of the album. In recent years, several cases have been brought by artists seeking to maintain control of their masters or to force labels to turn over past recorded masters. As Suge Knight boasted, "It's always better to own your masters."

Generally, there are three reasons for an artist to own his or her masters: to receive the bulk of the revenue associated therewith, to control the licensing and exploitation of that music, and to control future greatest hits or re-releases of those same masters. Once an artist signs with a label and records masters, the label generally owns those masters, and the artist is prevented from ever re-recording them for anyone else for a fixed period of time. This clause is sometimes described as the exclusive "re-recording restriction." The record company often will insist on including contractual language to prevent the artist from recording the same songs and masters for either five years from the date the album is delivered to the label or five years from the date the label actually places the album in stores for sale, known as the "release date."

Either scenario serves to lock up the masters for years while the label maintains its exclusive rights to exploit them as the sole beneficiary in the marketplace. Once the album is delivered, the label can pull any hit songs from the masters and re-release them, although the artist is still bound from re-recording those hit songs. Even if the artist terminates his or her contract and signs a new contract with a new label, the original label will reap millions from re-releasing the old masters and old albums.

Yolanda Adams had to deal with this situation when she signed with Elektra. Prior to her Elektra contract, she was a signed artist with Verity-Zomba and had minimal success. After moving to Elektra she scored a double-platinum album, and Zomba swiftly released a collection of greatest hits, "best of," and compilation albums featuring Adams.

As a result, Zomba saw a windfall of profits from the marketing efforts of Elektra. This situation has been a tragedy for many urban artists who have filed suit to gain control of their masters or the right to re-record their hits. Their former label makes the argument that it spent thousands of dollars on the artist and his or her records and it needs to recoup its investment.

Master P thought differently and set the newest trend of hip-hop artists demanding ownership of their masters. Master P found himself on the Fortune magazine top money earners list as a result of his cleverness. Essentially, he earned millions by retaining the ownership and copyright in the masters and merely licensing the masters to his distributors for sale in commercial stores. By virtue of licensing songs without relinquishing any ownership interest, Master P most likely saw his retention of the gross profits fall somewhere in the 70- to 80-percent ballpark. Had he not owned his masters, the label would have raked in the majority of the profits, and Master P would have been another "unrecouped" hip-hop artist. Suge Knight, another gangster-turned-record executive and CEO of Death Row Records, owned and licensed two Tupac albums to Koch Distribution and has made millions from these albums and prior Interscope masters that Tupac recorded.

Likewise, Shekani Akur, the mother of Tupac, also owns a number of her son's masters and each year earns millions in licensing them for re-release on "best of" albums. When the rap legend died, he had 154 unreleased masters recorded, according to his attorneys. Very wisely, LaPolt, discussed earlier, and Ms. Akur have used these masters to release ten albums since Tupac's death and set up a center in his honor.

Both Master P and Knight helped educate other urban artists on the importance of retaining rights to their masters. Unlike in the 1960s and 1970s, the trend today is to request either retention of the masters or their reversion back to the artist after the label exploits them for so many years. If an artist does not have the ability of Master P to license their musical masters and catalogs, one suggestion is to request what's known as a "reversion of masters" clause. A reversion clause inserted in a recording contract can provide that after so many years, the masters revert to the artist who created them. A reversion of masters clause might look like this:

SECTION 11. REVERSION OF MASTERS

<u>Reversion of Masters.</u> During the term of this Agreement and for a period of five years thereafter, Record Label shall own, free and clear, all of the rights to said Masters. Upon conclusion of said period, the Masters shall revert to artist and artist shall own the Masters free and clear in perpetuity, including all proprietary and intellectual rights therein.

This clause is established to provide the label with a window (five to ten years) to earn back its recording costs, marketing costs, and overall financial investment, plus a profit. Likewise, if it is agreed that at some point the label has fully recouped, as we discussed above, it is not difficult to assert that the artist should gain control of the masters. But I must warn you that this is not a clause that record labels will easily concede to unless you are an artist with great leverage and bargaining power.

GROUP ARTISTS AND LEAVING MEMBERS

In 2003, urban artist Justin Timberlake released a very successful solo album for Jive-Zomba Records. The record sold over 3 million copies and soared up the *Billboard* charts. Many industry insiders thought Timberlake would sign with another label for solo projects. I would assume his Zomba group contract prevented such. Jive-Zomba had signed *NSYNC, Timberlake's main performing group, to a contract years earlier and had sold millions of the band's records. Standard record company policy required that any group member seeking to do a solo project had to deliver that album through the Jive-Zomba label. Columbia Records most likely had a similar agreement with Destiny's Child that allowed Columbia to release the solo projects of current group members Beyoncé Knowles, Kelly Rowland, and Michelle Williams.

A recording contract generally has a clause somewhere toward the end of the agreement that addresses "group members" or "leaving members." This clause gives the label first right of refusal to release the solo project of any group member. It also allows the label to replace any group member who leaves. The clause generally reads as follows:

SECTION 12. LEAVING MEMBERS

Leaving Members. In the event any member of the group decides to leave the group, or is replaced or incapacitated, or relinquished from his duties as a group member for any reason whatsoever, the Record Label shall have first right to either sign the group member as an individual artist and/or to replace the leaving member as it deems in the best interest of the group and the label.

Based on this language, the label has the artists signed individually and collectively. The Temptations reportedly own their name so they do not have any issues with a record label regarding band members. However, younger artists like En Vogue and Trin-I-Tee 5:7 most likely need label approval to change members or record solo projects. Again, when signing a contract as a new group artist, the standard label policy is to secure the rights to everyone in the group for life, whether solo albums or group projects.

SIDEMAN RIGHTS

It is important to note that while major urban music companies require exclusivity, many labels will allow their artists to appear as a guest artist on other labels. Super-hot urban producer and performer Missy Elliott, an Elektra artist, will often appear on a song or in a video with another artist who is signed to Sony or BMG. Although Elliott is signed to Elektra, her contract allows her to appear in cameos with Beyoncé, Janet Jackson, and Alicia Keys, to name a few, as a "sideman," not the main star. Elliott's contract most likely has a sideman provision, which usually reads as follows:

SECTION 13. SIDEMAN PARTICIPATION

<u>Sideman.</u> During the term of this Agreement, Artist will not perform for the purpose of nor will Artist engage in making records for anyone other than Record Label . . . provided Artist is not prohibited from either producing recordings for third parties or appearing as a so-called sideman. In connection with any such recording for anyone other than Record Label, the following conditions shall apply: (i) Artist's name and likeness shall not appear on the front cover of any such recording; (ii) on any liner or insert Artist's name shall not appear in larger size type than any other sideman; and (iii) Record Label shall receive a courtesy credit that states that Artist appears through the courtesy of Record Label.

This provision requires her to acknowledge that she is signed to Elektra Records exclusively and can only appear on another label's project if the album includes a credit such as this:

> "Missy Elliott appears courtesy of Elektra Records."

In essence, Elektra is granting the courtesy to Elliott to appear on Columbia Records' Beyoncé album so long as the above tag line is used on the album credits. Elektra makes it expressly clear to Elliott in her contract that while she can appear as a sideman, she cannot be featured as the main artist or central figure in the overall promotion of the album. As a result, Columbia could not include an Elliott photo on the album cover, although her name might be included by adding "Featuring the Missy Elliott single . . ." to the promotional materials. Elektra's goal is to enforce its contract and reserve its exclusive rights to maximize the marketing and promotion of a future Elliott project.

BANKRUPTCY

About a decade ago, one of the top-selling girl groups in the history of urban music headed into bankruptcy court and shook up labels nationwide. After selling over 10 million records, Atlanta-based urban trio TLC—a/k/a Rozonda "Chili" Thomas, Tionne "T-Boz" Watkins, and the late Lisa "Left-Eye" Lopes—sought bankruptcy protection because they could not pay outstanding debt. This came as a surprise to the urban music community, but TLC proved they weren't too proud to admit they were broke despite having released two multi-platinum albums and half a dozen top singles. When the three women all filed for bankruptcy court protection, the music industry took notice.

TLC's then-manager, Pebbles Reid (then-wife of current Universal top executive Antonio "L. A." Reid) of Pebbitone Inc., and the group's record label, LaFace Records (owned by L. A. Reid at the time), both rejected the bankruptcy claims of the group members and contended that they attempted to file solely for the purpose of pressuring LaFace into renegotiating TLC's contract. The two parties ultimately resolved their differences and released subsequent hit albums. However, the case shook the music industry and exposed the connection between bankruptcy law and the music industry.

TLC's filing, along with a filing by fellow LaFace labelmate and diva Toni Braxton (who went on *Oprah* to make her case), reverberated through the offices of record labels. The labels feared urban artists would utilize the case precedent as a quick and efficient way to break their contracts. Few cases drew as much attention as TLC's plight because of the group's success at the time of the suit. The group's first 1992 album, *Ooooooohhh . . . on the TLC Tip*, sold nearly 3 million copies with three major hits: "Ain't 2 Proud 2 Beg," "What about Your Friends," and "Baby, Baby, Baby." TLC's second album, *Crazysexycool*, sold over 7 million records worldwide. After that, TLC popped up everywhere—in a cameo for the film *House Party 3*, on the soundtrack for the Janet Jackson film *Poetic Justice*, and on tours with the likes of MC Hammer and Bobby Brown.

Despite their worldwide exposure, TLC's contract was not a good one, based on every report on the case. Specifically, TLC's contract with LaFace gave the group 7 percent of the revenues from the sale of the first 500,000 copies of their debut and follow-up albums. That increased to 8 percent on sales over a million copies. However, even if the group completed their entire contract length of eight albums, TLC's percentage increased to just 9.5 percent on sales of more than a million copies. (See our chart earlier in this chapter and recall that TLC should have seen a base royalty rate at 10 percent and rising as high as 14 percent.)

As a result, the group felt it was the best financial decision to file bankruptcy. As discussed above, after paying the producers and deducting all fees, this 9.5 percent would have decreased to a fee of 3 percent to be divided among three group members. By filing bankruptcy, TLC hoped to either force LaFace to the renegotiation table or ask the bankruptcy court to void their recording contract. As a result of cases like this, labels now insert a bankruptcy clause to prevent an artist from using bankruptcy to cancel their contract. That clause might read:

SECTION 15. BANKRUPTCY

Bankruptcy. Notwithstanding anything herein to the contrary, if Artist files a voluntary petition, or is the subject of an involuntary petition, for relief under any applicable chapter of the Bankruptcy Code, 11 U.S.C. §§ 101-1532, Artist agrees to assume this Agreement in accordance with section 365 of the Bankruptcy Code. Artist understands and agrees that inclusion of the foregoing provision in this Agreement was a material inducement for Company to enter into this Agreement.

Section 365 of the Federal Bankruptcy Code currently allows the court to free debtors from burdensome or onerous contracts that impair their ability to make a fresh financial start if the court deems it fair to do so. Artists signed to horrible contracts sometimes look to bankruptcy court as a way out. For example, Profile Records argued this was precisely the goal of three members of the rap group Run-DMC, who filed for bankruptcy in August 1993. The performers insisted they were broke and asked the court to cancel their Profile contract. Within months, the group stepped out of court with a better agreement with Profile Records.

During that same period, five members of the R&B group Silk, discovered by Keith Sweat, fought for months with Sweat's label Keia Records about their contract. On March 14, 1993, Silk's members filed for bankruptcy in Atlanta and immediately asked to be freed of their Keia contract. On October 11, 1993, the court approved a settlement that gave the group a new, more advantageous contract with Keia.

Today labels have become wiser and include language in their contracts that essentially vitiates any attempt to file for bankruptcy and void the contract. Specifically, a label will not allow an artist to merely walk away from a deal after it has spent thousands of dollars in support. Labels will now include a bankruptcy clause in all standard contracts, and artists should read the clause closely and understand the implications. Added bankruptcy law expert, Reginald Greene, "TLC and Toni Braxton educated the music industry on the federal bankruptcy code and the legal ramifications of an artist filing for bankruptcy protection."

OTHER TERMS AND CONDITIONS

There are a litany of other clauses that we could discuss in this section. The "Guaranteed Release Clause," for example, is covered extensively on our website. We also did not discuss such clauses as coupling, video rights, merchandising, release requirements, assignments, warranties and representations, the governing law provision, the morals clause, suspension and termination, force majeure, joint recordings, or the standard boilerplate clauses that appear at the end of most recording agreements. For purposes of this chapter, we have covered the major terms that an artist should be concerned with if he or she is considering signing with a record label and the contractual language you will see from time to time throughout this book. If you would like to see helpful articles and sample contracts, please visit our website: www.thisbusinessofurbanmusic.com.

CHAPTER 3

Signing a Management Agreement

> *"A manager can make or break you in the music business."*
> —R&B LEGEND FREDDIE JACKSON

Freddie Jackson is an icon of urban music. His string of eleven number-one R&B hits in the 1980s and 1990s have included "Rock Me Tonight," "You Are My Lady," and "Love Me Down." To many, Jackson, along with the late Luther Vandross, is one of the godfathers of an era during which R&B crossed into the music mainstream and sold millions of records. As Jackson is quick to tell you, the real key to a long-term career and success is good management. The person or agency you hire can take your career to new heights.

For years we have heard stories of black artists being ripped off by their managers. The parties usually end up in court, at which time the existence and interpretation of the management agreement becomes critical. Often, the parties had a handshake agreement and the court is left sorting through oral testimony, documents, and other communications to determine whether a management agreement was, in fact, in effect and what remedies are available to the wronged party.

It is critical for artists to formalize an agreement in writing with their managers, according to Jeanine McLean of MBK Entertainment in New York, which manages Alicia Keys. This is even more important if that manager is a family member, best friend, former roommate, or member of the band. Without a written agreement it is difficult to know what the parties agreed to initially.

A standard management contract can range in length from one to five years, depending on the comfort level of the parties involved. Personally, I advise somewhere in the middle at around three years, unless the artist signs an exclusive recording contract during the management relationship. If this occurs, the management agreement automatically extends the manager's term to run concurrent with that recording contract. In this chapter, we look at signing up with a manager, the role of the manager, and the terms of a management agreement.

KEY CLAUSES OF A MANAGEMENT AGREEMENT

The key clauses of a management agreement include the following:

- Appointment
- Term
- Option and sunset provision
- Commission
- Territory
- Power of attorney
- Warranty and representation

+ Assignment
+ Indemnification
+ Governing law

APPOINTMENT

When an artist hires a manager as his or her representative, he or she needs to be formally appointed as the artist's sole and exclusive manager. Industry veteran Alvin Williams, manager of the likes of Jonathan Slocumb and Rickey Smiley, among others over the years, explained on a recent music industry panel, "When you sign a manager, make sure it is done in writing and a formal relationship that spells everything out . . . this way, there is no future confusion between the artist and manager."

It is important to note that various managers are involved in an artist's career (for example, personal manager, road manager, and business manager). It is also important to note that you need a qualified person to be a manager. Seasoned manager Michael Elder explained, "A manager plays a specific role and a record company, in general, does not like to deal with an artist directly." Elder advised against hiring your "boys," adding, "I would not recommend a family member. In my opinion this person should be a seasoned veteran of the industry . . . not Pookie or Ray Ray," or the old hangers-on from high school.

For purposes of this discussion we will focus on the agreement between the artists and his or her personal manager. Thus, the appointment clause in the management agreement would read as follows:

Section 2. Engagement Duties and Responsibilities.

2.1 Artist hereby engages Manager and Manager hereby accepts such engagement on the terms and conditions herein set forth. During the Term and throughout the Territory Artist hereby appoints Manager and Manager hereby accepts such appointment, as Artist's sole and exclusive Manager in connection with all of Artist's endeavors and interest in the entertainment industry.

2.2 Manager shall render such advice, guidance, counsel, and other services as Artist may reasonably require to develop and further Artist's career including but not limited to the following services:

- To supervise Artist's professional employment and, on Artist's behalf, to consult with employers and prospective employers so as to assure the proper use and continued demand for Artist's services;

- To approve or disapprove the exploitation of Artist's personality in all media and in connection therewith to approve and permit, for the purpose of trade, advertising, and publicity, the use, dissemination, reproduction, or publication of Artist's name, photographic likeness, biographical materials, voice, artistic, and musical materials;

- To engage, discharge and/or direct theatrical agents, talent agencies, and employment agencies that will be retained for the purpose of securing contracts, engagements, or employment of Artist; and

- To represent Artist in dealings with the Record Company and other users of Artist's products and services.

In this clause there are several contractually binding elements. First, the manager usually accepts such appointment and guides, revises, counsels, and otherwise provides whatever the artist may reasonably require to further his or her career. Generally, we limit the scope of this managerial service to representing the artist and negotiating the terms of agreements for the use, employment, or exploitation of the artist's services and products solely in the entertainment industry.

Secondly, this clause requires the manager to supervise the artist's professional employment in the entertainment industry and to consult with employers and potential employers to protect his client. The manager is also required to work hard to create demand for the artist's services throughout the world—i.e., "exploitation" of the talents of the artist.

Finally, by agreeing to the appointment, the artist must be available at reasonable times and places. The manager will confer with the artist on all matters concerning the artist's career when bookings and concert dates are offered.

As an aside, it is important to note that in some states the manager should be licensed to procure certain engagements for the artist. A couple of years ago, when Jennifer Lopez fired legendary industry manager Benny Medina and brought legal action, one of the main controversies centered around Medina securing work for Lopez allegedly without a license in the state of California. Lopez sought a return of commissions and to void the management agreement on grounds that Medina overstepped his rights as a manager when he negotiated film and other deals on her behalf. Medina, a manager for the likes of Will Smith, Mariah Carey, and Diddy, to name a few over the years, fought back, and the case was eventually worked out between the parties.

However, it is important to note the clever statutory license that Lopez raised initially in attempting to circumvent the management agreement. And, many years ago, in the same jurisdiction, the late comedian Richard Pryor took his manager to court for breach after losing millions of dollars. As a result of a multitude of cases, California has implemented certain restrictions and requirements of managers, agents, and the like that affect what types of business transactions they can perform for the artist.

Remember when signing an agreement you are appointing someone else as your "exclusive" representative to negotiate and handle all matters on your behalf. If you are not ready for management, then do not sign a management agreement, or simply limit the appointment clause as to what advice or matters the manager can handle.

In addition, do not appoint a manager to guide, supervise, negotiate, and manage your entertainment matters, if you plan to do the work of a manager yourself. Making calls to the media, record labels, promoters, concert halls, and booking agents are some of the duties you are delegating to your manager. The appointed manager will be ineffective if these duties are not truly assigned for his control.

Conversely, if you agree to take on the role of manager for an artist, understand that the artist expects you to spend each and every waking hour of the day calling, faxing, e-mailing, and mailing letters, photos, and the like out to everyone who could possibly put the artist on the map. If you do not have the personality, ambition, or determination as a manager required to "make things happen" (as the artist will challenge you to do), then decline the flattering offer and find another job.

TERM

One of the biggest legal problems for artists attempting to rescind a management agreement is its duration. How long was the artist supposed to be bound to the manager? As attorneys, we often struggle when we seek to terminate a management agreement the artist has signed with several options that the manager can unilaterally exercise at the close of the initial contract.

Unfortunately when this happens an artist has two options: buy out the manager or ride out the long-term agreement in misery. For an example, a couple of years ago, Baltimore teen heartthrob Mario filed a lawsuit to free himself from a long-term management and production deal signed when he was still a minor with music producer Troy Patterson. The suit was filed against Patterson and his Third Street Music Group, who Mario claimed made "hundreds of thousands" of dollars from Mario's multiplatinum album sales, and only paid Mario about $50,000 of the success. Patterson, who signed Mario in 2000, entered into a seven-album record deal for Mario with J Records. In the lawsuit, reportedly settled, Mario alleged that Patterson "insinuated" himself into Mario's life eight years previously, during a time when the singer's father was not in his life and his mother was addicted to drugs. Patterson eventually became Mario's legal guardian and acted as his personal manager, business manager, record company, and publisher. If this were the case, it is clearly too many titles for one entity or individual to hold without a conflict of interest. Mario would later join forces with manager Mathew Knowles (father of Beyoncé Knowles) and become an artist under the Music World/Sanctuary Urban Management team. Although he and Patterson resolved their differences, most likely with a buyout and future sharing of income with Patterson, it symbolizes the point of signing a bad long-term management agreement if you are not aware of the key terms and long-term problems.

In a standard management agreement, the initial term might be one or two years and up to five years, all depending on the manager's clout in the industry. However, the term is extended if during the period the manager secures a deal with a major record label or a major production company. For example, the manager can sign the artist on January 1, 2008, for two years. During those two years the manager secures a recording deal for the artist with Motown Records, so the contract with the manager will automatically extend, in some cases for three more years. In this case, it is also possible for the manager's agreement to extend to five years. The smart manager will make sure the agreement runs concurrent with the Motown recording agreement, so they share in the growth and hopeful future wealth and success of the artist.

It is very important for the artist to have a clear understanding of the contract language that spells out the term of the agreement. For an artist to avoid being locked into a seven- to ten-year management agreement he must first recognize the initial length of the agreement and the additional options.

OPTION AND SUNSET CLAUSE

Somewhere in the section of the agreement known as the term will be included the right of the manager to keep the artist signed for additional years after the term has expired. A typical management agreement will sometimes unilaterally allow the manager to exercise what's called an option, which is essentially the manager's right to keep the artist under contract for another year or two, depending on what the contract stipulates.

We highly advise our clients to give the manager a preliminary period. This period lasts between six months to one year, and during this period the artist and manager can grow together and see if there is chemistry and productivity between the two. Most important, the artist has the option to say, "If you get me a recording contract during the first year, then the management agreement will include an option clause to extend for another four to five years." This also gives the manager the opportunity to ask for one year to produce for his client. If he is unable to do so the agreement can be terminated.

The option is usually tacked on at the end of the term. As stated above, it is important to make sure there is some trigger language and/or consideration for this option. The option should not be given too easily. The manager should perform some service during the original term to justify the option. Says New Edition pioneer and former manager to Boyz II Men and tons of others Michael Bivins, "If a manager ain't performing, an artist does not need to give him options to extend for a longer term. The contract should expire after a brief period if the manager does not deliver a recording contract or some serious success for his client." Added Michael "Blue" Williams, who manages Outkast, Nick Cannon, and Nas, among others, "My role is to get the checks for the clients, and if I'm not delivering that, then there's no reason for me to be on the team for five years or even two years."

Within the manager's contract is another section known as the sunset clause, called that because the "sun goes down" on the monies that the manager is to earn. The sunset provision provides that at a certain specific date and time, the manager's commission on continued sources of royalties are reduced or eliminated.

An example of a sunset clause language might read as follows:

Section 3. <u>Term.</u>

If at any time during the Term of this Agreement, Manager is terminated or this Agreement shall expire, Manager shall only be due those commissions that were accrued and payable due for his services at the time of termination or expiration; (OR)

If Manager is fired, his commissions on any and all past deals and transactions shall be limited to two (2) years following the date of termination.

Keep in mind a sunset clause phases out the future earnings of the manager if the agreement is terminated. The manager will not receive a 10 percent commission for the life of the artist's career if he is terminated or the agreement expires and this clause kicks in motion. Our office has seen many situations in which a manager will work with an artist and as the artist's career takes off, for whatever reasons, he fires the manager. The former manager then argues his commission should run forever based on things that happened while he was manager, and in some cases, the manager is right. To avoid this, somewhere in the agreement under the commission clause, you want to make sure your legal representative places some limitations on how long the manager can financially ride the agreement if fired.

COMPENSATION

For years we have heard stories about managers exploiting their artists or producers. Rumor in the industry has it that Sean "Diddy" Combs allegedly takes nearly 30 percent of the earnings of the artists and producers he manages or controls. Diddy has repeatedly rejected any reference to ripping off his artists or producers. So what is a commission, and why is it the most uncomfortable word in the industry? A commission is the negotiated percentage the manager will receive from the artist's earnings. This percentage usually falls between 10 and 20 percent, according to industry manager Darren Hall. Here is a calculated example to help you better understand. If you performed on a tour and earned $5,000 per engagement, a 10-percent commission of $500 would be paid to the manager. It is called a commission because it is earned off of the fee the artist gets from a third party. Generally, the commission is based on the net earnings to artists versus the gross.

There are several factors to consider in determining the appropriate commission or fee to give the manager for services rendered. Those factors include experience, expertise, contacts, role, duties, and your needs. Sometimes, the commission can come later in the artist's career. Veteran industry manager Gwen Edwards, who managed Nancey Jackson for years, explained that "a beginning artist might be able to self-manage—or have a management consultant to whom he or she might negotiate a flat fee." Edwards added that, "as the artist steps up his or her game (mid- to higher levels) they should consider management on a commission basis as their ability to generate revenue (performance, recording, licensing, etc.) escalates."

Experience and contacts are the two most critical of these factors. If a manager has a track record of making hit R&B artists and has contacts in urban music, it is difficult not to give him a 20-percent commission on your earnings. However, if the manager is fairly inexperienced and has no established track record, he or she will generally accept a 10-percent commission of the artist's gross compensation.

In the management agreement, the standard compensation language should read:

Section 4. Compensation.

As compensation for the services of Manager, Artist shall pay and Manager shall accept the following:

Twenty Percent (20%) of Artist Gross Earnings from live performances and/or other work specifically contracted by Manager. Artist hereby irrevocably assigns to Manager the foregoing interest in Gross Earnings.

a) Artist Gross Earnings shall be paid to in the first instance to Manager, for Manager the portions of Artist Gross Earnings that equals Manager's compensation and such disbursement incurred by Manager on behalf of Artist, such amounts to be remitted to Manager with an appropriate accounting statement within five (5) business days of receipt. Whenever Manager receives Gross Earnings directly, Manager shall keep appropriate records and may withhold his compensation therefrom and may reimburse himself for any fees, costs, or expenses or loans advanced or incurred by Manager, and Manager shall render the balance to Artist or deposit the balance in an account maintained for the benefit of Artist within fifteen (15) days of receipt.

b) Artist shall be solely responsible for payment of all talent agency fees, union dues, publicity costs, promotion or exploitation costs, traveling expenses, and/or wardrobe expenses and all other expenses, fees, and costs incurred by Artist or by Manager on Artist's behalf. If Manager advances any of the foregoing fees, costs, or expenses on behalf of Artist, or incurs any other reasonable costs, fees, or expenses in direct connection with Artist's professional career or with performance of Manager's services hereunder (other than Manager's own legal, accounting, and/or bookkeeping or other general overhead expenses), Artist shall promptly reimburse for such fees, costs, and expenses.

c) The parties agree to keep complete and accurate books of account as to their respective financial obligations hereunder. Each part shall have reasonable access to the books of account and records of the other (including the right to inspect and copy supporting documents such as receipts and vouchers) for the purpose of verifying accounts, including the right to cause the other's books and records to be inspected and copied by a certified public accountant or an attorney.

It is very important to understand this section before signing a management agreement. Section 4a) gives the manager power to control the finances. By understanding this language as an artist, you will be able to make sure he does not step over his boundaries. First, under this section the manager collects your compensation. He is required to keep records, take out his fee or commission, and reimburse himself for any monies spent on your behalf or loan advances. It is important that you keep your own records and are aware of the "running tab" you might have with your manager when he is covering expenses. These expenses can include cab rides, plane tickets, hotel rooms, and other incidental expenses such as mailings or faxes. You could earn decent money for a performance but only receive a fifty-dollar check because of an outstanding debt with the manager for six months worth of work on your behalf.

Section 4b) above is also important for you to understand as a new artist. You may want to join the unions, the National Academy of Recording Arts and Sciences (NARAS) or subscribe to industry magazines such as *Billboard* and *Rolling Stone*. In the end it is you, the artist, who is footing the bill. Likewise, if the manager tells you, "I need to fly to LA to meet with 'some folks,'" under this same clause, he or she could seek reimbursement for that as well. Make sure to get an itemized advance itinerary from your manager with a detailed breakdown of what he is charging you for. Be sure everything is in writing and that you keep records during the entire term of your agreement with the manager appointed to handle your entertainment matters.

Finally, do not allow the manager to dictate to you as an artist what his commission percentage should be. Consider the factors above and if necessary call executives at urban labels or other R&B or hip-hop outlets to ascertain whether the commission is reasonable. Doing research before hiring a manager will help avoid trouble in the long run.

TERRITORY

The territory, simply put, is a limitation on whether the management agreement is domestic (only America) or worldwide. Is his or her appointment for worldwide services or is it just in a specific geographical area? For example, you could hire one manager to solely handle the United States music scene, then, after extensive research, an artist could hire the best management in R&B to handle his or her career overseas.

In a standard management agreement the territory clause is straightforward and will read as follows:

Section 5. Territory.

Artist hereby appoints manager to the following territory: Worldwide.

As you can see, in this clause, a manager is given the right to handle everything domestically and overseas during the term of the agreement. Given the need to synergize all efforts here and abroad, it is not uncommon for a manager to represent an artist worldwide. Most managers who have experience would reject a co-management status with another company overseas, although it is not uncommon for high-profile artists to utilize co-management.

POWER OF ATTORNEY

Once your career takes off as an artist, you may need a manager to hold what's called power of attorney. This allows another person the authority to sign and execute documents on your behalf and for it to legally bind the artist who gave this power of attorney. Power of attorney is a very sensitive matter, because everyone fears that their manager will abuse this power to sign off on a million-dollar check and flee to the Cayman Islands with the artist's cash.

This concern is both right and wrong for several reasons. Indeed, there are some horrible managers who have abused the power of attorney. However, there are a far greater number of credible managers that utilize this authorization for good reasons. They see to it that documents get executed in a timely manner and do not need to disturb the artist, who is normally traveling for weeks at a time, for signatures as paperwork arrives in the office each day.

Once an artist becomes a star, it is not uncommon to travel six out of seven days a week with each night in a different town and need a manager to handle office paperwork to keep the ball moving on other business matters. Specifically, I remember gospel sensation Yolanda Adams appearing one night at the Stellar Awards, at another gala a day or two later, followed by a few concerts in several cities, and then at the Grammy Awards just weeks later. This is the life that many successful urban artists will deal with if they are juggling TV, radio, and concert appearances and the like. This is why they will give power of attorney, while busy performing, like Adams.

It is not unusual to have a manager who handles some of the contracts and paperwork that needs to be executed in a timely fashion. The power of attorney clause is supposed to deal with this time crunch and authorize the manager to sign off and keep the career moving smoothly. This power of attorney clause usually reads as follows:

Section 6. <u>Power of Attorney.</u>

Artist irrevocably appoints Manager for the Term and for the Territory as Artist's true and lawful attorney-in-fact:

- To sign, make, execute, and deliver contracts for the rendition of Artist's services or the use and exploitation of Artist;
- To endorse, accept, and collect for deposit bills of exchange, check, notes, cash, or other payments or considerations received in connection with Artist endeavors or interests in the entertainment industry;
- To demand, sue for, collect, recover, and receive all goods, claims, money interests, or other items that may be due to Artist in connection with any service rendered or product created by Artist either directly or indirectly;
- To prosecute, defend, submit to arbitration and/or compromise, or settle all actions, suits, accounts, reckonings, claims, and demands whatsoever relating to any interest of Artist or Lending Company in such manner and in all respects as Manager in Manager's best business judgment shall deem advisable; and without in any way limiting the foregoing, generally do, execute, and perform any other act, deed, or thing whatsoever that reasonably appears to Manager ought to be done, executed, and performed relating to Artist's professional career and interests as fully and effectively as Artist could do if personally present; and Artist hereby ratifies and affirms all acts performed by Manager by virtue of this Power of Attorney.

Section 6 above is one of the most straightforward clauses in a typical music-industry management agreement. It is important to note several things from the clause. For instance, the appointment is irrevocable, meaning that you cannot take it back once you have signed the agreement and the agreement is in place. In addition, under this clause, you are granting the manager the right to sign, execute, deliver, endorse, accept, and collect among other descriptions on your behalf. The manager can also sue for, collect, record, and receive all monetary interest on behalf of the artist in connection with any services rendered or product created by the artist.

It is important to note that the manager can prosecute, defend, submit to arbitration and/or compromise, or settle all actions, suits, accounts, reckonings, claims, and demands whatsoever in the "manager's best judgment." As written, this clause is very broad. Depending on the experience of the manager, you may want to narrow this language or leave it as is. A seasoned manager would not abuse this clause but would use it strategically and wisely. However, a new or less experienced manager might overstep his or her boundaries and take advantage of this power.

As an artist you want to make sure this clause is specific to the entertainment industry. There have been many abuses by managers of their power of attorney rights. This happens when the artist has not clearly stated that the power of attorney is limited to the entertainment industry affairs of the artist. Specifically, the manager is only entitled to sign on matters relating to your career as an artist. "I tell artists all the time, you have to know what your manager is doing and make sure he or she is keeping you in the loop on everything," says Phillana Williams, a top manager who handles super-hot artist Ciara. Added Darren Hall, "With email and fax machines, a good manager can educate his or her artist daily on the work being performed."

In addition, the artist also wants to make sure the amount of weekly expenditures that the manager can sign off on is limited. You might recommend that your manager is only approved to spend up to five hundred dollars and anything higher will need your written approval as the artist. Or, you might require the manager to forward copies of any checks or contracts he executes, signs, or delivers to you within three days of receipt or execution. So, if your manager signs a check from Sony on February 1, by February 4 you should receive a copy of that check. This process will enable you to keep your own records accurate and up-to-date.

To specifically limit the breadth of the power of attorney clause, our office generally will include language as follows:

> e) Notwithstanding Section 6 above, pursuant to the power of attorney granted herein, Manager and Artist agree:
>
> 1) Manager shall not enter into any long-term contract for Artist's exclusive services without the express consent of Artist;
>
> 2) Manager shall not exercise any of the above granted prerogatives unreasonably, i.e., without seeking professional advice where advisable;
>
> 3) Manager shall not exercise any of the above granted prerogatives without consulting with Artist where reasonable and practicable.

While no contractual language is foolproof, here we have placed some requirements on the manager to exercise the power of attorney with rational judgment and reasonableness. Additionally, we have provided the language of consent for a long-term contract. There are countless rumors of managers signing off on cars, real estate, and houses claiming they had the power of attorney to do such deeds. With the artist consent required, it is difficult for a manager to enter into such a long-term contract.

A power of attorney clause is needed for the busy artist who wants his or her manager to keep the ball moving. Nonetheless, it is critical for you to keep up-to-date on all documents being signed on your behalf. Most importantly, it is critical to know about all checks tendered and cashed on your behalf.

The simple rules: demand copies of everything and an itemized weekly breakdown as you would require if there were a real attorney exercising matters on your behalf. Added Hall, "I photocopy everything and give my artists copies of any payment I receive or execute."

WARRANTIES AND REPRESENTATIONS

We have now discussed most of the major clauses in a management contract, but the warranties and representations clause is important from a legal standpoint and a key matter to discuss in reviewing your management agreement. In it you warrant and represent that you are free to sign the agreement and that there is no other previous agreement that you have signed. By "warrant" we legally mean that you represent without any hesitation that what you are stating is true. The warranty and representation clause is straightforward and usually has a clause that reads as follows:

Section 7. <u>Warranties and Representations.</u>

Each party represents and warrants to the other that he/she/they has/have the full right, power, and authority to enter into this Agreement and to grant to the other all of the rights purported to be granted herein.

Here you also warrant and represent that you are of the age necessary to sign an agreement of this sort. If you are a minor, you need your parents or guardians to sign or co-sign the agreement.

ASSIGNMENT

Another section to be aware of is the section dealing with what we call an assignment clause. You want to bar sale or assignment of your contract by the manager except to a firm in which he continues as a key person. For example, if you were managed by Benny Medina and he creates the Medina Group with other managers, he could assign your contract to the group, but he would be a critical part of the team and still provide you quality service. Essentially, you do not want a manager to build a company with you as a key artist asset, sell the company to a bigger conglomerate, and then he walks off and leaves you with a horrible conglomerate managing you. Thus, an assignment clause generally reads as follows:

Section 8. <u>Assignment.</u>

This agreement is personal to each of the parties, and neither party shall have the right to assign this Agreement to any third party without the prior written consent of the other, provided, however, that Manager shall have the right to assign this Agreement to a corporation that is substantially owned and controlled by Manager and that agrees to furnish the personal services of Manager to Artist for the purposes of this Agreement.

This assignment language prevents the manager from assigning the artist contract without your written consent. This is critical in the music industry because of the frequency with which labels are sold and transferred to other companies without any input from their artists.

INDEMNIFICATION

When it's raining outside you protect yourself under an umbrella. In the music industry, you protect yourself under the indemnification clause. Your manager wants you to open an umbrella over him when someone attempts to sue him for your deeds or misdeeds. The standard indemnification clause will read as follows:

Section 9. Indemnification.

Artist hereby agrees to indemnify and hold harmless the manager for any disputes, legal actions, or lawsuits that may arise in connection with this agreement as a result of the actions of the Artist, whether indirectly or directly.

Artists sometime forget contracts or agreements that they have made in the past. They often do not realize that we live in a highly litigious society. As a result, most managers will demand that they are indemnified or covered from any potential suits that may arise from the actions, or inactions, of an artist. For example, one well-known artist is known to skip his contracted performance dates and incite riots from town to town. His manager wants assurance that in the event a suit is filed and he or she is named as a defendant, that artist will cover the suit and pay all the associated legal fees.

GOVERNING LAW

This clause is very standard practice and deals with the interpretation and enforcement of the contract. Specifically, what state law will be applied, and what state courthouse will we, as the artist and manager, go to if we have a dispute. A manager will typically include his home state for preferential treatment or to avoid traveling a long distance in the event of a dispute. Alternatively, the clause might require the parties go before an arbitrator or arbitration board before heading to court. A typical governing law clause might read like this:

Section 10. Governing Law.

This Agreement shall be construed in accordance with the laws of New York State applicable to agreements, entered into and wholly performed therein. In the event of dispute, the parties agree prior to the commencement of a legal action, the parties will meet with an arbitrator, pursuant to the American Arbitration Association.

TYPES OF MANAGERS

Now that we have discussed management in general, it is important to distinguish the different types of managers: the personal manager, the road manager, and the business manager. Each of these plays a distinct role in guiding the artist's career.

PERSONAL MANAGER

The personal manager is the most influential in the artist's career. He or she would enter into the exclusive management agreement with you, subject to the terms discussed throughout this chapter. The personal manager does everything possible to make you a success, including, but not limited to, securing a recording contract, organizing a tour, arranging travel, coordinating media, and finding a financial advisor for you.

The personal manager oversees any other managers, lawyers, agents, accountants, publicists, and others who serve the artist each day. Outkast manager Michael "Blue" Williams explained in a recent interview that a personal manager must start with a game plan and "know your artists and what they're capable of, (and) what they will and won't do." Also, a personal manager's percentage can fluctuate between 10 and 20 percent or even higher, depending on experience. The good managers all rule by thinking wise, solving problems, and not solely flexing their power.

ROAD MANAGER

The road manager is generally sent out on the road with the artist. When the artist is on tour he or she travels from town to town with the artist. The road manager is usually on a weekly or monthly stipend and is paid a fee based on various factors. Those factors include, but are not limited to, the size of the tour, the length of the tour, the number of artists on the tour, and the experience of the road manager. Debbie May is one of the top road managers in the gospel and R&B industry. Having been on the road with Bobby Jones, Mary J. Blige, Jamie Foxx, and Fantasia, among dozens of others, May notes that "a road manager is the key to holding things together out on tour."

According to May, the road manager's job is to assure that every detail is covered while the artist is on the road. For example, the road manager would have all pertinent information required for the traveling plans. He or she will have the directions, transportation details, reservations, and all travel information. The road manager will ensure that if there are any details that the artist should be aware of before arriving in a given city—radio interviews, etc.—he or she has the information. The road manager plans several days ahead of arriving in a city and will have these plans written out in detail for the artist. If the show is a paying engagement, on some occasions, it is the responsibility of the road manager to collect payment from the promoter when the artist arrives at the venue. The road manager also makes sure the hotel rooms and all backstage details are in order. For example, some artists prefer their hotel room to be set at a particular temperature or need their dressing rooms to have certain lighting. Absurd or outrageous demands have become notoriously commonplace on performance-contract riders. This is an area that the road manager must assure is handled appropriately.

BUSINESS MANAGER

Two of the music industry's most successful business managers are Los Angeles–based Laura Gordon of Gordon and Associates and Bert Padell of the firm Padell, Nadell, Fine & Winberger. Gordon has served as business manager for Lou Gossett, David Talbert and Jamie Foxx to name a few. Padell has served as the business manager for the likes of Madonna, Wyclef Jean, and Alicia Keys. During a recent panel discussion at BMI, Padell shared with us that a business manager generally takes a 3- to 5-percent commission. The business manager will pay all of the bills. He or she will assure that all taxes are filed and that all monies are deposited into the right account. The business managers also take care of paying and withholding taxes and ensure that all health insurance and other types of filings are done appropriately. A good business manager will make sure that the artist sets up a retirement fund as well and has a retirement fund for years to come once his career slows down. All financial details go through the business manager, and he or she should be solely and totally aware of the artist's financial situation.

CLOSING THOUGHTS

There are literally thousands of things to tell you that artists commonly do in hiring a manager. Here are three closing thoughts from our experienced managers:

First, don't hire a manager who is the "flavor of the month." A manager who does phenomenal things for another artist may not be the manager for you. Finding the right fit is like having a tailor-made article of clothing. And get to know your prospective manager first.

Second-guessing management decisions on a regular basis breeds trouble, our second closing thought. Good managers juggle a lot of issues that you might not be aware of. If you don't have a comfort level with the manager, don't hire him. Trust is of the utmost importance.

Last, do not rely on the manager to bankroll and finance you. Establish the source of your own financial stability from the start and let the monetary issues in your artist/manager contract be clear.

In closing, I would amend the opening Freddie Jackson statement of this chapter to say, "A good manager and management contract" can "make or break" your career.

A SAMPLE MANAGEMENT AGREEMENT

Following is a sample management agreement that will be helpful to you in understanding how all of the clauses come together. Please be aware that you as an artist can have a management agreement exactly like or totally different from this agreement. However, the general terms should somewhat resemble the following and have the same overall intent and effect.

MANAGEMENT AGREEMENT

This Management Agreement (the "Agreement") is made this _____ day of _____, 2008 by and between _____

(hereinafter referred to as "Artist") and _____

(hereinafter referred to as "Manager"), having an address of _____

_____

RECITALS

WHEREAS, Artist performs as recording artist and musician and otherwise under the name "_____";

WHEREAS, Artist wishes to obtain advice, guidance, counsel, and direction in the development and furtherance of Artist's career as a performing and recording artist, musician, composer, arranger, writer, producer, publisher, and in such new and different areas as Artist's artistic talents can be developed and exploited, including but not limited to, the fields of motion pictures, television, radio, recording, legitimate theater, music and book publishing, advertising, concerts, and all other areas appurtenant to the entertainment industry (Artist's Career);

WHEREAS, Manager has acted as Artist's personal advisor and is willing to continue to be associated with Artist and to act as Artist's personal advisor upon the terms and conditions hereinafter set forth; and

WHEREAS, the nature and extent of the success or failure of Artist's career cannot be predetermined and it is therefore the mutual desire of Artist and Manager that Manager compensation be predicted on Artist's success or failure in the entertainment industry.

NOW, THEREFORE, in consideration of the mutual promises and agreements, the representations and recitals contained herein and for other good and valuable consideration, the receipt and sufficiency of which is hereby acknowledged and agreed not to be challenged later, Artist and Manager agree as follows:

Definitions: As used in this Agreement, the following terms shall have the following meanings:

Term: Shall mean a period of two (2) years commencing on the date first above written (hereinafter referred to the "Period"), provided, however that if Artist shall have received a bona fide written offer to enter into a "Recording Contract" (as hereinafter defined) or if Artist signs a Recording Contract during the Period, the Term shall be automatically extended and commencing on the date of the Recording Contract, and running concurrent therewith.

Territory: Worldwide.

Gross Earnings: Shall mean the total of all monies or things of value (whether in the form of salary, fees, royalties, advances against or guarantees of royalties, percentages, shares of profits or other contingent interests, merchandise, shares in ventures, products, properties) wherever and whenever paid or accrued to the account of Artist or a "Lending Company" (i.e., either during or after the expiration of the Term) from or connected with any of the following:

Contracts or commitments in or concerning the entertainment or amusement industries (whether oral or written and in whatever from) entered into by Artist or a "Lending Company" (i.e., a corporation set up to loan out Artist's services) or substantially negotiated for either of them during the Term for the full term (including extensions by option exercise or renewal) of any such contract or commitment; or

Services rendered or products of any kind created in whole or in part during the Term by Artist, whether individually, jointly, or through a "Lending Company."

Gross Earnings shall not include production expenses or distribution expenses paid by Artist to any third party and not retained by you or any such company as fees or profits.

> Lending Company: Shall mean a business entity formed for the purpose of and/or engaging in the business of furnishing, lending, using, owning, or exploiting any product or service of Artist.

> Recording Contract: Shall mean a written agreement under which an independent third party ("Record Company") agrees to finance the production of master recordings embodying performances of Artist and acquires the right to cause recordings of any kind or nature made therefrom to be offered for sale.

2. Engagement duties and responsibilities

Artist hereby engages Manager and Manager hereby accepts such engagement on the terms and conditions herein set forth for the Term as defined in Paragraph 1.1 hereof.

During the Term and throughout the Territory, Artist hereby appoints Manager and Manager hereby accepts such appointment, as Artist's sole and exclusive Manager in connection with all of Artist's endeavors and interests in the entertainment industry.

Manager shall render such advice, guidance, counsel, and other services as Artist may reasonably require to develop and further Artist's career including but not limited to the following services:

To supervise Artist's professional employment and, on Artist's behalf, to consult with employers and prospective employers so as to assure the proper use and continued demand for Artist's services;

To approve or disapprove the exploitation of Artist's personality in all media, and in connection therewith to approve and permit, for the purpose of trade, advertising, and publicity, the use, dissemination, reproduction, or publication of Artist's name, photographic likeness, biographical materials, voice, and artistic and musical materials;

To engage, discharge and/or direct theatrical agents, talent agencies, and employment agencies, which will be retained for the purpose of securing contracts, engagements, or employment of Artist; and

To represent Artist in dealings with the Record Company and other users of Artist's products and services, provided that such representation is not intended to include procurement of employment for Artist or any other services requiring Manager to be licensed in any state in which manager may transact any such business.

3. Power of Attorney

Artist irrevocably appoints Manager for the Term and for the Territory as Artist's true and lawful attorney-in-fact:

To sign, make, execute, and deliver contracts for the rendition of Artist's services or the use and exploitation of Artist's products in Artist's or, if appropriate, in Lending Company's name.

To endorse, accept, and collect for deposit bills of exchange, check, notes, cash, or other payments or considerations received in connection with Artist's or any Lending Company's endeavors or interests in the entertainment industry.

To demand, sue for, collect, recover, and receive all goods, claims, money interests, or other items that may be due to Artist or any Lending Company in connection with any service rendered or product created by Artist, either directly or indirectly or through a Lending Company.

(a) To prosecute, defend, submit to arbitration and/or compromise, or settle all actions, suits, accounts, reckonings, claims, and demands whatsoever relating to any interest of Artist or a Lending Company in such manner and in all respects as Manager in Manager's best business judgment shall deem advisable; and without in any way limiting the foregoing, generally do, execute, and perform any other act, deed, or thing whatsoever that reasonably appears to Manager ought to be done, executed, and performed relating to Artist's professional career and interests as fully and effectively as Artist could do if personally present; and Artist hereby ratifies and affirms all acts performed by Manager by virtue of this power of attorney.

(b) Notwithstanding subparagraph (a) above, pursuant to the power of attorney granted herein, Manager shall not:

enter into any long-term contract for Artist's exclusive services without the express consent of Artist;

exercise any of the above granted prerogatives unreasonably, i.e., without seeking professional advice where advisable; and

exercise any of the above granted prerogatives without consulting with Artist where such consultation is reasonable and practicable.

Artist will not exert any of the powers granted to the Manager by virtue of the foregoing power of attorney.

Artist agrees and acknowledges that the power of attorney granted to Manager herein is coupled with an interest and is therefore irrevocable.

Compensation

As compensation for the services of Manager, Artist shall pay (or shall cause a Lending Company to pay, if appropriate), and Manager shall accept the following:

_____ of Artist (or Lending Company's, if a Lending Company shall be used therefor) Gross Earnings. Artist hereby irrevocably assigns to Manager the foregoing interest in Gross Earnings.

Artist's or a Lending Company's Gross Earnings shall be paid to in the first instance to Manager, provided, however that if Artist, a Lending Company or any designee of theirs shall receive Gross Earnings directly, the recipient shall be deemed to hold in trust for Manager that portion of Artist's or the Lending Company's Gross Earnings that equals Manager's compensation hereunder and such disbursement incurred by Manager on behalf of Artist, such amounts to be remitted to Manager with an appropriate accounting statement within five (5) business days of receipt. Whenever Manager receives Gross Earnings directly, Manager shall keep appropriate records thereof and may withhold their compensation therefrom and may reimburse themselves for any fees, costs, or expenses or loans advanced or incurred by Manager, and Manager shall remit the balance to Artist or deposit the balance in an account maintained for the benefit of Artist within fifteen (15) days of receipt.

Artist shall be solely responsible for payment of all talent agency fees, union dues, publicity costs, promotion or exploitation costs, traveling expenses, and/or wardrobe expenses and all other expenses, fees, and costs incurred by Artist or by Manager on Artist's behalf. If Manager advances any of the foregoing fees, costs or expenses on behalf of Artist, or incurs any other reasonable costs, fees, or expenses in direct connection with Artist's professional career or with performance of Manager's services hereunder (other than Manager's own legal, accounting and/or bookkeeping, or other general overhead expenses), Artist shall promptly reimburse for such fees, costs, and expenses. Without limiting the foregoing, such direct expenses, costs, or fees incurred on behalf of Artist and travel and living expenses and costs whenever Manager travels on behalf of Artist. Manager agrees to discuss the incurring of such expenses (other than normal office expenses) for which Artist shall be responsible hereunder in advance with Artist whenever practical.

The parties agree to keep complete and accurate books of account as to their respective financial obligations hereunder.

Each party shall have reasonable access to the books of account and records of the other (including the right to inspect and copy supporting documents such as receipts and vouchers) for the purpose of verifying accounts, including the right to cause the other's books and records to be inspected and copied by a certified public accountant or an attorney.

Miscellaneous

Each party represents and warrants to the other that he/she/they has/have the full right, power, and authority to enter into this Agreement and to grant to the other all of the rights purported to be granted to other herein.

This agreement is personal to each of the parties, and neither party shall have the right to assign this Agreement to any third party without the prior written consent of the other, provided, however, that Manager shall have the right to assign this Agreement to a corporation that is substantially owned and controlled by Manager and that agrees to furnish the personal services of Manager to Artist for the purposes of this Agreement.

This Agreement shall be construed in accordance with the laws of New York State applicable to agreements entered into and wholly performed therein. In the event of dispute, the parties agree before an arbitration committee.

In making this Agreement each party has been advised by counsel of his or her choosing.

Neither party shall be considered in default of their obligations hereunder, unless the alleged aggrieved party shall give such party written notice of the alleged default and demand to cure, and unless such alleged default shall not have been cured within fifteen (15) business days following such party's receipt of the notice of default and demand to cure.

All notices required or desired to be sent hereunder shall be in writing and sent regular United States mail, postage prepaid, or delivered in person to both parties.

Artist is executing this Agreement and shall be liable for the performance of the obligations hereunder. If this Agreement is terminated for any reason whatsoever, it is agreed that this Agreement shall remain in full force and effect as to each of the undersigned with whom this Agreement is not terminated. If any provisions of this Agreement shall be deemed unenforceable for any reason, such unenforceability shall not affect those remaining portions of this Agreement that are enforceable, and this Agreement shall be deemed amended only insofar as necessary to remove such unenforceable provision.

In the event of legal proceedings between the parties under or connected in any way with this Agreement, the prevailing party or parties shall be entitled to their reasonable attorneys' fees.

5.9 This Agreement is the parties' entire understanding as to its subject matter, and all prior negotiations are merged herein and superseded hereby.

IN WITNESS WHEREOF of the parties hereto execute this Agreement on the date below written.

Artist   Manager

_____   _____

_____   _____
Social Security No.   Social Security No.

_____   _____
Date   Date

CHAPTER 4

Signing as a Group

> *"A group must always think as one."*
> —New Edition legend Michael Bivins on
> MTV's hot *Making the Band*

In urban and gospel music, there are many well-known groups from the past century. Since the 1960s, the three- and four-part harmonies from these groups have mesmerized the music industry and fans worldwide. Crossing genres, groups like Boyz II Men, the Four Tops, Jodeci, Trin-I-Tee 5:7, the Williams Brothers, New Edition, and Destiny's Child immediately come to my mind. But although they might sing in harmony, keeping that unity in the signing of a recording contract requires a number of special considerations, otherwise cacophony is inevitable. Specifically, whenever you are signing more than one person to a recording contract, there is a litany of legal issues that can arise. Former client, Isaac Caree of Men of Standard, once told me that a key for a group is that "the group must read and understand its contract before signing anything." In this chapter, we look at some of those issues and discuss in depth things to consider if you are an urban group, although what follows in this chapter applies to any genre.

Among the many issues, the key considerations are the following:

+ Who owns the name of the group?
+ Who owns the trademark?
+ Who owns the copyrights (to the songs)?
+ Who owns the tracks?
+ Should the group incorporate?
+ Should group members have individual attorneys?
+ Should group members have individual managers?
+ Who controls replacing members?
+ Who controls the distribution of solo albums (by group members)?
+ Who controls the image and development?

WHO OWNS THE NAME OF THE GROUP?

Everyone knows the Temptations from the group's heyday with Motown. During this period, they were one of the top acts in the music business, selling millions of records worldwide for the record label and its founder Berry Gordy. Over the years, owing to internal conflicts, drug abuses, and other issues, the group has splintered, renewed itself, and reassembled with different members. There have been a ton of legal battles regarding the Temptations and its group members, but because they reportedly own their name, they are allowed to do what they want with it and invite new members into the group. Specifically, they do not need permission from Motown to shuffle in a new lead singer.

Conversely, when Michael Jackson and the Jackson Five left Motown in 1975, the record label owned the very lucrative rights in the groups' "Jackson Five" name. As a result, when the group moved over to CBS with a new contract in the mid-1970s, they were recorded and released as the "Jacksons." Motown wisely retained the valuable intellectual property and the tremendous goodwill in the "Jackson Five" name. Even though the name was created by the success of the Gary, Indiana, Jackson brothers, to this day Motown still sells millions of *Jackson Five* records because Motown owns the name.

More recently, it was reported that Columbia-Sony announced that Destiny's Child would dissolve as a group. Over the years, the group has changed members quite often, keeping the core twosome of Kelly Rowland and Beyoncé. If, in the future, the group decides to reestablish itself with some new members, even without seeing the contract, it is plausible that Columbia-Sony would have the authority to determine the group's membership. The label could install three new members and still carry the name Destiny's Child forward forever with a revolving lineup, unless the group's contract provides otherwise. (Matthew Knowles, the brilliant father of group member Beyoncé, probably fought to keep these rights, but assuming he did not, Sony could legally replace Beyoncé, but I doubt they would!)

The ownership of the name is also critical with regards to marketing the brand for purposes of merchandising T-shirts, key chains, and other products. Many groups underestimate the importance of owning the rights to their name when signing a recording contract. Ten million records later, the record company will be able to take the name, change the group's membership, and continue to exploit the brand and its goodwill. Charles Graham, longstanding entertainment attorney, based in Atlanta, explained, "If you have a multiplatinum act selling ten million records, and the label controls the merchandising and name rights, they (the label) can see another fifty million plus in revenue." Even on a more modest scale, the sweat equity you put into establishing the group as an artist is priceless. You do not want to spend countless hours and resources literally "making a name" only to have a label or any other entity own the rights to that recognizable moniker should the relationship sour. Furthermore, merchandising is quickly becoming a coveted new domain for labels as they seek additional, viable revenue streams that can be generated by artists to bolster corporate profitability.

WHO OWNS THE TRADEMARK?

A *trademark* is simply a word, name, symbol, or device that is used in trade with goods to indicate the source of the goods and to distinguish them from the goods of others. Similarly, a service mark is the same as a trademark, except that it identifies and distinguishes the source of a service rather than a product. We discuss trademarks in much greater detail in Chapter Ten, so for the next page or two, I am only raising the issue as a key point of negotiations. Examples of marks are the brand names Roca Wear (the stylized RW), Bad Boy Records (the little boy with the hat turned sideways), and Phat Farm (the P in the circle with laurel leaves). If you are a boxing fan, you will recall Michael Buffer screaming, "Let's Get Ready to Rumble," before every big Mike Tyson or Oscar De La Hoya fight, a mark that has become his signature introduction worldwide. Buffer "owns" that catchphrase.

Likewise, an image of another device can serve as a trademark, as in the NBC's distinctive three-note musical hook. A name (the fictional "Five Heartbeats" or the legendary "Supremes") is important to both the artist and the record label. For purposes of this discussion, we use the word *mark* to discuss the importance of both service mark and trademark.

When consumers see or hear the mark, they recognize it, immediately understand what it represents, and attach feelings to the product at hand. This is the same phenomenon that happens with the service mark of a music group. Given this helpful fact, groups will often have a service mark or trademark (™) printed on promotional items.

The question for a new music group becomes who will own the intellectual property rights to the artist name or group name? When you are signing a recording contract as a group, it is best to retain these rights if you can. If immediate ownership of the mark proves to be a deal-breaking point for negotiations, then at least fight to have the rights to the mark revert to the group at some future time after the contract expires. The mark will last years after the group has retired. If the group builds up a successful name and goodwill, a mark can prove to be extremely lucrative. A recording contract will have language that provides that the group actually owns the name free and clear when signing the agreement reading as follows:

Section 10. Group Name. I/We warrant and represent that I/we own all rights in and to The Name and that I/we have the sole and exclusive right to use and to allow others to use The Name in connection with the manufacture, advertising, and sale of records. I/We hereby grant to company, and further warrant and represent that Company shall have, the rights to use and to allow others to use The Name for advertising and purposes of trade, and otherwise without restriction, in connection with the records made pursuant to this Agreement.

Another issue is the breakdown of the ownership amongst the group members. I always recommend that the group members own shares equally in the trademark or service mark and divide up the revenue accordingly. Thus, if Boyz II Men owns the "BIIM" trademark that appeared on their T-shirts and merchandising, then the group would split the income associated therewith equally. And, whether owing to forgetfulness or intentionally blind ambition, I do realize that some individual group members from time to time will feel like, "If I invented the logo or mark, why am I sharing the income with the rest of the band or group?" Simple answer: because you are a group, and it's the best way to keep harmony in business and avoid useless litigation, in-fighting, or bad blood amongst members.

Please note, as discussed below, a trademark or service mark identifies goods and services, while a copyright deals with works of original authorship—e.g., a song, a written book, or a TV script. However, it is still just as important to trademark your intellectual property, if you can, as you would copyright your songs as a songwriter.

We discuss trademarks in depth in Chapter Ten, but I wanted to briefly introduce you to the interplay between trademarks, service marks, and the group signing of a recording contract.

WHO OWNS THE COPYRIGHTS?

Copyright is one of the most critical discussions for any group and its members. In the music industry, when we talk about copyrights, we are talking about those copyrights associated with the songs written by the artist or his writers. We are also talking about the publishing income associated with those copyrights from sheet music, CD sales, DVDs, videos, and any other exploitation of the songs created by a group. Michael Jackson purchased the Beatles' catalog nearly twenty years ago for $47.5 million. Today, that catalog, reportedly co-owned by Sony, is worth $1 billion.

In our group discussion, copyright becomes an issue owing to the set-up in recording the album. Typically, the group will arrive at a studio and commence with working on a song. Various members will write lyrics or a "hook" for the song—i.e., the catchy phrase. As a result of the various lyrical contributions, all group members should own a piece of the song. However, unless it is spelled out beforehand, on many occasions, group members, the hot producer and the record company executive, and anyone else who might have been in the room to potentially contribute, will end up fighting over who owns the copyrights and who should share in the lucrative millions at stake should the song or songs become a hit.

I remember when the four-member group Shai was signed to MCA a few years ago. The group had a big hit called "If I Ever Fall in Love." While all of the group members sang different parts on the two-million-copy-selling song, only group member Carl Martin was listed as a main songwriter throughout the liner notes. I wonder if the other members knew when they recorded hours after hours and tinkered with the song in the studio that it would become a hit song worth millions solely to Martin, who owned the copyright. Even four years after the hot album was released, Martin, the smartest businessman in the group, was still collecting money in connection with the hit songs from the debut album and, most recently, the song was featured prominently on the MTV show *Making the Band 4*, and so Martin continues to make the dollars! (I should note that Martin is no longer a member of the group.)

To avoid this dilemma, the group members generally should agree to split publishing three or four ways and establish that all songs will be equally divided for the unity of the group. The group should also establish that each group will set up a publishing company with BMI or ASCAP to administer that individual group members' share of ownership.

Now, I should note, the group does not have to split the song copyrights or ownership equally by law and Martin was not required by law in the example above. I only recommend this to avoid a lot of bickering and useless discord in the group. However, if you want to specifically attribute the exact shares to the exact writer, simply take a sheet of paper and write down who wrote what portion or percentage of the song. Known as split sheets or cue sheets, the group can jot down as you record who wrote the lyrics and who wrote the music. If you do this, it will remain clear after the session is over who wrote this and who owns that. Among the writers, and without consideration of whether an official publisher is involved—in which case there is another 100-percent share breakdown between the publishers that is calculated—the total splits should tally to 100 percent. Generally, music and lyrics are equally split as the two parts, 50/50, that make up a song. So if you wrote 100 percent of the music but 0 percent of the lyrics, then generally speaking, you own 50 percent of the song. If you also contributed to some of the lyrics, your percentage would also increase from there. If you invite others to simply replay your vision and they are following your direction in the creation of music for inclusion in your song (i.e., bass line or horn part), then that would fall under "work-for-hire" and you still retain ownership of the copyright. This means they would be paid for their services as musicians and would not be eligible for any future royalties as it relates to the specific song. This should also be documented in writing to confirm their understanding. It is essential that the group members understand when someone creates a track, the creator of the track owns it, or else, as we discussed earlier, it is a work-for-hire. However, conversely, if you wrote 100 percent of the lyrics and 0 percent of the music, then generally speaking you own 50 percent of the song with additional splits if you also contributed to the music. And, unless a contributing writer is signed to you, any lyrical contribution is generally not considered to be a work for hire and should be considered in the calculation of the split breakdown. If you do not spell out on paper at the beginning who wrote what, eventually there will be an argument and/or an assumption made by someone in the group contending that they wrote the hook, the verse, the chorus, and/or that they wrote the remix and, in turn, are owed a different split—which may lead to smaller takehome for you. It's usually at this point that even if there wasn't any heat on the track, things start to get nice and funky.

And, we must also include the record label in this discussion on splitting of the songs. While the group member will sometimes struggle with who owns the publishing rights or copyrights to the songs, the record labels generally have no problem with demanding that they share in the copyright ownership or publishing income. Generally, the recording contract will have a clause that will require the group to convert a 50-percent share of its publishing to the record label. For example, the group might sign as an artist with Jive Records and simultaneously sign a songwriter publishing deal with Zomba Publishing (a sister company of Jive Records). As a result, Zomba Publishing will co-own the songs and collect 50 percent of the revenue. Says esteemed industry vet Larkin Arnold, "I always recommend that artists as songwriters keep their publishing." Added former ASCAP director Kenny Ferracho, "Publishing is the artist or songwriter's retirement money." We will discuss this more in depth later on in our focus on publishing and co-publishing deals in Chapter Nineteen: The Writer as Publisher (Self-Publisher).

For purposes of this chapter, realize that copyright is the key to the ownership of the publishing of your song as a writer. Therefore, as a group it is critical to clarify the ownership of the copyright before the album is released. A horrible fight and bitterness can ensue if you do not resolve this discussion early. Lastly, we will discuss copyrights and trademarks in great detail in later chapters, Chapter Ten,

Trademarking the Name, Logo, and Intellectual Property and Chapter Fourteen, More Than a Melody: Understanding Copyright Law, so don't fret if you are still confused over copyrights and trademarks.

WHO OWNS THE TRACK?

Similar to who owns the copyright is the question of who owns the production track underneath the song. Many times an artist will show up at the studio and someone will provide them with a musical track. My old college classmate Derrick "D-Dot" Angeletti of Bad Boy's Hitmen team is a producer who comes to mind for delivering hot tracks for various groups like 112, the LOX, and Biggie, just to name a few. But, even more specific to the group situation is when you have a group in which one member writes the track and the other members write the lyrics. This is also very common with Jodeci. Group member DeVante is one of the most prolific members of the group in the production of tracks and operating the studio sessions. DeVante was known to be the one who worked in the studio alone to produce the cutting-edge tracks for the group's albums. Thus, many artists will ask, "Does he own the tracks or does the group?"

It is essential that the group members understand that when someone creates a track, the creator of the track owns it, or else, as we discussed earlier, it is a work-for-hire. Under the law, if you commission someone to produce a track for payment, it is viewed as a work-for-hire, and the person who hired and paid them owns the rights. However, if this individual produced the track for you and there is no prior agreement, he or she many legitimately claim that he or she owns the track and therefore wants to own half of the song. Thus, in the creation of the music, a superstar artist/producer like DeVante or Diddy would own the track and the group or individual writer would own the lyrics written on top of the track—i.e., the hot music and bed of the song. Basically, the whole song would be split 50/50. Also keep in mind that a producer such as DeVante and/or Diddy are in the business of making hits and collecting royalties, including those royalties legitimately earned by writing songs and/or hooking up the artist. Before the comments flood in, this, of course, is not to say that you can't strike gold or platinum with an up-and-coming producer.

Regardless of the presence of a known hitmaker on the track, it remains a very critical point that groups establish the ownership of the track and confirm whether the group as a whole will share in the income associated with that track, the copyright registered for the track, and/or the overall exploitation of the track. Super producers like Dr. Dre, Trackmasters, Kirk Franklin, Kurt Carr, and Timbaland will happily produce a track for you (with the right payment). The key is to make sure it is clear who will own the track so that when it is time to exploit and pay royalties, the details are crystal clear to everyone involved.

SHOULD THE GROUP INCORPORATE?

Thirty years ago, very few artists in R&B or the gospel music industry had corporations set up to handle their business affairs. Many of the artists were intimidated by such corporate business planning. Sadly, most were only interested in singing and performing and ran away from setting up businesses or corporations. It was no different whether a soloist or a group; the trend was to shy away from setting up a business or corporate entity and the resulting horror stories, owing to their lack of executive involvement, still clutter the headlines. Now, it is very common for artists and groups to set up corporations for tax implications and the employment of their friends and family, among other perks. (We discuss this in depth in Chapter Eight, Selecting an Entity: A Corporation, Partnership, or LLC, but wanted to raise it as a serious consideration for groups in organizing themselves as a business corporation.)

A *corporation* is simply a legal entity that is set up with a group of shareholders who each own part of the whole. The shareholders realize that the corporation is an entity in and of itself. The corporation has what is known as "continuity of life," or continues on existing even if a shareholder dies. Corporations are not very costly to set up and they provide some great write-offs for taxes and cover the members from personal liability in case of a lawsuit. For example, if promoters are booking the group to perform, it is sometimes advantageous to have the contract drawn up between the promoter and the corporation. Sometimes a group will set up a corporation to sign the recording contract with the major label for the exclusive services of a group—i.e., a loan-out agreement. Likewise, any contracts entered into by the group for merchandising and other related matters would be in the name of the corporation. Each of these scenarios limits the liability and exposure of the group by having a corporation as the contractual party.

There are several legal entities that one can set up in regards to their career and their group. For example, many groups set up a *limited liability company*, or LLC. An LLC is a business ownership structure that offers its owners the advantage of limited liability (like corporations) and partnership-like taxation, in which profits are passed through to the owners and taxed on their personal income tax returns. However, an LLC does not have shareholders; it has members. For many groups, particularly those just starting out, an LLC may be the best way to set up and run the business aspect, depending on the laws of your state. Each of the group members can be LLC members and vote on all actions of the LLC and limit who can join the LLC membership. Similar to a corporation, the LLC is a good tool to use for purposes of avoiding direct exposure for the artist or group. So in the event that there is a dispute or altercation at a concert, for instance, if the contracts are done with the corporate entity or LLC, the liability to the group is very limited, and the corporation would be named as a defendant, not the group members individually.

If you are a group, it is important to set up a business entity for liability purposes, outside of just performing. For example, if you own a music studio and the studio is in your name, or a group member's name, you will leave yourself open to a lawsuit and the potential loss of income if someone is severely hurt while using your studio. Thus, it is important to consider setting up a corporate entity, whether LLC or corporation, that can partially shield you from liability and protect you in the event of an emergency.

Many groups have a business entity that will sign contracts for them. That entity will then loan out the services of the group. For example, Sony may sign a recording contract with Boyz II Men, Inc., after which Boyz II Men, Inc. delivers the services of Boys II Men the group. Regardless of which corporate entity you choose, it is important to understand that you do need to set up a business organi-zation and you need to understand that it is the music business, with *business* being the emphasized term.

Obviously if you sign as a group with a record label, you will divide your roy-alty rates in several ways. Generally, the royalty rate will likewise be split among the number of members in the group. Similar to our last section, we discuss corpora-tions and business entities in great detail in later chapters, so don't worry if you still have questions.

SHOULD GROUP MEMBERS HAVE INDIVIDUAL ATTORNEYS?

I remember hearing a story a few years ago about the group TLC, when they still existed as a recording group. The group had sold over 20 million records and con-sisted of three very popular girls: Lisa "Left Eye" Lopez, Rozonda "Chili" Thomas, and Tionne "T-Boz" Watkins. The three girls would meet regularly as a group and in some instances each member would have her entire staff with her or available for their meetings via phone. The group members had individual attorneys, individual accountants, individual managers, and individual publicists, among others. Why is this critical to our discussion? Because it is important to understand that when a group has the type of success that TLC garnered over the years, each individual member can become somewhat of a celebrity icon in his or her own right and a cor-porate enterprise with a bunch of handlers.

Therefore, it is critical that the group members begin to assemble their own teams. So Lisa "Left-Eye" might have had her own attorney working on her own label, her own nonprofit, her own corporations, her own real estate, and her own personal interests. Likewise, T-Boz would have the same kind of setup with her own legal team, managerial team, and real estate team overseeing her busi-ness interests. And group member Chili might have the same team working on her personal interests, including a book deal, production company, and clothing line. Label head L. A. Reid told the *Atlanta Journal-Constitution* "that we could round up these three very different personalities with these [contentious] things going on and get them back in the studio was a feat, to say the least," in the mak-ing of their 1999 multiplatinum-selling *Fanmail* album, which featured the hit "No Scrubs."

TLC had attorney Channing Johnson represent the group as a whole. But there is nothing wrong with group members having individual attorneys like Johnson on separate legal issues, so long as they find a harmonious way to have one attorney or law firm handle their group dealings with the record label. Interestingly enough, despite the presence of multiple attorneys protecting individual client interests, and massive and repeat chart success, TLC still blazed the headlines with news of their financial straits. The moral of that story is to stay involved. As artists *never*, repeat *never*, give 100 percent control to anyone without staying involved, aware, and with a working understanding of business documents, asking questions, and occasionally auditing to make sure you are covered and protected, especially as it relates to your business affairs.

It is important to understand that the separate attorneys would be able to protect each member's various interests outside of the joint recording contract with the label. Legal conflicts have a tendency to arise once a group has decided to sign a recording contract and is suddenly conducting itself as a moneymaking entity. The groups' single attorney will not be able to represent one member against another in a dispute because of the ethical concerns involved.

So, again, study carefully the timing of when a separate attorney is needed and then make the adjustments to find him. But, do it only when the economics and timing are right and the group is in a position to need separate counsel.

Indeed, it is not uncommon for group members to have individual managers at some point in existence. But if you are a new group still selling records out of your trunk or working in your garage trying to get a big break, it is unlikely to be economically feasible to retain separate attorneys. Most likely, you are utilizing whatever funds you do have to market or promote your album.

SHOULD GROUP MEMBERS HAVE INDIVIDUAL MANAGERS?

The hiring of separate managers for each group member is similar to the hiring of individual attorneys. Each group or band will have to decide at what point they have reached a level of notoriety where the individual members will be better served by individual managers. Also, realize the individual manager will cost you money, if you choose to hire her as group members.

For purposes of keeping this simple, going back to our TLC example, it is very common in a group like that for each woman to have her own manager. For example, Left Eye had industry vet Ida Harris helping her with managerial duties. And I recall talented manager Dolly Turner assisting T-Boz with her management needs. The manager's functions will vary from member to member, but generally the manager will oversee everything. It is important to understand that even though they have separate managers, the group still needs to come together and agree on many things as a collective unit. Thus, if you decide as a group to have individual managers, you need to be clear that the managers must work things out in a businesslike manner and not create a code of business that sends a wave of bad press through the industry for you as a group—i.e., "their team is so complicated and difficult"—and/or create situations in which the only way to get things done is for "my people to talk to your people to meet to set up a time to talk." Keep the layers thin to avoid clogging the machine with hangers-on who are only making it more difficult for things to get done. As a result, many groups will have one management company or person that might manage the entire "TLC" group, while individual personal managers will handle the women individually and their day-to-day projects and business interests.

It is important to note that the group, when choosing a manager, should look first for someone that the entire group feels comfortable with and can trust. If the manager makes any group member feel uneasy in any way, do not hire him. Second, look for a manager that really believes in the group as a whole and has the ability to motivate and inspire the whole group to reach its full potential. Finally, do your research and check out the manager's reputation. Does he/she have significant industry contacts? And does he/she have a reputation for making good deals, bad deals, or a reputation for being difficult in business negotiations?

Start by checking the manager's roster of clients and then consult your friends and acquaintances in the industry. A bad manager's reputation travels fast in the music industry. Also, make sure to get second and third opinions, but remember that certain insiders may see a talented manager as direct competition and have ulterior motives to also fill that slot. Before you hand off those duties to someone else, be aware of what they are doing on your behalf. Also, it is important to note that your manager will be your right-hand contact. As stated in Chapter Three, managers in the music and entertainment industries have chosen a path through which they can profoundly affect an artist's career. As Ida Harris explained to a packed law school class at the University of Connecticut, "The manager is respon- sible for counseling the artist on all aspects of the industry: how to deal with record companies, public relations, marketing, advertising, and merchandising" among other things. The manager is the artist's link to key players and influential power people in the music industry.

WHO CONTROLS REPLACING MEMBERS?

If you look carefully at some music groups over the years, you will see that the record companies generally control who will replace a leaving member. In other words, when Destiny's Child had four members and then went to three members, lost and gained a new member, and then went to another new member, they were fortunate that the record companies found a good fit with Michelle Williams. And, recall Elektra Records shuffling En Vogue for the departure of one of its group members. Even on the gospel side, groups will shuffle members or downsize on occasion. Men of Standard went from four members to three members and recently signed as a threesome with Sony Urban's gospel division.

Typically, in a recording contract for a group, there is a clause that deals with departing members. Unless, you are a superstar group, in all cases, the labels can remove or add a new singer to the group, pretty much without your input. The group usually has no control over this process. Sometimes the group can have key influence. For example, if the group has sold millions of records and established chemistry, the record label will look to the group members for input on selection of a new member. An example of this was seen in New Edition when they brought on Johnny Gill and he filled in as a member for the departed Bobby Brown.

Generally speaking, contractual language will state that the record company retains the authority to install a new member upon the exit of another. Please note that the right of the record label remains intact regardless of whether the exiting member dies, retires, resigns, or gets arrested. As a group, you can fight hard to retain some input or rights over changing members or adding new members, but at the end of the day, these rights are usually vested with the record label. The concept is this: If we are spending our record label funds to record you as a group, we should have final say on who exits or joins the group for purposes of maximizing our profits.

WHO CONTROLS THE DISTRIBUTION OF SOLO ALBUMS?

Several years ago in the urban music scene, *NSYNC's Justin Timberlake released a solo project. Timberlake's project was extremely successful. The project was also released on the same Zomba Records label as his group albums with *NSYNC. I raise this connection to only point out that most likely when he signed as a member of *NSYNC, Zomba retained the right to do any solo projects that a group member may do in the future, regardless of whether the group disbands or "retires," as the new trend seems to be among well-known acts.

So essentially, what happens when you sign a recording contract as a member of a group and then decide to release a solo album? The short answer: You are bound by the same contract you signed as a group member. Specifically, the record label normally retains the right to distribute or release the new solo recording, unless you negotiate this out of your agreement. The thought process behind this is that they do not want to build you up as a member of a successful group and then lose out on the individual projects. It is almost as if they are saying, "We want to make sure that we are along for the ride individually as a solo artist and collectively as a group."

This is standard operating procedure by a record label, particularly major labels. However, if your attorney is capable of doing so, you should seek to get released from such a clause or restriction for your solo project. It is highly unlikely you will be successful in this negotiation, unless your group has sold millions of records and the label agrees to renegotiate or in good faith allow you as a solo member to record separately for any label you choose. Again, this is highly unlikely, but worth a fight.

WHO CONTROLS THE IMAGE AND DEVELOPMENT OF THE GROUP?

In writing this chapter, I spoke to several clients who are a part of a group presently or at some point sang with a group. Almost unanimously, most desired the right to retain the image and development of the group. However, this is highly unlikely. Back to the days of Motown, where Berry Gordy sent artists to charm school, dance lessons, and media training and oversaw artists' development, the record labels would take control of the artist or group's national image. Antipas Harris, a lead member of hot gospel group A7, admits that the group "would like to retain as much creative control as possible," but concedes that to secure major label support, the group would have to adhere to a lot of input from the label in developing the group's image and makeup.

When Bad Boy Records signed artists in its heyday of the 1990s, it was not uncommon for the label to assemble an army of staff members to take a group shopping on Broadway in New York to buy them clothes and outfits to create the group's urban image. In R&B and hip-hop for example, the labels will commonly promote fancy cars, jewelry, big homes, and flashy clothes to develop a hip-hop image of success, despite the true financial condition of an artist. It is important to point this out, as groups sign with labels and deal with the struggles of "keeping it real" and striving to look the part or "image" being created by a label.

Keep in mind, if the label is spending thousands to make your album, it will feel it must guide the image and marketing of the group. As the group signs that multiyear album deal, realize the implications of allowing the label to develop your career, image, and marketing. At most, strive to have mutual creative input or mutual approval of the final image chosen for the group. What's unique in this situation is that as the artist, you know who you are and what you want to portray, but, on the label's end, they also know what's going on in the marketplace and want to do all they can to succeed with a project that will be right on time and just right for the masses—this is a combination of marketplace analysis and experience that will require balance and synchronicity for everything to align just right for that undeniable grand slam.

As an artist, your job is to know who you are, who your audience is, the way you dress, the style of music you do, etc. Harris, above, whose group had a top twenty single in 2007, added, "the group should not look to the company to make them a star or successful," but hopefully, both sides can work together to maximize the success of the group. We discuss the development of the artist in various chapters, but it is a critical for a group to consider this main point when signing as well. For more contracts and sample helpful information, please visit our website: www.thisbusinessofurbanmusic.com

CHAPTER 5

Signing with an Indie

"We do everything we can to make sure that the artist or label succeeds."
—CHUCK ADAMS, PRESIDENT AND OWNER OF
CENTRAL SOUTH DISTRIBUTION, ONE OF THE
LARGEST INDIE DISTRIBUTORS IN THE COUNTRY

When we talk about signing with an independent label, or "indie," we are talking about signing with a record company that does not have major distribution with one of the "Big Four"—EMI, SONY/BMG, Warner, and Universal. When we think of successful independents, we think of Ice Cube's label Lynch Mob Records or Master P's No Limit Records. We also think of labels such as Jermaine Dupri's So So Def Records, Eve's Ruff Riders label home, or Roc-A-Fella Records, once owned by Damon Dash/Jay-Z. On the gospel side, hitmakers like JDI Records, Bajada Records, and Pepperco Records all show that indies are powerful outlets for artists to grow and succeed.

As stated, an independent label is basically a label that is not affiliated with a major distribution company. For purposes of background, it is important to note that an independent label can have the advantages of reaping more of the profits when we think about selling the record at the local record store or over the Internet or through other channels of distribution. For example, digital downloading has given independents great standing to compete with the majors and be very financially solid. An independent label usually will cut an 80/20 deal with a distributor, which means that if there's a ten-dollar net profit or ten-dollar profit on a record, the independent label will keep 80 percent and the distributor will keep 20 percent. In some cases, the splits can be 70/30 or 60/40; it all depends on the leverage of the indie label as well as the way negotiations shake out at the end of the day.

The indie then takes that 60- to 80-percent share and signs artists to its label. The artist would receive a royalty rate from this percentage held by the indie, and most likely have no direct business relationship with the national distributor. In this instance, an artist could see a higher royalty rate from an indie than a major.

However, most artists that consider a recording contract often will overlook the indie label for a major. Specifically, the artist wants to brag to his friends that it has "signed a deal with J Records [Arista/BMG]" or that "Sony just inked me." Thus, it was important to write this chapter on the pros and cons of signing with an indie. I have heard many horror stories in which an artist will sign with a major label, but the album is never released to the marketplace. Or even if the label allows the artist to record a few masters, the album does not receive the promotional support it needs, fails to sell in large numbers, and ultimately the artist gets dropped by the major label and becomes financially bankrupt.

Every artist must consider these eight factors before signing with an independent label:

- What is the indie label's financial situation?
- The difference between an indie label and a major label
- What's gained and lost by signing with an indie label?
- What is the indie's expertise?
- Is it a mom-and-pop indie label?
- What's in the deal?
- Am I in a position to put money toward my album?
- How do I track the record sales and get accountings?

WHAT IS THE INDIE LABEL'S FINANCIAL SITUATION?

Most of my clients sign a recording contract and expect a label to shell out thousands of dollars, if not millions. If you are an artist signing with an indie label, you must consider that their financial situation will most likely be very different than one of the majors. As a result, as an artist, you have to be prepared to spend some of your own finances, as discussed below, and realize that the indie does not have the marketing strength of Warner Bros. The indie label may not allow you to examine their books and financial status; however, ask around and investigate the financial condition of the label as much as you can and make sure they are as secure as possible to help you reach success as an artist.

Numerous artists have had deals fall through because their indie distribution company gets financially strapped or goes bankrupt. Make sure that your contract contains terms that will release you from any further obligations if the indie label goes bankrupt. If this language is not found in your contract, you could be tied to a sinking ship until a court decides that you can be released. Going through this process can be really expensive for you because the clause you negotiated in your contract that said the label would pay court costs and attorneys' fees for any legal proceedings that arise because of something that is their fault will no longer be enforceable.

THE DIFFERENCE BETWEEN AN INDIE
AND A MAJOR LABEL

"Indie" is industry slang for independent. Central South Distribution (CSD) is one of the major companies that distribute small indie labels. Owner Chuck Adams explained that CSD has serviced projects for million-selling gospel artist Juanita Bynum and other artists like super hot Micah Stampley and award-winning choir James Hall & Citadel of Love, to name a few. In the music industry, many things are considered "indie," including independent record labels, independent publishing companies, independent distributors, and the artists signed to these labels and companies. An indie label often will not have the marketing, A&R, promotions, and publicity departments that a major label does. An indie label also outsources a lot of these departments and retains promotions and marketing experts as well as publicity types to help the artist succeed. Often, the costs of these various individuals are paid for and absorbed by the artist. Remember, indie labels tend to be small companies, in contrast to major labels that have a corporate owner overseeing their management and providing support. There are four dominant parent companies that control the majors are Universal Music Group, Sony BMG Music Entertainment, EMI Group, and Warner Bros. Music. In comparison to the majors, indie labels control less than 20 percent of all record sales in the United States. But, indie labels offer unique possibilities that might save you from the bottomless pit of a major label's roster.

Some indie labels focus their resources on developing niche artists, although their funds and distribution network tend to be limited. And, some indie labels have risen through the ranks and established a name that is almost as big as their major label counterparts. Death Row Records, Suge Knight's label, formerly carried artists such as Snoop Dogg, Dr. Dre, and the late Tupac Shakur. Russell Simmons launched Def Jam Recordings from his college dorm room and was initially called an "indie." Brick Records of Boston is another award-winning indie dedicated to releasing high-quality underground hip-hop.

WHAT'S GAINED AND LOST BY SIGNING WITH AN INDIE?

Often clients will ask me the gains and losses of signing with an indie. The short answer is that an indie label is typically on a shoestring budget, so you are not going to see a big six-figure or even five-figure advance. There will be no big meeting with an A&R department or marketing team, solely geared on maximizing your worldwide exposure and success when you sign with an indie. However, the gain is that you will get a label that really believes in the few artists that it signs.

For example, major labels effectively weed through the crowd by signing all acts that appear promising and then, in many cases, pull the funds on the acts that do not take off on their first album. Signing artists this way, the major label has insurance against the vast amounts of money they invest in the groups they sign. They count on a handful of successful "superstars" to counter the losses on the artists that do not succeed.

But indie labels will often have a different business plan and will seek out artists that they actually believe can succeed and not sign an entire roster of artists. Because their funding is limited, they typically can't afford to sign more artists than the ones they think will actually be promising. Most indies, with their money at stake, will typically follow through on the deals they make with an artist to turn a profit.

So in sum, the key differences between indie and major labels are: 1) the mission of the label, 2) the recording contracts employed by each and profit sharing therein, 3) their distribution channels, and 4) the amount of money that will be spent and how soon it might be recouped.

Without exhausting too much time on some of the self-explanatory issues regarding indie labels, it is important to point out that with regards to contracts, I have found that there is a big difference in terms of the recording contracts that each type of label presents. For example, major labels typically use archaic contracts that are over fifty pages long containing confusing terms and a lot of "legalese," and you will need a good attorney to read and interpret.

However, indie label contracts tend to be less intimidating. They are usually only about ten pages in length and consist of much simpler language. It is mandatory that you have an attorney to review any contract you sign, but an indie label deal is usually easier to navigate and negotiate.

While major labels also have access to a bigger distribution channel than indies because their parent companies own the distribution companies, there are several advantages to signing with indies. For example, indies typically use independent distributors, who focus only on smaller labels, like Central South Distribution, Koch, and Artemis, to name a few. Some independent distributors service only a few states or a region of the country, but independent distributors are a great resource for more specialized areas of music that the majors ignore because these areas are too small. Independent distributors can also offer a faster turnaround than majors because they are smaller and easier to manage. Also, independent distributors have better connections to the smaller retailers who carry the independent, harder to find, and non-mainstream music.

Some independent labels do have affiliation with major labels, or have access to the major distribution channels, but they do their own marketing and promotion. The obvious advantage to signing to an independent with major distribution would be the large market you would be able to reach. However, there might be more strings attached in terms of your creative freedom with your music and less flexibility in negotiating your deal.

Given the difference in the amount of money that indies and majors can spend on a single artist, there is a difference in the number of albums that must be sold before an artist will see royalties. The usual major deal has the label spending somewhere around $500,000 or much more on a new artist just to record, not even including the marketing costs. That means that at least 100,000 records or more will have to be sold before the label can hope to break even, and the artist's advance will be recouped (assuming the label is netting a minimum of five dollars per record). It is only after your advance is recouped that you will begin to see any royalty payments.

Indie labels naturally sell fewer records. Typically twenty thousand units is a positive *success* number for indies. Owing to their limited promotional and distribution power, indies typically cannot sell more units because they cannot reach a broader audience.

And, in the usual independent deal, the record company will spend only around ten thousand dollars on a new artist. That means the label can start turning a profit at two thousand records sold, and you can begin receiving royalty payments. However, this should be weighed against the fact that an indie label cannot necessarily be expected to reach more than twenty thousand willing buyers. This caveat is especially true for niche acts like gospel artists that may have a limited following.

Finally, the plusses and minuses associated with an indie label's distribution are elements that must be weighed when considering a deal. Major labels are distributed by one of the major distributors: EMI, Warner Bros. Music, Sony BMG, and Universal. Indie distributors fall outside of these umbrella companies. The independent distributors may own or share an ownership interest with an indie label, but typically they are completely independent. Major distributors almost always share an ownership interest in the major label, or vice versa. The other aspect of distribution to examine is the retail opportunities that the distributor can provide. The majors sell in all the major chain stores and retail outlets, while most indie labels sell in independent record stores and only some chain retailers. Increasingly, indie labels turn directly to the Internet for distribution.

Just remember, whether or not you are working with an indie, every ounce of money spent on you and your group (food, limos, new instruments, recording, videos, touring, all the engineers, producers, managers, and lawyers) must be recouped before the artists can be paid. This is true if your album sells no copies or a million copies. So it takes a level head to consider the deals being offered.

WHAT IS THE INDIE'S EXPERTISE?

As an artist you will want to consider the indie label's brand of expertise. Ask the label and your other industry sources about the following key questions, among others:

- How long has the label been in business? The length of time the label has been in business could be an indicator of the stability of the label. If the label has only been in business for a short period, you might be incurring a greater risk than if you were dealing with an indie label that has been in business for more than five or ten years.

- How many artists do they have, and what genre is their music? Considering the number of artists will give an idea of how much attention the label could possibly afford to focus on you. If you notice that the label consists of only a handful of people, but they have two or three times as many artists, they might not be able to give you the attention you need to produce a successful album. Looking at the genre of the other artists signed to the label will also help you determine how you fit into the roster, and it will give you an idea of whether the label has any experience dealing with music in your genre.

- How are their artists doing? The success and the activity of the other artists signed to the label can be an indicator of how the label focuses its energies. If the label has a number of artists on its roster, but only one or two are actually actively touring, recording, or selling records, then the label might only be concentrating on the artists they think are most promising, letting others fall to the wayside. But, if the label seems to have activity going on with most of its artists, it could be an indicator that the label is attentive to its artists and that the label has managed to maximize the success of all of its artists.

- What industry contacts do they have in distribution, recording, producing, etc.? A label's connections in the industry are essential to the successful release of an album. If the label has a good relationship with prominent distributors or producers, you will be able to receive better quality service and attention from those businesses, which will contribute to the overall success for your album.

- Do they understand your type of music? Needless to say, a label has to understand you and your music to help you be successful. Longstanding gospel independent Crystal Rose had great success with Ricky Dillard. Explained label head

Brian Spears, "You have to know the music and how to market the artist and his music when you are an independent, or you won't survive in the long run." As an artist, you should feel free to ask the indie label's president what he or she thinks your music is trying to convey, or what he or she likes about your music. The label is your means of communicating your message, and you need to make sure that it understands your message so that it can communicate that message clearly. You are essentially putting your career in someone else's hands. Before you agree to work with a label, you want to make sure that representatives are capable and that they will do the best for you and at the same time actually care about your music. True indie label executives go through a lot of heartache for their artists. They believe in the message and love the sound, but in the end, an album just may not have a paying audience. As a struggling artist, a nurturing label may be just what you need. This kind of attachment to the artists leads to advocacy and persistence through the hard times and poor sales. Although struggling financially, an indie will sometimes be more patient than a major. But remember that while the size is different for majors and indies, indies still remain a business. Heartfelt admiration for your talents is only profitable if the label has the connections to make your albums sell. They must be able to prove to the distributors that your albums are commercially marketable.

IS IT A MOM-AND-POP LABEL?

Generally, a "mom-and-pop" business is a indie company that was not created by a major financial backer, a celebrity, or well-known major label. It is created by a relatively unknown person who just believes in the music and his or her ability to get it out to the public. Whereas a celebrity or successful music business mogul might have opened the indie label as an addition to his or her own roster of successes that he/she has already achieved.

Consider the celebrity status of the indie as you shop your demo. You should focus your energy on labels that are more likely to fit you. If Suge Knight or Kedar Massenburg (a former major executive turned indie) runs the show, they will need some assurance that your talent is marketable, in the way a major label would consider you. If Jane Smith owns the label, she will probably be looking at your talent, your sound, and your goals. If you are a lesser-known artist, or if your music caters to a more niche market, you probably have a better chance of being signed to a deal at a mom-and-pop label.

WHAT'S IN THE DEAL?

Each month at our law office, some artist, whether R&B, hip-hop, or gospel, calls me and tells me he or she is signing with an indie. Specifically, most of our artist clients and friends are so excited and eager to sign a deal that an independent label from Paducah, Kentucky, can call and promise a deal and he/she would sign it. As a result, I often ask these artists to please review what's actually in the deal. Do not be so eager to put out a press release or Blackberry message that you signed a deal and not realize that it is really not a deal that benefits you if the terms are horrible.

Depending on the label you are dealing with, you may have more or less flexibility in your negotiations. Independent labels might be open to different possibilities, so you might have an opportunity to be creative and reserve rights to some things that artists signing a deal with a major label cannot. Use what bargaining power you have to obtain the best deal you can for yourself. In addition to negotiating for a higher royalty rate or a bigger advance, you might want to consider the following as goals for your negotiations:

- Try to negotiate a smaller number of required albums in the initial period, and limit the number of options allowed. As mentioned in Chapter Two, the length of your contract is often tied to your recording commitment and delivery of albums. The term and recording commitment clauses can be tricky, because if you do not deliver your albums on time, or if the album delivery dates are hard to meet, your contract could go on forever.

- Try to negotiate funding for tours. This may be difficult with the limited funding of an independent, but touring is an important part of record promotion. Make sure you discuss touring with your label, and see what kind of possibilities they offer.

- Record companies will often license out the use of your name or image for merchandise. Try to negotiate a royalty rate on those licenses.

- If you are a group, look back on the terms you discussed regarding how you would treat a member leaving your group. If that policy still works for you, try to incorporate it into your deal. Also, make sure that if one member leaves, the rest of you are not tied to a contract that you cannot fulfill, possibly preventing you from pursuing another career in music.

- Maintain your creative control. With an independent label, you might have the ability to preserve a portion of your creative control in producing and selecting the material for your masters.

I recommend taking the time to sit down and think through your identity and goals as an artist. Consider your contract with the label and what the label has to offer before you meet with your attorney and make your deal. Draw up some notes that will help you pinpoint what exactly it is you want out of your deal by following these suggestions:

Make a list of the things you do know and do not know about the label.

Go through their proposed contract and make a list of the following contract terms, or other terms that might appear in your contract:

- Term/length of contract
- Recording commitment
- Advances
- Selection of material
- Delivery requirements
- Ownership of masters
- Sound recording copyright
- Accountings

- Exclusivity and sideman clause
- Copyright/mechanical royalties
- Music publishing
- Warranties/termination
- Group members/leaving member
- Bankruptcy
- Merchandising
- Touring

Identify the section numbers in your contract, and write the gist of what your contract states for each. Chapter Two suggests some other possible terms and explains more about what to look for in each of the terms in your contract.

Next, rank the key items on a scale of what is most to least important to you.

It will take a few hours, but this knowledge is invaluable. It will also serve you well in the future when you are considering new deals as an established artist. Finally, take your contract to your attorney and have him go through it and describe what each of the sections mean for your deal. Having familiarized yourself with the contract, you will be able to follow along and better articulate your priorities to your attorney, which will enable him to better negotiate and plan for you.

AM I IN A POSITION TO PUT MONEY TOWARD MY ALBUM?

As I stated above, the indie label is not going to advance you a large check when you sign the contract. As a result, you have to think beforehand as to whether you will have the funds necessary to make the video, market your album, and truly break your record on radio and TV. Before hammering out the details of your deal with an indie label, look at your financial situation to determine if you have any extra funds available that you can put toward your deal and the touring costs and promotional costs. Putting additional funds toward the promotion of your album will provide more marketing opportunities and resources and will allow the label to allocate more of their overall budget to your recording budget. Or if you put your money toward the recording, the label can put their resources into the marketing and promotion.

If you consider these factors and determine that you are not in a position to put your own money into your recording, be prepared to possibly pass on signing the deal. If not, then you will have a contract in hand for bragging purposes, but in a matter of weeks and months, when no one sees your record in stores, most will know that you signed a bad deal and had no real money to promote and market your album.

WHAT ARE MY MEANS OF ACCOUNTING?

Last, but not least important, are your royalty statements and accountings. When you deal with some of the indie labels, they do not have an accounting department or mechanical licensing team or even a copyright administrator like some of the major labels. And, as discussed throughout this book, the majority of issues between artists and labels arise over two things: money and the payment of royalties. When are they due versus when do they actually arrive? Are the splits with other songwriters, group members or producers made accurately? If a check was sent out for an artist, did it get to the right address? A lot of confusion and frustration happens over the accounting, even years after the album was released and the tours have finished. R&B artist Teena Marie got into a dispute with Motown Records over her royalty payments. Signed as a relatively unknown artist, Teena Marie did not receive any payments until nearly six years into her recording contract. (See *Motown Record Corp. v. Brockert*, 160 Cal. App.3d 1231 [1984]). The O'Jays also complained that they were taken advantage of by their record company, Philadelphia International Records. But, the O'Jays lost their suit against Philadelphia International because they failed to make inquiries into the status of their royalty payments in the appropriate manner. (See *Levert v. Philadelphia International Records*, 2004 U.S. Dist. LEXIS 25244 [2004]). Royalties are an artist's bread and butter, so naturally it makes for a contentious issue.

Likewise, if you are signing with an indie, then you must inquire in advance on how they pay royalties and how you will be able to conduct an accounting. Also, talk to the other artists on the indie label to confirm that the label has paid them royalties properly in the past or if they have encountered any problems. Next, go to the better business bureau and research the label's business practices or any complaints, if you can find them. Finally, have your attorney look up any lawsuits filed against the indie label you are considering joining as an artist.

There are several other factors to consider in signing with an indie versus a major. Hopefully, this chapter has given you some insight in making that important decision.

Agents, Lawyers, Publicists, and Accountants: Understanding the Roles and Functions

"The key to the success of any artist is the team around him and whether he or she will listen to their team."

—BERT PADELL, BUSINESS MANAGER FOR
THE LIKES OF TONI BRAXTON, ALICIA KEYS,
AND DARWIN HOBBS, AMONG OTHERS

About fifteen years ago, Clive Davis telephoned Bert Padell with an important message. The message didn't involve a contract, or business matter. Instead, Davis called Padell, a longstanding friend, to jokingly tell him, "Bert Padell, you're famous!" However, Padell wasn't sure what the music mogul meant with the phone call. But, then Davis explained further: "Bert, your famous; you're on the radio on a Biggie Smalls–112 record." After laughing and hearing the record months later, with Biggie boasting, "I stash more cash than Bert Padell," the legendary seventy-year-old business manager and CPA had sealed his legend on the urban streets as the business manager of urban music's finest artists. Padell was and is one of the music industry's top business managers and icons. I tease him often that when you hear your name in the lyrics of a popular rap song, you know you have become *legend*! But, more important than Biggie riffing and using you in his lyrics is that you actually deliver the goods as a member of the team.

Padell has been a business manager and accountant for over forty years and has helped a Who's Who of the entertainment industry, from Biggie to Luther Vandross to Alicia Keys to gospel artist Darwin Hobbs. We have often shared clients, and I am amazed with how well he works as a business manager on top of the music, business, and personal issues of his clients. In this chapter, we will discuss lawyers, accountants, publicists, and agents, the people behind the scenes that keep the music industry artist machine rolling. We will discuss their roles, their fees, and a few helpful tips about each of their specialties.

THE ROLE OF THE LAWYER

In the field of urban music, there are so many great lawyers that I tried to feature a few examples of the role of the lawyer in helping the artist. Three lawyers I respect have highly different styles but show you the various styles of lawyering that can be effective for their clients.

First, there is Matt Middleton. He is the founder and managing partner of the Middleton Law Group in midtown Manhattan. His entertainment law practice focuses on providing counsel to recording artists, music producers, songwriters, production companies, independent record labels, record company executives, and professional athletes with respect to all facets of the entertainment business. Middleton's expertise in these areas has been utilized by an impressive group of clients including recording artists Chris Brown, Fabolous, DMX, Kanye West, Mario, Twista, Shyne, Rhymefest, Foxy Brown, Nelly, and Juelz Santana as well as Blackground Records (label home to Jo Jo, the late Aaliyah, Timbaland, and Toni Braxton). A native of Harlem, New York, Middleton attended Howard University in Washington, DC. He explained three things to remember in serving as the role of the lawyer: 1) maintain integrity, 2) always protect your client, and 3) remember your role as the attorney is to help the artist execute his game plan. As an example, Middleton shared how he helped DMX and Chris Brown build a team of agents, attorneys, and others to handle various issues as they arose from time to time. "If you are a good lawyer, you recognize things that you don't know and bring in key people to help fill in the gaps for the best success of your artist," explained Middleton, a master at organizing worldwide tours and merchandising deals for various hot urban artists.

Amy Goldson is just as sharp as Middleton. Goldson, based in Washington, DC, has represented not only many super-hot artists, but she also represented a number of high-profile media clients like ABC's first African American evening news anchor, Max Robinson, and former ABC weatherman Tony Perkins, to name a few. Goldson shared that the role of the lawyer is to guide the career of the artist on all negotiations and contracting matters. Goldson, with clients scattered all over the country, further explained, "A good lawyer knows how to close the deal for the client and teach the client or artist how to become an effective business person."

Lastly, Larkin Arnold must be included in the section on the role of the lawyer, given his history in urban music, or *black* music as it was called in his day, thirty years ago. Larkin recalled in an interview the days when he signed Luther Vandross and worked on the careers of Natalie Cole, Tavares, and Maze, among so many others in the late 1970s and early 1980s. Arnold, a Howard-trained attorney, was helpful in launching the first black-music department at Capitol Records. And, Larkin, recognizing Vandross's skills as an artist and songwriter, blue-printed the early Vandross albums and guided the release of the classic "Never Too Much" hit, which really became Vandross's first public introduction as a solo artist/songwriter. Arnold would advise Arista and work for CBS throughout an illustrious career that culminated with his being the executive producer on the *Thriller* album. In an interview for this book, he described the balance of using his legal skills and creative skills in working with a then twentysomething Michael Jackson and Quincy Jones on the top-selling album of all time. And, in discussing the role or duty of a lawyer, Arnold pointed out one key thing: "Always remember you could be on the other side of the table" when negotiating on behalf of an artist. Arnold explained that it is important for the lawyer to get a good deal for his client, but do not do it to the total destruction of the opposing side, and be considerate of future deals and relationships and working together with the label representatives or other attorneys.

The entertainment lawyer is one of the key components of any team because he or she should review any contractual matters. Anything you do as an artist that requires a contract or agreement should be reviewed by your lawyer. There are a variety of deals that the lawyer can look at, including the book deal, publishing deal, and recording deal. A good lawyer might also set up an estate for you and in some cases help you find a good accountant to take care of your taxes.

Conflict of Interest

Ethics prohibits attorneys from representing clients on both sides of a dispute. Unfortunately, in the tight-knit world of music entertainment, many record labels and artists share attorneys, and this problem is quite feasible. When a single attorney's two clients are involved in negotiations—or worse, a legal battle—this creates a *conflict of interest* for the attorney. Explained Goldson, "An attorney cannot sit on both sides of the table." Under those circumstances, one or both clients may have to find alternate representation or risk obtaining an unfair deal. Since the party who hired the attorney first is generally going to be the one to keep the attorney if a conflict arises, ask potential lawyers if they work with anyone you might have to negotiate with, like a record label or manager.

Fees

There are hundreds of lawyers describing themselves as entertainment lawyers and charging artists a variety of different fee arrangements. As an artist, be mindful of standard fees before you sign any retainer agreement with a lawyer. A retainer agreement is merely a one- to three-page agreement with the lawyer that sets forth his or her fees for the services they are providing you and spells out your authorization that he/she may state that you are officially a client. Most of these retainer agreements will set forth the hourly rate of the lawyer. Generally, a seasoned entertainment lawyer could charge between $300 and $600 per hour for his legal time. The hourly fee is higher depending on how long he has practiced, his reputation, his connections, and how experienced he is in entertainment law. In some cases, the entertainment lawyer might work for a percentage of the deal—i.e., a finder's fee of 5 to 10 percent. And, as Goldson explained, some lawyers will seek a *point* on a deal—i.e., when you secure your recording contract and the label outlines the points you will receive, you will share that income with the lawyer who brokered or worked on the deal. Always get an idea of how your attorney plans to bill you, and if he or she uses value billing, ask what the projected value will be.

I suggest asking for the fee agreement in writing because the last thing you want to do is litigate with an attorney. Also, pay close attention to his or her legal work to make sure that the work delivered is of the quality and standard that you expect. And don't assume that because you hire a popular, well-known entertainment lawyer you do not have to hold him accountable and stay on top of his work.

Importance

I really cannot overstate the importance of having a good entertainment attorney by your side. Even if you do not foresee any major conflict with your label, it is of utmost importance to have someone with experience fighting for your best interest. I can tell you a million and a half horror stories where record labels, managers, and other recording entities tried to take advantage of artists or producers and succeeded when the artist did not have good legal representation.

A conflict does not have to be monumental or involve large sums of money. One client that I worked with had produced an album for a famous gospel singer. He worked very hard on the production and our firm had helped him to secure a favorable contract. The contract required that the producer be mentioned in all media including articles and press releases about the album. When the singer issued a press release about the upcoming album, however, my client's name was nowhere to be found. In instances like that, it is the attorney's job, not the publicist's or agent's, to threaten appropriate legal action if the injustice is not rectified. (If you're interested, the singer subsequently submitted a new press release that included my client's name.)

THE ROLE OF THE ACCOUNTANT

The role of the accountant is pretty straightforward: make sure that the artist is financially viable for the rest of his life. The accountant should make sure that the artist understands where money is coming in and where money is going out. He also makes sure that if there are bookings, royalty statements, commissions, rents, and anything related to the artist's career, all of them have somewhere to be accounted for at the end of the day. In explaining the importance of being a good business accountant and business advisor, I have to go back to our introduction of Bert Padell in the opening of this chapter. Padell has worked as a business manager and CPA for nearly five decades. Padell advises three tips in hiring the accountant: 1) listen to the accountant, 2) make sure the accountant protects you and saves you money, and 3) do not hire family members. According to Padell, who, along with Vernon Brown of V. Brown Company and Laura Gordon of Gordon & Associates, are among the leading business managers for artists nationwide, "it's hard to have family members serve as your accountant or business advisor."

Padell, who was once Joe DiMaggio's batboy, teammate, and business manager and has been an accountant for Britney Spears, Alicia Keys, and Madonna, to name a few, explained further that many artists "hire family members who are clueless" but wear the title of "business manager. You can't fake it. I am a licensed accountant, and I really know what I am doing."

In a recent interview with *Velvet Addiction* magazine, Padell explained that "I look over everything my clients sign before they sign it and I care for them, and I am there for them 24/7." But, he also warned that if the artist will not listen to his or her accountant, it's hard to help. "Madonna came to me with nothing and no money. But, she listened and did very well for herself," Padell explained. "The most important thing an artist can do is to get the right professionals behind them."

While a lot of artists will hire the *in* lawyer of the moment, Padell cautiously stated, "Don't hire people who don't give a sugar about you, just because they have big names." He recommended further that you hire good people, regardless of their popularity. Padell also reminds us that an artist must remember that "Forty percent goes to income taxes, forty percent goes to themselves, and twenty percent for their savings." If you look at it this way, most likely you will not spend the forty percent that goes to yourself but will in fact save a great deal of money.

Choosing Your Accountant

As previously stated, your accountant should have a degree and experience. A Certified Public Accountant, although expensive, may be your best bet. Another important factor is whether the accountant you are considering has music industry clients. I suggest choosing one who does because he will be better equipped to work with the companies that pay you.

Conflict of interest applies to accountants, too, although not in the same way as it does to attorneys. Some accountants receive a "commission" from potential investment houses. Even though this is beneficial for the accountant, because he essentially gets paid twice, you should avoid using those who engage in this practice, because their kick-back might influence your investments in a negative way.

Managing Your Accountant

Before you hand over your money to an accountant, you should discuss and put in writing the sort of relationship that you hope to have with him. Contractually obligate your accountant to provide you with written monthly updates about your funds. If something begins to go wrong in business bank-account land, you want to know about it as soon as possible. Discuss whether you intend to allow your accountant to make investments with your money, and if so what kind of investments you (and him) are comfortable making. Finally, arrange to be able to sign your own checks. Oprah Winfrey often says that the most important advice she got from Bill Cosby was to "sign your own checks." When you are busy working on multiple projects and more than one check comes in, it is easy to lose track of your assets. When you lose track of your money, it is easy to *really* lose track of your money, and you may be left singing a sad tune, while your sleazy accountant reaps the benefits. If you have an agreement that you will sign all of your checks, and your bank does not accept checks that are not signed by you, you will be much more likely not to be robbed by your accountant, and that should provide a great deal of peace of mind.

Fees

If you are paying your accountant an hourly rate, make sure you know what that rate is before you hire him. On the other hand, some artists choose to pay their accountant a flat monthly fee or a percentage of gross—i.e., 3 to 5 percent, according to Padell. Others work on a percentage basis and incorporate a minimum; if you are just starting out, or do not need a lot of accounting work, this is not going to be cost effective for you. Whatever you choose to do, put it in writing to avoid confusion when it comes time to cut that check.

THE ROLE OF THE AGENT

Musical agents mostly work with clients on live performances and sometimes commercials and other forms of sponsorships. The agent fee can vary from 5 to 10 percent of your gross. There are different types of agents. For example, if you decide to branch out into other entertainment areas, like going from being an R&B singer to writing a book called *How I Became an Urban Music Sensation*, there are literary agents for these types of deals.

In the music industry you can also have a booking agent or a television agent. A booking agent might be from the William Morris Agency or ABC Booking or Alliance Booking. The job of the booking agent is to secure jobs, dates, and performances. A booking agent also tries to route concert tours and secure speaking engagements. The TV agent, however, works diligently to find TV and film gigs and also looks at scripts, much like a movie agent does for actors. Two of the top agents are Jodi Moniello from Alliance Booking and Charles King from William Morris. I have worked closely with these agents and know them well, and I can tell you that they are very good at what they do.

FEES

Since agents do not play a role in album production, it would be pointless to give them a percentage of album or recording sales. Aside from that, you will be happy to know that in most circumstances, except for personal appearances, agents cannot legally ask for more than 10 percent. Both your booking agent and TV agents normally collect a fee of 10 percent for their work in securing performance dates and television projects. Their fee is determined by the gross fee you receive for such performances. If you feel that your agent is not acting in good faith or is requesting more than the allowed percentage, feel free to check with local and state laws and union guidelines, if any, to make sure the agents are in compliance.

TERM OF CONTRACT

Agents like job security and a steady income as much as anyone else, so they will insist on signing the longest running contract, to bind you for years. It is in your best interest, on the other hand, to get the shortest contract term. A short contract will allow you to determine if the agent is doing everything that you would like him to do and it will also allow you the chance to renegotiate the agent's fees at a later date. Negotiate to the best of your ability (an attorney will be useful here). If you cannot find a good deal for yourself and your agent turns out to be a dud, do not worry; in a few paragraphs you will find out what to do.

EXCLUSIONS

You can and should exclude your agent from earning commission from certain areas of your business where he did not help generate financial success. Basically, your agent is only entitled to commissions that are stipulated in the contract that you both signed. You can exclude your agent from collecting for record albums, songwriting, and publishing. It is fair, of course, for your agent to be paid for the areas in which he helped you to reap financial rewards. For example, if you are a gospel singer with no acting résumé, and your agent got you a role in movie as a member of a gospel choir (like all of those singing extras in Queen Latifah's choir in the film *Last Holiday*), he should be paid for his effort.

TERMINATION

Even if you signed a contract for *x* number of years, you may be able to get out of it if the agent is not getting you work. Some agent union agreements allow artists to terminate contracts with their agents if the agent has not produced for ninety days. Keep in mind that this applies only if the agent has not produced any work at all; if he finds an offer in your professional range for you and you refuse to take it, the agent has satisfied his end of the deal. If, however, you are a gospel singer and the agent finds you a gig playing backup ukulele for Rolling Stone Keith Richards, or something equally outside of your professional scope, you would be justified in turning it down. On the other hand, it is important to be reasonable.

Geography

The bigger you get in your career, the more important geography or agent locations become. As your career becomes global, you will want representation in foreign markets that will be able to present you accurately to your international fans. Your domestic agent will want a piece of that action because that translates into more money for him. Most agents will insist that they represent you on a global scale, which means that getting an agent in Tokyo for your Asian market may be difficult. On the other hand, it is not an impossible task. A lot of larger agencies have offices or subcontractors internationally, and working with them may be easier than doing research about agents on an international scale.

THE ROLE OF THE PUBLICIST

As the urban music scene and hip-hop scene exploded in the 1980s and 1990s, along with the boom in gospel music in recent years, we've had a slew of individuals announcing themselves as "publicists." Be very careful when you allow someone the role of handling your media relations, magazine appearances, TV promos, and overall development of your image. In urban music, the queen bee of all publicists is Terrie Williams, who has handled everyone from Eddie Murphy to Janet Jackson to Diddy to the late, great Johnny Cochran, among tons of others. Williams and I sat down a few years ago and even attended Diddy's trial to watch Cochran at work. She has often been a trailblazer for the publicists of any genre, color, or shade. If you speak with her, she will tell you that a publicist is the key to help you promote yourself and your music. A publicist's key role is to generate publicity for his or her client.

A publicist will work to get you positive media attention, although some publicists swear by the adage "There is no such thing as bad publicity." When hiring your publicist, you should find out what their philosophy of fame is. If you are not the sort of person who feels comfortable with his or her picture on the cover of every magazine at the newsstand, your publicist should know that, or you may want to reconsider your career in entertainment.

A publicist can be beneficial if you have not hit it big yet. Your publicist will spend time writing press releases on your behalf. This will hopefully translate into greater media attention. I suggest going with a well-known PR firm. Just as a well-connected attorney will be able to get you better deals from record labels, so will a well-connected publicist get your picture and story into the hottest magazines. The other reason for using a well-known PR firm is that it will help to validate you as an artist in the minds of the public and media. To a publication like *Ebony* magazine, the fact that you, a new artist, have a PR firm with whom they have an established relationship may mean the difference between referencing your name or another newcomer's.

I spoke with publicist Elisa Keys of Events in the City, who has represented top names and projects in entertainment like *Fast and Furious: Tokyo Drift*, *Take the Lead*, *Final Destination 3*, *Silent Hill*, *Underworld: Evolution*, Virgin Megastores, New Line Cinema, Universal Pictures, Maya Angelou, Evander Holyfield, Earl Graves, Bob Watson, and the New York Yankees, just to name a few. After almost a decade in the business, Ms. Keys offered the following words of advice: "Make sure you are always prepared and polished. You never know who you might meet walking down the street or on the subway. Make sure you have your headshots, press kit, and promotional materials on point. Remember that your image is *who* you are." She also added: "The key traits for a publicist include excellent verbal and written communication skills, terrific people skills, and the unique ability to be in the *right place* at the *right time*."

It's also worth mentioning that record labels have their own publicists, many of whom are on staff, which means that they work directly for the label. These publicists make it their job to promote the artists on that label by coordinating with each individual artist's publicist. The downside of that is if you are a brand-new artist, it is likely that the label's publicist will not work as hard to promote you as to promote the label's other, more established, clients.

OVERVIEW

Let's recap, because let's face it, even the brightest minds sometimes need to hear things twice: Hire only people who you can fully trust, even for the smallest jobs or seemingly less important roles. Put all of your agreements, especially fees and duties, in writing. Do not feel hopeless. Even if the person who you hired does not work out for you, you can refer to professional organizations and unions for help.

And, in summary, Bert Padell said it best when he said that as an artist, you must "get people that care for you and not just the money you make, and who will nurture you and make sure you make the right decisions, and the money will take care of itself." He further explained that it is critical to "get the right lawyer, manager, business manager, publicist, and a good booking agency. . . . If an artist has this team, then he or she is going to be successful."

CHAPTER 7

Starting a Label: A Few Preliminary Points of Consideration

> *"I come from an entrepreneurial family, so it was logical to me that since my first love is music, I would start my own record company focusing on gospel music. After finishing graduate school, I was in debt with over $40,000 in student loans. That's when God told me to start JDI Records."*
>
> —JAMES ROBERSON, FOUNDER OF
> JDI RECORDS, A TOP GOSPEL LABEL

Many independent labels that have turned into companies with major-label power were started from meager beginnings by regular people. Sean John Combs founded Bad Boy Entertainment, one of the driving forces in hip-hop in the mid-1990s. P. Diddy first skyrocketed to fame when he worked with Mary J. Blige, Jodeci, and later Notorious B.I.G., and of course by releasing a myriad of his own hits including "Can't Nobody Hold Me Down" and "I'll Be Missing You" under the Bad Boy Records label.

Originally from Harlem, New York, P. Diddy got his start in the music industry when he gained a position as an intern at Uptown Records. Within a few short months, Combs was promoted to a position as an A&R executive and helped produce "Father's Day" (Father MC, 1990), "What's the 411?" (Mary J. Blige, 1992), and "Blue Funk" (Heavy D & the Boyz, 1992). Combs was fired from Uptown in 1993, but feeling no less determined to be a star of hip-hop, Combs set up his own label, Bad Boy Records, and soon signed Craig Mack and the Notorious B.I.G. In no time, both released hit singles that launched Bad Boy into fame. Diddy is recognized as one of the most successful entrepreneurs in the music industry. In 2002, he was featured as one of *Fortune* magazine's "Forty Richest People under Forty" list. He is recognized as such a powerful entrepreneur because he diversified his brand by adding an urban clothing line, Sean John, and the restaurant chain Justin's (named after his son). He is known to take lessons from Russell Simmons, another well-known entrepreneur in the hip-hop world.

Russell Simmons, along with his partner Rick Rubin, founded Def Jam recordings in Simmons's college dorm room while Simmons was studying sociology at the City College of New York. Def Jam is considered to be one of the first labels to take hip-hop into the mainstream. Together, Simmons and Rubin produced and released some of the first artists to create the hip-hop mainstream, including the Sugar Hill Gang, Run DMC, and LL Cool J. LL Cool J's first release, "I Need a Beat," sold 100,000 copies, bringing the label to the attention of Columbia Records, who began to underwrite the label's success. Over twenty-five years later, Def Jam continues to be a leader in mainstream hip-hop music. (Simmons and Rubin later reportedly sold their interests in Def Jam for $100 million each to Universal.)

The stories of P. Diddy and Russell Simmons demonstrate that anyone can start from meager beginnings to become a music mogul with hard work, diligence, and an ear for music. If you have always dreamed of running your own record label, you do not need be famous to get started. All you need is creativity and a plan, and you can build your music empire from the ground up. In this chapter, we look at the dos and don'ts of starting a label.

There are hundreds of labels in urban music, but few owners take the time to carefully plan out the necessary steps in forming the label. With a plan, it is not the most difficult thing to do.

The steps that follow apply to any genre. Every entrepreneur should follow these seven core concepts for planning and starting his or her own record label:

- Organize your dream into a reality.
- Research your start-up label.
- Design a business plan.
- Build your team.
- Find artists.
- Prepare for your debut.
- Premiere your label: showcasing your artists.

ORGANIZE YOUR DREAM INTO A REALITY

If you have always dreamed of starting your own record company, it is time to make that dream into a plan. Part of making your plan is determining what your ultimate goal is. Are you looking to create the next Def Jam on a national level, or is your goal simply to bring music to local ears? Whatever your goal, you need to determine how you are going to start and what steps you want to take to succeed in your dream. Start thinking about what it is you value most about offering your services as a record label. Are you looking forward to booking shows for your artists (look into whether your state will require you to get a license to manage)? Are you excited about helping your artists produce in the studio or mostly concerned with helping an artist get his or her music to the streets? Figuring out what aspect of starting a record label appeals to you most will help you organize the company.

What resources do you have to start with? Make a list of what financial resources you have, people who might be interested in offering you financial support, as well as existing connections within the industry. Come up with a hypothetical timeline for your company development, and make changes to it as you learn more about the business. For example, you may have to start your label in your bedroom, but set a goal for when you want to move your operation into a real office or a date by when you want to acquire your own recording studio. Also, create a list of things you will need as you are running your record label that you can adjust as you continue your research, such as equipment, office supplies, and services. "People have to understand, when you run a label you are running a business, so you have to come up with a business plan and do your research," says Monica Bacon, former VP for GospoCentric/Sony/Zomba.

RESEARCH YOUR START-UP LABEL

Whether you are an artist, producer, or simply an entertainment executive, or even a layperson, research the field you are getting into as a label owner. Most labels fail owing to lack of planning and research. As stated earlier, Sean Combs, a/k/a P. Diddy, spent time working with Uptown and learning the business before launching his Bad Boy imprint. While you might not be able to intern at Uptown or any major label, there is ample research available online and at your local library to understand the operation of a label and all that it entails.

Additionally, why waste time and money investing in a business as a prospective entrepreneur with no research or statistical data. Starting a record label is not for the faint of heart, but with a lot of work and research, as well as a solid business plan, anyone can be successful.

One of the best ways to do research on starting a business is to check out the competition. For example, if I planned to start a gospel label, I would do an extensive review of GospoCentric Records, Verity Records, EMI Records, Dexterity Records, and Malaco Records, to name a few major gospel players. I would look at a litany of factors, including the following:

How long have they been in business?
How many artists have they signed?
How many albums/artists do they release each year?
How were they funded?
How big is their staff?
How is their marketing and promotions handled?
How many flops have they had, if any, and why did the albums fail?
How are they distributed (independently or through a major—Sony, Warner, etc.)?
How is their reputation in the industry?
How have they expanded into other businesses (publishing, merchandising, etc.)?

These are only some of the major factors, but it is very critical to apply these ten considerations before you launch. For example, if you are going to compete with GospoCentric, you need to know if they have five or fifty people on staff. Did they invest their own monies as owners (Claude and Vicki Mack-Lataillade) or did they have major label financing? Did EMI Gospel release ten hit albums the past two years or did their second Smokey Norful album fail to reach expectations? And if so, what went wrong? Should Norful have kept his formula with Derrick "DOA" Allen to make another great album? Also, distribution is a key factor. Are they using Central South, Koch, or Artemis for distribution, or do they have distribution from a major like BMG, Warner, or Sony? And, how does that relationship work for them as a label?

By knowing your competition inside and out you can make decisions about how to set up your business and learn what strategies work and what strategies do not work for success in the long run.

First, you will want to create a list of other labels you want to research. Consider a range of different types of labels, and research some majors, some mini-majors, and independents. Do not just limit your search to labels that only produce records within the genre you think you want to your label to have. Create the list using labels that you already know of and by consulting industry classification manuals and search systems. You can consult the following manuals and research systems, many of which are available on the web:

- SIC—Standard Industry Classification
  (http://www.census.gov/epcd/www/sic.html)
- NAICS—North American Industry Classification System
  (http://www.census.gov/epcd/www/naics.html)
- U.S. Department of Commerce's National Technical Information Service
  (http://www.ntis.gov/)
- U.S. Industry & Trade Outlook, a resource for researching economic and high-level industry outlook
  (http://www.ita.doc.gov/td/industry/otea/outlook/index.html).

Once you have created your list of other labels, you will want to find more information about them. You can start your research on the web. Go to company websites, and look for any information they might provide about their companies. Also, be sure to read press releases if they are published on the sites. This will give you an idea of how to write your own press release in the future and for other nuggets of information about the company. Gather information that will help you put together what the business model looks like for each label.

Questions that I often ask clients to consider when looking at other labels are: Who is at the top of the company? What are the different departments of each company, and how do they function? Many major labels follow a similar business model and have similar departments, including A&R, Product Development, Marketing, Product Management, Public Relations, and Legal and Business Affairs. Look for contact information for key industry players, and contact the companies and request annual reports for financial information if it is available.

When you have received the financial information, you will want to make an analysis of each company's financials. You should hire a financial expert for analyzing the financial information. Try to figure out the reason for their profits.

It is also important to analyze the marketing strategies used in the industry. Think about what types of marketing techniques record labels use, such as advertising on TV, in magazines, and in stores. Touring and public appearances also serve as a form of marketing. If you have the funds, consider hiring a market research firm. Have the firm advise you on how to handle marketing expenses and the hidden tricks for success in that market.

Based on the information you gathered, analyze the business model. What about the business model works, and what aspects of the business model do you wish to adopt? Keep in mind what level of record company you want to start with (a label that is local and homegrown or one destined for major distribution), and determine what aspects of other models will work for your label.

Also, with your hypothetical business model in mind, begin researching and pricing some of the things you'll need to get your label started. Call around or look on the web to see how much studio time costs and how much time it usually takes to get in and out from start to finish. How much are duplicating and packaging services, or how much is it to buy the duplication equipment on your own? How much will it cost to produce promotional materials like stickers, posters, and flyers? Do you need a printer and stationary? Do not forget, you will need a website so that people can easily find you and your artists. Getting together a list of estimated costs will help you put together your budget and aid you in designing your business plan.

Many of these suggestions sound basic and common; however, most start-ups do not engage this level of analysis or research before announcing that they are the next new start-up on the scene. New Edition member Michael Bivins, one of the pioneers of urban labels, who discovered Boys II Men, says, "without a game plan, you won't go anywhere as a label."

DESIGN A BUSINESS PLAN

A business plan is a document written to organize your ideas for the structure of your business and to often attract potential investors. The business plan is about results and about making your business prosper. A plan will make your business better by allowing you to set priorities, manage numbers, and communicate your ideas and goals to others. Each section of your business plan should reflect the following attributes: credibility, objectivity, clarity, reasonableness, sufficient evidence, consistency, awareness of success factors, key risks, vulnerabilities, venture planning, and sound business analysis and judgment. Traditional sections of a business plan are as follows:

- Executive summary
- Table of contents
- Venture product
- Target market and competition
- Company description and venture organization
- Venture management
- Venture operations
- Venture financing
- Appendices and exhibits

If you are planning on presenting your business plan to an investment firm or other potential investors, you will want to consult some of the guides and books available on business plan writing. When writing your business plan, refer back to the lists you made of goals and priorities for what you want your label to be. You are going to want to integrate your goals and timeline into your business plan.

Decide on your business model. If you talk to Rodney Jerkins or Dallas Austin or Jermaine Dupri or Dr. Dre they would all tell you the things they would have done differently with regards to having a solid business plan. At a recent BMI Awards program, Jerkins told me, "you have to understand business to establish yourself, and if I knew then what I know now, I would do a lot of things differently."

Jerkins does not have funding issues, as he's been a multimillionaire since he was a teen. However, if you are limited on funding, you may want to consider some nontraditional business structures. For example, if you are really interested in producing albums with artists, you might want to consider only offering demo deals to start. A demo deal is an agreement to help an artist or group produce only one to three songs for an EP album. Or, if your goal is to start locally and help artists in your area become well known, consider offering deals in which you require the artist to have already recorded or pay for their own recording. One of the biggest expenses when starting a label is recording costs, so reducing the amount of time you spend and pay for the recording studio with your artists will be a huge part of keeping your budget small.

An important part of your business plan will be your budget. Based on your research, put together a budget that will help you determine how much money you will need to get started. Here are some items that you should consider for purposes of budgeting:

- Fees for registering your business entity and tax identification. Chapter Eight will discuss how to select and register your business entity, such as setting up a C Corp or LLC.

- Advances for artists. An important part of your budget will be how much money you give to and spend on your artists.

- Recording costs. These including studio time, fees for producers, fees for additional musicians your artist may need, and any necessary equipment rental.

- Duplication costs. These include the cost of duplication services or the cost of supplies and equipment if you plan on duplicating the CDs yourself.

- CD packaging costs. These include such items as jewel cases, shrink-wrap, barcodes, and inserts for liner notes.

- Marketing. Cost of advertisements, flyers, posters, stickers, and displays are included under this.

- Wages or salaries for employees.

- Bookkeeping and accountant fees. Of course, as a start-up, you may not have the ability to pay for someone to do your books, but if you do not have a lot of experience bookkeeping, you might want to consult an accountant on how to keep proper records and to ensure that you pay your taxes properly.

- Legal fees. You should consult an attorney when drafting and negotiating agreements for your artists.

- Rent for an office or storage space. If you are choosing to set up your label in an office space or if you need space to store CDs or equipment, make sure you set aside money in the budget for monthly rental payments.

- Website setup and maintenance. In the information age, a website is essential. Typically when setting up a website, you will need to pay to purchase a domain name, and unless you are an expert at web design, you may need to hire someone to design and maintain your site. You need a web presence so that fans can easily access information about your label and your artists. A website is a great way of communicating, selling merchandise, and cross-promoting your artists.

- Office supplies. You will need the equipment and supplies to communicate with your artists and spread the word about their music.

- Postage. You could end up spending a fair amount of money on postage sending out mailings for press releases and press kits for booking shows for artists, if you choose to offer management services.

This is by no means an exhaustive list of potential costs or issues, so be sure to think out your budget carefully as you are developing your business plan. One pointer for budgeting your expenses is that you should not keep more inventory than you can sell within a limited accounting period. So while some duplicating services or T-shirt printers might offer discounts for purchasing larger quantities, you will be able to keep your budget under control by ordering quantities that reflect your ability to sell your inventory within a given time period, such as a month or quarter. Also, put together a list of potential sources of income (such as CD sales, merchandise sales, and income from touring or management if you offer those services) with price points and estimate how much you will receive in revenues.

BUILD YOUR TEAM

CPA Vernon Brown was the genius behind P. Diddy for years, helping establish Justin's restaurant and other successful entertainment ventures for P. Diddy. LA-based entertainment lawyer Channing Johnson was the key legal person for GospoCentric. Laura Gordon was the key financial advisor for Jamie Foxx, and CAA super agent Andrea Nelson-Meigs is the dealmaker agent for Cedric the Entertainer, Beyoncé, and tons of others. And, of cource, where would urban music be without the great team of attorney-manager Ward White and Ms. Erykah Badu? The point: Put good people on your team to make it happen.

At first, you may not have the resources to hire any employees, especially not full time. But you should consider recruiting some friends or acquaintances to help you move merchandise at concerts and promote upcoming shows. For the start-up record label, a great source of labor is a "street team," i.e., a bunch of interns or young folks who plaster the city and marketplace with your flyers, marketing materials, and overall "street" presence and visibility efforts. Although you may have to do a lot of the initial promotional work yourself, as your label and artists gain notoriety, you can try to recruit a street team to help you promote your artists. Street teams can be a powerful yet inexpensive marketing tool for budding artists and labels. Street team members can usually be compensated for their work on promoting shows by offering them access to the artist, training at a business, free admission, and complimentary merchandise, and you can send them flyers and CDs for them to spread the word about your artists.

Once your label is up and running, you will want to begin employing a team to help you run the label and manage your artists. You can hire personnel to help promote the artists or to do more office management and administrative duties, or you can hire individuals to act as A&R executives and have them recruit and manage new artists. Just remember that while your friends might be banging down your door to help you out, you should be honest with yourself about how dedicated to your mission they will truly be. Good friends do not necessarily make good employees, so rather than hiring all of your friends, you might want to stick to asking them to simply continue spreading the good word and coming to shows.

If you find your label is expanding at a fast pace, and you need a lot of help, you should begin practicing some human resource techniques that will help you keep your employees motivated and in touch with the company. A few years ago, Brenda Culpepper was running the successful Pepperco Records gospel label (John P. Kee, East Coast Mass Choir). When the company started to grow, she quickly hired good staff and personnel to deal with the growth.

An employer can assist in an employee's transition into the workplace by investing a little time and guidance. A successful employee will translate into success for your company. By assisting the new employee, the employer is essentially preparing the company for his or her contributions. There are several ways an employer can assist a new employee in his transition to the work place.

OFFER AN ORIENTATION

Provide your new employees with a business overview, tour of facilities, and review compensation and benefits with them, and technical and administrative resources, as well as standard office and business procedures. This will also help your employee to be able to transition easily between job functions in case you have a need in the area that the employee does not normally fall under.

ARRANGE A "MEET AND GREET"

Introduce your new employees to co-workers and explain each co-worker's role. By meeting workers from other departments with whom he or she will be working on a regular basis, the new employee will feel more comfortable, will be able to perform better, and will feel comfortable asking for help when he or she comes across tasks that are difficult.

SET CLEAR EXPECTATIONS

Sit down early with a new staff member to ensure the individual knows exactly what the job entails. Remember that the employee is new and will not necessarily be able to adapt to your way of running the company without direction. Be sure to explain job functions thoroughly and point out any important office policies.

PROVIDE MENTORS

Pair new hires with seasoned employees so that they can share with newcomers their experiences with the firm and provide insight into working for your label. This will help ease their transition into the company.

MAINTAIN AN OPEN-DOOR POLICY

An employer or supervisor should make himself or herself available to the new employee. This will also help the new employee transition into your label.

FIND ARTISTS

Babyface and L. A. Reid discovered Toni Braxton and Usher. Top producer Jermaine Dupri brought us Kris Kross and Da Brat. Grammy-winning artist and producer Fred Hammond brought us Joanne Rosario. James Roberson of JDI

Records introduced us to Norman Hutchinson, the great gospel singer. Of course, the godfather of it all, Berry Gordy bought us the Supremes. NBA All-Star Allen Iverson once famously asked, "What are we talking about . . . practice ?" Well, in this section, we are talking about discovering talent—successful talent, that is.

It is important that you have a passion for the artists that you sign to your new label. Many people who open a record label get started with an artist that they know they want to sign right away. This is a great way to get started, but is not a prerequisite to getting your label up and running.

Needless to say, the most traditional way of finding your star artist is attending local shows and picking up an artist or group that you hear live and believe they can have commercial success. Pay close attention to artists in your area that have a buzz surrounding them, and a following. Signing an artist that already has a following will make it easier for you to get started.

You can also solicit press kits from local artists by putting up ads or bulletin posts on local music websites. Similarly, you can check social-networking websites for nearby artists who are getting a lot of hits or plays on their music. Once again, having an artist that is already somewhat established will give you a head start, and an artist that has a website with music samples available for upload is an artist that has already made an investment in developing themselves as an artist.

When you think you have found the artist of your dreams, you should schedule a time to meet and present her with information about your company, including your goals and what services you offer, and discuss common goals until you know each other better.

Have a good attorney prepare an agreement or deal memo for the artist when your gut tells you the feelings are mutual (a premature agreement will scare them away). For many artists, this will be their first time making an official agreement to have someone work on her music, so they will need terms explained. You should also advise her to consult an attorney, but consider having her sign a deal memo that outlines the basics of the agreement and follow up with your full-length agreement with more specifically negotiated terms.

Being a huge fan of the music is a paramount concern, but also try to get an idea as to whether the artist is someone that you think you can have a good working relationship with as a business partner. An artist that is difficult or has unrealistic expectations could lead to a lot of miscommunication and possible failure of your record deal with her. You and your artist should have a good understanding of what you both are expecting out of the deal, and as their record label, you need to work hard to fulfill what expectations your artist has.

PREPARE FOR YOUR DEBUT

Once you have an artist or two under your belt, you should prepare a marketing plan for announcing the debut of your label and your artists. You want to get a buzz going in your area about your record label. A lot of the buzz about your label will be through your artists. If you have established artists with a solid mailing list, you should send out an announcement to their fans that they have been signed to your label. If they have a website, make sure that they include information about your label and a link to your website.

Recall when Jimmy Jam and Terry Lewis brought us the Sounds of Blackness, there was a lot of pre-release buzz. The group went on to sell a ton of records and make noise worldwide. The group set the pavement for the urban contemporary gospel crossover sound that permeates urban radio now. None of this would have been possible had the label not done its homework.

A fun way to premiere your label is through a live performance showcasing your artists. The next section will go into further detail about how to set up your showcase. In this section, we will discuss the work required to launch your label's premiere. Your marketing plan for the premiere of your label should contain the components listed below. Create a timeline for your marketing plan integrating these components, using the showcase as the culmination of your marketing plan. You might need to allow several weeks to get everything together and get a buzz started. Center your timeline on the showcase and get all of the promotion and materials you will need together before the showcase.

PUBLICITY

The publicity component of your marketing plan is a crucial way of getting word out to the media about your label and your artists. Draw up a press release to send to local publications, especially those that focus on local arts and entertainment events. Also, try to notify local radio stations about the showcase and get them to add the concert to their list of upcoming events they announce on the air. (You may need to work with the venue to do this.) Explained publicist Kia Jones, "Without publicity, who is going to know your marketing or anything about your label or artist?"

ADVERTISING

If you have the ability to in your budget, create an advertising campaign to get the word out about your label and the showcase, starting with ads in local papers or on local radio. Make sure your ads start running soon enough before your event but not so far in advance that people are likely to forget about your concert.

STREET PROMOTION

Canvas your area with flyers and stickers to let people know about your artists, your label, and your showcase. Flyers and stickers placed in locations that people see every day leading up to your premiere will bring your label and artists to their attention and start to get your brand recognized, even if they do not attend the showcase.

WEB PROMOTION

Make sure that your website and your artist's website have information about the upcoming showcase and any available music and merchandise. If people see your flyers, they might surf onto your website for more information, so it is important that they can find what they are looking for.

MERCHANDISE AVAILABILITY

Having merchandise such as CDs, stickers, and T-shirts available at the time of your premiere will reinforce the buzz behind your debut and give attendees something to remember you for and share with other potential fans. Be sure to set aside room in your budget for giving out some merchandise for promotion prior to and at the premiere. Order merchandise relatively early in your plan so that it arrives on time and you can avoid costly rush fees.

LIVE PERFORMANCE/SHOWCASE PREMIERE

Debuting your label with a live performance will give people a taste of what your label has to offer. While it could be an expensive endeavor, it's a great way to get people excited about your artists and your label.

You can add or modify this list as you choose, but please think through this process of your debut and premiere.

PREMIERE YOUR LABEL: SHOWCASING YOUR ARTISTS

A few years ago, I remember attending a showcase for a sensational urban group Floetry. Their manager J. Erving put on an incredible showcase, and I have been buying their CDs ever since. An exciting way to premiere your label is to organize a concert or CD release party showcasing your artists. A live performance of your artists in one place will give your artists exposure and also give you an opportunity to advertise your brand, which you may not be able to do to the same extent as your artists go on to tour individually. Planning this event thoroughly is crucial, and you will need to work really hard to get people to attend. If you have the funds available, you might want to consider hiring an event planner, or someone who has experience hosting CD release parties or other concerts. Marvette Britto, Amy Bolsom, and Elisa Keys are the best in the industry if you can get them.

You can make this an event that exclusively shows your artists, or you can align yourself with another artist who is well established in the area by inviting him to perform at the show. By inviting an artist that is popular in the area and of a similar genre to your show, you will get his following to attend and see your artists. So, while you will have to share the stage, and possibly even pay him a fee or give them a cut of the door, you will probably be able to get a larger audience to fill the house.

To hold the concert, you will need to find a space for your artists to perform. If you are on a limited budget, look into spaces that are not normally used for concerts but may provide a suitable space. There may be an art center in your area that rents out space, and some fraternal societies offer spaces to rent as well. If you rent a space for your showcase, remember to hire or rent lighting and sound equipment and engineers to make sure that everyone who comes to the concert can see and hear your artists give quality performances!

You can also check out local music venues and see if they would allow you to buy time or if they would be willing to book your artists (which is where having a known name from the area might help you). If your artists have a separate manager, you will want to work with the manager to help arrange this, because the managers might have connections that you can use to book the showcase.

If you can, try to have your artists' CDs ready by the time the showcase comes around. The showcase can also serve as a CD release party, or you can follow up the showcase with a party celebrating the releases and the label's review. Having the

CDs available will provide another source of income at the showcase. You might also want to give some complimentary copies to your key industry people.

Because the showcase is a part of your promotion, you may not be able to sell as many tickets as you would like, so be prepared to consider the event as a promotional expense. When it comes time to start selling tickets, make sure that you give your artists some tickets to sell to their fans, family, and friends. As for your part of your publicity campaign, you should also target key critics and arts and entertainment reporters and send invitations to attend the showcase with a complimentary admission. Use what connections you have to spread the word and invite these key people. A big part of getting people to come is keeping in touch with them and following up on invitations you send out.

CLOSING THOUGHTS

We have discussed in depth several considerations for starting your own label. Remember, the first step is to organize your dream. After you organize, research everything you can about a label and then create a business plan. At the start of your career, you may not be able to afford the likes of Channing Johnson or Vernon Brown or other hotshots; however, build a solid team and listen to their advice.

After you have built the team, identify the artist(s), sign them, and prepare for your debut and the premiere of your label. While no one can guarantee success, it is safe to say if you take these steps, your investment and time will not be in vain, and you will be miles ahead of most other label owners.

PART II

CORPORATE MATTERS: RUNNING THE LABEL

CHAPTER 8

Selecting an Entity:
A Corporation, Partnership, or LLC

"If you are going to be in business, it's important for you to understand how to set it up the right way."

—RODNEY JERKINS, DARKCHILD PRODUCTIONS

A few years ago Jennifer Lopez a/k/a J-Lo opened her own clothing line, restaurant, and perfume line. Similarly, Madonna started Maverick Records. Michael Jackson has MJJ Productions. More recently, Rodney Jerkins began Darkchild Productions, and super-producer Dallas Austin started Darp Studios, the Atlanta-based hit factory for the likes of Monica and TLC, to name a few. Even Kirk Franklin stopped his "Stomp" dance for a minute to set up the super-hot Fo Yo Soul label. These are just a few of the corporate entities used by artists and producers to set up their corporate businesses and shield themselves from an array of legal and tax issues. They also serve as great tax write-offs for certain types of expenses.

All of these artists and their handlers figured out the critical importance of setting up their own corporate entities. While intimidating to some, selecting a business entity should not be a particularly difficult or arduous task. Various types of business entities exist, and in this chapter we will explain each one in nontechnical and basic terms. For the education of the artist and producer, we will discuss the pros and cons of each corporate entity. In this chapter, we cannot provide an extensive dialogue on the entities, but we will provide helpful examples of four primary options for you to consider in organizing the following:

- Corporation
- Partnership
- Sole proprietorship
- Limited liability company

CORPORATION

structure authorized by state law that allows a business to
al entity from its owners. A corporation is often referred
rson," meaning that, like an individual, it can enter into
l, and do the many other things necessary to carry on a
ve a rigid structure made up of shareholders, officers,
eir shares of stock, in most instances shareholders are the
oration, and the company is managed by the board of
ectors also appoints the officers who run the daily oper-
e., president, vice president, treasurer, and secretary. If
eople, don't worry. One person can serve as all three; so

technically, one person can be a corporation. (It is important to note we are not talking about non-stock corporations, i.e., non-profits or the like where in some jurisdictions like Connecticut you set up the non-stock corporation first and then apply for federal tax exemption).

For purposes of illustrating this point, let's assume Darkchild Productions was a one-man show. Darkchild Productions is the corporation and Rodney Jerkins serves as the president of the company, the director of the board, and the sole shareholder. Jerkins would hold a meeting as a shareholder to elect himself as the director. He would then call a meeting among the directors to manage the company and appoint the officers. From that point on he would serve day to day as the president and chief executive officer of the company. In some cases a person will serve as both president and secretary or some other simultaneous office, and the corporate records will reflect that person holding two offices. Because this is so important, I have attached a sample corporate resolution as an exhibit to this chapter.

Conversely, Rodney Jerkins could call together his brother Fred Jerkins, his wife, and his father, Rev. Jerkins, who manages the brothers, and form a four-person shareholder group. Each could sit on the board of directors and each could hold an office in the company. In this hypothetical, the corporate resolutions would state the following:

Be It Hereby Resolved that the Following Individuals Shall Serve in the Following Capacities as Officers:

NAME	TITLE
Rodney Jerkins	President
Fred Jerkins Jr.	Vice President
Fred Jerkins Sr.	Treasurer
Lynn Jerkins	Secretary

Signed by: _____   Date:_____
              Secretary of Darkchild Productions

These are just examples, and only Jerkins knows the true corporate structure of his company, but the simple underlying message is that the corporation can be owned by the four shareholders above or the sole shareholder (Rodney Jerkins) in the example prior. Many artists often wonder what the shareholder gets to prove his or her ownership. The simple answer: a shareholder certificate. When you hire your attorney, he or she will order a minute book, a black binder enclosed in a slide-in box with the company name printed on the outside: "Darkchild Productions." This minute book has certificates within its contents, and the attorney will type up the respective shares that you hold with your name on the front of a certificate. You would hold these certificates in a safe place and use them to prove how many shares you own or to show your interest if asked later in an audit or company buyout.

It is also important to understand that there are two types of corporations: C corporations and S corporations. The biggest difference is the way they file taxes and are treated by the Internal Revenue Service (IRS). All corporations are standard C corporations by default unless they elected to fill out the paperwork to become S corporations. When we say "C corporations," it is merely common business slang to distinguish a regular corporation whose profits are taxed separately from its owners under subchapter C of the Internal Revenue Code, from the S corporation, whose profits are passed through to shareholders and taxed on their personal returns under subchapter S of the Internal Revenue Code.

An S corporation describes a profit-making corporation organized under state law whose shareholders have applied for and received subchapter S corporation status from the IRS. Electing to do business as an S corporation lets shareholders enjoy limited liability status, as would be true of any corporation, but be taxed like a partnership or sole proprietor. That is, instead of being taxed as a separate entity (as would be the case with a regular, or C, corporation) an S corporation is a pass-through tax entity: Income taxes are reported and paid by the shareholders, not the S corporation. To qualify as an S corporation, a number of IRS terms must be met, including a limited number of citizenship requirements. Generally, with some exceptions, to be an S corporation a company is required to make this distinction on an IRS form 2253 usually immediately upon establishing the corporation. Simply put, it tells the IRS that the corporation is small start-up label or production company and not Sony, so don't tax us as such.

ADVANTAGES OF CORPORATIONS

There are many distinct advantages to becoming a corporation, if you are an artist or producer looking for a vehicle to limit your liability or possibly employ people and gain tax benefits. Thus, in our Darkchild example, Rodney Jerkins could set up the corporation and hire his relatives and friends to work in his studio. As a result, their salaries and expenses would be company expenses. Assume he grosses $1 million to produce Michael Jackson, Beyoncé, or Destiny's Child, with the salaries of ten people, office overhead, studio facilities, car service, food, and other miscellaneous expenses, this million-dollar figure could be trimmed significantly. Instead of being taxed on $1 million, Jerkins could be taxed on half of that amount or less, as long as his expenses are legitimate and approved under the IRS deductions standards. Some of these advantages are exclusive to corporations; others can be found in one form or another in other entities we discuss below.

It is also important to note that many artists have publishing companies set up as corporations. Stephen Hurd has Hurd the Word Music, Inc., which administers his music and song catalog. Gospel great John P. Kee has Kee Life, Inc. to administer his songs under a corporate umbrella.

Corporations are also more likely to receive tax breaks in various forms. Corporate income is not subject to the same taxes as your personal paycheck is, and avoiding those taxes can be a significant source of savings. Furthermore, if you have any employees, they will certainly demand health insurance, also tax deductible for corporate entities.

Another excellent way for corporations to save money is by incorporating across state lines. If you pay attention to the return addresses on credit card offers and other business mail that you receive, you may have noticed that many of them come from Delaware. Delaware has long been the nation's corporation capital because of favorable state tax conditions. As a matter of fact, at one point, over half of the Fortune 500 companies have been incorporated in the First State. Some corporations go so far as to have their headquarters in state A and keep an address in Delaware to keep their Delaware corporation status.

A great benefit to some is the fact that corporations are easily transferable in ownership and have an unlimited life. When a sole proprietor dies, his business dies with him, but corporations have the ability to live on forever.

Another very important benefit not exclusive to a corporation is the limited liability that it provides. This means that if the business is in financial trouble, the owners are immune to being held personally liable for any debt the corporation may have. For example, assume Janet Jackson is recording her latest album for your label and trips and falls on the way into your office. If she decides to sue, your personal possessions like your house, car, and bank accounts will be insulated from the suit. This also applies in the case of angry creditors and other entities that are hungry to get their hands on your money.

One last advantage that is popular amongst corporations is the ability to raise capital. Corporations have the ability to sell stock, and the owners of that stock become shareholders in the company. The money earned from the sale of stock can then be used to further the business pursuits. Another good way to raise capital is to get a business loan, which is also easier to do for an incorporated business. Finally, business funding firms are also more likely to give large sums of money to corporations because they assume corporations have better potential to repay a substantial loan.

DISADVANTAGES OF CORPORATIONS

The clear disadvantage of a corporation is that it is taxed twice. For corporations, profits are taxed as income of the company itself and then as income to the shareholders. If you choose to run an S corporation, the double tax is eliminated since it is passed on to the shareholders, but if only several people make up your corporation, this is not advantageous.

To explain this better, assume that Kirk Franklin's Fo Yo Soul corporation made $5 million last year. Let's assume further that Kirk took home a shareholder dividend or check for $500,000, 10 percent of that income. Under the IRS rules, Franklin would see a tax at the corporate level when the corporation files its tax return and he would be taxed individually when Kirk John Franklin, the individual, filed his taxes. This is why it's called "double taxation."

Another minor disadvantage to a corporation is the complexity and expense associated with forming and managing a corporation. By nature, corporations are difficult to set up because of the amount of paperwork involved. Corporations have to name an agent of representation and decide on a list of directors. Corporations also sometimes have to register with state governments outside of the state of incorporation as foreign corporations.

Even with the tedious, albeit simple, paperwork and foreign registrations for each state in which you plan to do business, it is still wise overall to consider establishing a corporate entity as an artist, producer, or businessperson in the music industry. The advantages outweigh the disadvantages. Additionally, hiring good people to deal with the paperwork, employment filings, and tax issues outweighs any of the disadvantages.

SOLE PROPRIETORSHIP

A sole proprietorship is a business owned and managed by one person (or for tax purposes, a husband and wife). For IRS purposes, a sole proprietor and her business are one tax entity, meaning that business profits are reported and taxed on the owner's personal tax return. Setting up a sole proprietorship is cheap and easy since no legal formation documents need be filed with any governmental agency (although tax registration and other permit and license requirements may still apply). Once you file a fictitious name statement (assuming you don't use your own name) and obtain any required basic tax permits and business licenses, you'll be in business. A sole proprietorship is the easiest kind of business entity to set up and run, but as with everything else there are some advantages and severe disadvantages to being a sole proprietor. Please keep in mind that although it may have been easy and inexpensive to form your sole proprietorship, that does not excuse you from other corporate and business law. You will still have to follow all local, state, and federal rules and regulations regarding your record label or entertainment company.

ADVANTAGES OF SOLE PROPRIETORSHIP

One major advantage of sole proprietorships is the ease with which they can be set up. Whereas setting up a corporation requires fees and a lot of paperwork, a sole proprietorship can be set up automatically.

Russell Simmons has a well-known international company called Phat Farm, the maker of all types of clothing lines. The company grosses hundreds of millions of dollars worldwide. For purposes of this section, assume Simmons never incorporated his clothing line but instead operated on his own out of his dorm room (as Def Jam reportedly started).

Assume further that Simmons was making millions and felt simply uninterested in hiring a good lawyer and incorporating himself. If he did not set up any corporation, he would be a sole proprietorship—i.e., an individual running a business behind which there is nothing filed with the state or town. Simmons would file taxes as an individual and sole proprietor and report all of the income he earned through his clothing line.

Many artists are sole proprietors and are not aware of it. For example, an artist selling T-shirts and CDs at a table on a street corner or at a church concert is a sole proprietor. Similarly, many of the vendors you see hawking goods in Times Square are sole proprietors.

Another advantage of a sole proprietorship is that you are your own boss, and there is not even a partner holding you back. I know this can be a relief to a lot of people, especially creative people whose craft can't afford to be micromanaged by a board of directors or a demanding business partner. Of course, as we discuss later, one can be one's own boss as the owner of a limited liability corporation, as well.

Another thing that you can do as a sole proprietor is form a "d/b/a," or doing business as. For example, you are Fred Hammond and you want to run a record label called Fred Jams Records or something equally clever. You could theoretically have a sole proprietorship as Fred Hammond d/b/a Fred Jams Records. This way, if you have established a name for yourself in the industry, you can use it as part of your business name, while retaining a unique identity for your label. As you will see below, this is doable but not generally advised by legal practitioners, owing to liability issues and tax consequences.

DISADVANTAGES OF SOLE PROPRIETORSHIP

The greatest disadvantage of a sole proprietorship is that sole proprietors take on personal liability for everything associated with their businesses. As a sole proprietor, if your label gets sued or faces financial difficulty, your personal finances may be compromised. So, in our Fred Hammond example, he might be succeeding as an artist and producer, but if someone decides to sue his Fred Jams Records as a sole proprietorship and he has no corporation or other entity to absorb the litigation, he exposes himself to serious liability and risks losing everything.

Likewise, if you are running a business as a sole proprietorship or d/b/a, the significance of filing corporate papers and shielding yourself from potential lawsuits and losses cannot be stressed enough. Even if you think you do everything correctly and have your bases covered, there is no such thing as a foolproof system, so remember that your sole proprietorship business life can leave you broke.

Another scenario is the most common occurrence. Fred Hammond starts his Fred Hammond d/b/a Fred Jams Records, invests borrowed money in a Detroit office, buys studio equipment, and eventually scouts and signs one musician with potential for a promising career. Hammond pays the artist's advance, records an album, and spends thousands advertising and marketing the album. The album is released and bombs terribly.

Unfortunately, Hammond had planned on repaying his debts after the release and huge success of the album, but now his personal funds are several million dollars in the red. Despite all of the wonderful praise and worship songs on the album, Hammond's creditors lose the faith and decide to file suit in court. In this situation, Hammond not only loses business funds, but the creditors go after his car, home, and personal bank accounts as well. Hammond's failure to incorporate as Fred Hammond, Inc. left him wide open as a sole proprietor (or d/b/a) for personal liability on the debt he incurred in making the album.

Overall, a sole proprietorship is a good initial way to get an introductory beginning. However, once you are up and rolling, it is important to find a lawyer and quickly incorporate yourself, particularly if the business you are in can leave you open to liability or other legal issues.

PARTNERSHIP

A partnership is an agreement between two or more persons to form a business. A partnership is different from a corporation in that there are no shareholders. It differs from a limited liability company (LLC, as discussed later) in that there are no members. In a partnership, you have "partners," and each owns part of the business. Generally, one partner is the general partner, or managing partner, who oversees the day-to-day matters and sets forth the company directive. The other partners can be active as well or silent partners.

When used without a qualifier such as "limited" or "limited liability," a partnership usually refers to a legal structure called a general partnership. This is a business owned by two or more people (called partners or general partners) who are personally liable for all business debts. To form a partnership, each partner normally contributes money, valuable property, or labor in exchange for a partnership share, which reflects the amount contributed. Partnerships are easy to form since no registration is required with any governmental agency to create a partnership (although tax registration and other requirements to conduct business may still apply). Although not required, it is an excellent idea to prepare a written partnership agreement between the partners to define items such as ownership percentages, how profits and losses will be divided, and what happens if a partner dies or becomes disabled. Partnerships themselves do not pay federal or state income taxes; rather, profits are passed through to partners, who report and pay income taxes on their personal returns. Explained former Mitchell & Titus Partner Tracey Mitchell, "Depending on your business, a partnership may be the appropriate corporate vehicle for you to set up."

ADVANTAGES OF PARTNERSHIP

Partnerships are as easy to set up as sole proprietorships. The most common type of partnership is a general partnership, but limited partnerships and limited liability partnerships also exist. (LLPs will be discussed in the limited liability corporation section.)

Using one of our examples, Rodney Jerkins and Fred Jerkins could have a handshake agreement that the two brothers will be partners in the Jerkins Partnership, a real estate company set up to purchase property on the East Coast. Fred Jerkins could be the general partner and oversee the operation, while Rodney Jerkins, as a partner, would share in the profits.

The obvious advantage of a partnership is the teamwork that it allows for furthering the development and growth of the company. Two heads, two points of view, and two wallets are always better than one. Additionally, it used to be that the death of one partner dissolved the company. However, partners can form an agreement that gives the remaining partner control over the company when one partner dies.

Legally speaking, there are not distinct advantages to a partnership like there are to a corporation or a limited liability corporation. Partnerships are formed by more than one person, by agreement, proof of existence, and estoppels.

It is not as common in the music industry for individuals to use this corporate model; however, it was important to discuss it as an option and for your understanding of this legal entity.

DISADVANTAGES OF PARTNERSHIP

Partnerships are a lot like marriage in that your fate is connected to that of your partner. This, of course, is a major drawback for the business-minded person. As in a sole proprietorship, a partnership leaves the partners open to liability stemming from the activities of the business. If one partner messes up, the others are personally liable. The question to ask before entering into a partnership is, "Would I give this person my bank account information, or the keys to my house or car?"

In our prior example, Rodney Jerkins and Fred Jerkins purchase some property and Fred decides to hire contractors to do work on the property. A month later, a construction worker is hurt in a fall on the job and his family seeks to come after the partnership for damages. Even though Rodney was off in LA recording a Destiny's Child album, he can still be exposed to some liability, and most important, be named in a lawsuit owing to the actions of his partner and brother, Fred Jerkins.

Another disadvantage that ties into the issue of trust is that in a partnership, not only real partners can act as authority figures. It is not uncommon for non-partners to legally gain partner status through their actions, like signing important documents or acting as a partner would. This leaves the real partners open to liability, as they become responsible for the actions for the non-partner acting as partner.

A litany of cases have dealt with an entire partnership being liable for the damage of one person, who acted like a partner or gained "partner" status. Said New York–based corporate and entertainment lawyer Heather Cunningham, "It is very important for artists and labels to understand the legal implications and liability issues when forming a partnership, whether on paper or with a handshake agreement."

LIMITED LIABILITY COMPANY

A limited liability company is a business ownership structure that offers its owners the advantage of limited liability (like corporations) and taxation like a partnership receives, in which profits are passed through to the owners and taxed on their personal income tax returns. Bad Boy Records is an LLC. It is also reported that LaFace, owned by Babyface and L. A. Reid and later sold to Zomba, is an LLC.

ADVANTAGES OF AN LLC

LLCs enjoy the advantage that the title of this entity promises: limited liability. When we say *limited liability*, we mean the maximum amount a business owner can lose if the business is subject to debts, claims, or other liabilities. An owner of an LLC or a person who invests in a corporation (i.e., a shareholder) generally stands to lose only the amount of money invested in the business. This means that if the business folds, creditors cannot seize or sell an owner's home, car, or other personal assets. If you plan to operate more than one business under the name of your record label, it would be wise to create a separate LLC for each one. If one of your businesses gets sued or faces debt, creditors will be able to take all of your assets under the LLC name. If, on the other hand, each business is a separate LLC, you will only lose the assets of the business that is in trouble, while the others will remain safe from the clutches of the creditors.

When Toni Braxton filed suit against LaFace years ago, the personal assets of Babyface and L. A. Reid were not at issue because of the limited liability their business afforded them. Instead, the company itself fought the lawsuit. (It was eventually settled, as we discuss later in this book.)

An advantage of setting up an LLC is the ease with which they can be created. As opposed to corporations, who must hold annual meetings and have shareholders, LLCs have only members and operating agreements. Another benefit is that every state allows an LLC to consist of just one person. Since Michael Jackson left his brothers (from the Jackson Five) and managing dad (Joe Jackson) and started his own empire, he could, for example, have his MJJ Productions configured with himself as the sole member of the LLC.

Tax breaks are also available to LLCs. Similar to our discussion about corporations, an LLC can elect how it wants to be taxed. For example, Michael Jackson's LLC run by one person can be taxed as a sole proprietorship, or he could choose to be taxed as an S or C corporation. LLCs that consist of more than one person are generally taxed as partnerships, but they can also elect the S or C corporation tax model.

By doing your homework and researching local laws, you can set up an LLC and protect your assets while getting taxed as a sole proprietor, thereby avoiding the double taxation that corporations face. This is one of the biggest advantages. In our Kirk Franklin example, we spoke of the double taxation, first to his Fo Yo Soul corporation then to him personally as a shareholder. This is not an issue with an LLC in this present discussion, but check with your local state corporate laws and a good local accountant.

It is also worth mentioning that a limited liability partnership, or LLP, is an option that is similar to an LLC in all major ways, except that it cannot be operated by just one person. It is less likely to be subject to state franchise taxes. Franchise taxes are something that you should look into before setting up your label, as they are a burden in more than a handful of states. It is also important to note that many major law firms, including ours, are LLPs and limit the liability of each lawyer for the work of another lawyer in the same firm. For purposes of this chapter, it is very technical; however, review your state's local corporate statutes and you will see a full breakdown of the various legal issues that collaborate with this discussion.

Disadvantages of a Limited Liability Company

There are truly not many disadvantages to operating an LLC. The only real drawback is that in some states, unlike corporations, LLCs have a limited life. This means the company can be dissolved if bankruptcy occurs or if a member dies. If you plan a long life for your label, beyond that of yourself, it is better to incorporate as anything but an LLC. If you are in a state that mandates operating agreements for LLCs, it is possible for you to establish a longer life for your company by writing a corporate-like life-span clause into your operating agreement.

Since LLCs are a fairly new concept (they did not exist in the United States until the 1970s) some states require LLCs to have what can become complicated operating agreements. The agreements outline the structure and business rules of the LLC and are sometimes more complex than the paperwork needed to form a corporation. Be sure to do your research to find out if your state requires such an agreement. If so, it may not be worth establishing your business as an LLC.

If LaFace is an LLC, most likely it has a great operating agreement. This operating agreement will set forth how the company should run, how new members are admitted, what happens when one member pulls out, dividend splits, any tax considerations, and when annual meetings are to be held, among other operating matters.

Another burden faced by LLC members is that in some states local officials and administrative offices are not familiar with the LLC model and members sometimes face bureaucratic red tape at the hands of ignorant officials.

In any event, the LLC, with its twofold benefit of limited liability and tax avoidance, is the most highly recommended business entity of counselors nationwide. Less than thirty years old, the law is still being defined, and there is great flexibility in using this entity for your first corporate business. Again, it is highly recommended that you understand the rules of your jurisdiction and hire a competent accountant and corporate counsel to handle these business affairs. Even the most seasoned entertainment law counsel may not necessarily be as up to speed on the workings of LLCs, and thus a corporate lawyer is appropriate.

BUSINESS INSURANCE

In closing out this chapter, it is important to point out a standard that is needed for all businesses discussed here. No matter what kind if business entity you choose, it is always smart to invest in business insurance. The varieties of business insurance that are most useful to record labels are property and liability insurance. Property insurance does for your business what it does for your home. Your property insurance should cover damage to your building(s) as well as damage to computer and recording equipment, fixtures, and furniture. As a record label, the most important thing for you to protect would be any and all expensive equipment.

Liability insurance may become even more useful than property insurance. Liability insurance will cover you if someone slips and falls in your studio, or if a sound guy gets electrocuted by your equipment, or anything of that nature. However, liability insurance will *not* cover your outstanding debts.

CLOSING TIPS

Regardless of where you are in your pursuit of setting up a record label, production company, publishing house, or non-entertainment industry venture, it is important for you to review closely the corporate entity that fits your needs—i.e., the corporation, the sole proprietorship, the partnership, or the LLC models discussed here. For purposes of tax reduction, expense write-offs, and legal liability issues in the event of a suit, it is important to establish one of the entities discussed. In this short chapter, we could not discuss all of the nuances of each of these corporations. Our hope is that you review this important chapter closely and visit your local library to find other interesting materials on running a business as well as the local laws of your state. A few websites to visit initially are www.sba.gov, www.smallbusiness.adp.com, and www.nfib.com.

The book is entitled *This Business of Urban Music*, and "business" is the most important word.

CHAPTER 9

Signing Artists to Your Label, Production Company, or Entity

"The record label can do a great job marketing and promoting a record, but the key to a label success is in the artist you sign."

—BERRY GORDY

Motown founder and industry giant Berry Gordy signed a string of hit artists from the Four Tops to Marvin Gaye to Diana Ross and the Supremes. He understood that his label's success rested not only on his brilliance but also on that of the artists that he signed. As America rolled out of the rock 'n' roll era and into the civil-rights movement of the 1960s, Gordy signed artists who captured the pulse of America. Forty years later, we are still singing, "I Heard It through the Grapevine" and "What's Going On."

In Chapter Two, we talked specifically about the provisions of the recording contract and the common terms and conditions found in that agreement. After that we discussed starting a label and choosing the corporate entity. In this chapter, we take it a step further and look at signing an artist to your label, production company, or corporate entity, be it a partnership, LLC, or corporation. We'll examine closely some of the popular labels and production companies in the marketplace and take a candid look at those that have worked and those that have failed. While it is true that starting and maintaining a label require trusting your gut and instinct as much as anything else, there are some suggestions in this chapter that will make your career running a label smoother, if you remember to take stock and consider all the options each step of the way.

First, we must distinguish between a label and a production company. A label is generally a company that has a staff, offices, an artist and repertoire (A&R) department that oversees the roster, and a full team of individuals working with the goal of nurturing and developing successful and—most importantly—profitable artists. Bad Boy Records is a label. LaFace was a label until it was sold to Zomba and the principals (L. A. Reid and Babyface) moved in other directions. Verity Records is the number-one gospel label in America.

A production company is simply an entity usually created by a hot producer for the purposes of recording and producing artists. Darkchild Productions, Trackmasters, and PaJam all come to mind when one thinks of hot production houses. These entities are usually headed up by a producer or two that have a reputation for producing big hits. For example, Darkchild is headed up by hitmaker Rodney Jerkins, and PaJam is headed up by Walter Kearny, James Moss, and Paul Allen. There are dozens of production companies in the industry, but only a handful are known on a one-word basis like these, and this is because of their track records.

In the music industry, when an artist has phenomenal success, on the level of Missy Elliott, Alicia Keys, Jay-Z, or Big Pun, he or she often decides it is time to sign musician friends to a recording contract or production agreement. A recording contract and a production agreement presented to an artist are very similar in terms of the development of an aspiring performer's career. However, a label would sign the artist to a recording contract and a production company would sign an artist to a production deal, both for the purposes of the long-term recording of those artists. The artists would then generally agree to record solely for that label or production company.

Because there are so many horror stories of artists signing with labels and production companies but never getting an album completed or much released to the general market, it is important to understand what to consider in signing an artist.

There are no doubt countless factors to consider if you own a label or production company, whether it is a corporation, partnership, or LLC. When considering these factors, it is the responsibility of the label exec to be realistic and consider those that are most critical in the presentation of a contract to an artist. With that in mind, here are the most important factors to consider before you sign artists to your label or production company:

- Label direction
- Genre of the artist
- Uniqueness
- Marketability of an artist
- Age
- Vocal skills/talent
- Training and grooming potential
- Financial investment/return

LABEL DIRECTION

A few years ago, we signed Stephen Hurd to Integrity Records, one of the largest Christian record labels in the world, which boasted a roster including Alvin Slaughter, Joe Pace, and Israel Haughton. Prior to the signing of the contract, talented Integrity executive Jackie Patillo invited us down for a chapel service, and Hurd attended. In all of the ten years prior I had worked in the industry, I had never heard of a label inviting an artist to such an occasion. That single act made it clear that this label wanted to sign artists that shared their purpose and direction—that ministry came first, and any artist signed to Integrity would have to agree to walk the walk and live the life that he or she sang about.

This also told my client the direction of the label, which is the first and most critical factor. So if you are setting up a label, you must analyze what is going to be your niche, your style. Are you going to be a gritty production house like Dr. Dre's Aftermath? Are you going to be an in-your-face outfit like G-Unit? Are you going to be urban and socially conscious like the Fugees? Are you going to have Bible studies and chapel services like Integrity Records?

Whatever the decision is, establish and write out the label direction and vision before signing any artist. An artist should be able to know exactly what you stand for and share your ideas for the direction of the label. As surprised as I was with the

Integrity meeting at the chapel service, it made it clear to me that president Don Moen had a direction and vision for the label. If my client was not interested in also *living* a Christian life, there would have been no reason for me to sign him to such a label.

GENRE OF THE ARTIST

In the 1960s and 1970s, when James Cleveland, the godfather of gospel music, recorded, there was a clear line between gospel music and secular music. If you turned on the radio you could clearly tell the difference between a gospel song and a Motown song. The line has somewhat blurred in the current music scene, causing controversy and confusion in many signings of artists to major labels and production houses.

For example, CeCe and BeBe Winans became urban inspirational to many, although they never lost their gospel roots. Kirk Franklin found his classics "Do You Want a Revolution?" and "Stomp" played in the nightclub. Howard Hewitt saw his "Say Amen" cross over between urban R&B radio and gospel radio. A crossover record is great for any label because an artist who reaches the masses is a goldmine for his label and usually enjoys longevity. However, with the success of crossover artists come a number of confused new start-ups trying to sign the next Kirk Franklin or Yolanda Adams, hoping to establish a hit in various genres. When starting, it is important to know who you are and remain true to that ideal.

Before signing an artist, be sure the artist fits your genre. If you are a gospel label, do gospel! If you are R&B/urban or hip-hop, then do R&B/urban and/or hip-hop. Do not try to sign an artist with the idea of merely "crossing over" to other genres. Unless you have an experienced track record of doing that, it is virtually impossible for an urban music label to meet this challenge. If an artist with real crossover potential appears, it will happen on its own. Don't force it.

Years ago, we administered contracts and mechanical licenses for a writer on the Yolanda Adams album. We represented songwriter V. Michael McKay, who wrote various songs for many of Ms. Adams's platinum selling albums. One night in Houston, over dinner, Ms. Adams told me that while many artists are trying to find their niche, "they have to be true to themselves and realize God crosses you over, and if he does, just let it happen."

The wisdom of Ms. Adams is the best advice I can give a new label owner or production company. Decide the genre and sign artists with that in mind. If you try too hard to cross over, your artist may end up with no demographic and reach no core audience. Remember, the key to any hot artist is their core fan base. Michael Jackson had a core base of Motown fans that carried him for years until he signed with Epic/CBS and recorded *Thriller*. Similarly, the artists that tour Vegas each year—Prince, Celine Dion, and Toni Braxton—built a core base first, and consistently sell out Vegas as a result. Even Kirk Franklin had to come back to his core church base fans on his third album after some criticism of his second album.

The genre, or style, of the artist also plays a major role in the label's decision to sign a that artist. The genre determines how the label should market the artist and the amount of finances needed to produce its goal to sell records. When an artist's genre is "hip-hop/R&B" and the artist's appearance and demeanor are not the accepted portrayal of such an artist, the label will factor the cost to change the artist's image. Also, if the label has traditionally signed gospel artists and the promising client is more "country" based, the label may not want to diverge from its fundamental design.

UNIQUENESS

When you sit down as a label head and dive into the dozens of demo tapes you have, or reflect on artists you have seen perform, a key factor to consider is "uniqueness." You don't want to sign an artist that reminds people of another artist already in the marketplace, as this will pigeonhole your success. Instead, you want to find that Nelly or Bow Wow or Tonex or even 50 Cent—the new voice that takes the industry by storm.

If you read a standard recording contract closely you will notice there is a clause that essentially says, "the services of the artist are of such a unique nature, that they cannot be replaced." This carefully worded language only tells a court that, in the event the artist attempts to breach the contract, he or she will have to perform his or her unique services. But, it raises a serious point: Are you sure the artist you sign is unique for purposes of promotion and marketing?

Outkast has sold over 20 million records. Whitney Houston sold over 100 million. Run-DMC has moved 20 million records. Public Enemy has sold over 10 million. The common element? When they peaked with chart-topping success, they were unique to the marketplace. It sounds very simple, but each year an artist that hits the marketplace catches the industry off-guard and surprises the A&R executives at the major labels.

For example, I remember when Missy Elliott, a native of Portsmouth, Virginia, first came on the scene. Elliott surprised many of us with her free-styling, in-your-face rapping, dancing, and singing hooks. Before her arrival, the industry had not seen a female with such unique talent. Millions of records and several platinum albums later she is still a major talent in the industry. But it took a wise executive like Sylvia Rhone at Elektra to see her Gold Mine label as the hitmaker it could be.

You want an artist that has a unique quality about them. This uniqueness creates buzz and industry "noise." This buzz will help win the marketing battle and break the artist in the long run.

MARKETABILITY OF AN ARTIST

Over a decade ago a client of mine, Dr. Bobby Jones, was handed a tape of a then-unknown artist named Kirk Franklin during a BET program. Dr. Jones played the tape in a boom box and realized Franklin was something special. Several labels had passed over Franklin, and he often played second fiddle to stars like Grammy-winning Hezekiah Walker and Donald Lawrence. However, one young start-up label, GospoCentric, saw something marketable in the gap-toothed, jheri-curled James Brown–like dancing choir director and songwriter. GospoCentric president Vicki Mack-Lataillade told me once over a lunch in Los Angeles, "I knew he was special when I first signed him." Ten million records later, Lataillade is seen as a marketing genius for turning choir director and dancer Kirk Franklin into the top-selling gospel artist of all time.

Similarly, Master P took a unique sound from New Orleans and captivated America, leading to the successful No Limit record label, a real estate company, a television team, and series of B movies. Meanwhile, his son, artist Li'l Romeo, has become an overnight success on Nickelodeon. All of this was made possible through very careful marketing, the second major factor to consider when signing an artist. "The marketability of an artist is probably the number-one factor in signing an artist," said former Def Jam marketing guru Johnnie Walker, who worked with LL Cool J and many of the popular Def Jam artists in an illustrious fourteen-year career at the label.

For the novice, successful marketing is simply the ability to promote and "brand" an artist for purposes of selling his or her product to the masses in a somewhat calculated manner. Done correctly it ultimately delivers a financial windfall. Arrested Development, Tracy Chapman, and Outkast are all artists that someone with marketing genius noticed. Those people convinced America to buy millions of records, and now those urban artists are stars.

Former Elektra president Sylvia Rhone (now running Motown) told me ten years ago, "in signing an artist, you are looking for that unique factor . . . something different." This is the key to marketing. You cannot market a five-member singing family from Gary, Indiana, with the little brother singing lead if Motown already has the Jackson Five on the scene.

Good marketing leads to appeal, and appeal leads to sales. Lots of sales. This is a very important factor in signing any artist to your entity, whether production company or label. Although often criticized, the marketing strategy of Bad Boy with Biggie, Craig Mack, and Faith was nothing short of genius. It resulted in Bad Boy selling over 40 million records in its heyday.

If the artist lacks either appeal or talent, the label must be able to foresee the artist developing the absent factor. In many cases, a label will have talent scouts known as artists and repertoire (A&R) reps, whose sole job is to discover raw talent that has the potential to sell to the public. After the A&R rep has prepped the artist for public consumption, the hope is that he or she is commercially viable to sell records worldwide.

Lastly, if possible, it is in the label's best interest to sign an artist that has sold records previously. This demonstrates that the artist does have the potential to sell many records with the appropriate marketing from a label or record production company. Also, it is beneficial to sign an artist that has a "buzz" in the industry. When people are talking about your promising artist, it is a good sign that he has been accepted by the public

Signing too many artists within a short time frame is a common pitfall of many record labels and production companies. Verity Records has dropped a series of major artists, including Taralyn Ramsey. When Ramsey won the VH-1 Diva Search, many critics correctly contended that Verity did not have the marketing expertise to break the artist—although no one knows precisely why Ramsey saw little success with Verity but exploded elsewhere.

The label must be patient and determine all the attributes of the promising artist prior to signing. Some questions the label or record production company may ask itself are: Is this artist a good fit to my entity? Is it possible to market the artist effectively? If there is any doubt to these questions, the entity should reconsider signing the artist.

AGE

In 2005, our law firm had the honor of organizing a Patti LaBelle concert at Foxwoods Casino in Connecticut. LaBelle started with a group in the 1970s called LaBelle and recorded such classic hits as "Somewhere over the Rainbow," "On My Own" (duet with Michael McDonald), and "Lady Marmalade," among many, many others. Another star artist of the 1970s, Freddie Jackson, is still packing them in all over the country. But, both artists are now over fifty, and the likelihood of a major label signing them to a long-term contract is very slim. Although this may seem shortsighted on some executives' behalves, I do understand the marketplace and the industry. And with that I give you the next key factor to consider when signing talent to your label or production company: Are they too old to break the marketplace or genre and really make a return on your investment? Remember, you don't sign an artist on personal taste; you sign an artist with consideration to sales and marketing, and age is often a key factor.

Travel through New York on any given Thursday or Friday night and stop by the Sugar Café, owned by Ashford and Simpson, or Nell's on Broadway, and you can find a bunch of singers and artists over fifty years old, who could blow both Alicia Keys and Beyoncé off the stage. However, because of age, they might not get any record deal or have any hot producers rushing contract papers to their attorneys or managers.

It is a very frustrating situation for many older artists, but it is critical for a record executive, such as you, to understand in signing artists. Nancy Wilson is over seventy years old and one of the most accomplished artists in jazz music, and I could listen to her perform all night at the Blue Note, along with R&B songstress Alyson Williams (of "Just Call My Name" fame); but there are some that would advise you not to sign her.

Last year, Blue Note Records signed Anita Baker to a contract, and the subsequent album release did not generate the type of sales customarily expected for an Anita Baker album. Some critics said age was a factor, that this new marketplace caters to the MTV generation and Baker's longstanding fans would either not jump aboard or the radio format does not cater to her music anymore.

In any event, while I don't necessarily agree with it, age is a key factor for any artist you sign. If you plan to be a hot urban label, the demographics support signing the artist popular with the 18- to 34-year-old group. If you are in gospel music, you have a little flexibility, but even that genre has altered its core demographics. Rarely will you see a label sign someone over forty years old, without great buzz or an established fan base.

VOCAL SKILLS/TALENT

Mariah Carey recently returned with a very successful album, *The Emancipation of Mimi*, and it went multiplatinum. Carey's legendary vocal range has catapulted her to status as the new Whitney Houston. Her tours sell out worldwide. Most interestingly, a few years ago, EMI gave Carey millions of dollars but later voided the contract after a lackluster album and an even worse movie (the clunker *Glitter*). However, many industry experts warned EMI that the vocals and talent were still there and that bad marketing and poor song choice were responsible for lackluster album sales, neither which were any fault of Mariah's. A few years later, armed with better songs, thanks to whiz producer Jermaine Dupri, Carey soared to the top of the charts again, as she had when she was discovered a decade earlier by Tommy Mottola.

When signing a singing artist, particularly in gospel music, vocal ability and talent are normally the most critical factors. Gospel purists will examine closely whether an artist is a great singer à la Donnie McClurkin, or should stick to song-writing and producing like super-hot producer Donald Lawrence does with the Stellar Award-winning Tri-City Singers.

Similarly, in R&B, vocalists like Kelly Price, Mary J. Blige, and India Arie emphasize the return to true singing. John Legend took the stage with Stevie Wonder at the 2006 BET Awards and held his own, one of the few young crooners who could do so with a legend of Wonder's stature. In this age of technology, drum machines, fancy keyboards, and music sampling, it was encouraging for many to see an artist sing in such a skillful manner.

In the gospel industry, the vocal talents of Smokey Norful gave EMI its first gold record in a long time. With the exception of some artists, most of the main gospel performers have a great degree of vocal prowess and skill.

As a result, I highly urge you to consider the vocal talent of any artist you plan to sign to your label and realize the competition to which they will be compared after releasing their initial CD. Not everyone is expected to riff like Vicki Winans; however, a good singer with an incredible range like Nancey Jackson can help make your label a success.

Usually the label's CEO will be a successful artist that will sign fellow artists and friends and have no difficulty finding great talent. However, if you are a budding label/music production company you may want to spend time in clubs and music venues listening to live performances. This will give you the opportunity to hear artists perform and forecast whether the artist will meet your expectation.

Often, start-up labels sign artists based on a look or style and overlook talent as a factor. Even Beyoncé, at the end of the day, is a strong vocalist. Without her vocals, Destiny's Child would have fizzled out like many other pop girl groups.

TRAINING AND GROOMING POTENTIAL

Before Jodeci was to give its first TV performance, P. Diddy took them shopping in New York City. Berry Gordy put the Supremes and Four Tops into choreography classes and media training. Verity Records hired industry veteran Jazzy Jordan, a marketing genius, to train its gospel artists. When signing an artist to your label, you have to consider two things in this regard: the need for training, and whether the artist will be receptive to such training. An artist must be able to take advice and allow the professionals of the label to groom her into stardom. More specifically, an artist that you are signing and investing thousands of dollars in has to be willing to take your counsel.

That training may include improving speech, singing, dancing, and performance presence. Typically the training is executed by an expert in the area of need and is taught within a short time frame. The label may also want to improve aspects of the artist's grooming, such as hair, makeup, wardrobe, and/or weight.

When a promising artist is reluctant to change her appearance, attitude, or singing style for the growth of her career, you should be wary of signing her to your production house or record label. Training and grooming are imperative for the overall success of an artist and label. During the courtship of an artist, make a few suggestions and see if the suggestions are welcomed or resisted. This is usually a key indicator of what it will be like to work with an artist in a label or production company.

The signing of a contract is not going to change the artist's refusal to listen to you. So spot a problem early on and think twice about signing an artist who is too difficult to market, promote, and eventually earn a return on your investment. Remember someone who is talented, driven, and easy to work with will be a success for someone's record label.

FINANCIAL INVESTMENT/RETURN

Def Jam Records was sold to Vivendi Universal in 1999 for over $100 million. Profile Records (once home to Run-DMC) also sold for millions. And Bad Boy was reportedly given over 10 million when it left Arista for Universal. Be clear that the artists you sign are the inventory and stock of your label or production company. A label signs an artist and markets his music in hopes of making a big financial return on CDs and DVDs of the recordings and performances and ancillary income, such as merchandising and publishing (which we discuss in a later chapter). But a label also signs an artist to build its catalog and masters ownership for long-term value.

The artist once again has the burden to perform successfully in order to sell recordings and repay the label and to see a royalty. Royalties are defined as a percentage of the net receipts paid to a composer or artist out of the proceeds resulting from the sale or performance of his or her work. A major label will typically give the artist 8 to 15 percent of the standard retail selling price of the CD—i.e., "the royalty rate" based on the artist's stature. The artist will receive full royalty rate for the CDs that were sold through a normal retail channel such as Borders, Tower Records, or Music Factory. However, when the sales of the CDs are outside the United States, sold at a discounted price, sold at record club sales, or any other retail channel that is not normal, the label receives a higher percentage of the sales.

After the label deducts its manufacturing costs, marketing and promotions, and other expenditures, it is probably netting four to five dollars a record, although this figure will be disputed vigilantly in hopes of painting a grim picture to the artist. Before you sign an artist and spend a ton of money to promote him, make sure you are clear on all of your fixed expenses for studio time, manufacturing, photos, videos, staffing, publishing/writer payments, and any other charges. These factors will ultimately determine the return on your investment.

For example, when GospoCentric recorded Kirk Franklin's *Revolution* album, they hired Rodney Jerkins. Jerkins had recently produced Michael Jackson and Destiny's Child. The production cost alone for Jerkins could have easily been $500,000 (a top-line producer can charge $75,000 to $250,000 per track, depending on the relationship the label owner has with the producer). Similarly, remember LaFace claimed it spent millions on recording Toni Braxton's album when she sued them for failure to pay her royalties. The label was basically claiming she was unrecouped.

Recently, we had the opportunity to work on several projects to be released under the Verity Records/Zomba/BMG umbrella. Verity releases a half-dozen or more albums each year. The budgets for these albums generally range between $100,000 and $300,000, depending on the artist. For example, they will spend $150,000 on a Richard Smallwood album, yet they may spend $500,000 or more on a platinum-selling Donnie McClurkin album. The obvious difference is that an average Smallwood album sells less than 200,000 records at Soundscan,[1] while McClurkin can turn any project into a gold or even platinum record. As a result, Verity, the gospel label giant, makes an investment that keeps this factor in consideration in deciding what to allocate for its albums on an artist-by-artist basis. Even though Verity might dispute this, it is clear in the writers and producers selected or hired on an A-list artist project (Donnie McClurkin, Kirk Franklin, etc.) versus those with a B-list artist (Keith "Wonderboy" Johnson, Marvin Sapp, etc.).

As you sign an artist, be mindful of overspending. Market, promote, and do all that you can to break the record or score a hit album, but be reasonable in your expectations. Similarly, as we discussed in Chapter Eight, look at what the other labels in your genre are doing and the monies they are spending. Oftentimes what works for another label may work for yours as well, especially if you seek the same success as the label you want to emulate.

CLOSING TIPS

There is no one way to scout and sign an artist. However, there are some basic business principles and tenets that you must to consider. The first thing to establish is the direction and genre of the label. After you get your direction settled and build your team, consider how marketable each artist will be in the long run. Ask friends who are objective and create showcases to gauge public response to your artist.

As much as we fail to discuss it in this industry, age and vocal talent are still critical factors to consider. Only Clive Davis could take a risk on some older acts and deliver platinum success (Luther Vandross, for example). Other labels will not take those chances, and you shouldn't either. An important related factor is the grooming and training necessary to teach and grow the artist.

Finally, consider the possibilities of a great return on your investment. You don't get into the music industry to be popular or to attend awards show (as some may think). You get into this industry to make money and to be a profitable label or production company. Study everything you can to understand which labels are making money and which labels are losing money. Then figure out what the successful they are doing differently to be profitable and make that a plan for your start-up.

---

[1] Soundscan is the system used to monitor record sales and purchases.

CHAPTER 10

Trademarking the Name, Logo, and Intellectual Property

"It is always wise for an artist to trademark his or her name to protect their intellectual property rights as their career grows and to capitalize on the income associated with the trademark."

—ATTORNEY ELLIOT ROBINSON, FORMER
TRADEMARK EXAMINER WITH THE UNITED
STATES PATENT AND TRADEMARK OFFICE

In 2006, flamboyant boxing icon and twentieth-century iconoclast Muhammad Ali shook up the world when he signed a contract that paid him more than any single fight had ever paid him. Entertainment and licensing firm CKX, Inc. bought the marketing rights to the name "Muhammad Ali" and paid the former Cassius Clay of Louisville, Kentucky, $50 million. The three-time heavyweight champion, who changed the landscape of boxing when he stunned the world and knocked out Sonny Liston in 1960s, sold the rights to his image and name in a cash deal that covered certain trademarks owned by the champ. No stranger to licensing the names of icons, CKX also controls the rights to the Elvis Presley image. In the music industry, most people do not emphasize the importance of trademarks and the value associated with such marks. Moreover, when we talk about trademarks, artists, producers, and label execs get confused, often saying the area is just much more confusing than its sibling copyrights, but some like Beyoncé, P. Diddy, and even Creflo Dollar, have registered trademarks for their names. In this chapter, we discuss trademarks in a very basic way to help you understand what a trademark is, how to file an application, and why it is valuable.

The term *trademark* is often used to include service marks, because there is no distinction in the protection granted to the mark, only in the nature of what the mark is protecting. In the music business, an album name could require a trademark whereas an artist name could qualify for a service mark; it all depends on what you *apply* for in the application.

In our Muhammad Ali scenario, the boxing icon, at sixty-five, and his wife, Lonnie, are expected to "actively work" with CKX to continue to promote Ali's legacy throughout the world and build on the goodwill in the trademark and image already established. When CKX signed Ali, they also announced it would create a new company called "Greatest of All Time," to take advantage of the moniker Ali once bestowed upon himself after beating Liston, Joe Frazier, and George Foreman, among others. In the deal with CKX, Ali is set to retain 20 percent of all monies, a considerable stake in the company.

Few artists will ever come close to the stature or fame of Muhammad Ali; however, that does not mean their names or images won't be worth millions with careful planning. The key is to recognize the value early on in your career and, if necessary, retain an attorney to register your name as a trademark.

As an artist, your name can become a commodity. It becomes a visual and verbal identification of you and your sound. Coupled with your music, your name provides a basis for creating your brand. Your name is and will be the means by which your fans identify you, locate you, find your albums, and tell their friends about you. It is a means of marketing within itself. Once you have that "cool" name—e.g., HezHouse, LaFace, Fo Yo Soul, Twink Twink Publishing—why not think about trademarks and service marks? There are numerous ownership rights that go along with adopting a name, and protection is available for maintaining your rights and preserving your brand. Understanding your rights and the protection provided them by trademark law is key to building and maintaining a strong brand and protecting it from piracy.

AN OVERVIEW OF TRADEMARK LAW AND REGISTRATION

Section 1 of the Trademark Act of 1946, as amended, provides "the owner of a trademark used in commerce may register his trademark with the United States Patent and Trademark Office (USPTO), if he files a written application with a drawing of the mark, along with specimens.[2] The entire process can be taken care of via Internet for a fee of $325 or, alternatively, $275 per class for a streamlined version of the online form. By "class," we mean the type or category your mark falls under when you go to the USPTO website. If you decide to file your trademark by mailing your application via snail mail, then the USPTO filing fee increases to $375 per class.

The registration also requires that the mark appear as a word(s), design(s), or a combination of the two. The mark can appear in the drawing in what used to be called typewritten form (for registration of words only), but now shows up as stylized typewritten form in a black-and-white ink rendition of the logo/design, or, if applicable, as a color rendition of the logo/design. The artist may then identify the mark, its class, and the register (principal or supplemental) and describe how it is to be used in what the USPTO calls "commerce." The benefits of getting a mark placed on the principal register include the notice to potential copiers that your mark is protected, the right to sue to stop copying, and the right to have the mark considered immune from certain legal challenge after five years. Registration also means that an infringer will be considered a willful infringer in case of an infringement lawsuit, which makes it a lot easier to collect large damages and possibly attorney fees. The supplemental register is the list on which nondistinctive trademarks or service marks are placed if federal registration is sought. Descriptive marks, surnames, and marks consisting primarily of geographical terms are usually placed on this register, which offers limited protection for marks.

It is important to note that the USPTO looks at a list of factors to determine approval, and it is important for you to remember these key factors as you explore registering your mark:

- The mark must be already be in use in interstate commerce, or
- There must be a bona fide intention to use the mark in interstate commerce, or
- Under certain international treaties you can apply based on registration or application in a foreign country, and

---

[2] Federal Trademark Act of 1946, §1.

- When you file based on a bona fide intention to use the mark, registration is not issued until the mark is used and proved

Once the mark is received the USPTO will assign your file a serial number, and send a confirmation of receipt, and normally within two months assign your file to an examining attorney. The mark is then searched and analyzed by the USPTO's office, through an individual known as a trademark examiner. If the mark is not rejected (reasons for rejection include existence of a confusingly similar mark or because the artist failed to fill out the application correctly) then the mark is published in the Official Gazette. This publication allows for the public to object to USPTO approving your mark by filing an opposition.

For instance, if DMX filed his name as a mark (three raised gothic letters, DMX), could the makers of the famous DMX keyboard (Yamaha) object? I doubt it, but this is an example of an opposition that might be made once a mark is filed for protection. However, if DMX filed a trademark application for musical equipment, say microphones (after all, he is an MC), then the keyboard maker might begin an opposition proceeding because those goods would move in the same channels of trade as the Yamaha DMX keyboard, according to Attorney Robinson, a former examiner with the USPTO office and a top trademark lawyer in the Atlanta area.

Anyone who takes advantage of the opportunity the USPTO allows for an individual or company to object to the registration of the mark by filing an opposition with the USPTO must file within thirty days of the publication. If an opposition is filed, there is a proceeding to determine which party has prior use of the mark. If there is no opposition to the mark, the USPTO will issue a certificate of registration about three months later.

Once your trademark has been registered, you should give notice of registration by designating your mark as "Registered in U.S. Patent and Trademark Office," which you will recognize as being shortened to ®. Under the Lanham Act, failure to give notice of registration by use of the ® designation prevents the registrant from recovering damages from infringement, unless the infringer had actual notice that the mark was registered. More importantly, do not use the ® designation prior to the official issuance of registration and certificate. Stick to using TM or SM before you file or while your application is pending. Misuse of the ® designation may result in fraud sanctions under the Lanham Act and possible notice from the USPTO that your use of the symbol is premature.

Trademark law is a little complicated, but it is important to note that your rights regarding a registered trademark can continue indefinitely provided that you continue to use the mark and file documentation of continued use in the USPTO. It can be complicated, so please see the info below for more in-depth discussion, or if you are a technically minded artist.[3]

---

[3] After five years, the trademark owner must file a Declaration of Continued Use or Excusable Nonuse, which is also known as a Section 8 Declaration. After five consecutive years of use, the owner may file a Declaration of Incontestability under Section 15 of the Trademark Act, but it is not required to maintain your rights. Between your ninth and tenth years of use, you should file another Section 8 Declaration and an Application for Renewal under Section 9. These should be filed every ten years to renew and maintain your rights in the trademark. Failure to renew will result in expiration and cancellation of your registration.

Many of my clients and friends in the entertainment industry do not understand the concept of registering their names (whether a pseudonym or not), or their logo. Those who do understand realize an artist is wise to consider having his name registered for the following goods and services directly related to entertainment services: live musical performances, a series of musical sound recordings, etc. Artists will also get protection for ancillary items like posters, lunch boxes, notebooks, and other merchandise. Registrations for single albums and song titles are generally not issued, as the USPTO will reject such filings as merely a single work. A song or album title can however be used on ancillary items like the posters, lunch boxes, and the like.

For example, Stephen Hurd has coined "Hurd the Word Music." Bobby Jones has *The Bobby Jones Gospel Show*. James Hall is known as "The Professor" in gospel music. Imagine, if twenty-five years ago, when Dr. Jones started his TV career with Black Entertainment Television (BET), he had registered his tag "Hey, hey, hey . . . it's the *Bobby Jones Gospel Show*." It's akin to Michael Buffer's trademarked phrase "Let's get ready to rumble" heard before every big fight. Dr. Jones could have earned millions from BET and others if the USPTO approved his mark. (I should note that Dr. Bobby Jones is a financially astute entertainer, so don't shed any tears for him in this example.)

A trademark certifies a certain quality of services and identifies the product's origins. Trademarks and service marks are created through use and can be registered instate or nationally. State trademark registration is often made through the local secretary of state. Federal trademark registrations offer the most protection for your name or logo, but to qualify, the mark must be used in interstate commerce. If you are operating locally for the time being and not performing or selling merchandise outside of your state, you can wait to register the trademark until you're ready to start selling your product outside of your state. However, given today's Internet-heavy traffic, most products do find their way into interstate commerce, the exceptions being restaurants and some other service-industry-related services.

Unlike other countries, the United States allows trademark rights to be acquired essentially by use. Registration enhances those rights. A federal trademark application, as highlighted above, may be filed based either on actual use or on a bona fide intent to use a mark in commerce. It is important to note that a trademark application based on bona fide intention to use still requires that there be actual use before registration is ultimately completed. However, once the mark is registered, priority is given to the mark and thus constructive use is established as of the filing date of the federal trademark application.

CKX plans to enhance the Muhammad Ali brand, so other marks will come into play. They might create an Ali video game, an Ali boxing glove, an Ali clothing line, or an Ali food line. As a result, there will be marks to be registered with the USPTO. The extent to which they plan to use the Ali name makes it critical for the CKX team to run trademark searches. Ali has been an icon for over four decades now, and it is important to make sure no former manager, attorney, agent, or handler registered any unauthorized or unknown marks on behalf of the champ. Trademark searches are recommended before commencing use of a trademark, whether or not one files an application for registration.

Commonly you will see the ® next to a trademark like Xerox® or Coke® or Motown®. It is important to note that this symbol ® cannot be used unless a mark is federally registered in connection with the goods or services with which the mark is used.

As stated earlier in this chapter, Ali will retain some rights in his new agreement with CKX. This is important because under trademark law, a trademark can be licensed to a third party, but the license requires quality control over the use of the mark by the licensor. Failure to monitor quality control may result in the loss of rights in the mark. Thus, any existing marks that Ali owns and has transferred for that $50 million need to be monitored to make certain that they do not fall into the public domain or lose protection. Examples of marks that fell into the public domain (a/k/a "genericide") because they were not vigilantly protected are "elevator" and "aspirin."

Another benefit of trademark protection is it allows you to sell or assign your trademark to anyone, with the requirement that it be accompanied by the goodwill represented by the mark. Goodwill is the value and intangible worldwide recognition Ali has put into his brand and associated image. When you hear "Ali" in this century, he is almost on the level of Ghandi or Nelson Mandela or Babe Ruth for his generation (we overlook his fights with the government that stripped him of his title in the late 1960s, when he refused to go to Vietnam). As a result of the goodwill Ali has created, when Ali took the megabucks from CKX, he transferred all of the intangible rights or goodwill he had built up over the years in his name, marks, and image.

BE SURE THE MARK IS DISTINCTIVE

As an artist or label you can seek legal protection from the USPTO based on how distinctive your mark is. The degree of distinctiveness may be classified in descending order of protection, from arbitrary or fanciful, suggestive, descriptive, or generic. Arbitrary or fanciful marks, which are both inherently distinctive, have the greatest opportunity for protection and the protection afforded them broadest in scope. The word *Nextel*, displayed on a Blackberry, is an example of a fanciful mark. Another is the flying symbol of Michael Jordan's "Jumpman" that accompanies the "Air Jordan" name. The Air Jordan Jumpman has become a mark known all over the world.

"Suggestive marks," marks that hint at but do not describe the nature or quality of goods or services, are able to be protected when first used, but the scope of such marks may be limited. Descriptive and ornamental marks are not able to be protected or registered initially but only become so at such time as they have acquired a "secondary meaning." This is accomplished when the public comes to recognize the words as a mark, rather than as its primary meaning. An example of an ornamental mark that acquired a secondary meaning is the "Nike Swoosh." According to representatives at the USPTO, the government will often refuse a mark as being merely ornamental when it is used simply as a decoration on the front of a shirt. An example is the initial meaning of the Nike swoosh symbol. Now, after hundreds of millions of dollars in marketing and advertising, we all know what the Swoosh stands for Nike and its motto "Just Do It." Generic marks,

marks that are the common commercial names for objects, e.g., "sugar" is generic for sugar, will probably never be protected.

One of my clients, Twinkie Clark, has a unique way of teaching songs to a choir. Her family, and especially her mother, Mattie Moss-Clark, created a school in Detroit. If the school set up a descriptive trademark—e.g., "Clark Sisters Singing" lessons—and this mark gained a secondary meaning, this mark could become protected under trademark laws. An example of a secondary meaning coming about would be a situation in which the community knew a certain style of singing as "Clark Sisters" singing. Arguably, after the mark acquired secondary meaning, it could be registered with the USPTO. Additionally, assume the Clark Sisters made a logo of a singer holding a mic to go with the singing lessons, album sales, T-shirts, etc. As this logo or mark became more and more popular it, too, could be registered. Depending on the nature of the hypothetical Clark Sisters design, the USPTO might register it without need for a secondary meaning, especially in relation to the services, if we argued that it was remotely fanciful and not ornamental and it could be used on the goods as well.

This can all sound a bit too technical for a new artist or start-up label. Understand the basics and hire someone who specializes in trademark law if you are interested in truly registering anything associated with your label, or your career for that matter.

FIVE FACTORS ON TRADEMARKS

Here are five factors to consider for purposes of a trademark or service mark.

A mark:

- protects you from others' infringing use of your mark
- helps to create a brand image
- creates a professional image
- prevents importation of foreign counterfeit goods
- provides a basis for filing trademark applications in foreign countries (so that your trademark will be safe when you're ready for foreign album and merchandise sales.)

As stated above, under the Trademark Act of 1946, more commonly known as the Lanham Act (Title 15, Chapter 22 of the U.S. Code), an artist can trademark a name, symbol, logo, or original work to identify a product or good, such as an album, T-shirt, or other promotional merchandise. Similarly, an artist can put a service mark on flyers or other items bearing her name to identify services—e.g., "Goodwrench," "Firestone" certified, or "Clark Sisters" as stated above. Because there is no distinction in the protection granted to the two marks, only in the nature of what the mark is protecting, the term *trademark* is often used to include service marks. In the music business, an album name would require a trademark, whereas an artist name would qualify for a service mark.

CHOOSING YOUR MARK

Successful artists and producers have distinctive names and symbols that serve to create an image and identity for their music. Begin by selecting a name and image to create an identity for your music. Your name and symbol are an important element of your "brand." Names should be unique and memorable. Choosing a distinctive name will reduce your chances of duplicating a name already in use. Start by generating a list of possible names that you feel represent you and your music. You can search the web to see if there are any artists or prominent business with the same name, or similar ones. You can also perform a search through the USPTO (www.uspto.gov) to see if any of your proposed names are already registered. Stay away from using names that are used by another business or entity, because it may be considered an infringement.

As I was writing this book, Apple Corporation (owned by the Beatles) was still fighting Apple Computers owned by Steve Jobs over the "Apple" use in both of their companies and the intellectual property confusion. Apparently, the companies had a "concurrent use" agreement that provided that Apple Computers would never go into the music business. Now that Apple's iPod has exploded on to the music scene, the Apple Corporation feels there is a ton of confusion between the two amongst consumers. It is a case that has gone on for years.

Traditionally, registering a trademarked name provided you protection in the specific area in which you did business. Many years ago the Apple Computer folks felt comfortable telling the USPTO that no one would mix up their computers with the Apple Corporation owned by the legendary 1960s group the Beatles. Now, forty years later, a good argument could be made that uncertainty does exist, particularly because both the Apple Corporation and now Apple Computers are huge players in the music industry. The uncertainty that may exist is cause for concern based on the Beatles' fear of dilution and confusion.

Dilution

About ten years ago, a new area was recognized in trademark legislation called dilution, which expanded the traditional scope of trademark protection beyond the trademark holder's specific area of business. A 1996 amendment to the Lanham Act created the first federal trademark statute addressing dilution. The theory is that by allowing two identical names in different areas of business, the value of the original trademark is "diluted" by the subsequent mark. This is essential to the Beatles' argument as Apple, with its iTunes, continues to be a major player in the music industry.

Legal scholars feel that this may include diminution of the uniqueness of the trademark, tarnishing of the well-known trademark, and a creation of a likelihood of confusion about the sponsorship or affiliation of goods or services under the second trademark. For example, if you wanted to use a name like Red Roof for your group, despite the Red Roof Inn being a major hotel chain, the hotel company might be able to stop you on the grounds that they cater to hotel and entertainment guests and your mark would dilute their uniqueness and reduce the value of their trademark, causing a lot of confusion to the consumer.

As an artist or producer, you will also want to create a design or symbol to accompany your name, which will enhance your artist identity. Diddy has done this with his Bad Boy Records, Sean John clothing line, and Justin's restaurant. Each one has its own goodwill and value, but all are created from his identity.

When you ultimately decide the name of your label or business and come up with a unique or distinctive design that everyone recognizes as your symbol, like Wu-Tang Clan's W symbol or the Def Jam recordings logo, you should begin protecting your mark immediately.

It is important to run an initial search to see if your name and symbol are already in use before using them because failure to do so may result in infringing on someone else's registered mark. Such action would force you to forfeit the use of your name and begin building your reputation again from the ground up. If your goal is to start a record label or production company, you might want to consult trade publications such as *Phonolog* or *Billboard International Buyer's Guide*. Further, when you become serious about registering your name and symbol, you will want to consult a trademark attorney who can help you perform the trademark search or hire a trademark search organization. Our firm often uses Thompson & Thompson (www.thompson.com), one of the leading trademark search companies in the land.

Ownership Rights in an Artist's Name

We already saw how Muhammad Ali created great value in the ownership rights to his name. We should point out even George Foreman received millions for the use of his name and image on a hamburger skillet. By using your name in connection with your music you are creating a right to use that name. When you see Beyoncé's image and likeness with makeup projects and Pepsi, realize she will make millions. Your rights to the name generally extend to the areas in which you have been using it.

For example, if you and a friend started a hip-hop group called "202" (no kin to the former hot R&B group 702) in Washington, DC, in 2002, you would have the rights to use that name in DC, assuming no other artists started using the same name there before you. As you became more popular, let's assume you started touring the East Coast, New York to Virginia, in 2003. As a touring artist, you sold your albums and your merchandise. But one day in 2005, as you attempt to sell some of your albums to a local record store in Newark, New Jersey, you see that the store is already selling an album by another group called 202.

If the group formed and started using that name in Jersey prior to 2003, they will have the rights to use "202" in New Jersey, and you will be unable to use that name there. However, if they formed after 2003, you could have the ability to file an action preventing them from using the name in New Jersey and in any other area where you have already put the 202 name into use. These conflicts can get pretty tricky, so you will definitely want to seek legal advice if you should ever encounter such a problem. To avoid this problem, make sure you find a name that is not already in use when you start using your name.

Record companies don't want to deal with these issues, so it is important that you deal with them as they arise. Do not simply ignore them. Let me repeat: DO NOT IGNORE THESE ISSUES. If your 202 competitors are from Reno, Nevada, you may think it's not necessary to get the rights to use the name in Reno because you're only touring and selling your merchandise on the East Coast. But, when you have a chance to sign with a label, they'll want to distribute your albums nationwide, and not handling the problem when it came up will create bigger issues and can stall or even kill a deal.

If there is an artist out there with your name, that artist could file an injunction preventing the record company from releasing your albums. If the record company is unable to release your records, they will then look to you to pay damages. Again, you will want to handle any conflicts as they arise. If you encounter this issue, there are several options to consider. If you're quickly establishing a strong reputation and an expansive fan base, offer to buy the rights to the name from the other artist. Or, if you're a group just getting started, you might want to consider changing your name, adding an element to it to make it different (for example, "202" could become "DC Music 202"), or allowing the other artist to purchase your rights. Even if you make this change, though, you are not guaranteed registration on the Principal Register. It is addressed on a case-by-case basis.

GROUP RIGHTS IN THE NAME

As we've discussed, there is a difference between a trademark and a service mark. A trademark identifies the origins of goods. Pepsi, Xerox, and Nike are trademarks. However, a service mark identifies services like those of your group—e.g., Backstreet Boys, the Five Heartbeats, and the Soul Singers. If you are a group rather than a solo artist, you will want to determine the nature of your partnership once you select a name. You will want to consider what to do if circumstances arise resulting in the breakup of your group, and who will get the rights to use the name.

Some factors you should consider are:

- What if the group breaks up and everyone goes their separate ways?
- What if the majority of the members leave the group to form another group?
- What if the lead performer or writer leaves the group?
- What if a supporting performer or writer leaves the group?
- What if the group breaks up, but one or two members want to continue a solo career using the name of the group?

Consider all possibilities and hire a good intellectual property lawyer to draw up an agreement that considers all imaginable possibilities. The main goal is to lay some basic ground rules for what to do in case of a breakup.

For instance, you might want to make an agreement that no one can use the name if the group breaks up, even if some of the members continue performing together. Another option is to allow the most business-savvy member of the group to use the name, so long as he or she agrees to pay a fee to the rest of the group. Or, if the marks are owned by the group's corporation or LLC (Boyz II Men, Inc. or Boyz II Men, LLC), then the member continuing use would pay a fee to the corporation and everyone would reap their share of the profits.

Without ground rules it is dangerous to assume that just because you came up with the name without the help of any other members of the group, you will be able to keep using it. When I was a student at Howard, a group of people in my fraternity devised the moniker "Shai" as the pledge name for a new brother being initiated into the fraternity. Two million records later, neither we nor our fraternity have received a royalty for the use of that name by three frat brothers, who later formed the former Gasoline Alley/MCA group that went double platinum. (Smile, guys; I told you I would mention you in the book!)

RECORD COMPANY RIGHTS TO THE NAME

For many years, I have known the Gordy family, particularly super-savvy business-man Kerry Gordy, the son who worked closely with his dad, Berry, then ventured off to build his own successful company. I've always asked Kerry Gordy about life at Motown. However, one question I didn't consider was whether Motown owned the name "Diana Ross and the Supremes" or just the "Supremes" name. When Diana left, she recorded under her own name "Diana Ross" (remember those classics "Muscles" and "I'm Coming Out"?).

Many recording contracts clearly provide that a record company owns the name the "Boyz" or the "Five Heartbeats" or the "Mary J. Blige" or "*NSYNC," unless these artists kept those rights during negotiations or registered their name prior to signing with the label. Record companies require an artist to assign the exclusive rights to the use of her name, biographical material, and likeness to the record company in the recording agreement. The record company uses these rights to freely use the name to disseminate and advertise the music made under the agreement. The use of the name does not have to be connected to a promotion for a specific recording. The record company also wants to protect its investment. If an established artist were to make recordings with another artist and use his or her name to promote that artist, the record company would be deprived of poten-tial income.

The label would claim, rightly so, that it is entitled to the income resulting from the use of your name because of the risk it took by making an investment in your music. The assignment of the rights is usually restricted to the duration of the agreement; however, a record company will want to retain its right to use your name once the agreement has expired in connection with recordings made while you were under contract with it.

PROTECTING YOUR MARK

You can designate your symbol and name as a trademark even before you officially register your mark. As stated earlier in this chapter, the designation "TM" should be used for a trademark, and "SM," or "S," in conjunction with a service mark. These designations are inserted next to the mark in a prominent place to serve as a notice of ownership. This is especially critical when you publish your first adver-tisement bearing the trademark or your first sale of products or services bearing the trademark. You should keep dated records and documents of your first use of the trademark both locally and in interstate transactions. You may also want to keep actual products, copies of flyers used for promotion, and photos of products and the mark as records. These records will provide evidence for your trademark registra-tion and evidence of your use of the trademark should you encounter any infringe-ment in the future.

Trademarks are protected under federal law by 18 U.S.C. §2321, and they are also protected in a number of states. These laws make it a criminal offense to infringe, imitate, or counterfeit trademarks or goods bearing imitation marks. To be found guilty of violation of the statutes, the offender must be found to have had a criminal or fraudulent intent.

Trademark owners can also file civil actions to protect their marks. Courts protect trademarks under the doctrine of unfair competition, which is closely related to trademark cases. In most cases, people suing for trademark infringement also make a claim for unfair competition. Unfair competition arises when there is a misappropriation or misrepresentation made as an individual or business attempts to sell a product or service of another business as their own. The legal test for trademark infringement requires that there be a likelihood of confusion about the origin of a product or service. This means that the representation by the infringer need only be capable of easily misleading the public into believing the good or service was sold or made by the original trademark owner. Take for instance designer-style handbags sold on the streets of New York. There is a fine line differentiating how similar the handbags sold on the street can be from the designs sold by the designer companies like Coach or Louis Vuitton, and they cannot bear the designer logos, which are trademarked.

A claim against an infringer might involve an injunction preventing the infringer from continuing to produce products or services that resemble your mark. You can also claim damages against an infringer for lost profits caused by the infringement.

The Lanham Act allows federal district courts to grant injunctions to prevent violation of the trademark owner's rights. If an infringement is found, the court can order the destruction of any infringing labels, packages, reproductions, signs, or other materials used to reproduce the imitation mark. If you file a claim under the Lanham Act, your recovery may include the following:

- Any profits made by the defendant while infringing on your mark
- Any damages you might have suffered as a result of the infringement
- Legal costs associated with your action against the infringer

The court will determine your award at its discretion. Your recovery may be adjusted if the court finds the profits to be too excessive or inadequate when compared to the severity of the infringement. The court is empowered to enter a judgment for a recovery of up to three times the amount of actual damages. In exceptional cases the court can also grant an award for attorney's fees, something usually not done in America. To recover the infringer's profits you will need to prove the amount he made in sales of the infringing product or service, but he will be allowed to prove deductions and costs against his sales.

Trademarks used by third parties for news purposes do not constitute an infringement. News gathering or news reporting uses are an exception to infringement when there is no indication of endorsement or sponsorship by the artist.

Take for instance the unauthorized biographical documentary of 50 Cent, *Shoot First*. The disclaimer that the documentary was "unauthorized" makes it clear that 50 Cent did not consent to the use of his name or likeness, nor any of the information contained in the video, so there should be no confusion when the consumer purchases the DVD.

INTERNATIONAL PROTECTION

If you're planning on performing or otherwise selling your albums and merchandise abroad, it is imperative you seek professional advice to register your trademark in foreign countries. Unlike in the United States, in most foreign countries it is not necessary to put the mark into use before applying for registration. Regardless of whether you have sold anything overseas, if you're on the cusp of hitting it big, you will want to take the time to register your mark internationally. If you become popular and do not, it is entirely possible for another to capitalize on your fame and register your mark in another country first, thus preventing you from registering your mark there. In addition, registration is also a method for barring importation of foreign counterfeit products bearing your mark.

CLOSING TIPS

It is unlikely you will be able to sell your image at age sixty-five for $50 million like Muhammad Ali or be asked to license your name for a hamburger grill like George Foreman and make millions. However, it is still important that you have some idea of the possibilities of revenue streams through the use of your name, likeness, logo, and image. (As I write this chapter, a Meineke commercial featuring George Foreman just flashed—need I write anymore about using your image and likeness?)

In the urban and gospel communities, there has not been a great deal of discussion on trademarks. However, as Ali (and Foreman) paved the way in boxing, you too could pave the way in urban music by creating a brand that sets the bar.

CHAPTER 11

Distribution for the Label: Taking It to the Streets

"Russell Simmons is the main reason for the financial success of the whole hip-hop/rap music culture; if he hadn't gotten into it when he did, who can guess where it would be today?"

—CLARENCE AVANT, FORMER RECORD
COMPANY EXEC, OFTEN CALLED THE MOST
POWERFUL MAN IN THE RECORD INDUSTRY

In the late 1970s, Def Jam founder Russell Simmons was just a skinny kid at City University in New York. The son of a college professor at Pace University, Simmons, a sociology major, decided to put on several rap concerts on the Manhattan campus at a time when rap music was only reaching into a few small sections of urban communities. Nicknamed "Rush" as a child, he used Rush Promotions to market and promote these landmark concerts.

It was during this time he met a white kid named Rick Rubin, also from New York, and also intrigued by the sound of poetic lyrics riffing over cutting-edge drum beats and scratching vinyl records on a turntable. The two young record label pioneers raised five thousand dollars and from their college dormitory built the Def Jam empire, selling thousands of records out of their trunks and everywhere else necessary to create a grassroots hip-hop movement.

By 1985, Def Jam went from a small college start-up to a record label selling half a million records a year. Corporate America took notice, and soon CBS Records offered the two brilliant entrepreneurs a $600,000 label deal with Def Jam that included marketing, promotion, and better distribution, all designed to grow the label into a multimillion-dollar empire in a short matter of time. In this chapter, we will look at distribution and how to get a record out to the masses.

Getting a record from the recording studio to the hands of the consumer takes a lot of work. There is a lot of critical thinking and much consideration that goes into producing a CD, manufacturing the product, and ultimately selling it. For small labels, the failure to obtain a solid distribution agreement with the distributor that will best represent your artists could be the difference between success and failure. The manufacturing and distributing processes require just as much of your attention as actually recording the album. Manufacturing and distribution are a fundamental part of your marketing plan. Without the right distribution, your album will be never be discovered by your target audience.

In this chapter, we'll discuss how to go about manufacturing CDs, how distributors work, and the details of distribution agreements and how to get one.

KEY CONSIDERATIONS IN GETTING
YOUR RECORDS TO THE PEOPLE

✦ Manufacturing CDs

✦ Distribution

✦ Pressing and distribution (P&D) deals

✦ Selling your story

✦ A sample distribution agreement

MANUFACTURING CDS (BEFORE DISTRIBUTION,
UNDERSTAND HOW THE CD IS MADE)

Many early-1980s records, including the Sugar Hill Gang's "Rapper's Delight" and Afrika Bambaataa's "Planet Rock," were manufactured at home studios and distributed on the street, at barbershops, or even corner stores in the old neighborhood. The early pioneers like Bambaataa, Grandmaster Flash, and Russell Simmons understood the importance of understanding how CDs were manufactured and then distributed. They also understood the importance of mastering.

Mastering is a huge component of manufacturing that can really help you perfect your record. The process of mastering resequences the songs, adds or limits compression to the music, and bolsters quality by using EQ on the highs, mids, and lows. Many DJs in the early days of hip-hop engineered and mastered early classics like "Sucker MCs" (Run-DMC) and "These Are the Breaks" (Kurtis Blow). Engineers know how to mix a recording according to the standards of the genre, leading to ultimate success. After the record is engineered and mastered properly, you are ready for manufacturing and distribution.

"If you do not have distribution, it is very hard to reach the masses with your CD," explains Bambaataa, whose yearly tours worldwide educate thousands on the music industry and his history as the songwriter of "Planet Rock" and "Looking for the Perfect Beat," still licensed for use twenty years later. He added, "Before you sign that distribution agreement, understand how these companies manufacture CDs and how the profits are made."

Bambaataa is correct; manufacturing, if done right, can have a career-altering affect on your CD release. Simply having first-class production and sound quality in the manufacturing is key in today's high-tech society. Also, a nicely designed package and insert will entice your target audience to pick up the CD and give it a listen.

Bambaataa shared with me horror stories of hip-hop artists over the past thirty years not understanding manufacturing and printing costs prior to signing a record deal with a major or an indie. So, before you get into distribution, try to get a thorough understanding of how the manufacturing process works. As you're shopping for manufacturers and materials, ask questions and try to build your manufacturing knowledge. Try to determine which options and manufacturers are the best values. Just because one manufacturer is expensive doesn't mean he or she offers the best quality product or the best customer service. Don't underestimate the value of gaining this kind of information, no matter what avenue of manufacturing you take. Getting the information from the start can help you plan for the future and learn while your label grows.

Recently, we were putting together a distribution deal for a gospel artist. The distributor offered our client, a well-known artist I am not at liberty to name, approximately five dollars a record. We realized that at that time to manufacture one CD was about $1.60. We also realized that we had to pay mechanical royalties and producer points, as discussed earlier, out of the CD sales. Thus, we asked the distributor to raise the deal to closer to seven dollars a record to our client, and they ultimately consented.

The budget for printing our initial CDs had to consider our return, and the higher the return, the better we did fiscally. Keep in mind that you may not be like our client, and the size of your budget may determine how you will produce your CDs. If you operate a label and have a relatively small budget with new artists who haven't hit it big yet, you might want to consider manufacturing their CDs yourself. You will need a burner, some blank CDs, jewel cases, and labels that you can print. A lot of these products can be found online at reasonable prices. You can also print CD inserts to make the CD look more professional, and even include lyrics and liner notes. You should consider investing in some design software that will help you design your CD insert and labels and a high-quality printer to print the final product.

If you have a larger budget, there are a lot of companies that offer manufacturing and duplicating services similar to those used in the example discussed above at or near $1.60 a unit. Duplicating services complete with printing, jewel cases, and inserts can fluctuate in cost, all depending on the quantity that you order and the company you use to manufacture the CD. Lots of duplication companies can be found online, or you can check the yellow pages in your area or ask at a local recording studio to find out who in the area provides these services.

While manufacturing may seem like the easiest and the least labor-intensive aspect of releasing an album, it actually requires a lot of attention and is a critical part of marketing an artist and selling the product as a label. Quality control is one aspect of manufacturing that you must not ignore. All CDs are not created equal! Many CDs from each printing are produced with defects in both appearance and quality. Some come with paper rips, ink smears, and logos printed off-center or not printed at all. Often, jewel cases crack during shipping. Manufacturers are responsible for monitoring their output and filtering out any defective pieces from any shipment, but it is the artist's job to hold them accountable.

Industry standards account for anticipated defects and shipments usually running about 10 percent above or below the ordered production amount. If you receive less than your ordered amount, you'll end up being short on product. If you receive more than the amount you ordered, you will have to pay for the additional product. When ordering, keep in mind the minimum amount of product you need, and make sure if you receive 10 percent under the amount of your order, you will still have enough product.

Although we tend to think of CDs when we think of buying a new album, there are still other formats available for manufacturing. You can get your artist's music reproduced as cassette or even vinyl. While at first it might seem like it would be a good idea to cover as many formats as possible, you should really consider your market: Some formats might be a waste of time or money, depending on your stage of development.

The first question to ask yourself is what are you releasing, an LP, an EP or a single? An LP is a full album and the most popular format no matter what genre. It also has the highest profit margin and is the format that distributors and retailers prefer to stock. An EP is an album that only contains a handful of songs, typically three to five, and is usually released by artists who are just getting started, many released by the artists themselves. Distributors and retailers are less likely to want to stock an EP because the profit margin for an EP is not as high as that of an LP. Stocking an EP can be much riskier for retailers. Although it occupies just as much shelf space as an LP, it does not make a as great a profit for a distributor and is typically not as popular with customers.

Manufacturing costs are about the same for LPs and EPs, so you won't save much money by releasing an EP, only in the recording costs. A single is just what it sounds like, one track (maybe two) that is released on its own. Hip-hop and dance markets usually thrive on singles, and a label can break an artist on a single. A single could be a good investment if you're working with a really talented hip-hop artist or group. Singles often work better as free promotional items, but do not sell as well as full albums.

Although it is great to appeal to as many people as possible, you don't have to have all of the various formats and lengths produced when you first start approaching distributors and place a manufacturing order. For instance, you can start with the CD format at first, and you can always produce other formats, like cassettes, later. It is best to wait until there is a demand for the product before you start producing it. Not only will this save you money up front, but it will also help you in terms of marketing. You'll be able to announce and promote the release of new formats.

DISTRIBUTION

During the late 1980s, Def Jam decided to renew the initial distribution agreement discussed earlier for nearly five times as much in money to Simmons and Rubin. At that time, CBS and Simmons set up a joint distribution deal that was considered a huge breakthrough for rap labels. Def Jam reportedly received a few million dollars for operating costs and day-to-day affairs, while the major label/distributor CBS collected the major profit and paid a royalty to Def Jam. Although I did not see the agreement, it was most likely an 80/20 split in favor of CBS, subject to the advance of $3 to $5 million to cover salaries, recording costs, marketing, etc. As a result, Simmons and his top executives and staff most likely received a salary and budget, from which he could pay all of the recording costs to make the albums for LL Cool J, Public Enemy (who were the label mainstays in the late 1980s and early 1990s), and a host of others.

Additionally, if the distributor was advancing these funds to Def Jam, the company most likely would not split the profits until some point of recoupment or break-even point was reached for CBS/Sony. (Simmons ultimately sold Def Jam, but for purposes of explaining distribution, it is helpful to understand the early days of Def Jam and its distribution scheme.)

Many start-up labels believe that once they have a distribution deal all of their troubles will just melt away. This is not true! Notice that Simmons and Rubin figured out distribution on their own prior to joining the CBS/Sony family as a label. Making a deal with a distributor before you're established can be a big mistake. Before you make an agreement with any distributor, learn as much as you can about distribution.

Most likely, CBS/Sony promised Def Jam that it would do the job of shopping Def Jam product to retailers and record stores and encourage them to stock Def Jam CDs for consumers to buy. GospoCentric president Vicki Mack-Lataillade, a pioneer in gospel music, once explained to me that "shelf space" was the whole key to a label: The most successful labels are the ones whose products are most prominently displayed. GospoCentric shattered industry standards with its gold and multiplatinum artists like Kurt Carr and Kirk Franklin. They went through distributors like Interscope and Zomba/BMG in continuing to expand a brand that started in a small building with a husband and wife team (Claude Lataillade and Vicki Mack-Lataillade).

Interestingly enough, GospoCentric began dealing with a small distributor, but as the company exploded, a larger distributor was needed. It is important to realize that distribution companies range in size from companies that support the major labels to small independent distributors who specialize in certain genres of music and regions. A distributor can be as simple as two guys selling CDs out of their trunk on a city corner. Midsize distributors are not necessarily entirely independent. Even though it may maintain its own business entity, a distributor will often use the facilities of other companies for warehousing and transportation. A midsize distributor can be a good option for the established label because it will generally have a better reputation than those small operations that consist of people who drive around in beat-up vans dropping CDs off at local retailers but can still give you the attention and specialization you need to get your record shipped and sold.

Of course, these services come with a price. Distributors take a commission on records sold by the retailers. You send them the recordings you've manufactured based on their estimate of how many they believe they will be able to ship, and they then ship the CDs to each of the individual record stores that have placed orders for your album. The distributor is then paid by the retailer for the shipment, and the distributor then holds the funds due the label. Typically, distributors pay labels in thirty-, sixty-, or ninety-day periods. However, in the United States music retailers are allowed a 100-percent return policy for shipments received from distributors. This means that a retailer can return an unsold CD or any quantity of CDs at almost any time, even several months or years down the road (although distributors will institute a marginal penalty charge).

Because of this possibility, it is important to not overestimate your potential sales. If as a label you do this, you will lose all of the revenue from those extra CDs, and you will take a loss on the manufacturing and production costs on each of those CDs. Also, many distributors will require you to pay the distribution fee despite the fact that the CD was returned; after all, they did distribute it for you, didn't they?

Because of this return policy, distributors like to hold onto a portion of the amount of money they owe you against future returns as "reserves." Then, once any unsold records are returned to the distributor, the distributor will return the unsold product to you.

MAJOR DISTRIBUTORS

Major distributors are the companies that get the product from the major labels into retail stores. In the music industry, there have been several major distributors like: EMD, WEA, PGD, UNI, and Sony/BMG. Labels like So So Def, Bad Boy, LaFace, Verity, and G-Unit are distributed by majors. The major distributors also distribute product from indie labels, but usually only the more established ones.

Admittedly, it is hard for a beginner, indie, or otherwise small label to get distribution from a major distributor. It happens from time to time if an indie produces a breakout hit. For example, Shekinah Glory and William Murphy had majors lining up to sign them after releasing the classic song and CD "Praise Is What I Do," produced by the incredible Rose Harper.

Usually, to be picked up by a major distributor, an indie had to work its way through the independent distributor channels. For an indie label, major distribution isn't necessarily better, but it can open a lot of doors and provide access to national retail coverage. Major distribution can also do a lot to boost the credibility of your label and help you become recognized as a successful, legitimate operation.

INDIE DISTRIBUTORS

James Roberson, the founder of JDI Records, encourages most small-record-label owners to highly consider the independent distribution route or indie distribution. Roberson explains: "One of the biggest advantages of using an indie distributor is the flexibility to get records out in the marketplace much quicker. With the major systems, there is usually at least a six-month lead time to schedule releases. With an indie distributor, I can get a record out on the streets in two months."

Independent distributors can have distribution networks that range in size from a small local circle of retailers (usually called "one-stop" distributors) to a national distribution system. Some of the national distributors include RED Distribution, Koch Distribution, Artemis, and ADA. Getting a national distributor to carry your albums takes quite a bit of marketing and a solid sales history. National distributors look for labels that have artists with a national audience. They don't want to spend time, energy, or money on a name that won't be recognized outside of a limited territory. Further, a national distributor needs to know that you have the resources to promote and market your record on a national level.

An obvious advantage to using a national distributor is that you usually have the ability to send your entire product to one location, rather than managing accounts with several regional distributors. A disadvantage to using a larger distributor is that you have no power over how many albums get shipped to retailers and even less power over how many get returned. The larger the distributor, the more units will be returned. A large distributor will be less conservative about the number of albums they order from you and less involved with your product and developing sales.

Midsize distributors are usually more involved with the labels and the albums they carry and typically specialize in particular genres of music. Small and midsize distributors will also be more conservative in the number of albums they order from you, which can minimize both your risk and theirs. A smaller or midsize distributor can be a good option for distribution for a label that has an established sales record locally or in a specific region.

One-stop distributors cater to mom-and-pop retailers. Because mom-and-pops serve a limited number of customers and are not part of a chain, they typically only require small quantities of each title they want to carry. Major and midsize indie distributors typically don't like to break up full boxes to ship to retailers, especially because they want to maximize the number of records they sell. Enter the one-stop. One-stops will sell major and indie titles to mom-and-pop retailers in small quantities—as little as five or ten copies. Using a one-stop can be a huge advantage for a budding label because of the level of involvement and the investment mom-and-pops have in the music they sell. Selling your record at a mom-and-pop can create a lot of buzz about your record.

P&D DEALS

If you are starting your label with a larger budget and more established artists, you might want to consider getting a "P&D" deal. A P&D deal is a pressing and distribution agreement in which a distributor agrees to manufacture your CDs and distribute them as a wholesaler, for a fee. Typically, you'll sell your CDs to the distributor at a wholesale price, minus a distribution fee ranging from about 15 to 20 percent, with the difference given to your production company. For example, on a CD with a wholesale price of ten dollars, 20 percent, or two dollars, would be paid to the distribution entity, and 80 percent, eight dollars, is paid to the production entity. The production entity will pay for manufacturing, mechanicals, artist royalties, and promotion and will, of course, cover all of their overhead. In the case of a small label like yours, the production entity will be you, as you will have paid for all of the manufacturing and packaging of your product. While this may sound like a prayer answered by heaven, know that this type of deal is not for a novice. P&D deals are difficult to obtain because you will have to come to the distributor with a "story" to sell.

Reportedly, executives of West Coast labels like Death Row and Ruthless Records were smart and savvy enough to sign P&D deals to maintain most of the profits themselves. Death Row founder Suge Knight often explains, "Why should we do all the work and give the record company or distributor all of the profits?" Knight, although often criticized, undoubtedly changed the landscape of West Coast distribution and business deals with distributors. He signed a number of artists like Dr. Dre, Tupac, Snoop Dogg, and even MC Hammer to his label. With his profit participation, he was able to maintain a larger percentage for Death Row and then pay the artists from his company's profits.

SELLING YOUR STORY

Distributors look for records that have a story behind them. Not a story in the traditional fairy tale sense, but a solid history of growth in sales, promotion, and marketing. Distributors want to know that your artists have a rock-solid audience who is going to go out and buy your records. They also want to know that your artists are going to continue to grow in popularity. Distributors do look to the label to see that the label is going to provide the support the album needs to succeed. One of the first things larger distributors look at is whether your label has financing or a strong financial portfolio. They need to know that you have the money to invest in the album before they do so. They look at the packaging and design of the product and the advertising strategies, and they want to be able to see that the label knows its market and how to reach it.

One major distribution executive pointed out that his distribution company looks for "all of the factors that make a label great, from creative packaging to creative ideas of advertising along with great music." The distributor also wants to "work with people who are determined to be successful and have the wherewithal of the experience in addition to the money to achieve success in a marketplace that's really dominated by the major record companies."

Before you start shopping your albums to distributors, put together a marketing plan and present your promotional strategies to them. Be realistic in your expectations, and be honest with yourself before you begin soliciting bigger distributors. Make sure your marketing plan matches the size and scope of the distributor you are targeting. For a national distributor, you will need to come to the table with a national marketing campaign.

Another important component of presenting your product to a distributor is to create a one-sheet. A one-sheet is a promotional instrument that is one page in length and describes your product. Your one-sheet should include information about your artist or group, a description of their music, excerpts of reviews that have been published about your artist, as well as a list of other press publications, a list of tour dates (both those in the recent past and the future, so that the distributor gets an idea of where your artist is known), radio spins, and any other promotional information that will persuade the distributor or retailer to carry your product. (When presenting your one-sheet, also be sure to provide the distributor with extra copies, because they like to use them as a marketing tool when selling your CDs to retailers.)

THE STANDARD DISTRIBUTION AGREEMENT

A year ago, we recorded gospel legend James Hall's album at Foxwoods Resort. We realized for Hall this would be the first time we self-financed his album and looked for a "standard distribution agreement." Says Hall: "I have recorded several albums over the years, but this time I wanted to record the album independently and seek a distribution agreement after we mastered the album." Hall admitted that when he was a young artist, he did not understand the importance of having good distribution.

A good distribution agreement should assure both sides a profitable participation when the record sells well in the marketplace. These agreements can vary in some ways but should contain some standard language. For example, most distribution agreements usually consist of the following terms:

- Term: Almost every agreement in the record business has a term. A term is the length of time the agreement will be binding. Most distribution agreements carry a term of about two years and may also provide several option periods that would extend the contract.

- Distributor obligations: The agreement will usually specify what services the distributor is required to provide you. In our example, the distributor agrees to provide the services of soliciting sales of the product to retailers, fulfilling orders placed by retailers, processing order returns (which everyone dreads), and billing and collecting records shipped to retailers. If you have discussed other possible services, make sure that these are also outlined in the agreement.

- Territory: The agreement will also address what territory the distributor is supposed to cover. This can be a critical term for your regional distributors. Make sure this term is clear and that the territory is limited to the area you negotiated. You don't want your regional distributor to stake a claim on regions in which they are not developed when you can work with another distributor who is more established in that area. Also, it is important to clarify from the onset whether the territory will be worldwide or just in the United States.

- Exclusivity: Most distributors will require an exclusive agreement that will prevent you from working with another distributor, especially in the same region. This is why it is important to make all of the terms in your agreement clear before you become stuck with one distributor who does not fulfill your needs.

- Distribution fees: The contract will also outline how much the distributor will receive for sales, or how much the label will receive for sales. The fee section might also address how accounting is done and how often payments are made.

- Reserves: Almost all distribution companies hold onto reserves. Reserves are monies a distributor owes the label for sales but withhold while awaiting the return of product sold to retailers. Make sure that the distributors reserve policy or "open invoice" policy is disclosed in your agreement so that you can know when you will be paid.

- Label obligations: The agreement will also outline the label's responsibilities during the course of the agreement. These obligations primarily refer to the label insuring the quality and legal soundness of the product being distributed. The distributor wants to make sure that it is not held responsible for bad dealings by the label and that it is not responsible for royalty payments to third parties. The label is therefore responsible for paying royalties to its artists, costs of promotion and marketing, recording and production costs, costs of manufacturing and packaging, and mechanical royalties.

- Representatives and warranties: Similar to guaranteeing that it will pay its artists, the label must also guarantee that the product will not violate any right of any person and that it has obtained all of the necessary licenses it needs to record, manufacture, and sell the product.

- Termination: The agreement will also cover what will happen in the event of a termination and under what circumstances a party may seek to terminate.

- Free goods: The contract will specify the quantity of product the label is required to deliver for promotion. Distributors like to have extra copies of an album on hand to help promote it. Promotional albums usually need to have the UPC barcode punched or drilled so that they cannot be resold in the retail market.

When you are presented with any distribution agreements, always read through them carefully. It is in your best interest to consult an attorney before signing anything such as a distribution agreement. The attorney can help you to avoid tricky clauses that could set you back. Make sure that your agreement with your distributor represents the terms that you expected and agreed upon. The distributor may not adhere to them strictly, so stay on top of your distributor. Also, try to keep track of sales, and negotiate how many records you send out to them before you send them to avoid costly future returns. If you are interested in seeing a sample contract or distribution agreement, please visit our website at www.thisbusinessofurbanmusic.com.

CHAPTER 12

**Bring the Noise:
Building a Studio**

"Without a good studio, it's hard to make quality music."
—TONY DOFAT, BAD BOY RECORDS PRODUCER AND HITMAN

A few years ago, MTV introduced a TV show called *Making the Band*, a popular program that featured an unknown group that signed to Bad Boy Records and put together an album in a state-of-the art studio. Led by a team of producers and record executive Harve Pierre, the young singers were guided into several studios, including the Hit Factory and Daddy's House studio in New York. These two studios have an incredible reputation for producing hits, and the studios likely cost millions to build and use (if you are an artist or label needing such). However, the days of needing a million-dollar studio to produce an album are coming to an end. In today's high-tech age, it is possible to build a studio for a lot less and still have the same quality.

"I built a studio in my home and still had quality mastering and recording," explains super-hot producer Nate Clemons, who worked with Mary J. Blige, Tyrese, and Dru Hill. Clemons, a native of Bridgeport, Connecticut, who relocated and built a studio in Raleigh, North Carolina, recorded dozens of projects in his home studio before moving out to a more commercial establishment. Nevertheless, he notes, "I only moved due to the heavy traffic coming to my home, not so much the quality of the equipment. It was just better for my family to take my studio business and recording projects to a commercial building, given the countless hours of recording. You can easily build your home studio and accomplish the same goals sound-wise and product-wise."

Since the days of Motown, the process of recording an album has changed dramatically. There was once a time when you had to rent or otherwise utilize a facility owned by the record label. Both methods were very costly, and an artist would spend thousands, if not millions, on the recording, depending on the nature of the project. However, the newest craze is building a recording studio of your own. Once you have your record label set up and ready to cater to artists, you should consider building a recording studio as well.

By operating your own studio you will save money when recording artists use your studio and generate extra cash flow. You can also ensure that the quality of the recording is up to your standards. Explained Derrick "DOA" Allen, an owner of the Designated Hitters production team and bass player for Lionel Richie, "Nowadays, with your own studio, you can deliver quality and a great record without compromising the artist's album." In this chapter we will discuss how to create your own recording studio as well as the advantages and disadvantages of building one for use with your artists.

In the early 1990s, it was common for urban artists to use studios in Manhattan like Daddy's House, Battery Park, or Quad Studios. I remember working with producer Donald Lawrence sitting behind the board of Battery Park on the west side in Manhattan producing Hezekiah Walker and the Love Fellowship Tabernacle Choir. This, like all studios, would charge an artist the room rate, plus engineering costs and any other incidental costs. It was not uncommon for an artist to see his recording costs rise to the level of six figures for the use of a top studio.

In hindsight, looking at the recording fees and expenses of the Love Fellowship album, I would advise the group and Lawrence to set up their own studios. So much has changed since Russell Simmons and Def Jam collaborated with CBS and Sony to establish hip-hop as a force for decades to come. On the gospel side, a lot has changed since the days of signing with Malaco Records or Benson Records and using its studios for your recording.

Now, one can set up a home recording studio, sometimes called a digital audio workstation, or DAW. Hezekiah Walker has a choir, so he most likely could create this kind of studio at his Brooklyn-based church facility. In addition, he would have saved thousands of dollars in studio time paid to Battery Park and its sister company Verity/Zomba/BMG for the recording costs.

This process of building a recording studio is the smart way to go for any artist or small label constantly in need of a studio. A gospel artist like Hezekiah Walker has probably spent over $500,000 in studio costs during the past ten years of recording. That same money could have been used to build the DAW discussed below. "Without a doubt, owning your own studio is the best way to go," says Tony Dofat, one of Diddy's legendary hitmen producers.

THE TECHNICAL STUFF

It's a little technical, but simply put, a digital audio workstation converts analog audio vocals and sounds from a musical instrument into a digital file that gets stored onto the computer's hard drive. It then provides editing, mixing, and mastering options for your song. Apple and Yamaha provide customer support in setting up the DAW. When building your studio, choose a computer that is equipped to satisfy your demands and the industry standards. For example, Apple Macs have become the professional recording industry standard. Macs are easy to set up, but they are costly. The Mac system is designed to have an inexperienced user utilize the program instantly. In the alternative, PCs are more affordable, but they require more work with the audio.

The boom in technology and the decrease in technological costs have made recording a song of commercially acceptable quality a possibility for the "little guy." It used to be that to record an album of radio quality, an artist would have to fly across the country to a state-of-the-art recording studio that cost millions of dollars to install. For example, the girls in the girl group on *Making the Band* find themselves in South Beach, Miami, at the Hit Factory. However, I shutter to think what the cost will be when they get their first royalty statement and see the costs of studio time and housing in Miami. Imagine if one group member had her own quality recording studio, or at least thinks to build a DAW before the second project.

BUILDING YOUR OWN RECORDING STUDIO

If you ask any major producer, he or she will tell you there are numerous advantages, as well as disadvantages, to having your own studio. In the following pages, we discuss some of the key factors on both sides of the spectrum.

ADVANTAGES

There are a number of factors to consider in building and owning your own studio, including but not limited to the following:

- No recording time limitations
- Saving money on studio rentals
- Privacy afforded when recording
- Spontaneity when you need to write or record
- Rental of studio for revenue

No Recording-Time Limitations. The most obvious advantage to owning your own studio is the lack of time constraints. When you pay for the use of Daddy's House or Quad Studios or Battery Park, you pay by the hour in most cases. Each hour can be up to hundreds of dollars. If you own the studio, there are no time limitations when recording or writing songs. As we all know, recording an album can be a long endeavor. It is not uncommon for artists to spend weeks or even months in the recording studio, often up to twenty hours per day. This is how a top R&B or hip-hop album can cost millions to record in studio time with a host of top-notch engineers, songwriters, and producers present.

For this reason, many artists, at the behest of their financial advisors, will rush through the recording process and sometimes come out with a mediocre product that could be improved by extra time in the studio. When you own your own studio, your artist can work "from home" in an environment that allows him to have the freedom to work at his own pace.

For years, Michael Jackson would record material at his Neverland enclave before delivering the final project to Sony. For Jackson it may have been for privacy or creative reasons. In any case, it allowed him to work unregulated by time and studio limitations a commercial facility might create (not that the lavish-spending Jackson would care anyway).

If you are a singer or songwriter, you spend the majority of your time in the studio either writing or recording songs. If you are a producer you may spend most of your time in the studio arranging and producing an album. In either scenario, thousands of dollars are spent on the use of a professional studio. However, if you own your own studio it will not cost nearly as much. Moreover, the artist or producer can concentrate more of his time on his craft without worrying about wasting time in a studio session. As a result, the artist or producer will not rush a project simply to avoid spending long hours, and big dollars, in a professional studio. Having your studio allows an artist the freedom to finish recording a song or to record a song several times on his terms until he or she believes the product is acceptable. Obviously, this delivers a better final product for the store shelves and hopefully sales.

Privacy. Your own studio also provides privacy for your artists. Many top-notch artists prefer to utilize a private studio versus a public or commercial studio because privacy means they are less likely to run into fans. A private studio is more preferred for a certain clientele. Artists are peculiar people, and any nuance can distract their recording or writing. A private environment can make the most of their creative gifts.

Accessibility. Having your own studio also provides you round-the-clock accessibility. I remember Kerry Gordy spending countless late nights in his home studio working with various Los Angeles artists. You can use a private studio any time you wish without having to schedule an appointment. You can leave as late as you want, and you don't have to hear the studio manager inform you the session is over.

Spontaneity. Songwriter Stephen Hurd once told me he was in an airport when a hit song came to him and he had to get somewhere to write it down. It ultimately went on his top-selling album using a top studio and paying for that studio, because he did not own his own facility. Spontaneity is important for many writers and producers, thus a studio of your own gives you that oft-needed quiet place to write down your ideas and thoughts; they come in the most unexpected moments.

Many artists or producers need to be inspired to create a song. Having a studio allows the artist or producer to enter the studio quickly when they feel inspired or if they have an idea that they wish to put in writing. Although some rock 'n' roll bands have written down their inspired lyrics on cocktail napkins, better product comes from professionalism. When an artist is inspired at 4 AM on a Tuesday while watching reruns of a favorite movie on HBO, he can go into his private studio and record a masterpiece.

If you are an aspiring artist who does not have a lot of money, you can save a significant amount of money recording at your own studio. For one, when recording your demo, you do not want to spend an excessive amount of money. You may want to start practicing at your home studio and then figure out which songs are suitable for the demo.

Rental Income from Studio. If you do not have a lot of artists signed to your label yet, or you feel that you will not get a lot of use out of your new recording studio, don't worry; there are other ways to recoup your investment. You can rent out your studio to other artists who are not signed to your label or to any label. There is a demand by artists for affordable professional-quality recording space. For example, artists trying to put together demo packages who are not yet signed to labels need a place to record their first few songs. Renting a recording studio can run between $45 and $1,000 an hour, depending on where the studio is located and how many staff members or engineers you need in the studio for your recording. The rule of thumb is that one minute of recording time equals an hour and a half of studio time. The good thing about renting your recording studio to third parties is that you can market your services to a wide range or artists.

Although you may represent urban and gospel musicians on your label, you can rent studio time to a wide range of artists, which will increase your target market beyond a narrow niche. Diddy, Destiny's Child, and Marilyn Manson have all used the same recording studio, which means that any number of musicians can use your studio.

DISADVANTAGES

There are a number of disadvantages to consider in building and owning your own studio, including but not limited to the following:

✦ Noise problems
✦ Safety concerns
✦ Costs
✦ Engineer costs
✦ Equipment cost

Noise Problems. Depending on where the studio is located and if your studio is soundproofed, you may have noise complaints from neighbors. Because of these complaints, you may only be able to use your equipment during the daytime. On the other hand, you can help yourself in several ways. You can invest in a home on a large parcel of land. With no neighbors for several acres, you will be free to record anytime, day or night. I can barely hear the sounds from my neighbor's studio; and even when I hear them, it's only when he is recording a large band. The other option is to use soundproof material in the construction of your studio. Although soundproof material works wonders, it can be hazardous. The epic fire that killed over one hundred people at Rhode Island's Station nightclub in February 2003 was caused by highly flammable soundproofing material.

Safety Concerns. Once again, this brings us to the issue of safety. If you are using the studio as a business to generate income, you will have strangers entering your home to utilize your studio. You will need some type of insurance for purposes of liability in the event someone is hurt. You should take the same precautions as you would when having any other strangers in your home.

Require individuals to provide some references, proof of income, and some historical data prior to allowing them to use your studio, whether at home or otherwise. Make sure you know who is coming into your studio as best as possible to avoid any future problems. It is less likely that a well-known studio will have problems, as most of its clientele are the artists referred by the record label backing them. However, if you survey some of the major New York studios, they will share a horror story or two on damage done to their studios by some of the major artists, funded by major labels.

Costs. Indeed, in the long run it is profitable to have your own studio, but some of the costs associated with running a studio can be quite high. You can spend an excessive amount of money in overhead expenses such as electrical bills and updating software, not to mention rent. In today's housing market, rent can be astronomical, especially if you desire a prime location for your studio space. I will discuss the importance of location momentarily. Remember that when rent is high, even if you don't own your own studio, you will be paying somewhere along the way. If you choose to rent studio time, your cost will reflect the real estate cost, but you will be paying rent for someone else's benefit, not for your own studio.

Engineers. If you are not an engineer, you will need to hire an engineer to assist in the mixing and mastering of your recordings. This can be a costly endeavor as well. As you may know from personal experience, it is expensive to hire a professional of any variety. On the bright side, you would have had to pay for the services of an engineer, even if that cost was hidden to you if you chose to rent studio space.

Equipment. Another disadvantage that is related to cost is the issue of equipment. Not only should you attempt to have the latest equipment, but it needs to be maintained. If equipment no longer works, you must spend additional monies to replace the broken or outdated items. This isn't meant to scare you, or to say that you can only have a successful studio if you have $1 million worth of equipment, but you should think carefully about the items you invest in. Do not buy some discount microphones from a 1970s estate sale; recording standards have changed. Also, do not buy equipment that is not of professional quality, as discussed later in this chapter.

Location. I previously mentioned the location of your studio is as important as the location of a home. As real estate agents say, location, location, location! Your studio does not have to be in an area with great schools and relaxed lease laws, but it does have to be in an area that is appealing and easily accessible to recording artists. If you live forty minutes off a major highway and the only way to access your house is by a bridge that has a tendency to get rained out, you may want to reconsider building a recording studio in your basement, because no one will show up. A good place for a studio is in a metropolitan area, or close to one where recording artists come for the dream of attaining fame. Your studio does not have to be in New York or Nashville, but it should not be in East of Nowhere, either.

STUDIO AND EQUIPMENT

Although recording studios have become fairly inexpensive to own and operate, there are still industry standards that you should follow. You don't have to have more than one recording space, but there should be a control room for each recording space you have. It is entirely up to you how large or small to make the recording space, but if you plan to record gospel choirs, make sure that the room can fit a choir. Remember that the size of the room and the height of the ceiling will influence the sound of the recording. When setting up a studio, you want to find a location that is free from excessive noise, echo, and a tendency to call attention to certain frequencies. For example, you do not want to have your studio equipment set up in a tiled room, nor do you want it in a carpeted room that absorbs high frequencies but emphasizes bass tones. It is ideal to have a room that is irregularly shaped accompanied by a mix of hard and soft surfaces.

You will also want to have isolation booths where one musician can record. Isolation booths are convenient for recording single instruments and should be big enough to house a piano or drum set. You will also want to provide your musicians with at least some equipment. A good place to start is with the drum set, since stage drums and studio drums are different.

Generally when recording, a CD, DAT, or computer-based recording will produce better quality than the old TDK cassette from back in the day. While you may want to offer cassette recordings as a novelty to outside clients, remember to record your record label clients on CD or DAT or the best technology at the time of your recording. The necessary equipment needed to record are microphones, headphones, monitors, microphone preamps, compressors, synthesizers, console, a computer with plug-ins (Macs are superior to PCs for creative endeavors), and a recording system such as Pro Tools®. I will discuss these technological requirements momentarily.

You should also create a website to list your floor plan, gear list, and specific breakdown of equipment. For example, if you click online and look at a top-notch studio, the website will show you their facilities and the gear list. It might provide something like the following (for you tech heads):

- 80 Input SSL 9000J Console
- Pultec (EQP-1, EQP-1A, MEQ-S, EQH-2x2)
- Universal Audio (LA-2Ax2)
- DBX—902 x2
- Drawmer (Dual Gate)
- API 550x4
- Yamaha—SPX 90, REV-7
- Lexicon—480L; 224xL, PCM-70, PCM-42x4
- Eventide H3500
- Roland Stereo Flanger
- Apogee
- Sony pCM-r500
- Alesis Master Link
- Tascam 122 MKII

This is just a sample state-of-the-art equipment listing (currently). You should make sure your gear list fits the hottest brands of the moment if you plan to offer your studio commercially for others. Explains top urban producer Sanchez Harley (Aretha Franklin and Shirley Caesar): "The gear list is critical when you look at whether a studio can meet the demands of your artists."

EDITING SOFTWARE

As you engage in building a studio, you must choose editing software. Most producers, both experienced and inexperienced, are using the popular software named Pro Tools®. This software allows you to cut and paste snippets and alter subpar sound recordings to produce a flawless piece of work. In one recent *USA Today* article, the owner of Pro Tools estimated that its product was used in at least 90 percent of all popular-music recording. Along with Pro Tools, there is other software, such as Cubase (for Macs or PCs), Sonar (for PCs only) and Logic (for Macs only). These four programs allow you to record audio, edit, mix, add effects, and create a master copy. In essence, you can make a gospel record at home that sounds as good as Fred Hammond's top-selling album or a hip-hop record that competes with Kanye West.

Here is a more affordable option to build your home recording studio for less than one thousand dollars. The first thing you will need is software. For example, Ecasound is a popular command-line sound recorder and processor. This software is used to record and playback tracks. When mastering a song you can use one of the following three pieces of software: Audacity, Ardour, or Ecasound. Audacity is entry level and is claimed to be easy to understand, yet powerful. Next, you will need hardware, preferably hardware that is equipped to store an excessive amount of data, such as a CPU with a dual-processor. To build a recording studio of maximum quality, you can buy an external analog-digital converter. However, the most inexpensive solution is to use a sound card. Finally, you need to purchase a microphone and position it near your amplifier or instrument or be able to plug your instrument directly into the sound card. Another option for sound card is to purchase a USB box, such as the Emagic 2/6, or to get a PCI card, such as the RME Hammerfall line or the Delta line. For a home recording studio, a full duplex sound card that comes with your computer, along with at least a 2.4 series Linux kernel and full-duplex sound card drivers, will be adequate.

Similar to software selection is the selection of the microphone brand that you install in your studio. A studio is not complete unless it has a microphone, and many artists will want the top of the line. Funny enough, when Luther Vandross died, *VIBE* magazine reported that his mother had his favorite microphone, the Sony 800 G, standing in front of his casket. He would apparently only record when using this microphone and brought it with him to his recording sessions.

Depending on your current budget you can get an affordable microphone for about one to two hundred dollars, plus sixty dollars for a cable and stand. (If you are like Luther Vandross, you can spend five thousand dollars and get his Sony 800 G.) The standard microphones used for live performances are Shure microphones. These mics are excellent for recording with limited money. An alternative are Condenser microphones, which are mainly for recording.

INTERFACE AND MIXERS

If you are a technology nut, you are totally enjoying this chapter by now. However, if you're not, it all sounds foreign to you. So, when we talk about "interface," you will be even more lost. Here is the simplest way to understand it. PreSonus Firepod, MOTU, Yamaha, or Digidesign, among others, make a device called an "interface."

The interface preamplifies the audio signal, converts it to a digital file, and transfers it to the hard drive for editing. In other words, the audio interface allows the sound to transmit into the computer. When you have installed your interface equipment you will need software for it. A good place to start is Cubase LE, which you can download on PreSonus's website (www.presonus.com).

For a more professional studio, you may want to invest in a mixer and studio monitors. A mixer provides power to your microphones and allows you to adjust levels and tweak equalization. The cost of a mixer can vary depending on its options, such as the number of channels, digital features, and quality of the electronics.

You can then connect keyboards, samplers, and other musical devices to the mixer. Once you have your microphone set up with your mixer equipment, you can adjust levels. This is very critical to the final mastered product that you produce for sale or distribution.

MONITORS

Other important pieces of equipment that you may want to invest in are studio monitors. Stereo monitors are designed to accurately reflect the recorded material. They are supposed to reproduce sound evenly and should accurately reflect your recording. The quality of your mixes can rely on the accurate monitoring of the sounds. Inexpensive monitors can give you an inaccurate mixing sound.

OVERVIEW

You are now ready to record your first artist. You can record songs of artists that are signed to your label or advertise the services of your recording studio to the public. A good place to start is the Internet. As stated previously, make a website for your studio and advertise your equipment and what services you can offer. With just a few artists, hopefully you can make your investment back in no time.

CHAPTER 13

Final Thoughts on Running and Maintaining a Record Label

"The key to the music business is building good relationships, nurturing talent, and understanding that it's a business first and foremost."
—LARKIN ARNOLD, FORMER CBS EXECUTIVE
AND EXECUTIVE PRODUCER OF *THRILLER*

In this chapter, we look at a top label executive, L. A. Reid, one of the premier music men in the industry, whose career epitomizes how to successfully run and maintain not just his LaFace label but also three others that are well known worldwide. Reid is known as a very smart executive who understands Business 101 in leading a label.

In the late 1980s, music legend Clarence Avant, a pioneer of so many things in black music and former chairman of Motown records, called the "Godfather" by most current black execs, arranged the 50/50 joint venture with Reid's LaFace Records and Arista that gave Reid his first major start in operating a label. That joint venture would yield over thirty-five number-one hits and millions of dollars in revenue for Arista and its parent company, BMG. Avant has always described Reid as one of the smartest people in the music business.

As a result of the phenomenal success of LaFace, Reid would be called in to take over Arista in the initial awkward retirement-demotion of music man and Arista Records founder Clive Davis, who was president and CEO at the time. At the time of hiring Reid, then BMG president and CEO Strauss Zelnick proudly exclaimed, "there were no other candidates. L. A. has a wonderful style, he's comfortable with the artists, and they respect him." BMG acquired Arista in 1979, and in 2000, Reid came in and continued the successful run for Arista, discovering and furthering the careers of Pink, Usher, and Avril Lavigne.

As a result of accepting the Arista post, Reid sold the remaining 50-percent interest of LaFace records to BMG for a reported $100 million after a ten-year run that dominated the music industry with hit after hit by Toni Braxton, TLC, Usher, and Babyface, among so many others. There were soundtracks to tons of movie hits like *Soul Food* and *Waiting to Exhale* under the LaFace Records banner. If Babyface is considered the "Paul McCartney songwriter of this generation," as L. A. Reid called him at a recent BMI awards program, then Reid himself would be the Berry Gordy executive of this generation.

Using many of the principles in the first few chapters of this book, Reid ran the LaFace operation with a business savvy uncommon for this generation. He found a way to keep budgets controlled, studio costs manageable, and most important, he maintained a wonderful relationship with the most important people: the artists. As he told *Black Enterprise* magazine at the time, "My job is to identify stars, find hits, and form relationships with creative people." Even during Toni Braxton's fight with LaFace and her ultimate embarrassing lawsuit, Reid managed to calm the storm, keep Braxton with the label, and even gain positive endorsement from Braxton in his move to Arista.

While Clive Davis ran Arista and the variety of labels that fell under its umbrella, it was the Reid's LaFace brand that delivered 50 million albums sold for Davis's midtown Manhattan label. When Reid took over Arista, he went from about fifteen artists under his helm to nearly sixty stateside and worldwide.

In the next five years, while leading Arista, Reid's hot streak would only continue, with two best selling albums for Usher and Outkast. Along with hit albums from Avril Lavigne and Pink, Usher and Outkast would sell over 25 million singles and albums, bringing in about $300 million in for the label, not to mention the monies brought in from publishing income as BMG publishing continued to grow.

Recalling when he took the job, Reid said "my guess is that I have about six months to make a difference, as opposed to the three to five years most CEOs get." Reid became one of the few African Americans to ever hold such a powerful position in the music industry. Only Sylvia Rhone had ever successfully managed such a high-powered position at a major label, and she endorsed the growing success of Reid and his ability to successfully lead Arista.

In 2005, despite his great success and track record, Reid was ousted at Arista, but he did not sit unemployed long. The once-top hip-hop label on the planet quickly grabbed Reid to come run the now-ailing Island Def Jam, home of past and present hip-hop superstars like LL Cool J, the Beastie Boys, and Public Enemy. Some questioned whether Reid's suave, smooth style could finesse and motivate the gritty street artists on Def Jam's roster. For example, while Russell Simmons applauded Reid for his accomplishments, he did express reservations at the time as to whether Reid could understand the culture of the rap label he helped co-found. Simmons openly wondered if Reid lived the life or could relate to Method Man, Beanie Seagel, Jay-Z, and Memphis Bleak, telling *Newsweek*, "I'm with rappers every day. Managing them is a cultural process . . . these are the things that made Def Jam."

Reid may not have hung with rappers all day in the ATL (Atlanta) while running LaFace, but his track record for good management and solid operation of a record label for the prior twenty years encouraged Universal, the parent company of Island Def Jam, to persuade him to run the label. And, wise as usual, Reid brought in an executive to head up Def Jam and get the once-powerful label back on its feet.

Reid pulled in hip-hop king Shawn "Jay-Z" Carter to help him run Def Jam, calling Carter "a genius." Reid also swiftly negotiated a deal to buy out Carter and Damion Dash's Roc-A-Fella Records. Reid was quickly reorganizing the Def Jam brass and reestablishing the once-powerful brand to its rightful place atop the Hip-Hop Nation.

Now that you've got your label up and running, it's time to take care of business and ensure that your label is here to stay. For purposes of this chapter, we zoomed in on L. A. Reid of LaFace, Arista, and Def Jam success. Here are six core concepts that you should take away from this chapter and the Reid story to help your label or company:

♦ Accounting

♦ Paying artist royalties

♦ Promotion

♦ Producing hits

♦ Dealing with artists

♦ Manufacturing CDs

ACCOUNTING

Accounting is a key element to keeping your record company successful. You must keep good records from the time you start up your label to avoid any encounters with tax problems and to keep up on your cash flow. Having good financial records can also help you troubleshoot and find areas where you are spending too much and help you allocate funds to more important areas of development. Make sure you record expenses and revenues, keep receipts, and issue receipts where applicable, then try to keep all of this information organized. If you are able to, hire an accountant to keep track of your finances.

If, in the beginning, you have to go it alone on your accounting, keep it simple. There are lots of budgeting and accounting software programs available. QuickBooks, Quicken, and Microsoft Money can all help you keep track of your revenue and expenses. You can also use accounting paper or ledgers that are available at most local office supply stores. Keep your receipts, write down all of your transactions (incoming and outgoing), and try to sit down from time to time and figure out how you're doing.

Daylle Deanna Schwartz, author of *Start and Run Your Own Record Label*, uses a ledger to keep track of her accounting. She says:

"I keep a column for each type of expense: manufacturing, advertising, printing, office supplies, mailing and shipping, phone, transportation, etc. Each check number is listed in the left column and I put the amount spent in the column it fits into. If a check covers more than one type of expense, I write each figure into the appropriate column next to the check number. Periodically, I tabulate totals to see how my expenses are running in relation to my income. At the end of the year, I total the columns and give the figures to my accountant so that he can file my income tax forms.

"When an invoice is paid by a store or distributor, I write the invoice number on the left and have a column in my ledger for each title. If a title's out in more than one format, I have separate columns for that title under CDs, records, and cassettes. I find it helpful to include the numbers of products sold and the amount received. When I get returns on products that have already been paid for, I list them in the appropriate column and deduct them."

Schwartz also recommends that if you need to pay cash for one or several expenses, pay cash out of your own pocket, then reimburse yourself with a check from your label. That will make accounting for cash expenses much easier on you.

Create a cash flow budget. Failure to monitor cash flow can lead to cash shortages. Or a company that keeps too much money in the petty-cash drawer for emergencies can potentially deprive your company of the opportunity to expand. A cash flow budget can allow you to accurately monitor cash needs, time cash disbursements, and plan ahead for cash shortfalls. In addition, the company is able to allocate cash to meet specific requirements.

Accounting and maintaining a company bank account is also important for building your company's credit. Credit is an essential factor for getting bank financing. Borrowing from a bank will help you to receive the funding you need to take the next step toward running your dream record company.

Notice in our Reid example, it was widely reported that he understood the business side and importance of understanding the books. His 50 million records sold at LaFace kept the doors opened in Atlanta for nearly twelve years, and his $300 million gross revenue for Arista showed his business savvy. You must do the same.

PAYING ARTIST ROYALTIES

Royalties are typically paid twice a year, or semiannually, on December 31 and June 30. For each of these periods, you must prepare a statement of earnings for them based on the amount of royalties they have earned under their contract. Compute the royalties based on the number of sales under the agreement, minus all deductions permitted under the agreement. In doing so, you can recoup all of your recoupable expenses based on that figure. Deduct your recoupables, so that you can earn back some of the money that you have expended on your artist.

When Toni Braxton sued LaFace, her main contention was that an album that sold over 10 million records did not pay her a single royalty. TLC would later claim bankruptcy and a poor payment of royalties by the label. Owing to Reid's practical understanding, these artists worked out their deals and stayed with the label. However, the damage done to the brand and litigation costs as well as overall negative publicity did not help the label and hindered its growth at one stage in the 1990s.

It is critical to establish a regular system of paying royalties or sending out royalty statements if the artist is unsecured and no payments are due for that quarter. Make sure the statements are accurate and fully detailed and account for all sales, minus returns and reserves, as we discussed in Chapter Two.

If you can, hire an accountant or a bookkeeper to help you with royalty statements. You do not have to keep him on your staff, or even keep using him year after year, but if you can get someone experienced to help you run through the books the first few times until you get a better financial understanding, you will be the better for it, and your accounting will be more accurate. This will help you and your artists in the long run.

PROMOTION

Promotion is a constant in the music industry. It is vital to growing your company and getting the word about your artists out there. As discussed in Chapter Seven, it is important to have a marketing plan for your company as well as for each album your record label releases. Several promotion avenues will lead to getting your name recognized as an authority in the industry. Your marketing plan should integrate each of these avenues, and each avenue should reinforce one another to achieve the fullest potential of your marketing plan.

PUBLICITY

Publicity, the "PR" component of your marketing plan, is the promotion you get through reporters and critics writing articles and reviews about your artists and your label. Or even better, getting mentioned in news segments on television or radio. It is important that you build and maintain a list of media contacts whom you can send press releases to as well as new albums as they are released. If it's in your budget, you should also consider hiring a PR consultant to assist you with getting your name and your artists out into the media.

Street Promotion. Getting the word out on the street about new artists is essential. Street promotion leading up to CD releases and concerts can really start a buzz about your artist. Print up flyers about upcoming shows and stickers for your artists. You'll want to distribute these at local clubs or hot restaurants where you know people go who will listen to your music or go to other concerts for similar artists. Try starting a street team of fans who support your artists to go to shows and clubs to hand out stickers, flyers, CDs, and even merchandise for you. Street teamers usually work for rewards like concert tickets, T-shirts, and CDs, and you can continually add street team members to your roster and meet them at shows.

ADVERTISING

As your artists become more established, taking out ads in industry magazines or on the radio to announce the release of a new album or major tour can be a good idea. You'll want to focus your ads on publications and programs where your artist's name might be recognized, which is why you should wait until your artist is established to launch an extensive advertising campaign.

WEB PROMOTION

Maintaining your website is an important part of promotion. Not only do you want to tell people about your label, but also you need to give them access to all of your artists and information about touring. If your artists have their own websites, or if you've decided to help them host one, make sure they incorporate a tour schedule, biography information, pictures, and, of course, music samples. Other popular ideas for enhancing a website are adding a blog for your artists to write about what they're doing and discussion boards for fans to share information. Your artists can even drop in and answer questions or post some thoughts. You also should set up an online storefront to sell CDs and merchandise. My longtime business associate Richard Byrd designs dozens of websites each year and insisted that I establish one. Explained Byrd, "without a website, an artist or business loses a certain marketing opportunity."

MERCHANDISING

A lucrative way to complement your promotional strategies is by creating an inventory of merchandise. What is great about merchandising is that fans pay for items that help you promote your artists, and it gives you an additional revenue stream. Merchandise can include T-shirts, stickers, posters, buttons, and just about anything you can think of. You should create these items for each of your artists to promote their concerts and CD releases.

LIVE PERFORMANCES AND APPEARANCES

Concerts and tours are a great way to reach new fans. There is no better way to show a new audience your stuff than by having your artists perform for them! Help your artists to perform as much as possible, and be sure to prepare for each concert by promoting each upcoming show. Teaming your artists up with popular local artists is another great way to promote your artist, your brand, and to reach a new audience. You can also have your artist appear in stores and other venues to reinforce CD releases or other big events or concerts.

PRODUCING HITS

The key to success in the music business is hits. Without hits on the charts, a label is invisible, and probably struggling. Take for instance P. Diddy's Bad Boy Records. Bad Boy hit its commercial peak in 1997 and had a brief period where it lost the flavor of hits from the likes of 112, Biggie, Craig Mack, and Carl Thomas. Many of its once-hot acts eventually vacated the label, while those who remained witnessed their sales fading. The label lost its relationship with Arista as the major partner and distributor. After a stint with Universal as a distributor, the label eventually ended up with Warner Music Group owning a major stake. At one point, the word on the street was that Bad Boy Records was done, but as Diddy always exclaimed, "I thought I told you that we won't stop [making hits]," and cranked out more hits. Behind the great minds of Diddy, Harve Pierre, the Howard-trained pulse of the label, and Derek Ferguson, the savvy Harvard-trained executive, the company returned to its 1990s success and stormed back in recent years with hits from Danity Kane, Da Band, and Cassie, among others.

When L. A. Reid was offered the helm of Arista and later Def Jam, obviously his track record for hits and music business management were the key. Keeping up-to-date with the times and pushing your artists to make hits can be a challenge even for the music moguls who have been most successful. If you are someone who has more of brain for business than an ear for music, it is worth the investment to consult or hire producers to help develop your artist's sound. Making those connections and having a professional find the strengths in your artist's music will help you find the hits that will make your label successful.

DEALING WITH ARTISTS

When I was in law school, Larkin Arnold came to speak to our law class. He explained what is was like dealing with Michael Jackson, Luther Vandross, Mint Condition, and other groups he worked with during an illustrious career at CBS and Epic and as a law practitioner. One of the key points of his visit was understanding the importance of learning your artist as a label or attorney.

If you are not careful, dealing with artists can be one of the most difficult and taxing parts of the job. Especially as a starter company, often times you end up with artists who are a little big for their britches and believe they're entitled to more than they are capable of financially paying for via their record sales. Needless to say, every artist thinks her music is the best and that she has the next hit, and while it may be true, sometimes it takes a while to convince the rest of the world!

When you sign your artists, lay out your ground rules. Help them have realistic expectations and stay on top of their concerns. Focus on letting your relationship grow and helping them with their music. Let your artists know why you've brought them to your label, and why you want to work with them, but explain that you're there to promote them and develop them as an artist. Artists are very protective of their creative control and generally don't like to be told what to do with their music, especially if it's coming from a non-musician. So, it's important that you let them know that their music will be subject to critiquing and changes—especially if you get them involved with a producer. When working with your artists, keep the lines of communication open. Keep your artists informed on their progress and maintain visibility.

MANUFACTURING CDS

Making sure you have product available to sell is an important part of being in business. No matter what kind of business plan you have, you will need CDs to sell to fans. The size of your budget will determine how you get them. If you have a relatively small budget with some new artists who don't really have their name out there yet, you might want to consider manufacturing their CDs yourself. You will need a burner, some blank CDs, jewel cases, and labels that you can print. A lot of these products can be found at decent prices online.

You can also print up CD inserts to make the CD more professional. If you have a larger budget, there are many companies that offer duplicating services and CD printing. Duplicating services complete with printing, jewel cases, and inserts can cost anywhere from five dollars to seventy-five cents per CD, depending on the quantity that you order. Lots of duplication companies can be found online, or you can check the yellow pages in your area or ask at your local recording studio, who might also offer these services.

If you are working with established artists, and have a larger budget, you can also consider using independent distributors or even major distributors to help you press and distribute your CDs. We discussed distribution in Chapter Eleven.

CLOSING TIPS

You may never be a Larkin Arnold or L. A. Reid; these great music men come once in a lifetime. However, you do have the chance to run and maintain a label, if you learn from the good and bad of those who came before you. If you learn the industry and read everything, you can learn and adopt what works for your company. Trust your instincts and apply Hardcore Business Principles 101 and you will do fine.

In the meantime, make the hits and pay your artists.

PART III

CHAPTER 14

More than a Melody: Understanding Copyright Law

"My songs deal with relationships, and whether they make you happy and whether you are happy with yourself, they are introspective and deal with self-realization."
—LUTHER VANDROSS, LEGENDARY SONGWRITER AND ARTIST

As executive vice president/head of Urban, Creative, West Coast for EMI Music Publishing, Big Jon Platt is arguably the most influential urban music publisher in the world and one of the most important music executives in the industry. Spending as much time in the studio as behind the desk, Platt, in addition to signing some of the biggest artists in music, advises, develops, and nurtures merging and established artists alike. But underneath it all, Platt is a part of a company that handles over a million copyrights worldwide. In the past decade or so, Platt has signed songwriting talents Jay-Z, Kanye West, Usher, Pharrell Williams (of the Neptunes), Young Jeezy, Snoop Dogg, Fabolous, Omarion, and the Ying Yang Twins, among so many others. And, each year, as Platt signs more songwriters, the copyright portfolio grows and grows. "I am always looking for talented songwriters who will write, produce, and develop great music," said Platt in a recent interview for this book. One such writer signed to EMI, with Platt's assistance, is Warryn Campbell (Mary Mary, Yolanda Adams). Campbell explained his trek to EMI in a recent interview: "In my situation, I hadn't had any songs out. I was just an up-and-coming writer and Big Jon signed me to a developmental type of deal to where he [helped] develop me as a writer. He started placing my songs and got me in the studio. He'd send them out and pound the pavement for placement. It took about a year and a half. He was grooming me and coaching me on my writing. But that was a unique situation and not a lot of publishers do that. A lot of them are not willing to take that route. I just happened to be in the right place, at the right time, with the right person. He saw something in me that I didn't see in myself."

There are a number of major publishing executives in urban music, including Richard Blackstone at Warner Bros. and Ethiopia Habtemariam at Universal Publishing. These companies are essentially managing millions of copyrights. Thus, it is important to anyone in the music business to understand the interplay with copyrights. Michael Jackson and his partners at Sony/ATV Music Publishing recently acquired some of the hit songs of Eminem (like the hit "The Real Slim Shady") when Jackson and company purchased Famous Music LLC from Viacom. The purchase granted Jackson the copyright ownership of songs by Eminem, Beck, Shakira, and Bjork. Explained Jackson, keenly aware of the intellectual property value: "The diverse collection of songs in this catalog range from timeless classics to contemporary hits, and I am pleased to add the acquisition . . ."

The public got a taste of copyright law during the Napster fiasco of the late 1990s. Unfortunately, stars like Mariah Carey, Britney Spears, Biz Markie, and Dr. Dre have been sued for copyright infringement; that is, artists using or performing a song in part or in whole that does not belong to them. In this chapter, we will discuss the basic and critical elements of copyright law. First we'll take a brief look at the history of American copyright law, which often differs greatly from copyright law abroad. Then we will discuss other necessary elements of copyright law, such as the methods in which you can copyright, as well as the ever-important work-made-for-hire doctrine.

WHAT IS COPYRIGHT?

Copyright is a form of protection provided by the laws of the United States to the authors of "original works of authorship," including literary, dramatic, musical, artistic, and certain other intellectual works. The most common types of copyrights for musicians lie in musical works, including any accompanying words, dramatic works, accompanying music, pantomimes and choreographic works, and sound recordings. Only expressions that have been recorded or otherwise noted are subject to copyright. This protection is available to both published and unpublished works. The owner of a music copyright generally has the exclusive right to do and to authorize others to do the following:

- Reproduce the work in phonorecords such as CD, cassette, LP, etc.
- Display the work publicly
- Prepare derivative works based on the work, such as songs that sample an earlier song
- Distribute phonorecords of the work to the public by sale or other transfer of ownership, or by rental, lease, or lending
- Perform the work publicly or broadcast an audio transmission.

It is illegal for anyone to violate any of the rights of the owner of copyright provided by the copyright law. This means that copyrighted works cannot be publicly performed by someone who is not the owner. If you hear Mary J. Blige performing another artist's song in concert, someone has to pay that artist for the right to do so under a license. Copyright owners can, however, sell their copyright or lend it at their discretion.

Have you noticed that when you go to popular chain restaurants for your birthday they always have a cleverly revised version of what used to be the "Birthday Song"? This is because the "Birthday Song," the one that you sang as a child, is currently owned by Time Warner. Since Time Warner actively enforces its license of the "Birthday Song," public performance of it is illegal unless a license is obtained from ASCAP.

A work that was created, a CD that was recorded, or sheet music that was written on or after January 1, 1978, is automatically protected from the moment of its creation and is protected for the author's life plus an additional seventy years after the author's death. In the case of co-ownership by two or more writers or composers, the term lasts for seventy years after the last surviving author's death. For works made for hire, the copyright will last for ninety-five years from publication or 120 years from creation, whichever is shorter.

COPYRIGHT INFRINGEMENT AND THE MUSIC INDUSTRY

Those in the world of music take copyright very seriously, as evidenced by the artistic response to free downloading on Napster. Artists were the first in line to bash users of the peer-to-peer sharing program, and the Recording Industry Association of America (RIAA) started a public push to urge consumers to "buy it, don't burn it." The most famous copyright infringement cases, however, involve famous artists who have themselves performed or sampled music that did not belong to them.

For instance, Dr. Dre became enamored with the introduction sound that is played before a movie begins in a theater. The sound, owned by THX, demonstrates the theater's capability to provide surround sound. Dre allegedly asked Lucasfilm, the owners of THX, for permission to use the sound on his song "Lolo," and when Lucas film denied him use of the sound, he sampled it anyway. Subsequently, Lucasfilm filed a lawsuit against Dr. Dre and his labels, Aftermath and Interscope Records.

Mariah Carey was also accused of copyright infringement on several occasions. On one such occasion, a songwriter named Rhonda Dimmie accused Mariah Carey of using "Be Your Own Hero," to which Dimmie claimed she owned the copyright as original songwriter.[4] In that case the court found in favor of Carey because it was determined that neither she nor anyone she associated with could have heard Dimmie's song and thus could not have stolen it.

One of America's landmark copyright cases involved famous Brooklyn rapper Biz Markie. He used a sample of a song by Daniel O'Sullivan. In reviewing copyright law, the judge in his opinion opened with the classic words, "Thou Shalt Not Steal" and went on to find the defendants guilty of copyright infringement. This case set the stage for the rule of sample clearances that many record labels follow today. In essence, when an artist turns a record in, the label will want to ensure that all copyrighted material used has been cleared so the label is not sued for copyright infringement as Biz Markie was. The label will have the artist confirm in writing that any song used on the album that is not a song written by the artist is being used with express permission of the songwriter.

WHO CAN CLAIM COPYRIGHT?

Copyright protection exists from the time the work is created in fixed form, such as written down or recorded. The copyright in the work of authorship immediately becomes the property of the author who created the work. Only the author or those deriving their rights through the author can rightfully claim copyright. The authors of a joint work are co-owners of the copyright in the work unless there is an agreement to the contrary (see Chapter Sixteen: A Thriller: Copyright Administration and Splits With Co-Writers). Not just anyone can submit an application to the Copyright Office. Only the author who actually created the work or, if the work was made for hire, the employer or

---

[4] *Dimmie v. Carey*, 88 F.2d 142 (2nd Cir. 2000).

other person for whom the work was prepared may do so. In addition, the copyright claimant who has obtained ownership of all the rights under the copyright initially belonging to the author, the owner of exclusive rights that make up copyright law, or an agent of any of these people may apply for registration. There is no legal requirement that applications be prepared or filed by an attorney, but the help of an attorney can mean the difference between a correctly and an incorrectly filed application.

HOW IS COPYRIGHT ACQUIRED?

Oftentimes, artists do not secure their copyright because of a false belief that it is too difficult to do so. This is a misconception, as the process is very simple. No publication, registration, or other action in the Copyright Office is required to secure copyright. Copyright is secured automatically when the work is created, and a work is created when it is fixed in a copy or phonorecord for the first time. My old great law professor Spencer Boyer, would use the acronym "TAME"—i.e., once the copyrighted material is placed in a fixed "**t**angible **m**eans of **e**xpression" (a tape recorder, sheet of paper, DVD, CD, etc.), copyright immediately exists. This means that a work must be written down as sheet music to be a copy or recorded as a CD or cassette to be a phonorecord. Registration, though not required, does provide certain advantages that may prove to be helpful if copyright is infringed. Registration affords you certain statutory damages and attorneys' fees in the event someone infringes your copyright.

PUBLICATION

Publication is defined as the distribution or sale of a tape, CD, or record to another party for the purpose of sales or performance.[5] It used to be that a work had to be published to obtain federal copyright protection. Before 1976, to acquire copyright, a singer/songwriter had to sell her CD to a store or a record label. A public performance in front of any number of people, even a crowded stadium, did not qualify as publication. As of 1976, this is no longer the case. However, copyright owners should not discredit the power of publication simply because it is no longer required. Publication is still important because even though copyright is acquired without it, it serves several purposes to copyright owners. First, works that are published in the United States are subject to mandatory deposit with the Library of Congress, and deposit standards differ for published works and unpublished view. A publication is also convenient because it displays the date of publication and the name of the copyright owner. Finally, the year of the publication helps to determine the duration of copyright protection, especially in cases of works-for-hire.

---

[5] The 1976 Copyright Act defines publication as follows: "Publication" is the distribution of copies or phonorecords of a work to the public by sale or other transfer of ownership, or by rental, lease, or lending. The offering to distribute copies or phonorecords to a group of persons for purposes of further distribution, public performance, or public display constitutes publication.

NOTICE OF COPYRIGHT

Much like publication, a copyright notice is no longer required under U.S. law, although it too is often beneficial. Since this is a newer law, notice is still required for copyright of older works. If you are creating music today, however, this isn't a concern to you. Use of notice protects your exclusive copyright privileges because it informs the public that the work is protected by copyright, identifies the copyright owner, and shows the year of first publication. Most important, in the event that a work is infringed, a proper notice of copyright appearing on the published phonorecord to which a defendant in a copyright infringement suit had access overcomes a defendant's claim that the infringement was innocent or accidental. This is because notice gives warning to potential infringers that the work is protected by copyright. Since notice is the responsibility of the artist or copyright holder, an artist can provide notice by including three elements on the back or another visible part of your CD or cassette.

- The symbol ℗ (the letter P in a circle)

- The year of first publication of the sound recording

- The name of the owner of copyright in the sound recording, an abbreviation by which the name can be recognized, or a generally known alternative designation of the owner.

Example: ℗2007 BMG Records Inc.

YOU CAN TRANSFER YOUR COPYRIGHT

Any or all of the copyright owner's exclusive rights may be transferred, but to be valid, the transfer of exclusive rights must be in writing and signed by the owner of the right. A copyright may also be conveyed by a will or pass as personal property as a gift; in such cases, state law applies. You may want to consult an attorney for the finer points of property law in your state. It is also helpful to see a lawyer about a transfer of copyright interests, as there is no federal form from the Copyright Office for such transactions.

SHOULD I REGISTER MY COPYRIGHT?

Yes. Although not required by law to be protected by copyright laws, registration is another useful tool in protecting your intellectual property. Registration is most useful in scenarios that involve lawsuits. For example, before you can file a copyright infringement lawsuit, your song must be registered, as this establishes a public record. This registration also provides "prima facie" or undisputable evidence of the true ownership of the copyright. Finally, registration will provide a basis for your attorneys to request statutory damages and attorneys' fees in a copyright infringement suit.

Also remember the general rule that the Library of Congress should have copies of your work within three months of its creation. You should also provide the Library of Congress with two copies of your phonorecord.

HOW DO I REGISTER?

To register your song, or collection of songs, just follow these simple steps:

1. Complete an application form.[6]

2. Write a check or money order to "Register of Copyrights" for an nonrefundable fee of forty-five dollars (as of 2007).

3. Compile the copies of your work that you must submit; the standard is three copies of sheet music and phonorecords.

4. Mail all of the above items in one envelope to:

    Library of Congress
    Copyright Office
    101 Independence Avenue, SE
    Washington, DC 20540-6000

A copyright registration is effective on the date the Copyright Office receives all the required elements in acceptable form, regardless of how long it then takes to process the application and mail the certificate of registration. The time the Copyright Office requires to process an application depends on the amount of material the office is receiving. You will only hear back from the Copyright Office if there is a problem with your application. You will also receive a certificate of registration indicating that the work has been registered. Conversely, if the application cannot be accepted, you will receive a letter explaining why it has been rejected. Do not continually call the copyright office asking for the status of your registration.

WORK MADE FOR HIRE

There is also the issue of writers who are contracted to write songs. These songwriters are considered to fall under the doctrine of "work-for-hire" or "work made for hire," as it is officially called.[7] (See a standard work-made-for-hire agreement at the end of this chapter.) A work made for hire is owned by the party who hires. In some instances, it is defined as a work prepared by an employee within the scope of his or her employment. A work made for hire can be specially ordered or commissioned. If the parties expressly agree in a written instrument signed by them, the work shall be considered a work made for hire, and any future confusion can be avoided.

---

[6] Get the relevant forms at:
www.copyright.gov/forms/formsr.pdf and www.copyright.gov/forms/formcon.pdf

[7] 17 U.S.C. § 101. Works Made for Hire—(1) a work prepared by an employee within the scope of his or her employment; or (2) a work specially ordered or commissioned for use as a contribution to a collective work, as a part of a motion picture or other audiovisual work, as a translation, as a supplementary work, as a compilation, as an instructional text, as a test, as answer material for a test, or as an atlas, if the parties expressly agree in a written instrument signed by them that the work shall be considered a work made for hire.

Work made for hire is a situation in which a composer is hired to write a melody or lyrics, but the composer does not retain the copyright.[8] The composer is paid, and the hiring party owns all rights to the song or work. Although this violates the basic principles of copyright law, that the creator of a work is the owner of it, it is perfectly legal. The writer of the song who works for hire may be credited in the liner notes as the writer, or he may not be, but regardless of that, he will not receive royalties from his work. In a sense, the work-for-hire writer is like a surrogate mother. He writes a song, and may even receive credit for it, but he will not reap any further rewards from it. This is a common phenomenon that is not widely known about. It often happens in work environments like advertising agencies, where an employee may write a commercial jingle, while his employer retains the rights to it.

Work made for hire is an important concept to know as a songwriter. If you're offered a great gig writing songs for Ashanti and you are given a work-made-for-hire agreement to sign, you *know* that you will receive no royalty payments when her album goes platinum, so don't expect a fat check in the mail.

In the music industry when an artist records for a label, it is considered a work made for hire. And the label would own all masters. Similarly, in many publishing houses, a songwriter might work in a work-for-hire scenario and receive a weekly stipend in exchange for releasing all rights to the underlying copyright. Take a look at the sample work-made-for-hire agreement located at our website www.thisbusinessofurbanmusic.com

---

[8] 17 U.S.C. § 201 (b)Works Made for Hire. "In the case of a work made for hire, the employer or other person for whom the work was prepared is considered the Composer for purposes of this title, and, unless the parties have expressly agreed otherwise in a written instrument signed by them, owns all of the rights comprised in the copyright."

CHAPTER 15

Joining a Performance Rights Society: BMI, ASCAP, and SESAC

"We are the people mostly responsible for paying you performance royalties based on the public performance of your songs. Therefore, if you have a song on the radio, in television, or at Disneyland or anywhere music gets played and there is a license for it, we are collecting it and we are distributing that money back out to our members."

—JEANNE WEEMS, SENIOR VICE PRESIDENT OF ASCAP

ASCAP has LL Cool J, Jermaine Dupri, 50 Cent, and Sean Paul. BMI has Twinkie Clark, Jennifer Lopez, and Kanye West, while SESAC has V. Michael McKay and Bob Dylan. Why are these songwriters and many others devoted to their performance rights societies? What do organizations like the ones these artists belong to do, and for whom?

"I needed a good performance rights society, so when BMI came along and told me what they could do as a performance rights society, I felt it was the time to make a change," explains Grammy-winning Twinkie Clark, a songwriter of such gospel classics as "Is My Living in Vain?," "You Brought the Sunshine," and "I'm Looking for a Miracle." Having had the pleasure of working closely with Clark and BMI representatives, I learned firsthand how important it is to have a good performance rights society for your career. Explains BMI's top executive Catherine Brewton, "when you are a top artist or songwriter, it is so important that you affiliate with the right society, whether BMI or ASCAP or SESAC." Brewton, a pioneer in establishing BMI's Atlanta presence and urban dominance, added, "If you want to have your monies collected and paid to you promptly, you have to be proactive and get registered and understand the business." Brewton and her partner Wardell Malloy have signed or worked with many of the heavyweights of BMI, including Rodney Jerkins, Clark, and Yolanda Adams, to name just a few.

Performance rights organizations are designed to represent songwriters and publishers and their right to be compensated for having their music performed in public. By securing a license from one of these companies, nonprivate music users (e.g., television and radio stations, auditoriums, gyms, restaurants, hotels, theme parks, malls) can legally play any song in the publishing company's collection. Without a license from a performing rights organization, music users are in danger of copyright infringement (again, remember the Napster craze in the late 1990s; artists were enraged that their songs were being used and they were not being compensated).

BMI, ASCAP, and SESAC collectively gross over $1 billion a year. But most gospel and urban artists couldn't even tell you succinctly what they do for those millions. Moreover, if you turn over the back of an album, you will always see BMI or ASCAP and the much smaller SESAC name listed as the publishing company. So what do those letters behind Grammy Award–winners Richard Smallwood's (Richwood/BMI/Zomba Publishing) and Shirley Caesar (Shu-Bel/Ascap/Caesar-Williams Publishing) really mean? Many young artists and songwriters do not know. In 2003, Richard Smallwood, the writer of songs like "Center of My Joy," "Calvary," "I Love the Lord," and "Total Praise" explained the role of BMI to a packed audience at BMI.

A world-class composer, pianist, and arranger, Smallwood changed the face of gospel music with his songs. "I felt it was important to do the BMI panel to explain what they do for me and how important it was for artists to understand the role of BMI or ASCAP in getting paid," explained Smallwood, who has been honored by the Smithsonian Institution as a "gospel innovator and songwriter." "BMI collects my royalties and makes sure that anyone who uses my music pays me," added Smallwood.

You read the back of gospel sensation Hezekiah Walker's album and you also see BMI's name after Walker's "Mokiah Publishing/BMI." This is an indicator that Pastor Walker has set up a publishing company and that he has signed with BMI to collect his performance royalties. And if you read the back of Grammy Award–winning Yolanda Adams's album, you'll see SESAC mentioned for hot writer V. Michael McKay, who wrote Adams's chart-topping "Through the Storm" and "This Battle Is the Lord." Finally, you'll notice the ASCAP moniker on Mary Mary's platinum-selling debut album.

In this chapter, we examine BMI, ASCAP, and SESAC and their significance to the artist, songwriter, and publisher. We will also discuss the importance of cue sheets, the main method for paying writers. I would encourage you to visit each of their websites for a full breakdown (www.bmi.com, www.ascap.com, and www.sesac.com). However, for purposes of this chapter, I will focus on some core concepts such as the following:

+ Performance rights societies
+ Royalty collections
+ Royalty calculations
+ ASCAP
+ BMI
+ SESAC
+ Soundexchange
+ Cue sheets

A GENERAL OVERVIEW

Performance rights societies are organizations through which songwriters, composers, and music publishers share their songs with the rest of the world in exchange for royalty payments. Performance rights societies also serve as forums where writers can exchange ideas and also receive insurance and other benefits that "regular folks" enjoy, according to BMI's Malloy.

Owing to court orders arising out of antitrust lawsuits, BMI and ASCAP follow a stringent code of ethics when it comes to recruiting and maintaining songwriters and publishers. To be a member of either of these societies, a songwriter must have at least one song that has the potential to be commercially distributed. It used to be that the song had to be used commercially for at least a year, but today, with the wide use of the Internet, having a song on your own website is enough to qualify you for membership. Almost anyone can join; BMI's website warns potential members under the age of seventeen that they must fill out a hardcopy form of their application. Be forewarned, if you have been a member of a performance rights society and are in the process of changing your membership, you will need to prove you terminated the prior company before you can join a different society.

For forty years, ending in the 1980s, BMI and ASCAP granted advance royalties to writers and publishers, which were taken out of their future royalty payments once their songs became hits. That service was ended after a court decision[9] that was unfavorable to the performance rights groups, and has never been reinstated, even after that decision was reversed by the court of appeals.[10]

Today, ASCAP and BMI are helpful in securing private and bank loans to members against future royalties. They provide all sorts of insurance, from medical and dental to insurance of musical instruments, studios, and tour liability. They also run credit unions and investment programs for members. Finally, they offer a slew of discounts on anything from musical equipment to rental cars.

Before we go on to discussing each performance rights group individually, please note that joining a performance rights group is not the only step to getting paid for your work. You will need to have mechanical licenses for your songs, which we will discuss in Chapter Twenty. I can spend a lifetime telling you horror stories about writers who wrote or co-wrote some of the biggest hits of the 1990s and today but have yet to see a dime because they failed to fill out mechanical licenses.

HOW PERFORMANCE ROYALTIES ARE COLLECTED

Once a song is registered, it becomes part of that performance rights agency's collection and is available to all of its users who pay a fee. Most of those users like radio stations and other major venues have a blanket license to use any or all of the organization's music. Some users, especially those with small budgets and smaller needs for music, license on a per-program basis and only pay for the music they actually use. Each performer's rights society use a slightly different system for calculations. For instance, ASCAP, whose calculation methods are available, either counts performances (like on TV) or does a sample survey (like radio stations).

For television and film performances, all performance rights groups depend on cue sheets (more on this later in the chapter) that program producers provide them for first-time broadcasts, and program schedules, network and station logs, and VHS tapes or DVDs of the broadcasts for subsequent performances. Additionally, for radio performances, performance rights groups do a sample survey of all radio

---

[9] *Buffalo Broadcasting Co., Inc. v. American Society of Composers*, Authors and Publishers, 744 F.2nd 917 (2nd Cir. 1984).

[10] *Buffalo Broadcasting Co. v. ASCAP*, 744 F.2d 917 (2nd Cir. 1985), cert. denied, 469 U.S. 1211 (1985) ("Buffalo Broadcasting II").

stations, including college stations and public radio. The sample survey is conducted with the use of a digital tracking system, station logs provided by the radio stations and their disc jockeys, and recordings of the broadcasts.

And, for live performances, performance rights groups review set lists provided by concert promoters, performing artists, and others, as well as printed programs that are handed out to the audience. Restaurants and bars are not surveyed and have to pay a flat rate that is distributed based on trends in local radio divided by genre of music. For example, a country-western bar would be subject to the playlists at the local country station, while a hot nightclub would use the local hip-hop station. Other venues like websites, zoos, parks, and malls provide lists of their music data to performance rights groups.

HOW PERFORMANCE ROYALTIES ARE CALCULATED

We will use ASCAP as an example for the calculation of royalties. ASCAP weighs different factors to come up with a song's total "credits," which then determines the song's royalty calculation. The song is weighed based on the type of performance, known as the use weight. The uses are theme, underscore, and promotional. A song that is used on TV or radio gets more weight than one that was played during a radio commercial or at a restaurant. The licensee (i.e., the venue that uses the music) is weighed based on its licensing fee. The licensing fee is based on the licensee's markets and number of stations carrying its broadcast signal. So, a media conglomerate like Radio One, owned by the incredible Cathy Hughes, may have markets from New York to Los Angeles and carry a higher licensing fee than a radio station that operates in rural Mississippi.

Another factor is the time of day the music is performed. Music played during peak times receives more weight; so music that is played during morning rush hour costs more for radio stations than music that is played at 8 PM. For television, however, peak hours are primetime, instead of the early morning. Songwriters and publishers are paid based on the medium from which the money came: Money paid out from radio stations is paid for radio performances, TV money is paid to television performances, and so forth. A general licensing allocation is included for fees that performance rights organizations collect from non-broadcast licensees like restaurants, parks, and malls.

$$\text{USE} \times \text{LICENSEE} \times \text{TIME} \times \text{WHO} \times \text{GENERAL} + \text{PREMIUM} = \text{TOTAL CREDITS}$$

The total number of credits is multiplied by the shares for the song, so if there is one writer and one publisher, each gets 50 percent. This number is multiplied by the credit value for the song. The credit value is the total number of credits for all writers and publishers divided by the total amount of money available for distribution for that quarter (three-month period). For example, if there are a total of 10 million credits for a quarter, and there have been $85 million collected for distribution that quarter, then the value of one credit for that quarter is $8.50 (85/10 = 8.5).

$$\text{NUMBER OF CREDITS} \times \text{SHARE (.50 OR .25, ETC.)} \times \text{CREDIT VALUE}$$
$$= \text{ROYALTY PAYMENT}$$

Royalty payment calculations vary slightly between performer's rights groups. When you are joining a performance rights group, the group will explain in further detail how they do calculations. To guide you in your selection, here is a brief overview of some of the distinctions between the societies. Keep in mind that you should call or e-mail their offices as well as visit their websites to get more information.

ASCAP

Created in 1914, ASCAP, the American Society of Composers, Authors, and Publishers, has nearly 300,000 U.S. composers, songwriters, lyricists, and music publishers of every kind of music, with a catalog and repertory of some 8.5 million copyrighted musical works. Legendary songwriter James Weldon Johnson, who, from an urban standpoint, wrote and composed the Negro National Anthem, "Lift Every Voice and Sing," was one of the early members and key founders in the establishment of ASCAP. ASCAP has offices all over the United States in New York, Los Angeles, Chicago, Nashville, Atlanta, and Miami, as well as Puerto Rico and London. Unlike BMI, ASCAP was created and is controlled by composers, songwriters, and music publishers, with a board of directors elected by and from the membership.

ASCAP protects the rights of its member composers by licensing and distributing royalties for the non-dramatic public performances of their copyrighted works. Like all performer's rights societies, ASCAP's licensees encompass all who want to perform copyrighted music publicly. ASCAP's repertory includes pop, rock, alternative, country, R&B, rap, hip-hop, Latin, film and television music, folk, roots and blues, jazz, gospel, Christian, new age, theater and cabaret, dance, electronic, symphonic, concert, as well as many others—the entire musical spectrum. ASCAP's members include Jay-Z, Stevie Wonder, Tito Puente, Duke Ellington, Beyoncé, and Marc Anthony.[11]

BMI

Broadcast Music Incorporated, or BMI, represents more than 300,000 performers and 6.5 million songs. Started in 1939, BMI represents songwriters, composers, and publishers from all genres of music. The license fees BMI collects for the "public performances"—including radio airplay, broadcast and cable television, Internet, and live and recorded performances—of its collection of compositions are distributed as royalties to the writers, composers, and copyright holders it represents.

BMI advertises itself as a place for artists, as well as a resource for businesses and broadcasters to find music that is right for their purposes. BMI's affiliated songwriters and composers include every style of music including pop, film and television, classical, commercial jingles, library music, musical theater, jazz, hip-hop, metal, meringue, classical, classic soul, rock, and reggae. Some of the musical legends represented by BMI are Chuck Berry, Mariah Carey, Carlos Santana, B. B. King, and Snoop Dogg, as well as John Legend, the Black-Eyed Peas, and Rodney Jerkins.[12]

---

[11] To join ASCAP as a writer, visit www.ascap.com/reference/writerapp.pdf
To join ASCAP as a publisher, visit www.ascap.com/reference/publisherapp.pdf

[12] To join BMI as a writer or publisher, visit https://applications.bmi.com/affiliation/joinen.aspx.

SESAC

SESAC was founded in 1930 as a performance rights society for European and gospel music. Today, SESAC has diversified to include today's most popular music, including R&B/hip-hop, dance, rock 'n' roll, country, Latin, contemporary Christian, jazz, and the television and film music of Hollywood's composers.

The smallest of the three performing rights organizations, SESAC has its headquarters in Nashville, with offices in New York, Los Angeles, and London. SESAC markets itself as an organization that allows songwriters and publishers to develop personal relationships with its staff. Some of artists who have used SESAC have been Usher, Bow Wow, Destiny's Child, Ludacris, Jimi Hendrix, and Christina Aguilera.[13] Said Trevor Gale, Vice President of Writer/Publisher Relations, "Songwriters must understand that they need a performing rights organization because while the songwriter creates and writes great music, we handle the licensing, protect their intellectual property, and make sure their royalties are collected and paid to them as the creator."

SOUNDEXCHANGE

SoundExchange is a performance rights group that was formed for the collection and distribution of webcasts and other digital performances. Broadcasters of digital performances of music, like web radio stations, must pay royalties to the songwriters and publishers. They must also pay royalties to the recording artists.[14] SoundExchange collects electronic play logs from cable and satellite subscription services, webcasters excluding request stations like Napster, and satellite radio stations on XM and Sirius. They then distribute the royalty payments directly to artists and recording copyright owners based on the data they have collected.[15]

SoundExchange is a nonprofit performance rights organization comprising recording companies and artists interested in receiving compensation for the licensing of their music in digital formats. Prior to 1995, sound recording copyright owners in the United States did not have a performance right to be paid royalties for digital performances of their songs. The U.S. Copyright Office recognized the benefits of SoundExchange's administration of royalties and designated SoundExchange as the administrative entity for subscription services' statutory license fees after the Digital Performance in Sound Recording Act of 1995 and the Digital Millennium Copyright Act of 1998.

---

[13] For information on the selection process for SESAC, visit www.sesac.com/writerpublisher/howtoaffiliate.aspx.

[14] Digital Performance Right in Sound Recordings Act of 1995.

[15] To join SoundExchange, visit www.soundexchange.com/members/become_member.html.

CUE SHEETS

Cue sheets are the most important step in getting paid for your music when it is used in film or on television. A cue sheet is a piece of paper that lists all of the music in an audiovisual program like a TV show, movie, or commercial and is used to determine how much royalties an artist will receive. Cue sheets are generally filled out by the music department of a production company, and while anyone can do them, the one submitted by the publishing company takes priority. See the sample cue sheet at the end of this chapter.

Cue sheets should be submitted to your performance rights agency as soon as possible. BMI and ASCAP recommend a time line of before the three-month mark after the original broadcast for a television program and before the first foreign theatrical performance for feature films. On that timeline, royalties will be paid within six months of the broadcast of the TV program or release of film. Cue sheets are not filled out for reruns, as the performer's rights society you use updates their database based on TV airings. Furthermore, only music that is not specifically written for the program needs to be registered; in other words, if you were hired by MTV to write the theme song to *Run's House*, you would not have to fill out a cue sheet.

Sometimes, songwriters run into problems with their production companies when the production company neglects to send the cue sheet in a timely fashion. In circumstances like that the songwriter should make every effort to contact the production company and demand the cue sheets. As a songwriter, you may want to include a cue sheet clause in your production agreement to insure that the production company will not neglect getting your payment. If the production company responsible for your cue sheets is no longer in operation, as a composer you can create your own cue sheet and submit it to BMI, ASCAP, or SESAC along with a VHS or DVD of the program for which you wish to get paid. Don't wait too long after the airing of the program to request your payment, as performance rights agencies only pay royalties for a certain interim beyond broadcast. If you receive an annual statement of your earnings and something is missing, contact your agency right away, because failure to do so may result in you not getting paid.

Cue sheets should include all of the relevant information so that the artist can receive royalties. Relevant information on a cue sheet for film or television will generally include the series, film, title (a/k/a Episode Title), the episode number, the air date, the show length, the music length, the production information, song title, composer, publisher, performing rights society, timing, usage, and co-writer, if any. These are all important elements on a cue sheet, and the absence of any relevant information will hold back your payments from your performance rights society.

WHY IT'S IMPORTANT

I was relaxing in front of the television one evening when a national commercial for a certain credit card came on. This new commercial featured an older song written by one of my clients. It took me several seconds to realize that my client never licensed this song to the company. I rushed back to my office and did all the necessary paperwork in order for my client to receive royalties for his work. Without the paperwork submitted and processed, he could not see a check. You may never catch every use of your copyright or work, but you can hire agencies and companies to monitor the use and infringement.

On another occasion, one of my clients had written dozens of mega-hits—songs that were performed and sampled by the likes of Janet Jackson, the Notorious B.I.G., Bobby Brown, and many other huge names in entertainment. You might think that my client is a millionaire as a result of his writing, but in fact, he has not seen any royalty payments from any of his songs. Part of the problem is that even though he is a member of ASCAP, he neglected to keep track of his mechanical licensing. This writer also owned his own publishing company and thought that he had covered all of his bases. The moral of the story here is that if you're a writer, and especially if you've taken on the responsibility of running your own publishing company, you have to be well educated on the process of collecting royalties. It's perfectly fine to be your own publisher, but if you are uncertain about the collection of royalties, hire someone with experience in the field.

Scenarios like these replay over and over again throughout the music industry. An unbelievable amount of songwriters do not receive royalties for their songs. Oftentimes the reason is that they serve as their own publishers and neglect to submit cue sheets for television and film performances of their music. Another reason is that some writers wrongly believe that their responsibilities end as soon as they join a performance rights society. Although joining a performance rights organization is a necessary step in getting paid for your music writing, it is not the only step.

CLOSING TIPS

Join a performance rights group as soon as you possibly can. Keep track of your finances, and if your music is used on television or in films, insist that the production company fills out your cue sheets. Don't get lazy; being a member of a performance rights organization does not guarantee that you will be paid. If you have completed all of the necessary steps to be paid, and you have received no royalties, don't dilly-dally and hope for the best; find out what went wrong. If necessary, hire someone to administer your music and collect your royalties. Do whatever you can to make sure that you are paid.

CUE SHEET

Series/Film Title: _____   Company Name: _____

Episode Title/Number: _____   Address: _____

Estimated Airdate: _____   Phone: _____

Program Length: _____   Contact: _____

Program Type: _____   Network Station: _____

Cue #	Cue Title	Use*	Timing	Composer(s) Affiliation / %	Publisher Affiliation / %
1					
2					
3					
4					
5					
6					
7					
8					
9					
10					
11					
12					
13					
14					
15					
16					
17					
18					
19					
20					
21					
22					
23					
24					
25					
26					
27					
28					
29					
30					

*Use Codes: MT = Main Title   VI = Visual Instrumental   BV = Background Vocal

VV = Visual Vocal   ET = End Title   BI = Background Instrumental   T = Theme

CHAPTER 16

A Thriller: Copyright Administration and Splits with Co-Writers

"It all starts with a song. Without a hit song, an artist has nothing."
—ANTONIO "L. A." REID

When Michael Jackson released his Grammy Award–winning album *Thriller* in 1982, he was credited as the writer of five of the nine songs on the album. The album has sold nearly 60 million copies to date, making it the number-one-selling album of all time. Many people were amazed with the tours, merchandising, videos, and other ancillary income Jackson received in connection with the legendary album. However, for purposes of this chapter, I want to zoom in on the quiet money Jackson and company hypothetically could have made as songwriters on this album under present royalty scales to get you to understand today's critical value of publishing income. Specifically, I want to discuss the rights of co-copyright owners and the revenue associated therewith.

As you may know, under copyright law, there is what is called the "statutory rate," which is the amount of money a record label or anyone is required to pay a songwriter for the use of his or her song on an album. I will describe statuary rates in more detail in the next few chapters, but for now you should know that starting January of 2006, the statutory rate was 9.1 cents for songs five minutes and under and 1.75 cents per minute or fraction thereof (whichever is greater), if the song runs over five minutes. (This is why record labels urge you to keep your songs under five minutes—they can pay less in royalties.)

Thus, at the writing of this book, the statute required a scale of pay as follows

Song Time and Pay

Up to 5:00 = $.091

5:01 to 6:00 = $.105 (6 × $.0175 = $.105)

6:01 to 7:00 = $.1225 (7 × $.0175 = $.1225)

7:01 to 8:00 = $.14 (8 × $.0175 = $.14)

Now, for purposes of this chapter, analyze and calculate the income associated with *Thriller* and the revenue received by Jackson and several other writers including Quincy Jones, James Ingram, and Rod Temperton. Using today's statutory rates for songwriters, if we calculated Jackson and his team's writing royalties under the statute, it would break down as follows:

Thriller Song List:	Songwriter:	Running Time:	Royalty:
"Wanna Be Startin' Somethin'"	(Jackson)	6:02	$.1225
"Baby Be Mine"	(Temperton)	4:20	$.0910
"The Girl Is Mine"	(Jackson)	3:42	$.0910
"Thriller"	(Temperton/Jackson)	5:57	$.1050
"Beat It"	(Jackson)	4:17	$.0910
"Billie Jean"	(Jackson)	4:57	$.0910
"Human Nature"	(Bettis/Porcaro)	4:05	$.0910
"P.Y.T. (Pretty Young Thing)"	(Ingram/Jones)	3:58	$.0910
"The Lady in My Life"	(Temperton)	4:57	<u>$.0910</u>
Total:			$.8645

This means that if _Thriller_ were released today, Michael Jackson and the co-writers or joint copyright holders would split more than eighty-six cents in mechanical songwriting royalties alone off of the sale of each album, not including singles. At 59 million copies sold, Jackson, the other writers, and the publisher would have made $51,005,500. That's not a typo; they would have made over $51 million on songwriting royalties as the copyright owners.

The _Thriller_ title track alone would have grossed the publisher and the writers a combined total of $6,195,000 (i.e., 59,000,000 units sold × .105 "Thriller" royalty rate). Notice that if Michael had forgotten to put his name on "Thriller," which he co-wrote with Rod Temperton, he would be out approximately $1.5 million or face an uphill legal battle to get back royalties.

Also, I should note that this 50-million-plus figure above is solely for the mechanical royalties. We did not run example calculations for sheet music, synchronization licenses for videos/DVDs, jingles, commercials, soundtracks, and dozens of other possible uses that could double this number, if the Jackson team exploited the catalog correctly. Again, this example is to solely teach you the importance of copyright.

Also, note that Jackson and Rod Temperton (a longtime Jackson co-collaborator) most likely have different publishing companies. So the divided copyright on _Thriller_ would be paid by various publishers. Jackson would seek payment from his publisher (Sony ATV) and Temperton would receive his payments from his publisher (Rod Songs). If the two publishers shared equally in the $6 million fee listed above for just the song "Thriller" on the 59-million-selling album, each publisher would have paid its respective writer (Jackson and Temperton) one-half of its mechanical license revenue. (Without knowing the writer and publisher ownership splits, it's hard to divide revenue accurately.)

The previous hypothetical scenario essentially highlights how two equal songwriters, signing different contracts and granting their publishing rights to different publishers (Sony/ATV and Rod Songs, respectively), would generate different shares for themselves. So, in this hypothetical, Rod Songs and ATV shared equally in the publisher's mechanical license fees payable for "Thriller." Jackson and Temperton, as writers, would split the writers' share equally. If Jackson and Temperton have co-publishing deals, they would get paid 100 percent of their writer's share and 50 percent of the publisher's share. In essence, they retain their writer's share and only split the publisher's share. This is the same rate and amount that would be payable to each writer if there were only one publisher and two writers—had the writers chose to have one publisher administrate. I strongly advise my clients to choose their own publisher in situations like this. (See Chapter Nineteen for a more detailed breakdown of the roles of a publisher.)

Note that Jackson owns the lucrative Sony/ATV catalog that features songs by the Beatles, Elvis, Babyface, Eminem, and Jackson himself. Using the chart on the previous page, you can run the numbers and imagine the near billion-dollar value of the entire Jackson catalog. Additionally, you can understand why Jackson paid $47.5 million for the Beatles' catalog and is considered one of the business geniuses of this industry. In addition, of course, he tremendously angered his friend Paul McCartney, who wanted to buy this catalog back after losing it in the 1960s. (I explain more on the matter in a later chapter.)

Moreover, the *Thriller* example is solely for the purpose of getting you to understand how important it is to a) register your copyright, b) understand the splits in ownership and who wrote what, and c) administer your songs properly with assistance, if necessary. It is also important for you to realize that being an artist is wonderful, but the true blessing and income is associated with who wrote the song. You could sing hit songs for the next twenty years and make a songwriter in Paducah, Kentucky, very wealthy if he or she did all of the writing and owned all of the copyrights for your hit songs.

Recently, Mariah Carey staged a comeback with the 5-million-selling *The Emancipation of Mimi* album. While her return to superstar status was incredible, it was even more impressive to learn that she had written many of her hit songs. If she never sold another record, her catalog alone is worth millions.

HISTORICAL ANALYSIS OF JOINT OWNERSHIP, CO-OWNERSHIP, AND "SPLITS"

In the music industry, we commonly ask, "What are the splits?"—i.e., how many writers jointly own the copyright as co-owners and "what right are you licensing" for a particular use? Prior to thirty years ago, no one ever used this terminology in the music industry or elsewhere, as the old laws did not allow you to split up your copyright. Specifically, a copyright was considered indivisible. After the Copyright Act of 1976, as amended, many of us in the field started teaching a theory of copyright as a "bundle of rights" that could be divided.

Thus, as of January 1, 1978, under the Copyright Act of 1976, the law allows you to divide the copyright so that any of the exclusive rights under copyright may be transferred or owned separately. Thus, Michael Jackson could sign a deal that allows Sony to license his mechanical rights but reserve another whole set of rights to another company. It is complicated but not difficult as you grow as a writer and exploit your copyrights with good help.

ASCAP, BMI, and SESAC can all guide you in handling your performance rights royalties and dealing with the issues affecting joint copyright owners. Similarly, the Harry Fox Agency (www.harryfox.com) is a helpful resource for handling mechanical rights and synchronization rights when you have joint copyright owners. In our example, I am certain that Michael Jackson, Rod Temperton, Quincy Jones, and James Ingram utilize these long-established companies to collect the royalties associated with their copyright ownership.

IN THE STUDIO: JOINT OWNERSHIP AND UNDERSTANDING THE COPYRIGHT ISSUES

In the urban music scene, many songs are the result of a factory-like setup. There is the hot producer, super lyrical writer, top beat maker, talented engineer, and great vocalist, among others, in the studio. These incredible talents come together to crank out a song that will eventually make its way to radio and become a hit. However, no one thinks of creating a split sheet or document identifying the splits on the songs. As a result, the copyright division is unclear. An entertainment attorney, record label, or Clive Davis himself cannot ascertain who owns the copyright or how the joint co-ownership of the copyright should be administered. Explains hitmaker Sean Garrett (Usher and Beyoncé): "You have to do business right and spell everything out in writing in terms of who owns what when you are writing and producing songs."

As we discuss in our chapter on mechanical royalties and publishing, it is critical to understand the monies associated with the song. For example, the LOX, a popular hip-hop group, went on New York radio not long ago and demanded that they share in more income associated with their hit song catalog. They contended that P. Diddy had ripped them off, exploited their copyrights for his own profit, and took enormous revenue from their publishing or copyright income. While the debate became bitter and P. Diddy vehemently denied their allegations, he ultimately rectified the situation by releasing them from some of the contractual restraints. However, it raised serious eyebrows and concern regarding ownership of your songs and what happens when you sign with a top record label/producer and co-write material.

Typically, in the excitement of producing an album, particularly the first album, the artist, as a writer, does not consider jotting down who wrote specific parts of the song. This is very disconcerting, as essentially you lose the statutory income that we discuss in Chapter Seventeen. For example, if you co-wrote Chris Brown's hit song "Run It," then you would share in hundreds of thousands of dollars in mechanical and performance rights royalties (see Chapter Eighteen). Says Brown attorney Matthew Middleton: "We never conclude with recording until all the paperwork is done correctly."

When Bad Boy released Biggie's album, the credits had a list of writers and producers, including D. Dot Angelettie, Tony Dofat, Harve Pierre, Ron Lawrence, and, of course, Diddy and Biggie himself. Each of these individuals understood the millions of dollars associated with the songs on the *Ready to Die* album and *Life after Death* (as well as 2005's *Born Again*).

Similarly, many of the thirty or more hits of Babyface and L. A. Reid were co-written, and each writer receives his share of the royalties. Each of the songs should be registered as "co-writer" Kenneth "Babyface" Edmonds and L. A. Reid. Without this registration, it is sometimes difficult to prove ownership in the event a dispute breaks out.

Babyface, as a joint co-owner of the copyright on songs like "End of the Road" (sung by Boyz II Men) and "Girlfriend" (sung by Pebbles) is free to use or license the use of the song without the consent of L. A. Reid or their partner songwriter Darryl Simmons, so long as the use of the song does not destroy or diminish the work. For example, I was watching BET/Showtime's *Soul Food* series produced by Babyface and his ex-wife Tracy Edmonds, and on occasion, I believe I heard songs written by Babyface and L. A. Reid. Most likely, this was welcomed by the co-writers, as the songs were not diluted or compromised.

Nearly twenty years ago, when Jimmy Jam and Terry Lewis produced Janet Jackson's mega-platinum album *Control*, the Minnesota production duo shared in a great deal of the writing credits, along with Jackson. Today, many years later, because they understood the importance of copyright and co-ownership guidelines, they are still collecting royalties on some of these early hits.

If you do not make it expressly clear on the writing of an album, it can sometimes lead to litigation. For example, in 2005, a New York jury decided quickly that superstar urban artist Ashanti, whose full name is Ashanti Douglas, owed her former producer $630,000 for breach of contract.[16] Genard Parker, who worked with the singer in 1996 and 1997 when she was a minor, let Ashanti out of her contract with him when she signed with a record label. According to the plaintiff, Parker, the two had agreed that he would produce two songs on her first album and receive $50,000 plus royalties. Most likely, he argued that because of Ashanti's breach, he did not earn some of the co-writing, publishing income he would have earned. As of August 2007, the case is in appeals, but it raises the serious point of how important it is to expressly spell out what the copyright and song agreement is for a given album.

WHO OWNS THE DRUM-RIFF COPYRIGHT?

Some common questions in the field of joint copyright are: Does the lyrical writer own 50 percent of the song for the lyrics and words? Does the musician own a piece for arranging the music or creating the musical accompaniment? How about the original drum beats; is there a copyright involved with the work performed by the drummer?

For example, twenty years ago, Run-DMC did the popular song "Sucker MCs" with the sound of a deep bass drum and loud ringing snare drum (boom-boom!, tat tat! boom tat! . . . Boom boom! Tat! Tat! Boom tat, followed by the clever, "Two years ago, a friend of mine/Asked me to say some MC rhymes"). This snare drum riff and breakdown became a nationwide anthem, recognized by teens immediately when played on radio, dancehalls, and nightclubs. Thus, I would argue a work of original authorship was created with the drumbeat by Run-DMC, and without question, the writers of the song should claim a copyright.

---

[16] *T.E.A.M. Entm't, Inc. v. Douglas*, 2006 U.S. Dist. LEXIS 9681 (D.N.Y. 2006).

Since then, that popular refrain and drumbeat rhythm has been sampled and sampled and sampled. Note that not every sample will possess the requisite degree of originality to demand copyright protection, even where the author places notice of the intent to do so. The sample taken from the live performance of a drummer, using a standard drum set, which is then edited and used as musical structure (i.e., background rhythm), is unlikely to stand on its own as an identifiable work of authorship. But the "signature sample," an identifiable sound of an artist, which is then dropped into a new Busta Rhymes rap composition, may possess the required degree of personality to warrant copyrightability, as is the case with the popular Run-DMC drum riff.

SPLITS

Writers should generally split the royalties of a song in equal shares if everyone contributed equally. For example, a lyricist and a composer will each receive 50 percent of the royalties of a song, unless there is an expressed understanding of a different split. If there are more than two writers, each will receive an equal share of 33 percent, 25 percent, and so on.

For instance, if there are three writers and two of them contributed the vast majority of the material in the song, while the third contributed 10 percent, it is possible to form a written agreement in which the two main writers will receive 45 percent each, while the third receives 10 percent. This is only an example. The breakdown will not necessarily be proportionate to the amount of work that the writer contributes. Although this violates the general rule on writers, if it serves to preserve fairness, it can be achieved with a contract. The issue of drummer-as-songwriter is debatable, but the general rule is, if the drummer creates a drum beat that is unique, then he can be a co-writer and own a portion of the copyright. It is fairly difficult to come up with a completely unique drumbeat though, so this may not be an option for many drummers.

Aside from that, music writers and lyric writers usually split the royalties 50/50 without distinguishing what is what. It is important to note that if you miss identifying the splits at the time of writing the song, it is very difficult for your manager, lawyer, or advisors to protect you later.

It is also important to note that in some cases, however—for example, if the song does not make it onto an album—that each writer can try to reclaim their contribution to reuse in a different composition. (See Agreement Canceling Collaboration form at the end of this chapter.)

HOW YOU CAN KEEP TRACK

Using our Biggie album example, take a look at the back of the top-selling Bad Boy album by Notorious B.I.G., a/k/a the late Christopher Wallace. The album has sold over 10 million copies worldwide. On the back of the album, you will see a litany of writers for each song, ranging from four writers to nearly ten writers.

It is very critical under this scenario that you have proper administration for each writer, whether he contributed 1 percent or 99 percent of the songs on the album. An administrator's role is to issue the mechanical license or contract for use of the song to the label. Thus, if writer Wallace is administered by Warner Chappell Publishing, a staff member at Warner Chappell would send a two- to three-page mechanical license contract over to Bad Boy Records authorizing the use of the song on the album and the copyrighted portion as owned by Wallace. Keep in mind that this is done even if Wallace's interest was 1 percent. Essentially, whether 1 percent or 99 percent, he is one of the copyright holders on the final song that made it to the album.

As a result of these various writers on the hit B.I.G. song, the copyright application filed would reflect all of the writers. Specifically, the Copyright Office of the Library of Congress requires the inclusion of all writers on the song prior to the approval of a copyright certificate.

Even though we see a list of ten writers on the Biggie album, I'm sure there are other writers who feel like they were overlooked and not included on the "split sheet," which identifies the writer splits. If you are in a studio and writing, it is highly advisable that you keep split sheets present. You don't have to call it a split sheet, but keep a piece of paper that indicates the participation of all the writers and composers who worked on a song. I have provided a co-writer contract at the end of this chapter for your convenience.

In addition to Wallace, the other co-writers would have their respective shares administered by various companies or individuals. It is also not uncommon for law firms or other professional companies to administer and collect royalties in connection with a given song.

Upon issuance of the mechanical license, which I will discuss in more detail in Chapter Twenty, Mechanical Licenses and Administration, each quarter after release of the album, the record label will send a royalty statement and, hopefully, a check to the administrator on behalf of the songwriter. So, in our example, the administrators for Biggie (a/k/a Wallace) would collect a check every three months for Wallace based on the mechanical license and deduct their fees, before ultimately sending Wallace his appropriate check.

On the gospel side, Donald Lawrence and Steven Ford come to mind as two top writers. Lawrence has a catalog of hit songs like "Stranger," "God's Favor," "Never Seen the Righteous Forsaken," and "The Best Is Yet to Come." His catalog was initially administered by his personal team, but he later signed a publishing deal with EMI Publishing in Nashville. As a result, EMI collects thousands of dollars annually for Lawrence as his publishing administrator. Keep in mind, the collection is done whether his song is the hit song on an album or merely appears on an album. Imagine if you wrote the eighteenth song on the super-hot Tri-City album that sold near gold. Your administrator would be happy to collect for that non-hit song you wrote. The royalties are payable to you as the copyright holder, regardless of popularity of song on the album. Ford, the top gospel producer for over twenty years, is a writer/producer for the likes of Vickie Winans, Donnie McClurkin, and Richard Smallwood. He does not have a publishing deal with a major like EMI, but he explains, "My staff and I work very hard to collect all of my royalties, and we use administrators for a small fee when necessary."

In addition to the mechanical license, the administrator would issue separate licenses for videos, DVDs, and sheet music, among other uses. Thus, a hit song for one writer could result in dozens of licenses per year as that song is used time and time again in various mediums (CD, DVD, soundtracks, etc.). One song's potential to spin off into dozens of other things is one of the key reasons why no contribution is too small. If you wrote the refrain on the next *Billboard* Top 100 hit, you can make a lot of money off of that contribution alone. The administrator's hard work and efforts pay off here, in catching all of the uses of a song you co-wrote. The key to a good administrator is to track the use of the copyright as owned by his or her writer and make sure the writer is paid for any and all uses.

Indeed, it is difficult to catch every single use of a song, but a good administrator should capture the widely known and highly publicized uses of a song or copyright. A young writer, or even an established writer, has to recognize whether he or she has the resources time or flexibility to collect the royalties.

Many young writers attempt to administer and collect their own royalties in connections with the copyrights, or rather songs, that they own. I highly advise against this option if you are a new songwriter. As a writer, or especially as one of several writers of a song, you may not realize when your material is being used, and you do not have the time and capabilities to track all forms of media.

As indicated in the example above, an artist can lose millions for lack of tracking capabilities, know-how, and specialized training in finding the royalties owed on a particular song. Thus, it is in the best interest of the writer to have an experienced administrator issue licenses and collect royalties in connection with a song.

IMPORTANT TIPS ON CO-PUBLISHING/CO-OWNING WITH A RECORD LABEL

A few years ago, I did a deal with Sony Integrity that required our client to license his songs to Sony under a co-publishing situation—i.e., Sony shared 50/50 in his publishing income. However, each time his album was released, Sony attempted to license the song at 75-percent versus 100-percent fee. This bothered me tremendously and created a conflict of interest for all parties.

Essentially, my client had agreed that Sony could share in his copyright income equally with him. However, if they requested and secured the use of his songs at 75 percent of the full rate, then he was only receiving 37.5 percent of the revenue. We later fixed this problem, but it created an awkward situation initially.

If you are going to share your copyright with a label, make sure the rate is full 100-percent statutory. Make sure that you do not reduce the rate and hurt your own interests. Also, make sure that you limit their share solely on albums that you appear on or write for them. Thus, if you write for another label or another artist's project, they should not share in that income.

OVERVIEW

As you see, writer royalty pennies add up into fortunes. Keep track of who on your team wrote what, and you will not be poor and embittered when that song you have been working on becomes the next big hit and you have no paperwork to get paid. Revisit the Michael Jackson example, the Biggie example, and the hypothetical example, and learn everything you can about publishing.

AGREEMENT CANCELING COLLABORATION IN AN UNEXPLOITED COMPOSITION

This will confirm our mutual agreement concerning the following unexploited composition(s):

_____

_____

_____

_____

All agreements between us hereto made concerning said composition(s) are cancelled and terminated.

The title, lyrics, and melodies of said composition(s) are deemed separated and the rights in said component parts shall be vested and owned as follows:

Title to: _____

Lyrics to: _____

Melody to: _____

Each of us agrees not to use or offer for publication or other purposes any of such component parts of said composition(s) which is herein transferred and released to other writer(s)

Dated: _____

_____
(Signature)

_____
(Signature)

_____
(Signature)

_____
(Signature)

SONGWRITERS COLLABORATION CONTRACT

The purpose of this contract is to give maximum flexibility to the original song-writers to generate revenue from a song. Any amendments to this contract must be signed by all of the original songwriters.

The following _____ (number) songwriters are referred to as the original songwriters for the song titled

_____ (Title)

List of original songwriters (Please include all information):

#1: Last: _____ First: _____ Middle: _____

Address: _____

City: _____ State: _____ Zip: _____

SSN#: _____ Phone: _____

E-mail: _____ Affiliation: _____

Signature: _____ Date:ₛ_____

#2: Last: _____ First: _____ Middle: _____

Address: _____

City: _____ State: _____ Zip: _____

SSN#: _____ Phone: _____

E-mail: _____ Affiliation: _____

Signature: _____ Date:ₛ_____

Song Title

Signature and Date of the Original Songwriters

Signature and Date of the Recording Songwriter and/or Contributing Songwriter

Terms:

Songwriter(s)—the author(s) of the song.

Original Songwriters—songwriters listed who originated the song. An original songwriter can not be added to this contract unless all original songwriters agree and enter into a new contract.

Recording Songwriter(s)—a songwriter who signs a "Recording Songwriter Contract" with an original songwriter and is the singer/performer who records the song that generates revenue.

Contributing Songwriter(s)—any songwriter who has signed a "Contributing Songwriter Contract" with an original songwriter.

Share—percentage of moneys retained from the revenue of a song.

Recording Songwriter Contract—a contract between an original songwriter and another songwriter who is the artist who records the song that is distributed to the public and generates income.

Contributing Songwriter Contract—a contract between an original songwriter and another songwriter who contributes to the song.

Original Songwriters Rights:

The original songwriters each retain full administrative rights to the song within the guidelines listed below. They do not need any additional permission from a songwriter.

Any original songwriter may alter the words or melody of the song.

Any original songwriter may enter into a "Recording Songwriter Contract" with a recording songwriter.

Any original songwriter may enter into a "Contributing Songwriter Contract" with a contributing songwriter.

Any original songwriter may release any royalties from the revenue generated from the performance of the song in competition. They may also release the use of the song when related to a competition.

Any original songwriter may sell or give out free copies of the song on home-created media without paying a songwriter's share (or any monies) to any songwriter and without obtaining their permission.

Any original songwriter may produce or record the song without any of the other songwriters' permission.

Any original songwriter may enter into a contract with any company regarding the song so long as the Songwriters Share is distributed as mentioned in the section titled "Songwriter's Share" and the ownership of the song is retained by the original songwriters.

Song Title

Signature and Date of the Original Songwriters

Signature and Date of the Recording Songwriter and/or Contributing Songwriter

Songwriters share:

The original songwriter that was instrumental in generating revenue from the song will disperse the revenue and make records available to the other original songwriters and recording songwriter.

Among the original songwriters, the songwriters share from a song will be equally distributed.

If a recording songwriter(s) is added, any revenue generated by his recording will be equally distributed among the original songwriters and the one entity of a recording songwriter(s). Therefore if there are 2 original songwriters and 2 recording songwriters then the songwriter's share distributed as follows: 33% to each original songwriter and 16.5% to each recording songwriter. 16.5% + 16.5% = 33% which is the one entity share of the recording songwriter(s). In this example there is 3 entities: the 2 songwriters and the 1 entity of a recording songwriter. Therefore, the songwriter's share is divided into 3 equal parts of 33%. Among the 2 recording songwriters, their 33% share is equally distributed into 2 parts of 16.5%.

Among the recording songwriter(s), the one entity of their share will be equally distributed among the recording songwriter(s).

For a recording songwriter to receive a portion of the songwriter's share, the recording songwriter(s) must be a key performer on the media that generates the revenue. Therefore the recording songwriter would receive no songwriter's share if another performer records the song that generates the revenue.

The recording songwriter's contribution to the song becomes property of the original songwriter to leave in the song or remove from the song whether or not the song generates monies.

A contributing songwriter's share will be distributed by the original songwriter who entered into the "Contributing Songwriter Contract" and will be paid by the original songwriter from his own share.

If any of the original songwriters or recording songwriters cannot be located with reasonable attempts, the original songwriter making the deal that generates money will hold the monies that should be distributed to the songwriters who can not be located and will make open to the songwriters who receive monies, the records showing the income.

Any of the original songwriters may allow a song to be sung by a performer in a contest and sign a contract that allows the organization/company holding the contest to retain all royalties from the competition and use the audio/video from the contest in any way they desire.

Publisher's Share:

Any original songwriter has the right to negotiate the publisher's share. The songwriter may also register the song with his own publishing company.

Any original songwriter has the right to enter into a contract with a publisher as long as the contract is not exclusive, therefore, other original songwriters may enter into contracts with other publishers simultaneously to try and get the song published.

Song Title

Signature and Date of the Original Songwriters

Signature and Date of the Recording Songwriter and/or Contributing Songwriter

Recording Songwriter Contract:

    On _____ (date) I,_____ (Recording Songwriter), enter into this "Recording Songwriter Contract" with the original songwriter _____ (Original Songwriter).

    I have read a copy of the "Songwriter's Collaboration Contract" that this contract is a part of and understand the conditions of this contract reside in that contract. I have also signed in the appropriate section of the table at the top of each page. I understand that the contract states that I will receive no monies (songwriter's share) unless I am the performer on the published song that generates revenue. I also understand that the contract states that the original songwriter that was instrumental in generating income from the song will disperse the songwriter's share according to the contract.

    Recording Songwriter   Date

    Original Songwriter   Date

Contributing Songwriter Contract:

    On _____ (date) I, _____ (Contributing Songwriter), enter into this "Contributing Songwriter Contract" with the original songwriter _____ (Original Songwriter).

    I have read a copy of the "Songwriters Collaboration Contract" that this contract is a part of and understand the conditions of this contract reside in that contract. I have also signed in the appropriate section of the table at the top of each document page. I understand that the contract states that any monies that I receive will come directly from the original songwriter that I have made this contract with.

    Contributing Songwriter   Date

    Original Songwriter   Date

The LOX vs. P. Diddy: Statutory Rate vs. Three-Quarters Rate— What Does It Really Mean?

"It's all about the Benjamins"

—THE NOTORIOUS B.I.G.,
A/K/A CHRISTOPHER "BIGGIE" SMALLS

In 2005, the urban music industry went primetime on the issue of songwriting and "publishing" and collecting your royalties when well-known hip-hop group the LOX stepped on the mic at Hot 97 in New York and lashed out at music mogul P. Diddy (a/k/a Puff Daddy, a/k/a Sean Combs) for his control over their publishing. Many people were very surprised by these allegations and even more shocked that the hip-hop group went public at a premier radio station in the number-one market to voice problems with their contracts. The group also took their protest to the streets by distributing T-shirts to fans that said, "Free the LOX" and "Let the LOX Go," which did much to impress and sway public opinion in their favor. In the end, the LOX, consisting of Shawn "Sheek" Jacobs, Jayson "Jadakiss" Phillips, and David "Styles P" Styles, successfully opened up a dialogue on music publishing that had never been heard before with such passion.

As their Bad Boy bio attests, LOX—an acronym for Living Off eXperience— was a Yonkers, NY–based rap trio who worked their way up and eventually grabbed the attention of Mary J. Blige, who forwarded their demo tape to Diddy. Impressed, the rap czar ended up signing the talented trio in 1998 as writers to his Bad Boy label and publishing companies, where they proceeded to write for and rap on hits by the likes of himself, the Notorious B.I.G., Mary J. Blige, Mariah Carey, and Mase, before releasing their debut album *Money, Power & Respect*. This debut real-ized high expectations, peaking at #3 on the *Billboard* charts.

Unfortunately, after a subsequent falling out, the group left Bad Boy to join the Ruff Ryders label at Interscope. LOX members appealed to the Bad Boy owner to also release their publishing. Not having seen their contract, the LOX were essen-tially seeking a termination of their publishing contract, simultaneous with the ter-mination of their recording contract. This type of request is sometimes known as a "co-terminus" clause, i.e., they both terminate simultaneously, according to top LA entertainment lawyer Courtney Coates.

Said LOX member Styles P to New York disc jockey and rap artist Angie Martinez, while millions listened on, "Imagine working for years, hard work, and somebody that has nothing to do with your songs that is getting the bulk of it. You'd be totally, utterly frustrated. And, you tryin' to get around it for years and you call about it with lawyers, but people are too powerful." The frustration Styles P and fellow group member Jadakiss were referring to was the contractual rights Diddy retained to all of the hit songs written by the LOX during their recording contract with Bad Boy.

These royalties would be payable under the statutory royalties provision of the Copyright Act of 1976, as amended. In this chapter, we look at publishing and how the law or statutes require a songwriter to be paid a certain rate per song. We also look at how much revenue Diddy potentially earned in sharing the LOX publishing. Specifically, we will discuss the "statutory royalty rate" versus "three-quarters stat" (three-quarters of the full rate).

FULL STATUTORY RATE

The full statutory rate, called "full stat" for short, is the ceiling for royalty payments to writers and publishers under the Copyright Act of 1976, as amended. The statutory rate applies to all audio recordings that are made and distributed from the time the new statutory rate goes into effect until the time it is upgraded, regardless of the date of the mechanical license or the date that the particular recording was initially released.

For instance, if Kanye West released a new album in the United States in 2006, and a song on that album was licensed at the full statutory rate, the publisher and writer of the composition would receive a combined 9.1 cents for each album sold during the years 2006 and 2007. Once the statutory rate is changed, they will receive the new royalty, unless an agreement with the distributor or label provided otherwise.

So, one way that record labels get around a full statutory rate is by negotiating to form an agreement with the publisher and songwriter to use a fixed rate for the future payment of royalties. Under a fixed rate, the record label can grant the songwriter the full statutory rate today, but that rate is fixed for the future. So when the statutory rate changes at a future date, the songwriter will continue to see the same royalties as before. This is most common when the songwriter is an artist looking for a record deal or a record producer who writes songs for the album being produced.

Every two years, the statutory rate is raised as a result of the Copyright Act. This rate started at two cents per copy sold, due and payable to the songwriter or copyright holder. Until 1978, the most that a songwriter or publisher could expect to be paid was two cents per song. The Copyright Act of 1976 raised that rate, and it changes every two years as part of the Mechanical Rate Adjustment Proceeding of 1980. In 1988, the Consumer Price Index started to be used to adjust the statutory rate. By 1998 the Mechanical rate Adjustment Proceeding of 1997 began to be used.[17] Currently, the statutory rate is .091 (9.1 cents) for songs five minutes or under and 1.75 cents per minute or fraction thereof over five minutes. For example:

Up to 5:00 = $.091

5:01 to 6:00 = $.105 (6 × $.0175 = $.105)

6:01 to 7:00 = $.1225 (7 × $.0175 = $.1225)

7:01 to 8:00 = $.14 (8 × $.0175 = $.14)

---

[17] To see the history of statutory rates, visit www.copyright.gov/carp/m200a.pdf.

THREE-QUARTERS RATE

Unless you are one of the industry's top songwriters or artists (who is also a writer), it is extremely difficult to command the full statutory rate. Record companies are in the business of making money, so a lot of the time labels negotiate with songwriters to reduce the royalty rate that they will receive. This is a particularly common strategy practiced on new songwriters who have not yet established a name for themselves.

This reduced rate is known as the three-quarters rate or "three-quarters stat." Under three-quarters stat, a writer would receive .06825 (6.8 cents) of a .091 (9.1 cent) statutory rate. Some people in the music industry may tell you that songwriters never receive the full statutory rate and that it is common knowledge that the three-quarters rate is the going rate for songs. However, it's important to stress that this contractual detail would be determined on a case-by-case basis and that well-seasoned writers will rarely work for three-quarters rate. When I am negotiating the rates for top songwriters on the popular gospel albums called *Wow Gospel*, I often secure full statutory rate, even though the labels will vehemently argue for a 25 percent reduction to three-quarters stat. This reduction saves the labels thousands of dollars in royalties if a song is licensed more cheaply.

DIDDY VERSUS THE LOX: THE FIGHT OVER THE STATUTORY BENJAMINS

In addition to the royalty rate, you also have to consider the publisher's split. A typical record label contract like Bad Boy/ LOX would call for the group to turn over 50 percent of its "publishing" to Diddy or his publishing companies (look in the credits of any song or composition and in addition to the writer names, you will also see their publishing company administrator and performing rights organization affiliations—e.g., for Bad Boy you will see Justin Combs Publishing). Now, if the LOX album sold a million copies or went double platinum like most of Diddy's projects, the statutory publishing income is phenomenal. Here is a breakdown of the songs on the *Money, Power & Respect* album released on Bad Boy and how you would calculate the "publishing" income at the heart of the fight between the two parties a few years ago:

The LOX Track Listing:	Writer(s):	Timing:	Royalty:
1. "Yonkers Tale (Intro)"		1:45	$.0910
2. "Livin' the Life"	Combs, Frierson, Jacobs, Phillips, Styles	3:36	$.0910
3. "If You Think I'm Jiggy"	Appice, Blackmon, Jacobs, Phillips, Stewart, Styles	4:40	$.0910
4. "Money, Power & Respect"	Angelettie, Jacobs, Lawrence, Phillips, Simmons, Smith, Styles	4:30	$.0910
5. "Get This $"	Combs, Isle, Isley, Jacobs, Phillips, Styles	3:58	$.0910

continued

The LOX Track Listing:	Writer(s):	Timing:	Royalty:
6. "Let's Start Rap Over"	Blackmon, Claxton, Gaynor, Jacobs, Phillips, Spalding, Styles, Walker	4:28	$.0910
7. "I Wanna Thank You"	Jacobs, Myrick, Phillips, Radcliffe, Scott, Styles	4:02	$.0910
8. "Goin' Be Some Shit"	Broady, Emcee Dee, Jacobs, MC Lyte, Myrick	4:20	$.0910
9. "The Heist, Pt. 1"	Carter, Combs, Jacobs, Phillips, Styles	2:51	$.0910
10. "Not to be F#%#ed With"	Blackmon, Styles	4:23	$.0910
11. "The Setup (Interlude)"	Non-Paid	:48	$.0910
12. "Bitches from Eastwick"	Angelettie, Hayes, Jacobs, Phillips, Styles, Thompson	4:13	$.0910
13. "Can't Stop, Won't Stop"	Angelettie, Combs, Jackson, Jacobs, Jordan, Phillips, Styles	3:38	$.0910
14. "All for the Love"	Dean, Phillips	3:33	$.0910
15. "Mad Rapper (Interlude)"	Non-Paid	1:15	$.0910
16. "So Right"	Combs, Harris, Jacobs, Lawrence, Lewis, Phillips, Styles	3:30	$.0910
17. "The Snitch (Interlude)"	Non-Paid	1:31	$.0910
18. "Everybody Wanna Rat"	Blackmon, Fields, Jacobs, Phillips, Styles	4:17	$.0910
19. "Interview, Pt. 1"	Non-Paid	:39	$.0910
20. "Interview, Pt. 2"	Non-Paid	:14	$.0910
21. "We'll Always Love Big Poppa"	Blackmon, Jacobs, Phillips, Styles	5:00	$.0910
TOTAL		63:11	$1.91

IF DIDDY AND BAD BOY PAID FULL STATUTORY RATE

There are several things to note about the chart above. First, although there are twenty-one songs, no songwriter will get paid for the interludes or interviews (i.e., tracks 11, 15, 17, 19, and 20). So we reduce the payment scale for these adjustments. Now, since we are specifically talking about the concerns of the LOX, we have to gather how much they made and would be due. If you look carefully at the chart, you will see Jacobs or Styles and/or Phillips are credited on fifteen of the twenty-one songs or interludes, etc. So, the first thing we do is add up their collective publishing interest. We next divide their interest in half, if they assigned 50 percent of their publishing when they signed the recording contract. We do this by going through each individual song and dividing the .0910 by the number of writers on that given song. So for example, in song 2 above, "Livin' the Life," there are five writers, so you divide .091 by five, which comes to .0182 per writer. The LOX would receive three times this amount as three of the writers for a total of .0546 on song number two ("Livin' the Life"). If they signed a publishing deal, this figure would be split in half as .0273 to the LOX and .0273 to Diddy's publishing entity. The chart would then be modified. First, we remove the non-royalty-paying songs or interludes like tracks 11, 15, 17, 19, and 20. So the chart now reads as follows for the fifteen songs that have writing credits from the LOX members and we add Bad Boy's percentage:

The LOX Track Listing:	Writer(s) (Only Songs that Contain the LOX as Writers):	Timing:	Royalty:	LOX %	Bad Boy %
2. "Livin' the Life"	Combs, Frierson, Jacobs, Phillips, Styles	3:36	$.0910	$.0546	$.0273
3. "If You Think I'm Jiggy"	Appice, Blackmon, Jacobs, Phillips, Stewart, Styles	4:40	$.0910	$.0455	$.0227
4. "Money, Power & Respect"	Angelettie, Jacobs, Lawrence, Phillips, Simmons, Smith, Styles	4:30	$.0910	$.039	$.0195
5. "Get This $"	Combs, Isle, Isley, Jacobs, Phillips, Styles	3:58	$.0910	$.0455	$.0227
6. "Let's Start Rap Over"	Blackmon, Claxton, Gaynor, Jacobs, Phillips, Spalding, Styles, Walker	4:28	$.0910	$.0341	$.0170
7. "I Wanna Thank You"	Jacobs, Myrick, Phillips, Radcliffe, Scott, Styles	4:02	$.0910	$.0455	$.0227
8. "Goin' Be Some Shit"	Broady, Emcee Dee, Jacobs, MC Lyte, Myrick	4:20	$.0910	$.0546	$.0273
9. "The Heist, Pt. 1"	Carter, Combs, Jacobs, Phillips, Styles	2:51	$.0910	$.0546	$.0273
10. "Not to be F#%#ed With"	Blackmon, Styles	4:23	$.0910	$.0455	$.0227
12. "Bitches from Eastwick"	Angelettie, Hayes, Jacobs, Phillips, Styles, Thompson	4:13	$.0910	$.0455	$.0227
13. "Can't Stop, Won't Stop"	Angelettie, Combs, Jackson, Jacobs, Jordan, Phillips, Styles	3:38	$.0910	$.039	$.0195
14. "All for the Love"	Dean, Phillips	3:33	$.0910	$.0455	$.0227
16. "So Right"	Combs, Harris, Jacobs, Lawrence, Lewis, Phillips, Styles	3:30	$.0910	$.039	$.0195
18. "Everybody Wanna Rat"	Blackmon, Fields, Jacobs, Phillips, Styles	4:17	$.0910	$.0546	$.0273
21. "We'll Always Love Big Poppa"	Blackmon, Jacobs, Phillips, Styles	5:00	$.0910	$.0682	$.0341
TOTAL		58:19	$1.365	$.6766	$.3383

Now, to explain this chart, let's go step by step. What we have done is isolated the fifteen songs that include one or all of the LOX members. We then add up the entire percentage, top to bottom, and we figure out that the total timing on all of their songs is 58.19 minutes and their total payment on the remaining fifteen songs would be $.6766. Remember, we are assuming for purposes of this hypothetical that the LOX were paid at the full statutory rate of .0910 (approximately nine cents per song) × (times) fifteen songs. So, for each CD they sold, Bad Boy would pay a total of $1.365 (approximately a dollar and thirty-six cents) to the writers together. Each song would be divided based on the ownership shares. And, if the LOX appear as writers together on twelve of the fifteen songs jointly, then they would receive their pro-rata ownership share. Thus, assume further that the album was double platinum as reported. This would calculate as follows:

$1.365 (combined full stat. payment) × 2,000,000 (units sold) = $2,730,000

Yes, that number is correct. If the group wrote the entire album and Bad Boy Records paid the LOX what's called the "full statutory" rate under the Copyright Act, the group would be due $2.73 million.

Now, if their contract called for three-quarters rate, then you would adjust that figure by 25 percent, and instead have a total of $2,047,500 (a reduction of 25 percent per album sold as "publishing" income). The rate would be reduced to .06825 (i.e., 75 percent or three-quarters of the .0910 full rate). To illustrate:

$10.23 (3/4ths of stat. for all songs) × 2,000,000 (units sold) = $2,0475,000

CO-PUBLISHING DEAL

For purposes of the examples, it is important to note a few things. In the event the group signed a recording contract that included a "co-publishing" split to Diddy, this would require the LOX to share with Bad Boy, or its "related entity" Justin Combs Publishing, much of this income. Diddy or his companies would share 50/50 in the income associated—i.e., half of the publishing. Thus, if the songs were paid at full stat (.0910 per song), then Diddy and company would receive half of the $2.73 million publishing income. Likewise, if the songs were licensed at three-quarters of the statutory rate, then Diddy and company would split the $2 million figure in half and share equally on that income.

CONTROLLED COMPOSITION CLAUSE AND MAXIMUM TWELVE SONGS

It is important to note that most labels will not pay a songwriter/artist on more than twelve songs. So, if an artist attempts to record twenty songs and get paid mechanical royalties at full statutory rate for all twenty songs, a label will include a clause in the recording contract that states in no uncertain terms, "despite the number of songs contained on any master, artist shall only be paid mechanical royalties on a maximum number of twelve (12) songs."

Thus, looking at our hypothetical above, even though there were seventeen songs on the LOX album and four interludes and interviews, Bad Boy contractually probably only had to pay mechanicals on twelve of the songs. Thus, the publishing income would be as follows for full statutory rate:

$1.092 (12 songs) × $2,000,000 (units sold) = $2,184,000

Notice this figure on twelve songs is over a half million less in publishing income to the writers. Also note that the label can calculate it as either twelve songs times the full statutory rate or divide the $1.092 by all fifeen songs. Either way, they are only going to pay for a maximum of twelve compositions or songs written on the album. And this is the figure that ALL writers would be paid out of at full stat.

Now, do note, if the LOX, in their agreement, licensed twelve songs at three-quarters rate, the equation changes tremendously also. This agreement would calculate as follows:

12 songs $\times$ .06825 (per song) = 0.819 $\times$ 2,000,000 (units sold) = $1,638,000

So, on a double-platinum (2 million sold) project, let's financially recap, with a chart to see what's really happening:

# of Royalty-Paying Songs	Rate	Gross Publ. Income	50% Diddy's Share
15	Full stat	$2,730,000	$1,365,000
15	Three-quarters stat	$2,047,500	$1,023,750
12	Full stat	$2,184,000	$1,092,000
12	Three-quarters stat	$1,638,000	$819,000

I must emphasize that Diddy's share could be lower or higher, depending on what the recording contract specifically stated with regards to the publishing owned by the three members of the LOX. All we know is that according to published reports and the common practice of the industry, Diddy or his publishing companies participated in the lucrative revenue associated with the songs written by the LOX. In some cases, it's a straight 50/50 percent split down the middle on all the publishing income. In some cases, it's 50 percent of the publisher's share, but the artist as a writer keeps his writer's share. It's a little complicated, and we discuss it more in depth in our publishing chapter ahead; however, understand this: We are talking millions of dollars in connection with these fifteen songs written on the LOX album. And, I must be clear that we are examining the songs, the timing, and the royalty rates speculatively, without access to the signed contract between the LOX and Bad Boy. Thus, our numbers are solely estimates using general industry standards.

Also keep in mind that the publishing income goes beyond just the CD sales. You also earn publishing income from ringtones, remixes, jingles, commercials, sheet music, downloads, videos, digital gaming, soundtracks, and tons of other uses for a given hit song. One look at the above-listed chart and it's easy to see how artists can underestimate the splits and overspend their projected income. As Biggie said, it is all about the Benjamins—getting and keeping them.

TYPES OF ROYALTIES

The LOX example above is helpful for you to understand the millions of dollars we are talking about when we talk "publishing" in this industry. However, realize that there are other types of royalties, depending on how your music is performed and distributed. Licenses fall into five major categories:

- Mechanical licenses/mechanical royalties
- Performance rights and licenses/performance royalties
- Synchronization rights and licenses/synchronization royalties
- Print rights and licenses/print royalties
- Digital recording-fund licenses/digital-recording royalties

A mechanical license is permission to reproduce music into a CD, cassette, LP, or other form of media for public distribution in stores. The music publisher grants permission for the musical composition to be reproduced. The mechanical royalty is paid to the recording artist, songwriter/composer, and publisher based on the number of recordings sold. I will discuss this in further detail in Chapter Twenty, Mechanical Licenses and Administration, but for the multiple songs recorded by the LOX on their *Money, Power & Respect* album, there would be a mechanical license agreement for each song.

A performance rights license allows music to be performed live or broadcast on the radio or in malls, restaurants, and other businesses. These licenses typically come in the form of a "blanket license," which gives the licensee the right to play a particular performance rights organization's (ASCAP, BMI, SESAC; see Chapter Fifteen) entire collection in exchange for a fee or an individual license for use of individual recordings. The performance royalty is paid to the songwriter and publisher in equal shares when a song is performed live or on the radio or other venue.

Likewise, a synchronization license is needed for a song to be used in a television program, film, video, commercial, or on radio. The synchronization royalty is paid to songwriters and publishers for use of a song in a movie, TV show, or commercial. I will discuss this in further detail in Chapter Twenty-Two, Amazing Grace: Public Domain and Gospel Music, but note that if there were a LOX video or DVD, you would need synchronization licenses as well for the same songs listed earlier.

Print rights and royalties are paid to songwriters and publishers based on sales of printed sheet music. I will discuss this in further detail in Chapter Eighteen on songwriter contracts and publishing deals.

A digital recording license requires that the manufacturers of digital audio recording devices and the manufacturers of blank recording media (blank cassette tapes, blank CDs, blank DVDs, etc.) pay a percentage of their sales price to the Register of Copyrights to make up for loss of sales owing to the possible unauthorized copying of music through piracy and peer-to-peer programs like Napster.[18] The money paid by these manufacturers is dispersed between two funds. The Sound Recording Fund receives two-thirds of the money, which goes to the recording artists and record companies. The Musical Works Fund, which receives one-third of the money, splits it between the publisher and the songwriter.

---

[18] Audio Home Recording Act of 1992.

HARRY FOX AGENCY

It is important to include a little tidbit on the Harry Fox Agency (HFA), or Harry Fox, as it is commonly known. HFA is the foremost mechanical licensing, collections, and distribution agency for U.S. music publishers. It is to publishers what ASCAP, BMI, and SESAC are to writers.

Established in 1927 by the National Music Publisher's Association, Harry Fox is an information source, clearinghouse, and monitoring service for licensing musical copyrights for music publishers. Harry Fox licenses the largest percentage of the mechanical and digital uses of music in the United States on printed media, collectively known as phonorecords.

Although Harry Fox resources are available to anyone with access to the Internet, to gain membership to Harry Fox, music publishers must have current record activity, such as a song released on a third-party record label. This means that if your songs are recorded on your own record label, you cannot become a member of Harry Fox.[19] Once a music publisher qualifies for membership, Harry Fox covers the issuance of mechanical licenses, synchronization licenses, and electrical transcription licenses and collects royalties that are earned from licensing.

STATUTORY RATES THROUGHOUT HISTORY

If you think that writers are being ripped off by record labels, consider yourself lucky to be in the business in 2007. It is only recently that statutory rates hit an all-time high; as a matter of fact, they did not change a cent from 1909 to 1978. For almost seventy years, song writers were paid the same royalty. Here is the history of increases in the rate:

---

[19] For information on becoming a member of the Harry Fox Agency, visit: www.harryfox.com/public/index.jsp

From	To	Rate
1909	December 31, 1977	2.00 cents for all songs
January 1, 1978	June 30, 1981	2.75 cents for songs 5 minutes or less or 0.50 cents per minute or fraction thereof for songs over 5 minutes
July 1, 1981	December 31, 1982	4.00 cents for songs 5 minutes or less or 0.75 cents per minute or fraction thereof for songs over 5 minutes
January 1, 1983	June 30, 1984	4.25 cents for songs 5 minutes or less or 0.80 cents per minute or fraction thereof for songs over 5 minutes
July 1, 1984	December 31, 1985	4.50 cents for songs 5 minutes or less or 0.85 cents per minute or fraction thereof for songs over 5 minutes
January 1, 1986	December 31, 1987	5.00 cents for songs 5 minutes or less or 0.95 cents per minute or fraction thereof for songs over 5 minutes
January 1, 1988	December 31, 1989	5.25 cents for songs 5 minutes or less or 1.00 cents per minute or fraction thereof for songs over 5 minutes
January 1, 1990	December 31, 1991	5.70 cents for songs 5 minutes or less or 1.10 cents per minute or fraction thereof for songs over 5 minutes
January 1, 1992	December 31, 1993	6.25 cents for songs 5 minutes or less or 1.20 cents per minute or fraction thereof for songs over 5 minutes
January 1, 1994	December 31, 1995	6.60 cents for songs 5 minutes or less or 1.25 cents per minute or fraction thereof for songs over 5 minutes
January 1, 1996	December 31, 1997	6.95 cents for songs 5 minutes or less or 1.30 cents per minute or fraction thereof for songs over 5 minutes
January 1, 1998	December 31, 1999	7.10 cents for songs 5 minutes or less or 1.35 cents per minute or fraction thereof for songs over 5 minutes
January 1, 2000	December 31, 2001	7.55 cents for songs 5 minutes or less or 1.45 cents per minute or fraction thereof for songs over 5 minutes
January 1, 2002	December 31, 2003	8.00 cents for songs 5 minutes or less or 1.55 cents per minute or fraction thereof for songs over 5 minutes
January 1, 2004	December 31, 2005	8.5 cents for songs 5 minutes or less or 1.65 cents per minute or fraction thereof for songs over 5 minutes
January 1, 2006	December 31, 2007	9.1 cents for songs 5 minutes or less or 1.75 cents per minute or fraction thereof for songs over 5 minutes

CLOSING TIPS

Although the statutory royalty rate assures payment to the songwriter, do not expect that you will receive the full rate. Also remember, if you are offered a contract to receive a full statutory rate, but it will be fixed in time, you might be better off with a three-quarters rate that is not fixed. Since the statutory rate changes often, you do not want to be locked into one rate permanently.

Furthermore, keep track of your licensed music to ensure that you collect all the royalties due to you. Take advantage of resources like the Harry Fox Agency to figure out the royalties that you should collect; or better yet, hire a copyright administrator for your catalog. As long as you understand how your royalties are calculated, collected, and distributed, you are ahead of the game. Keep as your motivation the unfortunate stories of other artists who let copyrights lapse on valuable compositions because of delayed or inaccurate paperwork details—be aware, and stay on top of your filings. Especially in a group or collective writing situation, maintain awareness of and involvement in the administration of your individual split.

Whatever you do, understand what you are signing and have good legal representation. The LOX were lucky and fortunate to have the power of Hot 97 in New York to reach Diddy and resolve their contractual publishing issues. Most artists or songwriters do not have this opportunity. As we discussed in Chapter Six, dealing with agents, lawyers, publicists, etc., surround yourself with qualified and experienced folks who can make a positive difference in your long-term career—financially and otherwise.

If signed to an affiliated label and publisher, consider splitting the administration of your master versus songwriter royalties to separate entities. As Monique Headley highlights, "Publishers perk up and are swayed by a label signing because, as an artist, it make you more financially viable with a relatively immediate revenue system in place to assist in the promotion of your music and generation of royalties. This kind of machine and level of business partner make you increasingly attractive to publishers."

If you do sign a deal with affiliated label and publisher, have your attorney include a co-terminus clause in your contract, so that when the fat lady sings for your label recording career, so will she signal the close to the publishing side of things, too. This step will renew to you the maximum freedom to shop for a better and more inclusive deal with the momentum you've been building with the previous label and publisher.

CHAPTER 18

**Songwriter Contracts and
Publishing Deals: What Are They?**

*"If you are thinking about signing a publishing deal, you have to decide if
that's something that's right for you at that time in your career. But whatever you sign, inspect what you expect."*
— SEAN GARRETT, TOP SONGWRITER FOR USHER

In June 2006, well-known artist and super-writer Chamillionaire signed an
exclusive publishing deal with Universal Publishing, home to such great writers as
Ice Cube, Mariah Carey, and Ludacris to name a few. A few years prior, 50 Cent
had also signed a publishing deal with Columbia. Gospel sensation Kirk Franklin
was signed to Lilly Mack Publishing for the first ten years of his career under a joint
artist-publishing deal. And, of course, everyone knows Rodney Jerkins was only
seventeen years old when he signed his lucrative multiyear, multimillion-dollar
deal with EMI Publishing.

Regarding these deals, I am commonly asked by young artists and songwriters,
"What is a publishing deal? Is it good for my career?" In this chapter, I hope to provide an overview of music publishing, the signing of a publishing deal, and the various types of publishing deals.

Although a bit complicated, music publishing remains one of the most financially lucrative areas in the music business, and one of the few areas in which artists
can survive if he or she takes the right path. As a result, this book would be sorely
lacking if we did not provide the critical information needed for recording artists
and songwriters to protect their publishing rights. For our purposes, the term
"publishing deal" refers, rather broadly, to any kind of deal whereby some individual or company (other than the songwriter) obtains the right to receive a share of
the songwriter's music publishing income (for example, mechanical royalties from
the use of songs on records, public performance income from BMI and ASCAP for
radio airplay, and synchronization income from the use of songs in films, television
shows, computer games, etc.).

There are four major types of deals: 1) the traditional exclusive publishing
deal; 2) the co-publishing deal; 3) the administration deal; and 4) the sub-publishing, or "sub-pub," deal. Additionally, there are some less common deals like
investor deals, step-up deals, and single-song deals.

Although there are countless small publishers, five majors publishers dominate
the industry. The so-called majors: BMG Music Publishing, EMI Music
Publishing, Sony/ATV Music Publishing, Universal Music Publishing Group (used
in this discussion), and Warner-Chappell Music Publishing.

All of the majors publish various styles of music writers, and right now urban
music is among the most popular. BMG Music Publishing publishes writers like
Nelly, Keyshia Cole, Foxy Brown, R. Kelly, and Justin Timberlake. EMI Music

Publishing publishes Nelly Furtado, Shakira, Yung Joc, Kelis, and Sean Paul. Sony/ATV Music Publishing, a joint venture between Sony and Michael Jackson, publishes such writers as Lyfe Jennings, Wyclef Jean, Lauryn Hill, Maxwell, and Mikkel Erikson, who has written for the likes of Rihanna, Kelly Rowland, and Beyoncé Knowles. Explains Jennings: "A publishing deal can be a great thing if you understand business and understand your role and the role of the publisher in maximizing your songwriting royalties and profitability."

EXCLUSIVE PUBLISHING DEAL

Let's take one of the major urban publishers and dissect an exclusive publishing deal. Universal Music Publishing Group (referenced throughout the book as "Universal" or "UMPG") is one of the majors, with urban writers Prince, Ashanti, Mary J. Blige, Eve, Musiq, and Brian McKnight, to name a few. The company administers more than 1 million copyrights in nearly fifty offices worldwide. In the early days, before the invention of the phonograph, songwriters earned income by relying on music publishers to sell sheet music copies of their songs. Well-known singers like Billie Holiday and Mahalia Jackson used established songwriters to develop hit songs. But, in the 1950s, we saw Elvis and rock 'n' roll, then later the Beatles and pop music and ultimately the Supremes with black music. More and more, well-established acts were writing more of their own songs. As the music industry became a multibillion-dollar worldwide conglomerate, the role of publishers was still needed for the great growth of writers.

UMPG also administers the prestigious sixty-thousand-title Rondor Music catalog and also owns or administers a multitude of prestigious catalogs including those of Interscope and Def Jam Music, All Nations Music, Charlie Daniels, Matraca Berg, Forerunner Music, Epitaph, Greenwich/Barry, Momentum Publishing, and John Philips. UMPG also owns or administers the works of Leonard Bernstein, Holland/Dozier/Holland, and Henry Mancini.

Given the prolific history of UMPG and the success of Chamillionaire, a partnership is understandable. When Chamillionaire's deal was signed it was described as an "exclusive publishing deal." Chamillionaire's *The Sound of Revenge* album was certified platinum, and his hit single "Ridin'" held down the number-one spot on the *Billboard* Hot 100 for two weeks. It was no surprise when Universal came along, like many others, and offered him an exclusive publishing deal.

The exclusive deal provides cash paid at the signing and yearly installments thereafter. Most likely, because Chamillionaire is a hot songwriter, his attorney would negotiate a publishing deal incorporating an upfront, high-six-figure or seven-figure advance. If that attorney is clever, he or she can seek a non-recoupable advance in total or ask that some portion of an artist's advance be non-recoupable. In the 1980s and 1990s heyday of the rap world, a publishing deal might have contained a large cash advance. However, given the economics and the drastic changes in today's music industry, an advance can be reduced to the range of twenty-five thousand to fifty thousand dollars, and you will only see five hundred thousand or more advances, if you are a super-hot writer with many hits coming to the deal upfront.

Because Chamillionaire had a successful track record, he may have gotten a very substantial advance up front, with additional advances each following year that Universal exercises its option for another year. Each publisher has a sophisticated formula in determining the year-two advance. It could be based on net profits, the number of songs turned in (as discussed below), or revenue streams.

In addition to his entire catalog, the exclusive publishing agreement gave Universal the rights to all compositions and copyrights written and created during a specified number of years into the future. Normally, an agreement will be for an initial one-year period (with the writer obligated to deliver a certain number of songs to the publisher in that one year), followed by several consecutive one-year options (usually as small as three years, but as high as six years in some cases). Even though the term of the agreement may be only a few years, without a reversion clause (where the rights revert to Chamillionaire as discussed below) the publisher will be the owner of those songs for a much, much longer period of time, sometimes until they go into public domain many years later.

The creative director at UMPG, who most likely put the deal together, like Kamala Gordon, formerly at Warner-Chappell, or Brian Jackson and Evan Lamberg at EMI, will expect Chamillionaire to submit songs throughout the year. Additionally, to assist this great writer, the UMPG team will send him a "who's looking list" of all of the various projects presently being considered by labels and the types of songs they are looking for from songwriters.

A "who's looking list" might say, for example, that Arista is looking for a slow ballad for Whitney Houston's next project (similar to "Saving All My Love"), or Motown is looking for a "neo-soul" song for the next Erykah Badu project. Or, alternatively, Beyoncé is looking for a track for her upcoming solo project similar to her smash hit "Bills, Bills, Bills" with Destiny's Child. The key is for Chamillionaire as a writer to go to work and crank out a hit for the powers that be at UMPG.

If he delivers a hit, the two parties will split the income, the songwriter's share of the royalties being 50 percent, while the publisher Universal also receives 50 percent. The splits are larger than the other deals discussed below because the publisher in this deal is supposed to be more proactive in getting placements for the songwriter on other artist's albums. It is critical to understand in an exclusive publishing deal, where a songwriter assigns his copyrights and compositions, the publisher must be proactive and actually secure placements for you. If Beyoncé records a Chamillionaire song on her next album and the album goes platinum, the publisher would share in the nearly $100,000 due to Chamillionaire (assuming the song was licensed at full statutory rate of 9.1. cents per CD sold, as we discussed in the prior chapter) for that single track. In that case splitting is appropriate, since UMPG did the work in getting the song placed in the first place.

Another value of such an exclusive relationship with a publisher is that Chamillionaire is guaranteed steady income. Remember, even though he is a great songwriter and/or artist, without a deal such as this he won't be paid until his CD comes out and starts selling or if he has songs on other projects. In addition, since it can take six months to two years for royalties from record sales and performances to reach Chamillionaire, the advances, whether distributed monthly or annually (sometimes known as a "writer's draw"), can lend a great deal of financial security in the time the artist is waiting for royalties to be collected and processed.

But keep in mind that these advances to Chamillionaire will be deducted from any royalties that become due from record sales, downloads, sheet music, commercials, home video, television, and motion picture synchronization fees, as well as from any other source of income that the publisher controls. This is all determined by the deal that you put together with your publisher as negotiated by your lawyer.

CO-PUBLISHING DEAL

Using our same Beyoncé example, Universal would not see an equal fifty thousand dollars or 50-percent split on the platinum song written by Chamillionaire. Instead, Universal would see twenty-five thousand dollars as its share. In a co-publishing deal, the writer's share is still 50 percent, but the publisher's share is split in two; 25 percent to the publisher and another 25 to the writer. This is because in addition to acting as the writer, in a co-publishing deal Chamillionaire's publishing entity will split the publisher's share equally. It's a little tricky, but in a "co-pub" deal, the writer generally retains the entire writers' share and splits equally with the publisher on the publisher's share, as we discussed in earlier chapters. So, if a song pays ten cents in full, the writer keeps five cents and splits the remaining five cents. These publishing deals may cover all songs written by an artist or just those songs commercially released over the course of the agreement.

In the language of the music industry, we refer to a 100-percent writer's share and a 100-percent publisher's share. You will see this language in various agreements. Essentially, although confusing jargon, it means simply that a song is divided into two shares of 100 percent each. So, when a songwriter signs a co-pub deal, he is keeping his 100-percent songwriter's income and only sharing half of the 100 percent going to his publishing company or publishing designee. Thus, in the example above, Universal would split the fifty-thousand-dollar publisher's share with Chamillionaire's publishing company—i.e., Chamillionaire Music. No matter how you do the math, it works out to 75/25 in favor of the writer.

In such a setup, the songwriter receives an advance but generally negotiates the other services that the publisher will provide. Since the publisher is only getting paid half of the standard percentage, the songwriter may be left doing some work for himself that publishers would ordinarily do, like shopping demos. Co-publishing is wonderful because it gives you more control over your songs and you relinquish 25 percent versus 50 percent of the income, but it will add to an artist's responsibilities.

A co-pub deal is also commonly used for writers who are in groups already signed to a record deal. Many of the groups signed to labels such as Jive or Zomba have this type of arrangement. This type of agreement covers the original material on the group's records. Normally, all of the members of the group who are songwriters will be signed to this type of agreement by the same publisher. It is important to limit the co-pub deal to only the material the group writes for, e.g., Zomba, leaving out material written by group members for projects outside of their album.

For groups newly signed to major label record deals the initial advance from a major music publisher is typically in the $100,000–$500,000 range and can be higher, with additional advances being paid if and when the publisher exercises its options for the follow-up albums. Please note, these numbers are not set in stone, and with good counsel an advance can be higher (and, with bad counsel, I must confess, could be even lower).

Do not overlook the possibility of establishing an agreement with the publisher/record label that allows for a reduction on album number two as well as any subsequent albums. For example, the co-publishing deal could provide that Zomba is to share in the publishing on the first album but reduce its take to four or five songs on the second album, three or four songs on the third album, and so on. We call this a "phase-out" deal, where the publisher, affiliated with the record company, is eventually phased out in its take of the publishing income. The logic is, since the publisher is doing very little work, the reductions are not unreasonable as the group grows in stature.

The songwriter normally transfers one-half of the copyright ownership to the publisher and retains the other half. In other words, the song is co-published (and the copyright is co-owned 50/50) by the third-party publisher and the writer's own publishing company. In a co-publishing deal, Universal, as Chamillionaire's publisher, would collect all income and then pay the songwriter and the songwriter's publishing company 75 percent of all publishing income.

Similar to a traditional exclusive publishing deal, the term of a co-pub deal can be one to six years, depending on the results of the negotiation process. As already mentioned, co-publishing agreements are usually for a certain specified number of albums.

ADMINISTRATION DEALS

Over the past few years, much attention has been placed on the near billion-dollar catalog owned by Michael Jackson and his ATV/Sony arrangement. Years ago, Jackson, ironically educated in part by Paul McCartney on music publishing, purchased portions of the Beatles catalog for $47.5 million. Jackson then went on to buy up other catalogs and build one of the most powerful music catalogs ever assembled. When he partnered with Sony, it was reportedly an administration deal, not an exclusive publishing deal.

One of the main functions of a publisher is to properly administer the songwriter's catalog. Sometimes all that a songwriter needs is administration, particularly if the songwriter is established and does not need a lot of promotional help from the publisher. A publisher that handles purely administration will keep track of the collection of royalties and send the writer a check every few months. Administration deals can be negotiated so your publisher only earns a small portion of your royalties instead of the standard 50 percent, again maximizing your earnings.

It is usually advisable to sign an administration, or "admin," deal if you are a songwriter like Jackson with a bulk of songs returning a great revenue and do not have the time or energy to self-publish by registering with the collecting societies and tracking royalties yourself. Under an admin deal, the publisher, like Sony with Jackson, signs on to administer the artist's songs. Sony would most likely appeal to

Jackson as a publisher collecting royalties and handling the various paperwork (for example, the BMI/ASCAP song title registrations, copyright applications, and the issuance of licenses). It is important to note that in an admin deal Sony would take no interest in the artist's copyright ownership but simply prepare the paperwork to license the use of the songs.

The assumption in an admin deal is that these songs are already copywritten, preexisting as part of the artist's catalog. In MJ's deal, he probably did not assign his copyright to the publisher, as no writer should do in such a deal. And, with Jackson's savvy, he would not easily agree to any reduction in his copyright ownership either.

For a specified period of time, usually between three and five years, Sony can license the use of Jackson's songs in recordings, tapes, CDs, television series, motion pictures, DVDs, commercials, and video productions and collect royalties from all music users. In return for its services, the publisher will receive an "administration fee," usually ranging from 10 to 15 percent of the gross income earned during the term of the agreement. It is important to note that in a typical admin deal, the artist does not get an advance. However, if you wear a white sequined glove on one hand and your name is Michael Jackson, you most likely got millions from Sony in your admin deal, considering the revenue associated with your catalog and that of the Beatles.

As part of the deal you can ask to be consulted on any controversial use of your songs—for instance, in a violent computer game or an inappropriate advertisement. In an admin deal the publishing administrator collects income and also helps promote the songwriter's catalog. An administration deal may last for a specific period of time (e.g., three years) or for one year with several options to renew. When the term is over, all rights revert to the artist.

Essentially, a publishing administrator pays itself by deducting a percentage of the income it collects on behalf of the artist. After deducting this administration fee (10 to 15 percent), the administrator distributes all of the remaining net income to the songwriter(s). As an incentive to promote an artist's songs, some administrators may also charge a slightly higher collection fee for income earned from cover songs.

And while it has been widely reported Sony advanced Jackson millions to administer his catalog, that is *not* a common occurrence in an admin deal. For catalogs generating a modest amount of income, usually no advance is paid. For more profitable catalogs, usually an advance will be paid, with the amount to be determined on the basis of the income that has been generated in recent years. But nothing in the range of what Michael Jackson earned in his admin deal.

THE SUB-PUBLISHING DEAL

For purposes of this section, assume that in our Michael Jackson example above that MJ wanted Sony/ATV to be a company that found new ways to earn income from his extensive Beatles catalog (among other songs). In a sub-publishing deal, or "sub-pub" as it is called, you have a hybrid of sorts, partly an exclusive publishing deal like Chamillionaire's and partly the admin deal that Jackson reportedly has. In this case the songwriter doesn't want to assign all copyrights but does want the publisher to look for new ways to earn income from their songs.

In a sub-pub deal, it is common for a writer like Jackson to transfer some of the copyright ownership. There may be no advance, or Jackson might negotiate an advance depending on how much of the rights are being assigned to the Sony publisher. Generally the advance in a sub-pub deal would not be as significant as an exclusive deal, since the writer would only assign some of the rights and the sub-publisher would not see the same money that, say, Universal expects in its exclusive deal with Chamillionaire. Even so, the amount of the advance would be negotiated by the legal representatives of the party,

Sub-publishing deals are often favored by smaller publishers who want to operate abroad but do not have the means to start a company overseas. Here, the publishers keep the rights they have but grant the overseas company the right to use some or all of those rights in the foreign country. A brief visit to Diane Warren's website shows that she has EMI Publishing administer some of her overseas licenses. One wonders if this is a situation in which Warren and EMI work overseas together in finding sub-publishers to collect her top-selling worldwide catalog.

There are other types of deals, including the following.

THE STEP-UP DEAL

There are a few other types of deals, which don't require a lot of commentary in this book, but will be cited for your general information. First, there is what some call a "step-up deal." This type of deal is for situations in which a songwriter is not yet signed to a record deal but may later enter into one. The contract here will provide, in effect, that the deal will be the "traditional" deal mentioned above but will automatically transform into a co-publishing deal if and when the songwriter is signed to a record deal. These deals serve as good motivation for the writer to continue to develop him- or herself.

INCOME-PARTICIPATION DEAL

There is also the income-participation deal. This deal is a "publishing deal" only in the sense that it involves a share of future publishing income. This deal is used to cut someone in on a share of future revenues associated with the catalog. A savvy business person or experienced music industry veteran will use this deal to accommodate his fees for finding a deal for you.

Generally, these deals are for specific songs and involve set time frames. Essentially, the writer uses another individual to find a deal, and, once secured, that individual takes a percentage of the deal and participates in the income. Here the intellectual property remains in the ownership of the songwriter, thus there is no assignment or transfer of the copyright. The tradeoff as a songwriter is that you receive no cash advance.

SINGLE-SONG ASSIGNMENT

The "single-song deal" is not as popular as it used to be, but I have used it for clients who have placed a song on a top album or have a song already soaring up the charts and are in dire need of income. One of the top writers in the gospel industry, Melvin Crispell, wrote several classics like "Wonderful Is Your Name" for Hezekiah Walker. On one occasion seven years ago, Crispell requested a single-song advance, and we found such an arrangement. In this scenario, the rights of a song are assigned to the publisher or investor and the publisher or investor hopes to find as many uses for the song as possible. There may be an advance, but it's likely to be small, unless the parties negotiate otherwise.

Also, in this scenario, Crispell and I decided the assignment was not for the life of the copyright but on a single use and album. This is critical to understand; you would never want to assign your copyright in a one-song deal and allow a publisher or investor to share seventy-five-plus years in the life of that copyright, especially for only a small advance. If you have a hit song and you are going to allow a publisher or investor to share these extensive long-term rights, be wise and make sure the publisher pays you top dollar. Remember the publisher is like an investor and will also share in all forms of use of the songs (CDs, DVDs, synch licenses, mechanical, etc.). Lastly, make sure you maintain some control over the song, such as the right to approve any changes to the lyrics or approval for use in a movie, play, TV commercial, or jingle. Lastly, the single-song deal is a good option when you sign different publishing deals in different territories. This is especially useful if you are more successful in one part of the world than you are in another.

In closing, these deals differ from one another in many respects. Most important, when considering the different possible deals, ask yourself the following questions:

- What percentage of copyright ownership, if any, is given to the publisher?
- What share of future publishing income will the publisher get?
- What functions will the publisher perform?
- How long will the agreement remain in effect?

When you get to the answers of these questions, the deal best suitable to you will be apparent.

SELF-PUBLISHING

It is important to note that despite the great number of publishing deals executed each day in the music industry, a publishing deal is not a requirement. A publishing deal is not for every client or songwriter, and I often advise clients against them. Instead of a publishing deal, songwriters have the option of self-publishing. Although I discussed this in further detail in Chapter Nineteen, The Writer as Publisher, there are some benefits and some challenges to being your own publisher, and you should know about them if you are considering that option.

LEGAL DISPUTES

Although this is a book about urban music, the Axl Rose case is helpful to understand the fights around publishing. A couple of years ago it was announced in all of the trade magazines that the well-known Guns N' Roses star had signed a multi-million-dollar publishing deal. Apparently this news did not sit well with his former Guns N' Roses bandmates.

The deal with music powerhouse Sanctuary Group covered both the back catalog, which includes hits such as "Sweet Child o' Mine," "Paradise City," and "November Rain," as well as Rose's future material, including dozens of new tracks he recently recorded for Universal Music. After burning up the charts and selling out stadiums around the world in the late 1980s and early 1990s, Guns N' Roses endured a bitter split, leaving only Rose and keyboard player Dizzy Reed to soldier on under the GNR banner. Former members Slash (Saul Hudson) and Duff (Michael) McKagan, now part of the band Velvet Revolver, filed a lawsuit against Rose, who controls the rights to the old GNR songs. At the time of the deal, McKagan's lawyer, Glen Miskel, expressed surprise when told of the Sanctuary deal. He believed Rose, Slash, and Duff were members in a partnership and "neither Sanctuary nor Axl Rose have provided the remaining partners with a copy of that agreement." The suit was still pending in mid-2007.

The point of this story is whether in gospel or rock, urban or hip-hop, be clear in a publishing deal about which songs are being turned over (past, present, and future) and who owns the catalog. If these things are not made clear, a very expensive legal battle can ensue, and a publisher can back out of any deal.

THE ROLE OF THE PUBLISHER

The publishing deal is the most common way for a record company or publishing company to share in the copyright income derived from the use and exploitation of the writer's copyrights. Rodney Jerkins has produced hits like "Say My Name" for Destiny's Child, "Top of the World" for Brandy, "If You Had My Love" for Jennifer Lopez, and "You Rock My World" for Michael Jackson. He is considered one of the top producers of the last decade. As a result, EMI Publishing, seeing a goldmine in writing income, signed the teenaged Jerkins to a publishing deal.

Do not expect this deal. No matter what a particular company offers you, it is imperative you do your research and know what to expect. Just like in any other field, there are good companies and there are bad ones in the music industry; knowing the difference can make all the difference. Each publishing company is different and each specializes in different services. You need to decide what publishing company services are important to you before you commit to a publisher.

The following are some of the duties and roles of a publisher.

MAINTAINING PROPER ADMINISTRATION

One major role of the publisher is to maintain what is called "proper administration" of your songs. Proper administration includes all of the things that a layperson (and most songwriters) would not know to do. This includes registering copyrights, communicating with performance rights societies, and checking royalty statements to ensure royalties are being paid on time and appropriately.

I mentioned it earlier, but in case you missed it, I repeat: Registering your copyright with the U.S. Copyright Office provides added protection to copyright holders and can permit the copyright owner to recover statutory damages and attorneys' fees if the copyright is subsequently infringed. It is estimated that there are $2 billion of unclaimed royalties floating in the land of missing payments (or more likely in some record label's bank account). For that reason, proper administration is critical. The publisher should be your general champion and cheerleader by negotiating licenses for you, keeping track of your finances, and collecting your royalties.

PAYING ADVANCES ON ROYALTIES

Most music publishing companies offer advances on future royalties. As you may recall, performance rights groups used to offer advances, too, but have not done so for several decades, with very few exceptions. Advances are recoupable, meaning that the publishing company will collect all royalties earned by a song until the advance has been paid back. There is no standard advance amount; it is something that must be negotiated by your representative based on your earning potential. Clearly, an established artist like Usher will be able to get a bigger advance than first-time writer (and no-name) John Smith.

SONG PITCHING, SHOPPING, OR PLUGGING

A good publisher, like Barbara Slane, formerly of EMI Music Publishing, spends countless hours, days, and weeks, shopping your songs or "plugging" your songs to artists, labels, and producers. Since publishers directly benefit from your success, it is in their best interest for your songs to make it to as many listeners as possible. For that reason, some publishers will pitch your songs for use in movies, on TV, and in commercials. Publishers may also work on persuading well-known artists to record songs of songwriters with whom they are not typically affiliated. Publishers may also authorize translations to generate income from cover versions of a particular song in foreign countries. This may involve convincing popular artists to cover your song. Kurt Carr said his album *One Church* was being covered in eleven different languages.

PROVIDING PROTECTION FROM INFRINGEMENT

A large part of the 50 percent of the songwriting royalties a publisher receives is spent on monitoring the use of your songs and protecting them against infringement. Since it happens very often that songs are used inappropriately, a publisher has the arduous task of enforcing your copyrights. But it is important that you stay on top of your catalog as well. Do not expect Universal Music Publishing Group, with millions of licenses and the recent signings of Ciara and Chamillionaire distracting them, to give your small catalog the same priority. They are just as likely to inadvertently overlook an infringement of your copyright as you might be without paying careful attention to your rights.

NETWORKING

Since publishing companies earn money based on the sales of an album, the success of a song is critical to their profit margins. For that reason, some publishing companies will work to team their songwriters with other writers, from inside their own publishing company and with artists from affiliated companies. By introducing phenomenal writers to each other, great ideas are born, and with them hit songs produced. For Beyoncé's last album, Jerkins and his publishing squad put together a reported "boot camp" of writers to develop some hits for the talented singer.

COLLECTING BMI, ASCAP, AND SESAC PUBLIC PERFORMANCE ROYALTIES

A copyright owner also has the exclusive right to authorize any "public performance" of that work. Even though music publishers do not collect the performance rights income, publishers in some cases remain entitled to 50 percent of the money received by societies such as BMI, ASCAP, and SESAC. Thus, a good publisher will make sure they establish a strong relationship with performance rights societies and be sure to register songs with these organizations.

OTHER HELPFUL ROLES OF A PUBLISHER

Some publishing companies will help singer/songwriters finance demo recordings, and they may offer access to the publisher's recording studios. The idea here is that a demo recorded at a professional studio will sound better than something that the writer could muster alone. In turn, record labels will be more likely to sign the singer or songwriter, and the publisher will see revenue from royalties. Furthermore, since promotion is one of the keys to a successful record, and a successful record means a lot of money for a publisher, some publishers share development costs with a record label that agrees to sign the songwriter. Development costs can include everything from advertisements to radio promotions.

KEY TERMS OF A PUBLISHING DEAL

In the course of my career I have had the professional pleasure of working with many talented songwriters. A key component to working with these well-known writers has been the negotiation of publishing deals. The following pages detail a favorable deal secured by one of my clients who has written songs for almost every name in gospel music. Pay extra-close attention to the songs that are covered by the agreement, as well as reversion-of-copyright clause. Although you may want think the advance is the most important part of the contract, don't be fooled; it isn't. The songs covered by the deal, and the eventual reversions, are just as important, if not more.

Imagine you are a young writer just starting out. You sign a poorly written publishing deal with a small local publisher that lasts for three years. At the end of those three years you move on to bigger and better things, eventually becoming famous.

Now imagine you have a new publisher and think that the big bucks are going to start rolling in. *Wrong.* It turns out that the contract you signed with the first publisher, way back before anyone knew your name, tied your copyrights up for your lifetime, plus for seventy years after your death. Not only will you not receive your full royalties, but your children and grandchildren will also be missing out on these. If this sounds to you like something that could never happen, keep in mind that it is the story of many a famous artist.

Here is a sample deal memo for a publishing deal:

EXAMPLE DEAL MEMO FROM MAJOR PUBLISHER

To: Attorney James L. Walker, Jr.
Re: Sarah Songwriter
Date: January 15, 2008

Terms

Co-Publishing Deal: Worldwide Territory
Term: Two (2) year deal
Songs: Certain songs written prior to and during Term.
   1) Min. of eight (8) wholly owned songs delivered, four (4) released.
   2) Credit songs from past catalog.
First-Year Advances: $100,000 upon signing
Second-Year Advances: 2/3rd prior year earnings with the following min/max
   schedule, $200,000 minimum and $350,000 maximum per writer.

Copyright Terms

   1) Limited Term of Copyright (ten years or reversion at some recouped point)
   2) 75/25 mechanical
   3) 50/50 publishing/performance
   4) 60/40 synch
   5) 75/25 all other

Discussion: Let's flesh out each term below!

CO-PUBLISHING DEAL: WORLDWIDE

This is the territory that your publishing deal covers. As I explain throughout the book, publishing deals can be split into sub-publishers, meaning a writer will have different publishers throughout the world. The term "worldwide" means that this publishing deal covers international licensing, not just songs used in the United States. Specifically, the publisher has signed (or is offering the songwriter) a deal that entails the publisher collecting monies worldwide. Likewise, the publisher will share in the income from all sources worldwide.

Term: Two (2) Year deal

The term serves several purposes. First and foremost, it defines the number of years the songwriter will be required to write songs for the publisher. In this example, the songs requirement is eight per year. The term is also critical because during this time (if the deal is exclusive) the songwriter cannot sign a publishing deal with any other publisher. A two-year term spans an appropriate length of time because it will give you the option to renegotiate your contract in a reasonable period of time. Another way of looking at it is that a short-term deal is a sign that you are successful and that a publisher believes that it will be able to recoup the costs of signing you within two years.

> Songs: Certain songs written prior to and during Term.
> 1) Min. of eight (8) wholly owned songs delivered, four (4) released.
> 2) Credit songs from past catalog.

The "songs" section of the deal references the songs that are covered by the publishing agreement. Since a songwriter may have hundreds of songs in his catalog when signing a publishing agreement, it is necessary to determine which songs will be covered. Section 1 does this (minimum of eight [8] songs must be delivered from the songwriter to the publisher each year of the contract). Additionally, the songwriter must make sure four of those songs are actually released. In essence the publisher wants to be sure that songs are placed on albums or CDs that will actually show a return on its investment and cash advances.

Section 2 of the deal provides that the writer can receive credit for past songs written. In other words, he will not have to deliver eight totally new songs each year. Instead, if negotiated well, some of his past catalog could be used to credit him with songs delivered.

> First-Year Advances: $100,000 upon signing

This is generally the most negotiated part of a proposed deal. The label will base these numbers on: (i) pipeline income; (ii) past catalog; (iii) industry credibility of the writer, and (iv) future potential revenue based on their success and your collaboration. The publisher will throw out an initial number to get the negotiation started. Your attorney will work closely with them to finalize an actual bottom-line cash figure. The advance is what most songwriters covet; a large advance is proof of having arrived, having made it. As you can see, a range of $100,000 is given upon signing and where the actual advance falls on that range is determined by the writer's earning potential. For example, a barely known writer would earn an advance at the bottom of the range, while a hit-maker will earn the full $250,000 or more.

A key term to remember here is "pipeline income." This is the income still coming in from past songs in the songwriter's catalog. Before a publisher makes an offer to a songwriter, the publisher will look closely at the pipeline income to determine what revenues will still be coming in for the songwriter in the days, months, and years to come. For example, if you took over Michael Jackson's catalog, based on the existing licenses and uses, pipeline income should be in the millions, if the catalog is properly exploited.

> Second Year: 2/3rd prior year earnings with the following min/max schedule, $200,000 minimum and $350,000 maximum, per writer.

This section is pretty self-explanatory. The publisher is using a formula that locks in a low-end of $200,000 (minimum) and $350,000 (maximum) to the songwriter.

The key is the prior year's earnings and revenue. A good prior year for the songwriter, with regards to revenue, and the advance will obviously be higher for year two. If the first year is slow, then the songwriter should expect only a minimal advance.

F. Copyright Terms

1) Limited Term of Copyright (ten years or reversion at some recouped point)
2) 75/25 mechanical
3) 50/50 publishing/performance
4) 60/40 synch
5) 75/25 all other

This is also a critical deal point to understand, so let's flesh it out carefully. First, a "limited term of copyright" of "ten years or reversion" means that the songwriter will enter into an agreement in 2008 and in ten years, 2018, any copyright assignment or rights that he shared with the publisher will return to the songwriter or, "revert," under the "reversion clause" of the agreement. This is imperative, as a failure to limit the copyright sharing could result in publisher sharing in royalties for many decades to come.

Secondly, the publisher is offering a 75/25 split on mechanical royalties. The amount of money a record company must pay for a mechanical license is generally set by the government's Copyright Royalty Tribunal. This rate is sometimes referred to as a "statutory" rate. The current statutory rate is nine and one-tenths cents ($.091) per song. This means that a single song can generate up to $.91 in mechanical royalties for every ten records sold, payable by use of a mechanical license.

Mechanical royalties are, simply put, royalties that are paid whenever a song is performed through any medium. Years ago, "mechanical royalties" referred to royalties paid whenever a song was reproduced by a mechanical device (under the Copyright Act of 1976, as discussed in Chapter Sixteen, recall that one of a copyright owner's exclusive rights is the right to authorize the reproduction of her work). Additionally, the term "mechanical royalties" was applied to the reproduction of songs in music boxes, player piano rolls, and, later, phonograph records. In the music industry today, this term now refers to royalties paid for the reproduction of songs on CD, DAT, audiocassette, flexi-discs, musical greeting cards, and other devices sold on a "per unit" basis.

Next, the deal calls for an equal split on public performance monies—i.e., BMI, ASCAP, etc. The writer and publisher will split the performance royalties 50/50; when the writer's song is publicly performed, both parties will receive an equal share. This includes the use of the music on radio, in concerts, or anywhere considered "publicly performed." Note here that the publisher is trying to assure it earns enough to cover its advance; first from mechanicals, then, if not, from performance royalties.

Another area in which the publisher hopes to recoup its monies is synchronization royalties. Under the deal memo, the writer gets 60 percent of the synchronization license royalties. Whenever a song is used with a visual image, it is necessary to obtain a "synchronization" (or "synch") license permitting the use of that song synchronized with the image. Music publishers issue synch licenses to television advertisers, motion picture companies, video manufacturers, and CD-ROM companies.

The last clause in the deal memo requires the songwriter to share 75/25 on "all other sources," which is a catch-all phrase that allows the publisher to collect 25 percent from "all other sources" and the publishers' safety blanket for profitability, if it does not recover the advance and make a profit on mechanical, synch licenses, and performance royalties. Merely breaking even is unacceptable.

PRINT LICENSES

Although not specifically mentioned in this deal memo, it is important to mention print licenses for sheet music and folio books. Most publishers license print rights to companies that specialize in printing music. The print licensee will usually pay the publisher a royalty of 10 to 25 percent of the retail price for the published piece. This is usually between sixty and eighty cents for the printing of one song; if the printed piece is a song book comprising many songs, of course the retail price and the royalty will be different. The publisher usually receives 50 percent of the publisher's royalties, after all expenses have been deducted, of course. Sometimes publishers have deals with the songwriter in which the publisher pays the songwriter 10 percent of the wholesale price of the sheet music. Since sheet music is generally sold to school bands and fans at home who want to practice their favorite musician's songs, print royalties are not usually a significant source of income. Sometimes, as is case the for rap music, print music may not even be available. Although sheet music sales have diminished over the years, many songs are still available in print form. These include books of songs by specific artists, instruction books, or compilations of hits within a given genre (e.g., *100 Greatest Country Hits of All Time*). In print licensing, the music publisher issues print licenses and collects this income from the sheet music company, while the songwriter receives a small royalty derived from the sale of his or her song in print.

FOREIGN LICENSES

Foreign countries sometimes have different laws governing the collection and distribution of mechanical royalties. As a result, it is often necessary for publishers to enter into agreements with foreign publishers (or "sub-publishers") to collect a songwriter's mechanical royalties in that territory. After the sub-pub takes a cut (anywhere from 15 to 25 percent) the rest of this foreign income is divided between the publisher and the songwriter according to their agreement.

The key point to remember here is what is termed the "at the source" calculation. As a songwriter, you want to make sure that calculations for your payment of royalties are calculated before deductions like foreign taxes and fees are charged. Failure to do so will reduce your royalties significantly.

ROYALTY STATEMENTS

Royalty statements are accompanying documents to your royalty payments. Although your publisher generally keeps track of your royalty statements, you should maintain a record of them as well. Remember, a publisher sometimes has hundreds of clients to keep track of and will often prioritize each based on the amount of income he or she generates. You, on the other hand, only have one artist to be worried about: YOU!

Royalty statements come every three months, and although they are not very detailed they can account for hundreds of thousands of dollars in income. Ignorance about royalty statements can only hurt you. Many otherwise intelligent and business-minded songwriters have lost out on thousands of dollars because they could not properly read and decipher royalty statements. When you receive your royalty statement, make certain all of your songs that you know are being used are included. Also, if you co-wrote any song, make sure that the writer splits are appropriate.

DRAWBACKS OF SIGNING WITH A RECORD LABEL AS YOUR PUBLISHER

GospoCentric Model

Prior to joining the Zomba Gospel family of labels, GospoCentric was one of the top gospel labels on the planet, with artists like Kirk Franklin, Trin-I-Tee 5:7, and Kurt Carr. The label required most, if not all, of its artists to sign with the GospoCentric label, a strong independent, and its sister company, Lilly Mack Publishing. I highly advise against an artist signing with both a label and its sister publishing company. Specifically, in my classes, I often warn my students of cross-collateralization—i.e., a label dipping into all incomes if the record is unrecouped. Many of the artists did not realize by signing these two agreements they were sharing in their future hits for many years to come.

Even if Kirk Franklin and Kurt Carr were offered substantial advances for signing with both GospoCentric and Lilly Mack Publishing (owned by GospoCentric founder Vicki Mack-Lataillade), they should have been advised against such business dealings because of the following:

If GospoCentric signs an artist to a recording contract and a songwriting deal, they can then reduce the amount of money payable to that artist from record sales (since GospoCentric would get to keep 50 percent of the "publisher's share" of mechanical royalty income). You might understand now the "reason why we sing," as the songwriter once wrote.

As a young company birthed in the 1990s, can GospoCentric really promote its artists' songs outside of the songs' appearance on the artists' own projects? In essence, will GospoCentric, or its sister company Lilly Mack really get the songwriter placed on other projects? Or do they lack the experience and resources to promote the artist's songs as an independent publishing company could?

Will GospoCentric really provide accurate accounting updates and highly scrutinize its sister publishing company (Lilly Mack Publishing)? In the end, Kirk Franklin signed with GospoCentric as an artist and with Lilly Mack as a songwriter. It is highly likely that an independent publisher would have a stronger incentive to monitor all royalty statements, demand accountings, and make sure the songs of Kirk Franklin, Kurt Carr, or other GospoCentric songwriters are paid whenever and wherever used.

It may actually be in Franklin's, Carr's, or your interest to retain these copyrights and enter into an administration deal instead. Reportedly Kirk Franklin has sold 10-million-plus records. If you do the math from our *Thriller* example, that's millions of dollars in publishing royalties shared or co-owned by GospoCentric/Lilly Mack.

CLOSING THOUGHTS ON PUBLISHING

SHOULD I BE IN A PUBLISHING DEAL?

Generally, I am reluctant to advise my clients to sign publishing deals, unless money is needed and the publisher is a solid company that will expand the client's songwriting presence in the industry.

The purpose of this book is to present to you, the aspiring urban artist, the materials herein and provide you with the necessary knowledge to do what's best for your career. Whatever you do, be smart when signing publishing contracts, and give yourself options to renegotiate later by signing the shortest contract possible. Remember, just because your publishing contract expires doesn't mean that the publisher doesn't still own your songs. Be sure to insist on a clause that will revert your songs to you in a short period of time.

Don't fall prey to song sharks; if you can't find someone to pay you for your work, keep trying. It will happen! Check out the resources provided in the next section. Many of these companies specialize in publishing urban music. The main reason publishers are investing more time, money, and effort are the potential for a great return and the overall growth of the urban music scene. Music publishers may be willing to pay a substantial cash advance for a songwriter's past, present, or future material. In exchange, the publisher will own a percentage of that artist's musical copyrights and keep a percentage of the money that these songs earn.

Of course, publishers are unlikely to pay an advance unless they believe they can make a profit in the deal. Like everyone else in the industry, music publishers are in the business of buying something of yours in order to sell it to others at a profit. Unfortunately, many artists do not realize how valuable their publishing rights are. The history of the music business is littered with sleazy publishers or investors who paid pennies for songs that later generated millions in income.

It is worth repeating that not every artist needs a publishing deal, and some artists may be better off by avoiding a publishing deal altogether. Chamillionaire felt it was good for him, so he signed with Universal. This may not be the case for you as an artist or songwriter.

Many different publishing options are available to an artist today. Some publishers may be willing to enter into a more limited co-publishing deal, and administration deals may be available for independent artists who seek to retain their valuable copyrights. Also, it may be wiser to first obtain a major record deal before finding a music publisher, because publishers may want nothing to do with an artist who doesn't yet have a record deal or some other guaranteed way to generate income. Likewise, some artists may prefer to hold onto their copyrights and let the administration agencies collect their publishing income.

As this book was going to press, we learned that mega-hot R&B artist Ciara had signed with Universal. MTV.com reported that the "And I" singer signed an exclusive worldwide publishing deal with Universal.

Hopefully, she examined all of the various types of deals and negotiated the best structure for her deal, whether admin, co-pub, or exclusive publishing deal.

CHAPTER 19 — The Writer as Publisher (Self-Publisher)

"Just because you are a great artist does not mean you are a great song-writer."

—DIANE WARREN, LEGENDARY SONGWRITER

In our last chapter, we talked about signing a publishing deal. We looked at the pros and cons of a publishing deal and the various types of publishing deals that exist. Also, as you know from Chapter Seventeen, in a traditional publishing deal, the songwriter and the publisher split the royalties 50/50. And in a "co-publishing" deal, the writer keeps 75 percent and the publisher takes 25 percent (i.e., 50 percent of the publisher's share). But, there is another alternative for purposes of handling your songs and publishing income, known as "self-publishing."

Self-publishing is the practice of issuing your own mechanical licenses and synchronization licenses and maintaining overall control of your songs without a major publisher (e.g., EMI, Sony, Universal). The best example to outline the advantages of self-publishing is Diane Warren. As the most sought-after writer in R&B, Warren has authored hundreds of hits for the likes of Debarge, Patti LaBelle, Chaka Khan, and Brandy. If self-publishing is a real option for you, Diane Warren is the model to follow.

DIANE WARREN: AN EXAMPLE OF ONE OF THE LEADING SELF-PUBLISHERS

Clive Davis describes Diane Warren as "the greatest writer of this generation and one of the greatest of all time." Davis, who has relied on Warren for artists such as Toni Braxton, Whitney Houston, and Monica, has a standing appointment with the songwriter when he visits Los Angeles each month. "Diane is able to combine tremendous feel for melody with lyrics that deal with genuine emotions, and she is able to do it time after time," Davis explained in a recent magazine interview. Even *American Idol* had a "Diane Warren Night," featuring her songs and Warren serving as a judge. Warren is considered to be the most successful songwriter and self-publisher of this generation. Over the past twenty years, she has had more than a hundred songs on the top of the charts.

A quick glance at her list of top-ten hits shows that she can write across a range of musical genres and diverse styles. It is somewhat hard to believe, but Warren is the composer of classic hits for Trisha Yearwood, Patti LaBelle, and Mark Chestnutt. It is important as a self-publisher to have a great range of songwriting talent, as this will help to get your music placed with as many artists as possible.

Warren developed her songwriting talents decades ago while growing up in Southern California. "I grew up on Top Forty radio; it's what I was exposed to and what attracted me," she explains. "I was fascinated with writers like Carole King, Lieber and Stoller, and Burt Bacharach . . . these were my idols."

While her mother could not agree on her career choice, her father, recognizing her potential, purchased Warren her first guitar at age ten. During the mid-1970s, David Warren would take the teenage Diane to meetings with Los Angeles music publishers. Years later, in 1985, after scoring a hit for Laura Branigan ("Solitaire"), Warren composed the classic "Rhythm of the Night" for R&B group Debarge, which hit #3 on the *Billboard* Hot 100 Chart and #1 on the *Billboard* Adult Contemporary Chart.

Since the beginning of her career, Warren has been writing for the world's most notable artists. Warren's hits have been penned for the likes of Aerosmith, Elton John, Tina Turner, Barbra Streisand, Aretha Franklin, Patti LaBelle, Roberta Flack, Celine Dion, Whitney Houston, and Roy Orbison. "Diane Warren is one of the most incredible writers you will ever see in this lifetime and one of the few who is able to self-publish so successfully," said Johnnie Walker, former top executive with Def Jam and a longstanding industry veteran of the music community.

Recently, Warren has worked with some contemporary artists like Lenny Kravitz, the Pussycat Dolls, Carrie Underwood, Joss Stone, CeCe Winans, Christina Aguilera, Jessica Simpson, and Mary J. Blige. "I just love writing a great ballad, something so essential that it reaches across genres and touches a lot of people," explains Warren.

One label, Warner Bros., recently decided to pull together a collection of Warren hits and release them, titling the project *Love Songs by Diane Warren*. This CD scored #1 songs in many Asian countries and, according to Warren, charted in the top five in Japan. Patti LaBelle recorded her hit song "If You Asked Me To," previously recorded by Celine Dion, for the project.

Eight different artists, from Tina Turner to Ace of Base, have recorded her song "Don't Turn Around." And, her #1 pop hit, "I Don't Want to Miss a Thing," performed by Aerosmith for the movie *Armageddon*, not only received an Oscar nomination but simultaneously hit #1 on the Country Charts with a version sung by Mark Chesnutt. As if her greatness was not already evident, Warren's songs have been featured in nearly one hundred motion pictures.

Not limited to film, Diane wrote her first television theme song for *Star Trek: Enterprise*, which was also the first theme song for the *Star Trek* series. To date, Diane's songs have been nominated for four Golden Globes, six Academy Awards, and nine Grammys.

Says gospel songwriting legend Kayla Parker: "Diane Warren is the standard that we all strive for as songwriters . . . making music that crosses all lines and reaches millions."

Diane has been named ASCAP's songwriter of the year six times (five times for pop and one time for country) and *Billboard*'s songwriter of the year four times (one time as Hot Country Songwriter, two times as Hot Singles songwriter, and one time as the number-one songwriter for pop and R&B). Diane also received a coveted star on the Hollywood Walk of Fame and has been inducted into the Songwriters' Hall of Fame.

ABOUT REALSONGS: A SELF-PUBLISHER

Realsongs Music Publishing was established in 1985, shortly after Warren's big hit with Debarge. She had also scored top hits with "I Get Weak" (Belinda Carlisle), "Nothing's Gonna Stop Us Now" (Starship), and "Who Will You Run To?" (Heart). As a result of a legal battle, and in order to hold the exclusive rights to all of her compositions and music she created, Warren launched her own company.

Essentially, whenever someone sings a song that Warren has composed, her Realsongs (www.realsongs.com) is contacted and negotiates the rate (whether statutory, three-quarters rate, or other) for use of that given song. Warren's office or legal team drafts the licensing agreement and monitors the sales and statements thereafter.

"I definitely recommend you self-publish, if you can," explains Warren. "When I first started out, I had a publishing deal to get some of my early hits like 'Rhythm of the Night' by Debarge, but as my career grew, I became a self-publisher." That hit for Debarge was in 1985. A decade later, Warren would write Toni Braxton's "Unbreak My Heart," which sold 10 million copies and earned Warren millions as a self-publisher.

According to Warren, before becoming one of the top music publishers in the industry, Realsongs started as a one-person shop operating out of Warren's home. *Billboard* named the company the Singles Publisher of the Year, choosing Realsongs over some of the major publishers in New York and LA, most with a roster of writers.

Realsongs has also been named one of the top-five music-publishing corporations and is the most successful female-owned and -operated business in the music industry, exclusively working the catalog of Diane Warren. She has a staff of ten to twelve people that includes an executive vice president, a senior vice president of creative affairs, a vice president of music administration, a director of royalties, and an operations director. Abroad, Realsongs gets some help from EMI Music Publishing in foreign collections. In addition, Warren uses the Alfred Publishing Company in Miami to help her with print licenses. (We discuss these positions and others in more detail later in this chapter.)

A FEW POINTS ON SELF-PUBLISHING

Warren explains candidly that self-publishing is not for everyone. She admits in the early years she utilized a publisher to help her secure song placement on albums to expand her exposure and build her name. But, she suggests several factors to consider about publishing and/or self-publishing.

First, Warren advises young songwriters to develop their gifts or talents and to know their personalities. "Learn how to write a chord progression," she advises, a reference to the widespread use of music sampling in the industry over the past twenty years. Warren, a student of music, urges musicians and songwriters to gain an appreciation for true music and writing, which will in turn help them develop as strong songwriters.

She also carefully notes that talent alone is not the key to being a successful self-publisher. To self-publish, you have to promote yourself more than anyone else is willing to promote you. "I am the best person to sell me," explains Warren. "I reach out to labels when I think I have a song that can help an artist's career. You have to be the best person to sell yourself and prove that you have a song to bring an artist to a new level." She points out that many great songwriters are not completely comfortable with selling and marketing themselves, but some of this is necessary to get songs placed on given albums. Specifically, if you are a self-publisher you do not have Universal Publishing or EMI Publishing or Sony Publishing shopping your songs daily to artists. Therefore, as Warren emphasizes, "you need to push you."

Acting as a self-publisher is similar to acting as a salesman for your music. You will need to find out who might be willing to use your songs, either to record or exploit commercially. You will have to develop relationships with record labels and TV and film execs to shop your songs to them and to their various artists. The footwork associated with this self-promotion can be extraordinary. Our law firm has assisted dozens of self-publishing writers, and just the necessary mailings and phone calls can be a full-time job.

As an example, Warren shares how she knew the classic hit "Unbreak My Heart" would take Toni Braxton to another whole level. "It was a special song, and I knew it could be huge, so I reached out to Clive and we made it happen," she recalled. The song has been covered by others and used dozens of times over in every setting imaginable.

Warren also suggests that having a publishing deal early on in your career is not a total curse. "Sometimes, when you're just getting started, it's okay to have a publisher to help open doors for you and get your songs placed," she recalls. Warren, who has been writing since she was ten years old, urges young writers to remember that they are always developing as artists. When she was signed to a publisher, she continued to develop as a songwriter under the tutelage of the major publisher.

A third suggestion from Warren is after you are established, try to keep all your publishing rights. In her career, she incorporated Realsongs and built a team around herself to control her publishing. In controlling her publishing, she can keep the 25 or 50 percent of revenue normally given over to a publisher. However, she warns, it is a lot of work, and she works tirelessly to keep her songs placed.

Because Warren holds on to much of the publishing rights, she maintains the greater share of her royalties and only pays a portion of them to staff or administrators. She retains all of the copyrights to her songs and the salaries she pays are far less than 25 or 50 percent of the royalties from them. As your catalog and reputation excel, self-publishing should be the ultimate goal. "I do a lot of different things at my company and wear a lot of different hats," she says, in explaining the hands-on involvement she has with her business. So if you plan to be a self-publisher, know your personality and whether you can multitask and play a variety of roles, if needed, for the success of your publishing company.

Please keep in mind that Warren and her team assume all publishing responsibilities, including copyright registrations, review of statements from labels, accountings, and any tax obligations. Keep in mind that, unlike many writers, she can afford a full staff to service her songs.

To make things easier on yourself, you can hire these people as you would any office worker and pay them by the hour. If you cannot afford to pay salaries to employees, it is common for publishers to pay the administrators a percentage of royalties, starting at 10 percent but not exceeding 25 percent. Your administrator does not have to be an attorney or a CPA, but he or she should be a competent person who has experience in the world of publishing. The advantage with this sort of set up is that you can get help from a professional while maintaining maximum control over your songs, all while reserving time to write music and hone your craft.

You can also put together a co-publishing arrangement with a traditional publisher for overseas collections. Warren used the global division of EMI Publishing for worldwide administration.

"It has really worked out well having EMI assist me with overseas collections," says Warren who has written worldwide hits for Celine Dion, Trish Yearwood, and Brandy, among others.

Of course I am not privy to Warren's deal, but most overseas publishers will handle administration in exchange for a percentage of royalties. Unlike the administrator, the co-publisher is also equipped to promote your songs, thereby generating more money for you both. In some cases, you will have to relinquish some control over the use of your music, as the co-publisher will probably want to license your songs far and wide.

Lastly, Warren suggests that you learn how to read a royalty statement or, alternatively, hire someone who is competent in reading the various statements from record labels and other users. "We have a person on staff who handles our royalty statements and overall royalty collections," Warren points out. "As a songwriter, you are very busy and you need someone to stay on top of royalty statements and things of that nature."

You may also consider sub-publishing for print music. Warren uses Alfred Publishing Company. Alfred Publishing is a company with over eighty years in the business and represents a Who's Who of songwriters (see its website at www.alfred.com). Print music might not be a huge money maker for you, but it is something that exists and if your music is used in print you want to be paid for it. To establish a sub-publishing relationship you will need to contract a major print publisher who will pay you a royalty based on the sales of your sheet music.

Warren also uses the Harry Fox Agency to issue some licenses. With a standard license form provided by Harry Fox you will be able to start collecting mechanical royalties. Harry Fox will collect these royalties for you, for just 6.5 percent, and using them can be a great way for small self-publishers to generate income.

The advantages of self-publishing are almost endless. You keep a higher percentage of the money, you get more say in how your music is exploited, and you can even get some help from outside sources when you need, all while reaping these benefits.

A FEW STEPS ON SETTING UP SELF-PUBLISHING

Until you enter into a publishing agreement and assign your publishing rights to a publishing company, you own the publishing rights to any song you have written and the income associated with those rights. Until your songs are covered by a publishing agreement, you own 100 percent of the writer royalties. Much like copyright, owning publishing rights as a songwriter is automatic. There are, however, steps that you should take to seal the deal and ensure your royalties as a writer/publisher.

First, you should set up a publishing company. It is much more professional to do business as Smith Music Publishing than as John Smith the individual. Typically when signing with BMI, ASCAP, or SESAC, they will ask you about your publishing company and whether you have established one. We have explored the world of publishing companies, but to recap: Stephen Hurd has Hurd the Word Music, Donald Lawrence has Songs by D. Publishing, Kirk Franklin has Kerrion Publishing, and phenom Rodney Jerkins has Darkchild Publishing.

Owning your copyright and serving as your own publisher are not mutually exclusive. When you are making a decision about whether to self-publish, or to publish others, you need to decide whether you have the time, resources, and drive necessary to properly administer your songs.

For example, one resource needed is a studio. To fulfill your duties as publisher, you will need to shop demos to record labels. Thus, unless you have access to a studio, you will need to purchase some studio and recording equipment of your own. Warren spends countless hours in the studio laying down songs for potential placement.

As you are shopping songs, you will need to make many copies of phonorecords or digital music, and for that you will need duplicating equipment. You will also need photocopying equipment and all other office supplies that make an office run effectively. In the age of technology it is easy to get equipment like this (computers and fax machines are readily available), but be aware that there are overhead costs associated with self-publishing. Because of these costs, it may not make financial sense to establish an entire company just to administer one song, Make sure before doing so that there are enough songs at our disposal to make it profitable to do so.

STARTING A PUBLISHING COMPANY

Once you've decided that you have the right personality, drive, and equipment to self-publish, you can think about starting a publishing company. Start your company off on the right note and affiliate with performance rights societies like ASACP or BMI. Generally, once you register your publishing company separately with the society they will let you know if someone with your company name is already registered. If two or more Smith Music Publishing companies are registered, then there is a chance that royalties could be paid to the wrong publisher. You're going to get a chance to submit three different names to these organizations, just in case the first (or second) you select is taken. As you submit your names, remember this is the name that will appear on future CDs, DVDs, and other licenses of your music.

Keep in mind that if you're affiliated with a performance rights agency as a songwriter you must affiliate with the same one as a publisher. If you plan on publishing the songs of other performers, you will have to affiliate with all of the performance rights agencies as a publisher because the agencies insist on having a song's publisher affiliated with the same society as the writer. Registering yourself with a performance rights group should not be confused with registering songs with that same group. When you register a song, you register it as either the publisher, or the songwriter, not both.

As a publisher, the registration for performance rights groups is as simple as it is for writers. The only thing you need to remember when doing so is to provide information about all of your songs, as well as any other relevant information (for example, if you have any foreign sub-publishing deals).

FORMING A PUBLISHING COMPANY

As discussed in Chapter Eight: Selecting an Entity, the formation of your business is critical. When starting your own publishing company, the first question to ask yourself is, "Do I want to incorporate?" Refer to Chapter Eight for more information on the difference between the various business entities. Remember, it costs money to form and maintain a corporation, so you must decide whether your publishing will be substantial enough to be worth the expense. Often, songwriters do business as a d/b/a (doing business as)—i.e., John Smith d/b/a John Smith Music.

One of the main benefits of a corporation is protection of the individual members in the event of a lawsuit. As a publisher with a place of business you face the same legal risks as every other business: the mundane things like trip-and-fall accidents, but you also face the risk of copyright infringement. If like many urban and hip-hop writers your music depends greatly on sampling or quoting the works of other writers and performers, you may be at risk for a copyright infringement suit. If you are unsure about the legal status of your songs, seek the advice of an entertainment attorney before proceeding.

Reread Chapter Eight and determine closely if you need to formally incorporate your publishing company. In the beginning, it may not be necessary. However, as your publishing catalog grows, it is a critical step to consider.

COPYRIGHT REGISTRATION

As you know, a songwriter retains copyright as soon as the song is written. When becoming a publisher, however, you will need to file an assignment to transfer the songs that were copyrighted to you to your new publishing name. After you and your songs are registered with a performance rights group, you're ready to issue licenses. You can now do everything that we discussed in earlier chapters, which publishers do. Start issuing mechanical licenses to record companies that want to release a record with your song on it.

CORPORATE STRUCTURE

After you've started to successfully exploit songs as a publisher, you may want to consider signing other writers to your company. Warren uses Realsongs to promote her catalog alone, not dabbling in the music of others. However, she could always grow the publishing company to publish other writers' works. In this scenario you need to understand the structure of large publishing companies before you can create a successful publishing empire. In any event, here are some of the individuals and positions you should consider for your self-publishing company or corporation:

PRESIDENT AND CHIEF EXECUTIVE OFFICE (CEO)

As in all companies there is a president or chief executive officer who uses charisma, power, leverage, and experience to seal deals, figure out business moves and acquisitions, and set the general tone for the operations of the company. If you have ever attended business school, you know that the culture of the company is set by the CEO. A good CEO will generally have honest, hardworking people, and you will need the same for your publishing company. In our Realsongs model, Diane Warren serves as the president and CEO of her company.

CREATIVE DEPARTMENT

The title of this department is a little misleading; because they do not actually create anything. Instead, members of the creative department listen to new material and go to performance venues to make recommendations on which artists and writers to sign. They also absorb the trends in music to help writers structure their songs and make them more commercially appealing. Some creative departments are also charged with producing or co-producing demos for singer/songwriters. As stated above, Warren has a vice president of creative affairs for her company, and this person works daily on finding and placing songs with artists and labels. The role of this person is to drive the company's creative wheels, increasing revenue and expanding the catalog.

PROMOTION DEPARTMENT

A huge part of publishing is promoting the music of your songwriters. The promotion department is responsible for promoting the catalog of songs by designing and preparing promotional CD packages, songbooks, and other items for distribution to entities who may be interested and using the songs. These entities may include recording artists, music producers, other media producers, and ad agencies (for use in advertisements). Diane Warren uses a publicity firm and other marketing resource to promote her brand worldwide.

BUSINESS DEPARTMENT/BUSINESS AFFAIRS

The business department, or business affairs, negotiates, drafts, and generally creates all of the legal documents that are necessary to run a publishing company. Because whoever handles the business will need to have extensive knowledge of the law, particularly contract law, it would be smart to designate an entertainment attorney to run your business office. This can prove handy because the business department also offers general legal advice to the rest of the company about anything from music licenses to sexual harassment.

Warren's company uses an outside lawyer and a vice president of music administration. The two may overlap in some ways, but contractually, Warren can be assured that she is covered in all legal dealings.

LICENSING DEPARTMENT

The licensing department takes care of all of the licenses for mechanicals and synchronizations. This department can be split into two sections, mechanicals and synch, or it can be kept whole. The employees who issue mechanical licenses fill the requests for songs used on phonorecords of all variety. They also keep track of the goings on of the Harry Fox Agency and do everything else that is necessary to issue licenses.

The members of the synchronization license team issue licenses for the use of songs in television programs, commercials, home video, motion pictures, and other audiovisual projects.

In addition to issuing licenses, both departments negotiate the fees for the use of compositions, keep track of options for additional media, and follow up on all music licenses that have expired or are about to. Remember, one song could have dozens of licenses if it is continually being used by different artists. Diane Warren had eight different artists sing her classic hit "Don't Turn Around." Thus, her licensing team would need to issue a mechanical license and synchronization license for the CD and DVD or video featuring her song.

FINANCE DEPARTMENT

The finance department does everything from issuing advances and royalty checks to ensuring the payment of taxes. They also do all of the budgeting, fiscal planning, and handle all mergers and acquisitions. Finally, they take care of all of the mundane payments like payroll, petty cash, and other overhead expenditures. Some publishers will have a person on staff that takes care of finance; others will have an outside company or CPA handle these financial matters. Warren's team handles some of this in-house, and she uses a CPA on certain matters.

COPYRIGHT DEPARTMENT

Registering songs can be a fulltime job, and the copyright department is the one that takes care of it. This department is responsible for the proper registration of compositions with the U.S. Copyright Office. They also provide copyright notices for all print and phonorecords usages and register songs with performance rights groups. Finally, they issue copyright renewals and do everything else to make sure that no copyright is infringed. Warren's music administration department would most likely handle the task of assuring all of her music is properly copywritten. If you cannot afford a staff person to handle copyrights, visit the Library of Congress website and go to the Copyright Office page to download the appropriate forms before handling the copyrights yourself.

INTERNATIONAL DEPARTMENT

The international, or foreign, department notifies a publishing company's representatives or subsidiaries throughout the world of new record releases and film or television uses so that songs can be properly registered with the local performance rights societies. This department also keeps track of the signings of new writers or recording artists, ownership percentages of songs controlled, and the acquisition of catalogs. Finally, they answer questions from foreign territories concerning the songs in the catalog.

ROYALTY DEPARTMENT

The royalty department is the heart of any publishing operation. Without the royalty department, no one gets paid. This department checks the royalty statements that come in and makes sure that the proper amounts are being paid out. They then distribute all of the money accordingly to writers. Lastly, they follow up with any user or company that has either not paid or has paid incorrectly. As mentioned earlier on this chapter, Warren's company uses a royalty's director to track all of her royalties. With one hundred major hits, she will see a royalty statement from the dozens of labels and companies using her music each quarter. The director of royalties will go through each of these statements to assure accuracy.

COMPUTER DEPARTMENT

There are computer programs in existence that will help you do everything from balance your checkbook to keep track of royalties. One well-known software company is Righttracks, based in California. They can provide you with software for tracking all royalties and managing month-to-month royalty distributions and statements. You will also need an information technology expert to handle computer and server issues or a team of programmers who help to develop better and more efficient software for keeping track of royalty statements and other entertainment industry needs. Publishing programs can contain a catalog by a particular artist, several catalogs by genre of music, royalty accounting, or songs in order of licensing popularity.

FINAL THOUGHTS

Being your own publisher can be as hard or as easy as you want it to be. Diane Warren and her Realsongs is a great example for you to look to for guidance and information. There are also plenty of resources available for songwriters who want to publish either their own music or the music of others simply by searching the Internet.

Just remember to be serious about setting up your publishing company; don't cut corners on anything, from registration to paying taxes. With the right motivation and the right people helping you along the way, you may be able to turn your small publishing company into Sony/ATV or Warner-Chappell.

For your convenience, I have included a list of some key publishing terminology to get you familiar with many of the terms you will see in the world of music publishing and self-publishing.

CHAPTER 20

Mechanical Licenses and Administration

"It all starts with a mechanical license when we talk about songwriters and record sales. Without it, you can't get paid on your songs."

—BIG JOHN PLATT, SENIOR VICE PRESIDENT OF URBAN MUSIC, EMI MUSIC PUBLISHING

A few years ago, Lauryn Hill and her group the Fugees made a hit recording of the classic Roberta Flack song "Killing Me Softly (With His Song)." The song sold millions of copies worldwide and is owned by writers Charles Fox and Norman Gimbel, according to BMI records. It became a classic when recorded by Flack, and dozens of others, including Johnny Mathis and Luther Vandross. And, we know from our prior chapter on royalties and statutory rates, that whoever is the songwriter should have received mechanical royalties. So for the purposes of illustrating the key points of this chapter, we will *hypothetically assume* that Flack owned the song and licensed it to Hill for use on the hot-selling *Miseducation of Lauryn Hill* album.[20] The agreement that would have been used between the parties is what we call a "mechanical license agreement."

When I was a young attorney, a very senior attorney told me to "learn how to use mechanical licenses" and collect your clients' songwriting royalties. We have talked about copyright, joint ownership of a song, administration, the statutory rate, and the signing of a publishing deal. All of these situations will eventually involve the issuance of the mechanical license. This license will set forth the terms and conditions of the use allowed for a given song or copyright. For example, the agreement, as pointed out below, tells the writer how much he or she will receive per copy sold upon distribution and sale of the project. In this chapter, we look at the mechanical license and how it works for the songwriter. We will also examine a mechanical license agreement and the relevant terms and provisions of the agreement. Key concepts for this chapter are the following:

+ What is a mechanical license?
+ What are the parts of a mechanical license?
+ When is a mechanical license required?
+ A mechanical license dissected
+ A discussion on Harry Fox Agency

---

[20] For a full reference of the writers and publishers of the song, please visit www.bmi.com. The above is solely for hypothetical illustration.

WHAT IS A MECHANICAL LICENSE?

A mechanical license gives the licensee or the holder permission to copy phonorecords off of a master record of a song. This is only necessary for songs that the licensee did not write or compose and to which she does not own the copyright. The mechanical license is an agreement with the copyright holder, the publisher, or the songwriter that allows the licensee to record and reproduce the song. Included in the world of mechanical licenses are compulsory mechanical licenses, necessary when permission from the original author is not required. However, despite the lack of consent on the part of the original composer, she will still receive royalties from the use of the song.

Thus, in the example of Lauryn Hill and Roberta Flack, Arista Records, as the distributor of the Fugees, would send a request for permission and a mechanical license to Flack's publishing company or administrator. Assuming everything goes smoothly, Flack's team would send over a two- to three-page agreement that would set forth the rate Arista would pay to Flack for the Fugees CD that features the licensed song or songs. Keep in mind, if Hill did a cover, Flack cannot deny such use under the law and would simply issue a mechanical license for the straight cover of the song. In the event the song was sampled or changed in some way, Flack, as the owner, would have to grant approval to Hill and Arista or they would be in violation of the copyright owned by Flack.

Although it sounds technical and not quite as exciting as, say, shooting a music video, it is important to understand that a mechanical license is one of the most important documents in the entertainment business. Far too often writers lose track of their songs and end up not getting paid. This can be avoided simply by understanding the importance of this agreement.

THE PARTS OF A MECHANICAL LICENSE

To grant a mechanical license, the administrator of the song in question must fill out some critical information. We will discuss the importance of this later, but for now we'll attend to the information that is necessary, and why it is so.

The initial page of the mechanical license agreement shall set forth the following descriptive sections. We break them out below and then provide the overall agreement in the pages to come.

Composition Title. This part of the Agreement would set forth Lauryn Hill's title, "Killing Me Softly." This is the title of the song for which she would have sought the mechanical license from Flack. In this case it is straightforward, but often it is not so. In jazz, for example, the same artist may have recorded the same song several times on different albums, each with a different band. Obtaining a mechanical license for that song would require listing both the title and the album on which it originally appeared, or the date of the performance at which it was recorded. When doing this part of the agreement, be as specific as you can be.

Licensee Information. This is the name of the entity that obtains the license for the song. In Hill's case, it would most likely be Arista Records as her then-label.

Note the "licensee" can be a record label or an artist who is not signed with a label. The licensee should include his name or company name and d/b/a, if applicable. Also, the address and phone and fax numbers for the licensee should be included, as well as other relevant contact information, like an e-mail address. As the owner of the song, you want to make sure you have the specific name of the distributor or entity printing and selling the CDs here so there is no confusion later in enforcing the agreement and collecting royalties.

Performing Artist's Name. This is the name of the artist or band who will be recording the song. In our example, the artist would be "Lauryn Hill and the Fugees" or simply the "Fugees."

Record ID Number. When record labels release an album, they usually have a product ID number. In the case of the Fugees' album, the product ID number was B000002B5L. This is important because for purposes of collecting mechanicals and other royalties the specific product number is often required, particularly when calculating royalties based on unit sales.

Recorded Play Time. This is the exact time of the song. The song "Killing Me Softly" is exactly 5:40. It is critical for the purposes of determining royalties, especially if the song exceeds five minutes. Play time should be noted in minutes and seconds.

Release Date. This is the expected date that the album will hit stores. It is important to know when the clock starts ticking for purposes of paying future royalties to the songwriter. As the label, Arista would most likely start paying Flack royalties in the quarter that begins after the album has been released, or as specified in the Mechanical License Agreement.

Royalty Rate. As stated in prior chapters, it is in the Royalty Rate section that Flack would set forth whether she is charging the full statutory rate at the time of the license or if she will reduce it to three-quarters stat (3/4th), as some writers will (see P. Diddy vs. the LOX discussion in Chapter Seventeen for a reminder). Most likely, because of Flack's stature in the industry and her standing as an established songwriter, she would get full rate.

Type of Album. This is simply the format of the phonorecord to be released, whether it's LP, cassette, or, as is most likely the case, CD. The Fugees released the CD and most likely a limited number of cassettes and the mechanical license would most likely cover both CD and cassette.

FINAL LOOK OF MECHANICAL LICENSE AGREEMENT

When you compile the information above into the cover page of the mechanical license agreement, the agreement for Lauryn Hill using Roberta Flack's song could look like this:

Album entitled: *The Score*

   (A) Composition Title: "Killing Me Softly"

   (B) Composer: Roberta Flack

   (C) Artist: The Fugees

   (D) Royalty Rate: $.078 (full stat for over five minutes)

   (E) Record Number: B000002B5L

   (F) Payment Percentage: 100%

   (G) Release Date: February 13, 1996

   (H) Playing Time: 5:40

WHEN ARE MECHANICAL LICENSES REQUIRED?

Mechanical licenses are not required for an artist who is recording and distributing his own work. So, if you wrote a song, and then recorded it and put it out yourself in the local community, it would be silly to issue a license to yourself. However, if you shopped your CD to a label and the label loved it so much that they signed you to a recording contract and kept your music on the final album, then your publishing company would issue a license to the label for the song(s) you wrote.

Also, if the song is considered in the public domain, a license is unnecessary (See Chapter Twenty-Two, Amazing Grace: Public Domain and Gospel Music). To see if a song you want to record is available in the public domain, check out www.pdinfo.com.

EXAMPLE OF A MECHANICAL LICENSE

Below are the remaining portions to the Arista and Roberta Flack mechanical license, which are favorable to the songwriter. I will go through each clause and explain its significance. Remember that although this is just an example, if a record label tries to convince you that this is not industry standard, don't be fooled; they just want a more favorable contract for themselves!

Album entitled: *The Score*

   (A) Composition Title: "Killing Me Softly"

   (B) Composer: Roberta Flack

   (C) Artist: The Fugees

   (D) Royalty Rate: $.078 (rate at time)

   (E) Record Number: B000002B5L

   (F) Payment Percentage: 100%

   (G) Release Date: February 13, 1996

   (H) Playing Time: 5:40

MECHANICAL LICENSE AGREEMENT TERMS AND CONDITIONS

We are the publishers who own the copyright or control the mechanical recording rights in and to the copyrighted musical work named herein (the "Composition").

You (Arista) have advised us (Roberta Flack Publishing) that you wish to use the Composition under the compulsory license provision of Section 115 of the United States Copyright Act of 1976 (the "Act"), as amended from time to time.

Upon your doing so, you shall have all the rights which are granted to, and all the obligations which are imposed upon, users of the Composition under the compulsory license provision of the Act after phonorecords of the Composition have been distributed to the public under the authority of the copyright owner of another person, except that with respect to phonorecords thereof made by you.

1. Arista shall pay royalties and account to us quarterly within thirty days after the end of each calendar quarter, on the basis of phonorecords made and distributed.

This is pretty self-explanatory. For the administrators of Flack's catalog to keep track of royalties due accurately, they need to receive the royalties from Arista in a timely manner. By adding a clause in your mechanical license that makes it mandatory for the licensee to pay you in a timely manner, you will be more likely to see more of your royalties. Without this clause, it is possible that the licensee could withhold the royalties due to you for many months.

2. Within respect to all such phonorecords, the royalty rate hereunder shall be the compulsory mechanical royalty rate contained in the Act, which is effective at the time such phonorecords are released.

This paragraph is critical to establish that the royalty rate will be paid based on the statutory rate at the time of release. So even if the album is recorded in 2000, if the statutory rate of 2008 is ten cents per record sold and that's when the album ultimately hits the stores, then that is what Arista would pay Flack's publishers. Even though there is a statuary rate, as you remember, that is not always the rate that is paid to writers. By clearly stating the royalty rate that you will be paid according to the contract, you will ensure that if you agreed to the full rate, you will receive it.

3. This license covers and is limited to the particular recording of the Composition performed by the Artist named in (C) above and on the phonograph identified in (E) above and this license does not supersede nor in any way affect any prior license now in effect respecting phonorecords of the Composition.

This clause limits the use of the song to protect the writer's interests. It limits the mechanical license to the phonorecord named. As stated above in Sections (C) and (E), you are given the artist's name, i.e., the Fugees, and the record number.

Note, this is only for the record number above, if Arista does a *Greatest Hits of the Fugees* that would be a new album, new record number, and of course, new mechanical license agreement.

> 4. In the event you (Arista) fail to account to us and pay royalties as herein provided, we shall have the right, in addition to any other rights or remedies which we may have in such event, to terminate this license by giving you written notice to such effect. Such termination shall render the making and/or distribution of phonorecords for which royalties have not been paid, actionable as acts of infringement under and fully subject to the remedies provided by the Act.

This clause serves as motivation for Arista to pay royalties honestly every quarter. This is because the last thing a record labels wants to do is have to pull a released album off of record store shelves because of a lawsuit. This security blanket for the writer ensures that if the licensee does not pay the promised royalties the writer has the right to have the phonorecords removed from stores. This is very costly to record labels. Imagine spending millions to make the Fugees album and Arista, after months of marketing, has to pull it off the shelves because of a royalty dispute and possible infringement claims. An action like that would be a heavy blow to even the richest of record labels.

> 5. You need not serve or file the notices required by the Act.

Consider this a gift to the licensee. The Copyright Act of 1976 is very serious in protecting the rights of writers. The Act sets forth a need for licensees to provide notices to copyright holders. Here, Lauryn Hill and the Fugees, in agreement with Arista, are waiving said notice requirements under the law. Also, since a mechanical license is being issued, the writer and publisher are already aware of the particulars and therefore do not have to be notified.

> 6. You will provide to the publisher five (5) copies of the works as described in (A) above, within thirty (30) days of release date.

This clause makes it mandatory for Arista, as the licensee, to provide Flack with copies of the song via CDs as will appear on the album or single release. This way Flack, as the hypothetical copyright owner of "Killing Me Softly" in this example, can know how her song sounds as a final product. It is also just the courteous thing to do in the event you are doing a cover of such a classic like "Killing Me Softly."

> 7. This license is for use of the song worldwide.

This is pretty straightforward. Arista has entered into a mechanical license agreement with Flack for the use of the song in the worldwide exploitation and distribution of the Fugees album. In some cases, a mechanical license will set forth that the use is solely for the domestic United States or other limited uses.

8. Appropriate credit shall be given hereunder on album and single packaging in the United States. Such credit shall be in substantially the following form:

"Written by Roberta Flack for Flack Music Publishing/BMI."

This hypothetical credits clause ensures that the writer or writers will be properly credited in the liner notes of the album that uses the song that has been licensed. This is not only a matter of what is right (giving credit where it is due), but this also gives the writer a chance to further his or her career. By being credited on a major album, writers are able to advertise their catalog. Other singers and artists will know what publisher to call for use of a given song.

With respect to each statement rendered by you (Arista) hereunder, we shall have the right at our sole cost and upon reasonable notice to you, to conduct an examination during usual business hours for your books and records with respect to such statement but not more frequently than once per year and we may designate an accountant or an attorney as our representative to make such an examination on our behalf.

This is a very standard protection for the writer and administrator. To make sure that the record label is honest in its accounting practices, Flack, or the administrator of the catalog, may have to check the label's books and records. In this case, Flack's administrator can go once a year during normal business hours to verify the accuracy of royalty statements.

If at any time during the duration of this license, the works, as referenced in (A), are certified Gold and/or Platinum by RIAA, you agree to forward to our office the Gold and Platinum certification plaques, as are customarily used in the Recording Industry, at our expense.

This is just a matter of pride for the songwriter. The songwriter is the one who creates the song, the moving words, and the memorable melody. When a song sells a million copies, the writer's role should be acknowledged. The best way to acknowledge a writer of a song for his contribution is by giving him or her the plaque that is awarded by RIAA for platinum record sales. A record label may wish to keep the attractive plaque, but this clause makes the label turn it over to the one who most would contend deserves it most, the songwriter.

You (Arista) may not assign or otherwise transfer this license or your rights hereunder.

Under this clause, if Arista obtains a license for the Fugees to perform Flack's "Killing Me Softly" on their album, Arista cannot assign or pass this license on to someone else. This protects writers from having their songs exploited without compensation.

IN WITNESS HEREOF, the parties have signed below as authorized representatives of the entities listed below.

This last boxed text is usually on the closing page, and it is where legal counsel for both the user and owner of the song indicate their respective acceptances by signing beneath these words.

THE HARRY FOX AGENCY: THE LEADING AGENCY FOR ISSUING MECHANICAL LICENSE

The Harry Fox Agency (HFA) is a great resource for all mechanical licensing questions. Harry Fox allows users to request a mechanical license for any song that has more than five hundred units printed.[21] HFA is the premier U.S. mechanical rights organization and represents over 28,000 U.S. music publishers as their mechanical licensing agent. Formed in 1927, HFA is a fully owned subsidiary of the National Music Publishers Association (NMPA). The company's services on behalf of its affiliate publishers include the following:

MECHANICAL LICENSING

The licensing of copyrighted musical compositions for commercial reproduction and distribution for private use. This includes physical formats such as CDs, records, tapes, SACD, and other emerging physical configurations, as well as full-length digital downloads and other methods of digital reproduction and distribution, such as on-demand streaming, limited downloads, and ringtones. HFA also licenses and collects royalties for the use of musical compositions in recordings made outside of the United States and imported into this country for sale.

INTERNATIONAL REPRESENTATION

Through reciprocal agreements with foreign rights organizations, HFA also provides collection and monitoring services to its U.S. publisher clients for music distributed and sold in over seventy-five territories around the world.

ROYALTY COMPLIANCE

HFA conducts royalty compliance examinations of licensees utilizing in-house staff and outside accountants to review the accuracy of royalty statements reported and payments remitted by licensees. Royalty compliance also seeks to verify that

---

[21] For more information, visit: www.HarryFox.com

mechanical licenses have been obtained for all phonorecords released by the licensee. HFA works with licensees by providing education on current licensing terms for new configurations. In addition, an examined company receives the latest information on current licensing and royalty payment processes.

ROYALTY COLLECTION AND DISTRIBUTION

Mechanical royalties are due from licensees to HFA on a quarterly basis, which are then distributed to the publishers of the licensed compositions.

NEW BUSINESS OPPORTUNITIES

HFA actively pursues new opportunities for mechanical licensing, such as ringtones, digital music services, Express Live CDs and downloads, and multi-session recordings.

HFA also promotes anti-piracy measures and supports the NMPA's legal efforts to protect and uphold copyright law. To sustain these activities, HFA charges its affiliated publishers a commission for its services, which in 2007 was set at 6.75 percent. HFA discontinued its synchronization licensing (the use of music in commercials, TV, and film) services in 2002 but continues to collect and distribute monies for licenses that were granted prior to that date.

HFA may represent any publisher who owns or controls one or more compositions currently being physically or digitally reproduced by a third party. Its affiliate publishers range from some of the largest music publishers in the world to one-person operations that control the works of a single composer. With its current level of publisher representation, HFA licenses the largest percentage of the mechanical and digital uses of music in the United States.

FINAL THOUGHTS

Mechanical licenses are very important to understand as a songwriter and as an artist. Even if after reading this book you think you know everything you should about mechanical licenses, it can never hurt to get an entertainment attorney to draw a mechanical licensing agreement up for you or to advise you before signing one. Or, you can always contact the Harry Fox Agency. Keep in mind that if you refuse to grant a mechanical license, the licensee will just obtain a compulsory license; however, a compulsory license cannot be obtained instead of a synchronization license. (See Chapter Twenty-One: Synchronization License: Music and Movies.)

CLOSING TIPS

A mechanical license agreement is one of the most critical contracts a songwriter and artist must understand. If you write a great song but do not understand how to contract for it, you will never see the royalties associated with the CD sales. Record labels hold millions of dollars in escrow and trust accounts as a direct result of the failure of songwriters to submit mechanical licenses. For your convenience, I have attached a full sample mechanical license agreement.

MECHANICAL LICENSE AGREEMENT

Roberta Flack
Flack Publishing
800 Main Street
New York, NY

Arista Records
808 Broadway
New York, NY 10012

Dear Sir/Madam:

We are the publishers who own the copyright or control the mechanical recording rights in and to the copyrighted musical work named in (A) below (the "Composition").

> Album entitled: *The Score*
> (A) Composition Title: "Killing Me Softly"
> (B) Composer: Roberta Flack
> (C) Artist: The Fugees
> (D) Royalty Rate: $.078 (full stat for over five minutes)
> (E) Record Number: B000002B5L
> (F) Payment Percentage: 100%
> (G) Release Date: February 13, 1996
> (H) Playing Time: 5:40

You (Arista) have advised us (Roberta Flack Publishing) that you wish to use the Composition under the compulsory license provision of Section 115 of the United States Copyright Act of 1976 (the "Act"), as amended from time to time.

Upon your doing so, you shall have all the rights which are granted to, and all the obligations which are imposed upon, users of the Composition under the compulsory license provision of the Act after phonorecords of the Composition have been distributed to the public under the authority of the copyright owner of another person, except that with respect to phonorecords thereof made by you.

1. Arista shall pay royalties and account to us quarterly within thirty (30) days after the end of each calendar quarter, on the basis of phonorecords made and distributed.

2. Within respect to all such phonorecords, the royalty rate hereunder shall be the compulsory mechanical royalty rate contained in the Act, which is effective at the time such phonorecords are released.

3. This license covers and is limited to the particular recording of the Composition performed by the Artist named in (C) above and on the phonograph identified in (E) above, and this license does not supersede nor in any way affect any prior license now in effect respecting phonorecords of the Composition.

4. In the event you (Arista) fail to account to us and pay royalties as herein provided, we shall have the right, in addition to any other rights or remedies that we may have in such event, to terminate this license by giving you written notice to such effect. Such termination shall render the making and/or distribution of phonorecords for which royalties have not been paid actionable as acts of infringement under and fully subject to the remedies provided by the Act.

5. You need not serve or file the notices required by the Act.

6. You will provide to the publisher five (5) copies of the works as described in (A) above, within thirty (30) days of release date.

7. This license is for use of the song worldwide.

8. Appropriate credit shall be given hereunder on album and single packaging in the United States. Such credit shall be in substantially the following form:

"Written by Roberta Flack for Flack Music Publishing/BMI."

With respect to each statement rendered by you (Arista) hereunder, we shall have the right at our sole cost and upon reasonable notice to you, to conduct an examination during usual business hours for your books and records with respect to such statement but not more frequently than once per year, and we may designate an accountant or an attorney as our representative to make such an examination on our behalf.

If at any time during the duration of this license, the works, as referenced in (A), are certified Gold and/or Platinum by RIAA. You agree to forward to our office the Gold and Platinum certification plaques, as are customarily used in the Recording Industry, at our expense.

You (Arista) may not assign or otherwise transfer this license or your rights hereunder.

The following accurately describes the title, writer(s), publishers, controlled percentages, timing, and the rate for purposes of this license:

IN WITNESS HEREOF, the parties have signed below as authorized representatives of the entities listed below.

ARISTA RECORDS

By _____
Federal ID number: 111-22-3333
FLACK MUSIC PUBLISHING

By:_____
Federal ID number: 111-22-3333

CHAPTER 21

Synchronization License: Music and Movies

"To work in the music business, a lawyer must know what a synchronization license is."

—BILL KRASILOVSKY, ATTORNEY OFTEN
REFERRED TO AS THE "DEAN OF MUSIC LAW"

Music is an essential component of motion pictures. Without music, many famous scenes in the movies would be without their feelings of sadness, suspense, and joy. Music adds character to film and completes the Hollywood experience. However, the relationship between music and movies is reciprocal. Movies provide a lot of exposure and promotion for upcoming artists and new songs, and they can even revive old songs.

Hip-hop, gospel, and R&B music have become popular resources in Hollywood. Hip-hop and R&B music have proved that they can help fill the seats in theaters worldwide. One of the best-selling soundtracks of all time was *The Bodyguard* featuring "I Will Always Love You" by Whitney Houston, who was also the star of the movie. It sold over 37 million units worldwide.[22] This was not the only one of Ms. Houston's successes on the silver screen. *The Preacher's Wife*, starring Whitney Houston alongside Denzel Washington, grossed over $48 million in the box office[23] and had one of the best-selling soundtracks of all time, selling over 6 million copies worldwide.[24] Movie soundtracks can generate a lot of money for songwriters and artists. From *The Preacher's Wife* soundtrack, Malaco Records made about $400,000 in synchronization licenses and royalties from three songs that were featured on the soundtrack.[25] Betty Fowler of Malaco remarks, "It's not really getting your songs in movies. You've got to have good copyrights and good masters."[26]

Soundtracks are often a big bonanza, with very little production cost on the part of the artist, but big returns based on the exposure of a hit movie, DVD, and other cross promotions. Films like *The Big Chill*, which featured the Motown Sound, *8 Mile*, which featured Eminem's music, or *Boyz N Da Hood*, which featured Ice Cube's gruff rapping, all relied on music to guide the thematic progression of

---

[22] en.wikipedia.org/wiki/Whitney_Houston_chart_records_and_achievements

[23] www.movieweb.com/movies/film/77/2177/summary.php

[24] en.wikipedia.org/wiki/Whitney_Houston_chart_records_and_achievements

[25] weeklywire.com/ww/06-01-98/nash_music-industry.html

[26] weeklywire.com/ww/06-01-98/nash_music-industry.html

the movie. In our last chapter, we used urban R&B examples Lauryn Hill and Roberta Flack to fully explain the use of a mechanical license. In this chapter, we travel a similar pattern and utilize Yolanda Adams and the hit movie *The Gospel* to explain the use of what's called a synchronization license. As you read through the example below, hopefully you will gain a clear understanding of synchronizing music to moving footage and the need to comprehend this type of license as a music industry person.

For an artist, a synchronization license, or "synch license," can be almost like a renewable source of income, especially if an artist's song is placed in a major motion picture. When a publisher issues a synch license on behalf of one of its artists to a film production, the royalties don't stop on the big screen. In this chapter, we will discuss synchronization licenses and walk through an example of synchronization license agreement, music composed specifically for a motion picture, as well as other opportunities for synchronization licenses.

KEY CONSIDERATIONS IN LICENSING MUSIC FOR MOTION PICTURES

+ Obtaining synchronization licenses
+ Composing: employee-for-hire
+ Don't forget the performance license
+ Television and other opportunities
+ The standard synchronization license

OBTAINING SYNCHRONIZATION LICENSES

In the movie *The Gospel*, Yolanda Adams sings a song called "Victory," written by Fred Hammond and featured on the movie's soundtrack. The movie was made by Rain Forest Films. Similar to the issuance of a mechanical license, Hammond as the copyright owner will issue a synchronization license for the use of the music to a synchronized material in the form of video and film.

However, synchronization licenses often do not just cover the release of a movie to the big screen. As anyone who's bought their favorite blockbuster movie on DVD or video knows, once they've left the silver screen, movies become available in forms that every fan can take home and watch. Once a movie has left the theaters, in the United States or around the world, they usually become available on pay-per-view. Then they become available on DVD or VHS and available for rental at Blockbuster Video, Hollywood Video, or Netflix, and are also licensed to free TV, basic cable, and premium cable for broadcast.

A synchronization license is required for each of these releases and formats, unless Hammond gave the movie makers a blanket license that covered all sources of future distribution. In a small-budget film like this one, it is common for the synch license to include all of the possible exhibitions and exploitations of the movie.

When a motion picture production company selects a piece of music to accompany their production, they must seek out the copyright holder, which is often the publisher or the record company that released the song. Up until 2002, the Harry Fox Agency used to assist production companies in obtaining and negotiating synchronization licenses for music to be used in conjunction with motion pictures. "We made a company decision not to issue synch licenses," says Laura Jacobsen, a top executive with HFA. As a result of this discontinued service, it is now up to the production company to contact the songwriter's publishing company directly.

In our example with *The Gospel*, Fred Hammond directed the music team in pulling together the soundtrack for his Verity Records label. Most likely, once the overall songs were chosen, Rain Forest Films, Verity, and Hammond met to negotiate all of the synch licenses. Generally, the publisher (F. Hammond Music) seeks a very limited scope of the license to reserve the right to future licensing fees. However, Rain Forest Films, as the producers, most likely sought the broadest and most inclusive license possible. As a producer, its main goal is to keep costs down and request that Hammond grant a license that would cover all possible forms of media in all possible locations throughout the world.

In some cases, the two sides, Hammond and Rain Forest Films, will work out a license that includes a flat fee. It will all depend on whether the songs as written by Hammond are simply instrumental or include a singing or vocal accompaniment. Visual performances require a higher fee than background performances.

Fred Hammond, the artist and songwriter, is signed to Verity Records. He has recorded a number of albums for Verity, and they co-publish some of his songs. As a result, the executives at Verity could also license a song or master for use on the songtrack without Hammond's approval, if his publishing contract gives them such right. Most likely, if his contract is prepared correctly, Hammond would be notified of Verity's intent to use a song on a given video, movie, or soundtrack, and he would have final approval. And in most cases, the record company, recognizing the opportunities made available by film, will not limit the usage of recordings by contract, especially when it comes to newer artists. However, with more established, veteran artists, the contract may require that the artist approve any and all deals. The producer will then need to obtain consent from the artist.

Another concern that the producers of *The Gospel* and the label had to consider involves the popular-music unions and the fees for second use. Specifically, the American Federation of Musicians (AFM) and the American Federation of Television and Radio Artists (AFTRA) maintain union agreements that require a record company to pay reuse fees if the original recordings its union members contributed to are used in other forms of media, which include films, television, and commercials.

Verity Records would be liable for reuse fees in an amount equal to union scale fees for the services previously performed, if Hammond were a member of the unions. Reuse fees vary and may be substantial, depending on the union members that performed in the original recording and what part they played in the original recording. Waivers of these fees may be waived if the film is nonprofit and public service–oriented, which producers usually must apply for prior to releasing the film.

As a side note, it is important to point out that if Verity plans to release the soundtrack to the movie *The Gospel* worldwide, it must make sure it does not violate any assignment of the foreign recording rights. Specifically, record companies may grant exclusive foreign recording rights to a foreign record company or an artist may have signed an agreement for foreign rights with an overseas outlet. Thus, allowing a soundtrack album to be released would be a conflict of such an agreement. If this were the case, the synchronization license among Hammond, Rain Forest, and Verity Records would have the appropriate language that either limits the license to the United States or Verity Records and that the artist retains the consent of the foreign record company.

DON'T FORGET THE PERFORMANCE LICENSE

In addition to a synchronization right, a producer must also obtain a performance right, which is the right to publicly perform that music selected for synchronization with the motion picture. While it is usually necessary for the venue in which the music is being played or broadcast to obtain a performance license, U.S. movie theaters are the exception. According to BMI representative Wardell Malloy, courts have held that performance licenses are not required for theaters under antimonopoly laws. A performance license is required of the film's producers instead. In foreign markets, movie theaters typically are granted blanket performance licenses by the local performing-rights society, which is usually a small percentage of net box-office receipts. These local performing rights societies have permission from BMI and/or ASCAP to collect these license fees on behalf of the BMI- or ASCAP-affiliated music.

Thus, in our example above, the synchronization license by and between Fred Hammond's publishing company and Rain Forest Films would include the fees for the performance license. There are various ways to incorporate this fee, but generally a performance license fee is up to one-half of the U.S. segment of the worldwide synchronization fee. Canada can also be considered one-tenth of the North American portion of the synchronization fee, but this segment is subject to negotiation, especially if there is a separate publisher who controls Canadian rights. The key here is to make sure your publisher understands how a synch license works and secures the maximum standard fee in closing the deal.

COMPOSING: EMPLOYEE-FOR-HIRE

Many movie producers also hire composers to make music specifically for a film. Deals with composers to create music for a specific film are known as work-for-hire agreements. We discussed work-for-hire in an earlier chapter on copyrights, so I will not expand in great detail here. However, the basic concept is that the producers of the film will pay Fred Hammond a flat salary or budget and he will be "commissioned" and will deliver all of the songs for the soundtrack on time and on budget. Sometimes the producer will try to come in lower than the budgeted amount to keep some of the overage money for himself. For example, if Hammond were given a budget of fifty thousand dollars and he can use his own studios and engineering team, he might be able to complete the project a little cheaper.

Keep in mind, as we discussed earlier, in a work-for-hire situation, the producers or hiring party will own the final product. Many of the established songwriters/producers will object to turning over work or songs they created and avoid a work-for-hire scenario. But, it is not totally uncommon in the music business.

Under the work-for-hire agreement, the producer becomes the copyright holder and is entitled to all rights the writer is normally entitled to under copyright law. But, keep in mind, twenty-eight years later, the Copyright Act provides specific renewal obligation by the producer, and it can become very tricky to retain such rights. Visit www.uspto.gov to gain more info on copyrights as we discussed earlier.

Payment under Work-for-Hire Agreement

Obviously, most individuals want to know what they are going to be paid in a work-for-hire scenario. Generally, with some exceptions, the work-for-hire agreement sets forth the rights granted to the producer and the royalties, if any, granted to the composer or "employee" for hire. In some situations like soundtrack albums, the agreement will also include mechanical licensing terms and will most likely ask the songwriter to grant the song at three-quarters stat. (See Chapter Seventeen.)

Also, under the work-for-hire agreement, the composer is paid royalties for printed editions of the score. Typically the composer will receive six to nine cents for piano copies and 10 percent of wholesale price for all of the printed editions sold in the United States and Canada. For foreign printed editions, 50 percent of royalties received by the publisher is standard. The composer is also paid 50 percent of mechanical licenses. In the case that there are lyricists who contributed to the work, composer royalties are split evenly.

In most cases, composers are not provided with a recording artist royalty. However, for more prominent urban music composers, like Terence Blanchard or Steven Ford, the agreement will usually allow for some royalty payment of about 6 percent of the retail list price of records sold in the United States, with a lower rate for overseas and record club sales. And, if the composer is also an artist, he or she will normally seek a royalty of 8 percent, but no greater than 10 percent, subject to reduction based on royalties payable to other artists and recoupment of reuse fees to union artists. Essentially, the producers of the film do not want to agree to paying a royalty fee to twenty different composers or artists that raises the budget and reduces the profit margin from the soundtrack side.

BMI representative Preston Pearson pointed out that for music that originates in film, BMI makes a special recognition of its value, and it pays twice the regular performance royalty rate for performances on television and radio, not including U.S. theaters. If you visit www.bmi.com, you will see a litany of workshops and seminars for aspiring film composers to learn more about the performance royalty aspects of film scoring.

TELEVISION AND OTHER OPPORTUNITIES

Television

If a television show wishes to play music in conjunction with its motion picture, it is also subject to synchronization and performance licensing. Often our former client Afrika Bambaataa will have his music ("Planet Rock" and "Looking for the Perfect Beat") used on various television shows. Television synchronization license fees are typically based on the rights granted by the license. For free television (FOX, NBC, CBS, ABC) and basic or satellite cable (MTV, Nickelodeon, Lifetime, USA) the fee is usually about three to seven thousand dollars for a blanket-fee five-year license, where the song is aired on episodic television, subject to all types of conditions and renegotiations. A license in perpetuity, which will last forever, usually starts around seven thousand dollars and will range up to about nine thousand dollars—depending on who handles your negotiations and secures the best fee possible (lower if you're the network; higher if you're the songwriter). Pay television (HBO, Showtime, Cinemax) usually commands about the same fee for the same time period.

COMMERCIALS

An average song used in a commercial can be very lucrative to a songwriter. A song used in a commercial with a national audience can fetch a fee anywhere from $10,000 to $500,000 for one year. With our standard synchronization television license for commercials, we generally have a time frame that the song can be used in the commercial and an option period at a fixed rate. Also, keep in mind, here I reference an "average" song. I am not referring to a hit song, like the Motown songs used in the popular raisin commercials or Madonna and Missy Elliott performing a song in a Gap advertisement a few years ago. Songs that are very popular or performed by mega-star artists in ad campaigns launched by major companies might get fees into the millions, although the typical range for a well-known song is about $150,000 to $350,000.

TV ON VIDEO

When a television show is released to video or DVD, producers will usually offer a buyout fee. The reason for this buyout fee is to avoid paying future royalties to the songwriter. However, it is in the artist or publisher's best interest to delay the producer's home video option, because the publisher might be able to get a better rate for the music after the television show has had a chance to grow and develop. In essence, if the show becomes a hit show, and you have music on the show, you can get a better price prior to the printing of the DVD, unless you waived those rights. Alternatively, once the producer has the home video rights, if the show becomes a hit, he pays only the amount agreed to prior to such success.

VIDEOS

Video and DVD sales and rentals are a huge market in the film industry. Videos and DVDs when first released typically retail for about fifteen to twenty-five dollars in "sell-thru" marketing to the consumer.[27] Rental stores typically must pay about seventy dollars per DVD or video they carry for rent. A higher price is designated to video stores because each copy of a movie they carry can be viewed hundreds of times, and the video store is looking to make a profit off of the rentals.

---

[27] Krasilovsky, M. William. *This Business of Music*. New York: Billboard Books, 2000, p. 263.

Producers of movies look to have the synchronization license include video rights and might include an extra fee for those rights. Video rights might also be included in the synch license as an option, where the producer has the ability to secure the video rights within a given period. However, I generally suggest a fee be included for the video rights option, if exercised.

Keep in mind, the producer will offer a negotiated "buyout" of these video rights for a flat fee, to avoid paying anything later. But, the best way to proceed is to get an advance against future sales, maybe 10,000 units, 50,000 units, or 100,000 units, depending on the magnitude of the song at stake, the producer's track record, and what is needed to close the deal. If you ask for too much, you can kill the deal altogether. For example, when the film is scored entirely by one composer, the publisher would look for a figure that is double the statutory royalty rate times the number of units sold. Once the film is ready for video, the publisher would receive an advance of about $9,100, which breaks down as follows:

Statutory Mechanical Royalty Rate:	$0.091
Doubled:	x 2
	$0.182

$0.182 \times 50,000$ (units sold) = $9,100.00

If a publisher is unable to negotiate a rolling advance, the buyout rate ranges from five to fifteen thousand dollars, depending on what the producer expects the video will sell and the importance of the score to the film. In the case of individual songs, the fee is likely to be less.

VIDEO GAMES

As video game technology and graphics get more advanced, the demand for popular, hit music increases. The gaming industry is quickly outpacing other media and entertainment industries in the United States, exceeding $10 billion in sales.[28] In this booming industry, it is estimated that there approximately 18 million gamers who spend up to fifty hours per week playing video games, which translates to up to 900,000,000 of advertising impressions, which includes the music featured on video games.[29] A study of one thousand gamers by Electronic Arts and Ziff-Davis showed that 40 percent of players who hear a song on a game will purchase it on a CD.

In many ways, video games are similar to films. Music can be written for a video game, or a video game company will seek out new songs from popular or undiscovered artists to complete the video game experience and get their target market hooked on their game. One video game series notorious for its use of music is Grand Theft Auto. Grand Theft Auto, which has the player acting at times as a

---

[28] en.wikipedia.org/wiki/2005_in_video_gaming

[29] Bloom, David. "New Kind of Playlist." Radnor: *Video Business*, 10 Feb 2003. Vol. 23, Iss. 6, p. 12.

car-jacker, allows the player to listen to the radio while driving the stolen car. The game provides multiple radio stations with all sorts of music from different genres and eras, often the 1980s or the 1990s. This music is also organized by a fictitious radio station onto a multiple-disc CD compilation.

Video games are an excellent opportunity for exposure and income for a blossoming recording artist. Not only does the artist stand to gain from the income generated directly from the synchronization licenses, but they have the opportunity to gain new fans, sell their own albums, and have even bigger audiences on their tours.

THE STANDARD SYNCHRONIZATION LICENSE

Synchronization licenses are highly informational agreements that film or television production companies send to the publisher of a particular song to gain permission to set the song to their motion picture production. Synch licenses provide the publisher with a lot of the details about the nature of the use. Here are the key clauses:

License and Territory. This clause specifies that the license will be granted to the licensee and also lays out the territory under which the license can be used. This clause will also lay out to which media formats the license extends. Most licensees will want the license to extend to all forms of media possible and all possible distribution channels, which would include not only films as projected at movie theaters across the country and around the world, but pay-per-view, DVDs, videos, video/DVD rentals, satellite, and the right to air the film on cable or free television. Below is a Standard Synchronization License Agreement with an explanation after each clause.

EXAMPLE OF A SYNCHRONIZATION LICENSE

In Consideration of and conditioned upon the payment of the sum as listed herein as a recording right license fee being paid to the undersigned and/or his/her representatives upon execution and delivery hereof, the undersigned PUBLISHER Publishing (referred to as the "Licensor") hereby gives to LICENSEE COMPANY (hereinafter referred to as "Licensee") the non-exclusive rights: Worldwide; Perpetuity; All Broadcast, non-broadcast/non-theatrical and Home Video/DVD devices (including, but not limited to Free TV, Basic Cable, Pay/Subscription, Closed-Circuit, Pay-Per-View, Satellite/DBS [Direct-by-Satellite], common carriers, military base, in-store, libraries, educational, oil rigs, hotels and all forms of Home Video/DVD devices); in-context ad and promo use permitted in all media including radio and website, provided that it be used in the same context as it appears in the Production and in non-downloadable formats.

Description of the Song and Usage. In this section, the details of the song and its publishing information are given, as well as information about the program or film in which it will be used. This also provides information about the television show or film that the song will be aired in, as well as a description of the scene so that the publisher will have an understanding of the context in which the song will be played, as well as the number of times the publisher can expect the song to be aired or played. This section will also specify the term, which is the length of time the agreement will be binding, and the territory, which is also described in the prior clause.

EXAMPLE

1. The composition covered by this synchronization license is:

SONG/VISUAL VOCAL:	"SONG TITLE"
PERCENTAGE OWNERSHIP:	100%
ARTIST:	ARTIST NAME
WRITER:	SONGWRITER NAME
TITLE:	TITLE OF FILM, TV SHOW, OR PRODUCTION
USAGE:	No more than 3 uses in the episodes/no use to exceed sixty seconds. Fee to apply to use within Episode, plus an additional in-context use with Re-Cap, Clip, or Reunion Episodes.
PROGRAM:	Ten one-hour long episodes series for UPN entitled "TV SHOW TITLE"
SHOW DESCRIPTION:	A reality television show starring CELEBRITY
SCENE:	DESCRIBE SCENE IN WHICH MUSIC WILL BE USED
TERM:	Three uses in episode
TERRITORY:	Worldwide

Limitation on Program/Film. This clause specifies the name of the television program or film in which the song can be used. In this case, it is a television program. It is important to include this clause so that the agreement cannot be construed to grant the licensee rights to use the song in conjunction with other works.

EXAMPLE

Said musical composition may only be recorded in a visual TV program entitled: PROGRAM TITLE

Limitation on Musical Composition. This clause limits the use to the recording specified in the agreement. This ensures the publisher that the licensee can only use the song specified, but it also protects the licensee from infringing.

> **EXAMPLE**
>
> The type of use to be made of said musical composition for such recording is limited to embodiment of the song as set forth herein.

Licensing Fee. This clause specifies the amount of the license fee, which will encompass all uses of the song in connection with the film or television program. In the case of a film agreement, this clause might also specify advances for future DVD or video sales and rentals, as well as other programming of the film on television.

> **EXAMPLE**
>
> In consideration for this use and license, the Licensee agrees to pay the Licensor for the use of the song expressed herein its prorate share of Two Thousand Dollars ($2,000.00).

Termination. The agreement also contains a "What will happen in the event of a breach of contract?" clause. In the event of a breech, under this example, the non-breaching party can notify the breaching party that the contract will be terminated if the breach is not rectified within a certain period of time.

> **EXAMPLE**
>
> Without limiting or affecting the rights or remedies that either party may have under this Agreement or at law or equity, it is agreed that in the event of a default or breach on the part of either party, the non-breaching party will notify the breaching party in writing of such default or breach and the breaching party shall have thirty (30) business days from receipt of such notice in which to cure such default or breach, provided that such breach is capable of being cured in such 30-day period. If such breach or default is not curable or if not cured within said (30) business day period, this Agreement shall automatically terminate.

Assignment or Transfer. This clause allows the licensee to assign or transfer the license to another party, although it specifies that the terms of the agreement will still be applicable to the assignee.

> **EXAMPLE**
>
> The Licensee may assign or otherwise transfer this license or your rights hereunder to its assigns, licensees, etc., but such transfer will not alleviate Licensee of its obligations under this agreement.

Performance Rights. This clause does not give the licensee permission to publicly perform the song, and it requires the licensee or any parties who display the film or television show (if applicable) to obtain a performance rights license.

EXAMPLE

The right to publicly perform said recording of said musical composition for the fees and royalties hereunder does not include public performance fees that may become payable by any establishment by reason of its public performance of the Composition. Any party publicly performing the Composition is required to obtain a public performance license from Publisher, Publisher's designee, or its performing rights society.

Creative Control. This clause does not grant the licensee creative control over the song and prohibits the licensee from changing the song from it original composition.

EXAMPLE

Neither license hereunder authorizes or permits any substantial change to be made in the lyrics or in the fundamental character of the music of said musical composition.

Representatives and Warranties. The licensor must guarantee that it has the right to license these rights to the licensee. This protects the licensee in the case that there is a claim by another party for infringement.

EXAMPLE

The Licensor makes no warranty or representation, express or implied, except that the Licensor warrants that it has the right to grant such recording right and performing right licenses subject to the terms, conditions, limitations, restrictions, and reservations therein contained, such licenses being granted without recourse for any other cause or in any other event whatsoever; the total liability of the Licensor under each such license being limited in any event to that part of the consideration paid hereunder by the Licensee to the Licensor for such license in respect to which such breach of warranty may relate.

Retaining Rights. This clause specifies that the licensor can retain rights to license the song to other parties, including synchronization and performances licenses, and prevents the licensee from making a claim that it has exclusive rights to the song.

EXAMPLE

The Licensor reserves to itself all rights and uses of every kind and nature whatsoever in and to said musical composition other than such limited right of recording and performance specifically licenses hereunder, whether now or hereafter known or in existence, including the sole right to exercise and to authorize others to exercise the same at any and all times and places and without limitation.

CLOSING TIPS

A synchronization license is very important for purposes of protecting your rights when licensing your music for TV, movies and videos, and other forms of media. My good friend Sean Johnson, who runs BET, points out often how much confusion exists in TV networks when lawyers forget to handle the "synch license." Also, the next time you visit a movie theater, stay five minutes afterward and read the music credits. Most likely, you will see the names of the songs, the artists who performed them (if vocals were used), the publishers, and some language indicating that permission was sought and obtained. And realize that songwriters likely sitting thousands of miles away are being paid based on that movie score and soundtrack.

CHAPTER 22

Amazing Grace:
Public Domain and Gospel Music

"He took the church music, spirituals, and hymns and pepped them up and put a rhythm to them and called it 'gospel.' Before Mr. Thomas Dorsey, they didn't call me a gospel singer. I was just a spiritual singer, a revival worker."
—WILLA MAE FORD DESCRIBING THOMAS
DORSEY, THE FATHER OF GOSPEL MUSIC

A few years ago, Donnie McClurkin recorded the album *Psalms, Hymns and Spiritual Songs* on Verity Records. Standing before five thousand fans and worshippers at the Rock Church in Virginia Beach, Virginia, and backed by a live orchestra, McClurkin sang a litany of popular hymns and spirituals from the black church, including "Draw Me Close," "I Am Thine Oh Lord," and "Draw Me Nearer." Although there were several original songs on the album, the 2004 release featured a great number of songs in the public domain. As a result, most likely, Verity Records did not have to pay a royalty on those songs. The use of songs in the public domain is very popular for songs commonly featured in the gospel-music industry. Songs like "Amazing Grace," "Precious Lord," "Near the Cross," and "What a Friend We Have in Jesus" are all considered public domain songs. Songs in the public domain are songs that have aged or originated as a state interest and are no longer protected by copyright, which makes them free for use by any artist.

Many gospel songs are created out of works in the public domain because gospel steeps Christian hymns, or "church music," in spiritual jazz and blues rhythms. The first composer to successfully publish gospel was Thomas A. Dorsey, a native of Villa Rica, Georgia. In 1930 he wrote "Take My Hand, Precious Lord," one of the most frequently recorded gospel hymns in history. In George T. Nieremberg's 1983 documentary *Say Amen Somebody*, Willa Mae Ford credited Dorsey with being the pioneer for the success of gospel music and many of the public domain hymns we sing today. In this chapter we'll discuss the use of a song in the public domain and give a brief overview of what the public domain is.

KEY CONSIDERATIONS IN USING MUSIC FROM THE PUBLIC DOMAIN

✦ What is the public domain?
✦ Why is there a public domain?
✦ Finding a work in the public domain
✦ Gospel and the public domain
✦ Registering a copyright for your arrangement
✦ Royalties for using works in the public domain

WHAT IS THE PUBLIC DOMAIN?

A work in the public domain is a work that is not tied to any private property rights under copyright law. Unlike a song protected by copyright, anyone can use it without any restrictions and without having to pay any royalties for using it. Public domain comprises the body of knowledge and innovation (especially creative works such as writing, art, music, and inventions) in relation to which no person or other legal entity can establish or maintain proprietary interests within a particular legal jurisdiction. This body of information and creativity is considered part of a common cultural and intellectual heritage, which, in general, anyone may use or exploit, whether for commercial or noncommercial purposes. As we discussed in Chapters Fourteen and Fifteen, copyright is only granted for a limited period of time. Works become a part of the public domain once their copyright expires.

Prior to the Copyright Act of 1976, any works that were published without notice of copyright became subject to the public domain. It was difficult to argue copyright for works that did not give notice of copyright, and thus it was hard to regain a private interest in the work. After the Copyright Act of 1976, and until the Berne Convention Implementation Act of 1988, works published without copyright notice were still considered a part of the public domain, but it was easier for the writer to regain ownership of the work. Following the Berne Act, the necessity of copyright notice was eliminated. However, it is still important for writers to obtain a copyright registration and proudly display their copyright when their work is published to give notice to others.

Under current copyright law, songs that are fixed in tangible form for the first time after January 1, 1978, are protected from the moment of their creation until the author's life plus an additional seventy years. In the case of a joint work, copyright protection lasts until the death of the last surviving author plus seventy years. In the case of works-for-hire, and for anonymous and pseudonymous works, the duration of copyright will be ninety-five years from publication or 120 years from creation, whichever is shorter. Works created prior to January 1, 1978, are eligible for copyright protection for a period of up to ninety-five years, and the rights are not measured by the life of the author. Songs from foreign countries might be subject to different copyright rules. In many foreign countries, the copyright term only lasts for life of the author plus fifty years. Here's a sample chart, which shows you in summary how to understand public domain:[30]

---

[30] Used with permission from www.unc.edu/~unclng/public-d.htm as prepared by Professor L. Gasaway.

Date of Work Created	Protected From	Term
Jan. 1, 1978 or after	When work is fixed in tangible medium of expression	Life plus 70 years (or, if work of corporate authorship, the shorter of 95 years from publication or 120 years from creation)[31]
Published pre-1923	In Public Domain	None
Published 1923–1963	Date When Published with Notice[32]	28 years + could be renewed for 47 years, now extended by 20 years for total 67 years; if not so renewed, falls into public domain
Published 1964–1977	Date When Published Notice	28 years for first term; now with automatic extension of 67 years for second term
Created Before Jan. 1, 1978, but not published	Jan. 1, 1978, the effective date of the 1976 Act, which eliminated common-law copyright	Life + 70 years or Dec. 31, 2002, whichever is greater
Created before Jan. 1, 1978 but published between then and December 31, 2002	Jan. 1, 1978, the effective date of the 1976 Act, which eliminated common-law copyright	Life + 70 years or Dec. 31, 2047, whichever is greater

---

[31] 17 U.S.C. Section 302(c).

[32] Under the 1909 Act, works published without notice went into the public domain upon publication. Works published without notice between January 1, 1978 and March 1, 1989, effective date of the Berne Convention Implementation Act, retained copyright only if efforts to correct the accidental omission of notice was made within five years, such as by placing notice on unsold copies (see 17 USC Section 405).

UNPUBLISHED WORKS

Keep in mind, the chart primarily focuses on published works, and there are a number of other situations in which songs created in 1890, for example, but unpublished could still be given copyright protection. For example, if Thomas Dorsey, the Godfather of Gospel Music wrote a song in 1930, but it was unpublished—i.e., never released—then those songs would still have copyright protection. Under the law, unpublished works with a known author are granted the life of the author, plus seventy years, so as of January 1, 2007, an author who died pre-1937 would see his work fall into public domain, as the seventy years would have expired.

Also, note as stated above that unpublished anonymous and pseudonymous works and works made for hire (corporate authorship) gain 120 years from the date of creation, so as of January 1, 2007, works created before 1887 that fall in these categories would no longer be protected.

Lastly, it is importantly to note that if a song were created before 1978, and published after 1977 but before 2003, it would not fall into public domain. The copyright lasts the life of the author plus seventy years, or December 31, 2047, whichever is greater. And, the soonest these songs can enter the public domain is January 1, 2048. Good examples would be hits written by the Clark Sisters, the Hawkins Family, and the Winans in the 1970s. If one of those acts created a song that was published after 1977 but prior to 2003, it would have copyright protection for another forty or so years (2048) before falling into public domain.

It is very complicated, so hire a good intellectual property lawyer or entertainment lawyer if you are considering the use of a song and cannot figure out whether it is still under copyright protection or under public domain.

WHY IS THERE A PUBLIC DOMAIN?

Songs and the creativity behind their conception are considered to be part of a common cultural and intellectual heritage. During the first years of the song's lifetime, it is a commonly held belief that the author or artist should be entitled to reap the benefits of its creation and should be entitled to the rights to perform that work exclusively. Allowing the author to benefit from his work exclusively for a period of time, though limited, gives artists and authors an incentive to create new works. If all works were automatically entered into the public domain, and the artists were never paid for their work, there would be no reason for artists seeking a livelihood to create new work and share it with the world. The reasoning as to why the song or work should then be turned over to the hands of the public is not just so that the world can enjoy an unlimited ability to perform the song but also for a more economic purpose. Before the Copyright Act of 1976 was passed, the Copyright Office released a study that gave the reasons for limiting the term of a copyright:

> Once the work has been created, and the author protected for a sufficient time . . . the work should become available to be freely used by all. There is believed to be a greater probability of more varied editions of works of lasting value, and a wider opportunity to distribute existing works competitively, and use them as a basis for new creation, if they are freely

available. It is basic to our economic system that profits in this area should be gained by more efficient manufacture, better distribution, and the like, rather than by perpetual protection, once the purpose of the protection for a limited time has been achieved.

Today's copyright law strikes a fair balance, which allows an author to have time during his life to enjoy the benefits of having created his work, as well as a reasonable amount of time for his heirs to also enjoy the benefits of his estate and the income generated from his copyrights. Yet, our copyright policy still gives an opportunity to the public to embrace its heritage and reinvent works and perform them freely, without the risk of infringement.

FINDING A WORK IN THE PUBLIC DOMAIN

There is no single entity that keeps track of all of the works in the public domain. So, tracking down the origin of a song to find out if it's free for use can be a daunting task. Even more confusing is that there are many songs that are in the public domain that have new versions or editions that are copyrighted. However, there are some ways to track down the origin of the hymn you might want to share with your congregation or song you might want to rejuvenate on your next album.

THE U.S. COPYRIGHT OFFICE

Keeping a record of all works that are in the public domain is not the responsibility of the U.S. Copyright Office, so you cannot rely on them exclusively for information as to whether a song is in the public domain. Once a copyright expires, the Copyright Office reportedly discards manuscripts and music deposited in its vaults. However, you can request that the Copyright Office perform a search to determine copyright status of a particular work. However, these searches can be costly—upwards of thirty dollars per hour. Also, despite the big expense, the Copyright Office will not certify that the song is in the public domain. There is a search engine available online to look up copyrights; however, this listing may not be comprehensive.

THE LIBRARY OF CONGRESS

The Library of Congress will sometimes keep copies of works deposited with the U.S. Copyright Office when a work is registered. The Library of Congress serves as the research branch of Congress. It is the largest library in the world, holding over 130 million items within its 530 miles of bookshelves. The Library of Congress holds more than 29 million books and printed materials, 2.7 million recordings, 12 million photographs, 4.8 million maps, and 58 million manuscripts. It is the mission of the Library of Congress to make its resources available to Congress and the American people and to preserve a comprehensive collection of knowledge and creativity for future generations to enjoy. There is no guarantee that even though the Library of Congress holds so many volumes of information that it will have what you need to determine whether the song you are seeking to perform is in the public domain, but it's worth a look.

PERFORMING RIGHTS SOCIETIES

As collectors of performance license fees, ASCAP, BMI, and SESAC keep meticulous lists of the works of their artists. Oftentimes, they will also keep track of whether the work underlying a song is part of the public domain. You can contact ASCAP or BMI to determine whether there is a copyright claim on a particular song you are seeking to perform. While the information provided by a performing rights society is helpful, it is not definitive. However, if you find that your song is still under copyright, you'll have an idea of who you might need to pay royalties to when you perform or record the song.

THE HARRY FOX AGENCY

As stated in Chapter Twenty-Two, the Harry Fox Agency is a company that offers mechanical licensing, collections, and distribution for publishers in the United States. Harry Fox maintains extensive records of information about songs and their copyright status for the purposes of their licensing services. You can make an inquiry to Harry Fox about the status of a song. They are available on the web at www.harryfox.com.

SHEET MUSIC

A piece of sheet music from an old song can easily indicate whether the song is now in the public domain. If the song is dated more than seventy-five years ago, you can assume the song and lyrics are now mostly likely in the public domain in the United States, unless there is an exception as stated above.

Another way to ensure that you are not infringing is to compile as many versions of a public-domain work as possible, using only the passages contained in every piece of source material. Expert musicologists can also offer helpful insights into determining what is within the realm of the public domain.

The New York Public Library for the Performing Arts at Lincoln Center in New York City has a vast assortment of popular songs from throughout the ages. You can browse their collection to help find early editions of songs. Information about their collection is available on the web at www.nypl.org/research/lpa/lpa.html.

THE PUBLIC DOMAIN REPORT

The Public Domain Report is a subscription newsletter that has been circulating since 1993. The information provided by the PDR is usually very reliable and is a great resource for advertising agencies and film companies who need assurance that songs they are including in their projects will not give rise to any infringement claims. The PDR is available online at www.pubdomain.com.

THE MINI-ENCYCLOPEDIA OF PUBLIC DOMAIN SONGS

The Mini-Encyclopedia of Public Domain Songs by Barbara Zimmerman is a publication of over eight hundred songs that are in the public domain. This is a great, easy resource that will provide you with an extensive list, and it is one of the least time-consuming and cheapest options for getting a quick answer on the status of a song. This publication currently runs at a price of about ninety-nine dollars on the BZ/Rights website: www.bzrights.com.

OTHER THOUGHTS ON USING WORKS IN THE PUBLIC DOMAIN

Although the underlying source for a song might be in the public domain, contributions and new editions made based on the original may be copyrighted by the contributor. Make sure that if you wish to make improvements to a classic hymn in the public domain you work with the original and do not incorporate any of the changes by a latter contributor (unless of course you obtain a license to do so). You should also be sure to place a new title on the song so that you avoid confusion when it comes time to collect your royalty checks.

REGISTERING A COPYRIGHT FOR YOUR ARRANGEMENT

When you file a copyright registration application, you must disclose if you have used any contributions from any other authors, including if any of your work is based on a public domain work. To register a song that has not been recorded, you can use form "PA," for Performing Arts. If your song has been recorded, you can use form "SR," for Sound Recordings. The fee for copyright registration is currently forty-five dollars. If you're short on funds to copyright all of your projects, you can copyright multiple works on one application fee—you do not need to register each work separately. For more information, check out the U.S. Copyright Office website: www.copyright.gov.

ROYALTIES FOR USING WORKS IN THE PUBLIC DOMAIN

Usually if you record a song that is in the public domain, your record company is not going to want to pay you mechanical royalties, because you're not the writer and there are no other writers who can make a copyright claim on it. However, if you provide them with a new twist on an old classic—e.g., by recording a new arrangement—you might be able to get your record company to compromise and pay you a mechanical royalty rate proportionate to your use of the song in the public domain. This proportion would mirror what ASCAP or BMI would pay you in performance royalties. So, for example, if BMI would pay you 50 percent of performance royalties, your record company would pay you 50 percent of the mechanical royalty rate ($0.091 \times 50\% = \$0.0455$). I must warn you this can be a difficult legal fight.

CLOSING TIPS

In the gospel industry, it is common to sing popular hymns and spirituals that have fallen into the public domain. As a songwriter or artist, whether gospel or urban, it is important to understand what public domain means and how it operates in the music we so love. This chapter is just a brief introduction; please contact an intellectual property attorney or expert on public domain if you choose to endeavor deeper in this area.

PART IV

MARKETING AND OTHER HELPFUL TIPS

CHAPTER 23

Marketing Urban Music

"It is difficult to define the elements of success in the music industry, but if you start with passion, talent, commitment, and luck, I think you are on the right track."

—SYLVIA RHONE, PRESIDENT, MOTOWN RECORDS/UNIVERSAL

Sylvia Rhone, former chairman and CEO Elektra Entertainment Group (EEG), has had a distinguished thirty-year career in the music business. She began her music career in 1974 with Buddha Records. Fourteen years later, she would become the senior vice president of Atlantic Records, a trailblazer for women and people of color everywhere. Just two years after, she became the first African American woman to head a major record company, when she was appointed president and CEO of EastWest Records, a division of Atlantic. Under her leadership, the label would see revenues of $100 million.

A year later, in 1991, she was promoted to chairman and CEO of the combined Atco/EastWest, which eventually became EastWest Records America. During this time she successfully worked with several super-hot urban talents like En Vogue, Gerald Levert, and even non-urban acts like Simply Red.

In 1994, Rhone became chairwoman and CEO of Elektra Records. Under her great leadership, several labels, including Elektra, EastWest, and Sire Records were consolidated into one powerful brand: Elektra Entertainment Group, or EEG, as it was called, whose roster included rapper Missy Elliott, Metallica, Fabolous, and Yolanda Adams. Rhone's marketing genius has also helped the likes of several artists at EEG, including Staind, Third Eye Blind, and Tamia, attain a level of sales previously thought out of reach for them. Long known throughout the industry as a keen developer of music talent, she was also instrumental in the continued success of platinum-plus artists like Metallica, Tracy Chapman, Bjork, Keith Sweat, and Natalie Merchant. She has the amazing ability to understand how to break an act at the marketplace, a very difficult task in urban music. As the head of EEG, Rhone had the company gross $300 million in revenue in the 1990s.

In 2004, Elektra was dismantled by its parent company, Warner Music Group. But Rhone, very much in demand as a marketing whiz, was soon called to the Universal team and asked to head Motown Records, where she remains today as CEO of the former Berry Gordy label and as an executive VP of Universal Records.[33]

---

[33] Universal Music Group consists of A&M Records, Decca Record Company, Deutsche Gramophone, Geffen Records, Interscope Records, Island Def Jam Music Group, MCA Nashville, Mercury Records, Motown Records, Phillips, Polydor, Universal Records, and Verve Music Group as well as a multitude of record labels owned or distributed by its record company subsidiaries around the world. The Universal Music Group owns the most extensive catalog of music in the industry, which is marketed through two distinct divisions, Universal Music Enterprises (in the United States) and Universal Strategic Marketing (outside the United States). Universal Music Group is a unit of Vivendi Universal, a global media and communications company.

Explained Mel Lewinter on her hiring: "Sylvia's enthusiasm for discovering a diversity of artists and her unique vision regarding the complexity of new platforms and formats that drive our industry make her a natural to lead Motown's evolution into the future."

By day, Sylvia Rhone is one of the music industry's most seasoned, savvy, and brilliant executives. The Wharton School alumna can be found daily attending staff meetings, reviewing sales reports, finalizing album budgets, and handling countless phone calls and meetings. Through it all, she remembers to stay connected to the street and the latest buzz affecting urban music. Rhone understands that you can't market music without knowing your marketplace.

URBAN MUSIC TAKEOVER

In just over two decades, black music (as it was once called) has been renamed "urban" music and is now the most popular and influential music movement of this generation. The urban scene—broadly covering hip-hop, rap, and R&B—is firmly at the heart of mainstream culture, from McDonald's commercials to Gap ads to Diddy performing at the NFL season opener.

As of 2007, urban music accounts for over 25 percent of industry sales. I remember in October 2003, when for the first time all the artists with top ten singles on the *Billboard* charts were black. As super-producer Rhemario "Rio Beats" Webber pointed out, "When you see Britney Spears hiring Pharrell and the Neptunes and Justin Timberlake hiring (hip-hop producer) Timbaland to produce his album, it shows you the reach of urban music and hip-hop."

Urban artists like Beyoncé, Outkast, and Ciara, have dominated the charts. In late 2003, Outkast spent nearly two months at either #1 or #2 on the singles chart and on the top of the albums chart. What is more, the reach of urban music is worldwide. New urban artists have won the United Kingdom's Mercury Music Prize for the best album of the years for two straight years. Chris Blenkarn, an editor with urban magazine *Touch*, points out that a new generation of music lovers grew up on hip-hop and have caused the sales surge.

The pattern of evolution—with black music being adopted by the mainstream—has been around since jazz and blues spread in the early twentieth century. Modern hip-hop music was born in the mid-1970s when the vibrant funk, disco, and soul scenes collided—helped by rapidly developing technology that spawned synthesizers and drum machines. R&B music has taken a different path, growing out of the soul of the 1960s and 1970s and combining the vibe of gospel singers with a more sleek and romantic sound.

Now, the two styles have come together, giving R&B a harder edge and, in turn, making hip-hop more polished and commercial. Beyoncé, an R&B singer, and rapper Jay-Z found that this formula worked very well when their collaboration "Crazy in Love" became a global smash in 2003.

WHAT IS MARKETING?

If you spoke to a thousand people in the music industry you might hear a thousand definitions for marketing and what it means to market an album, an artist, or a song.

Antonio "L. A." Reid, the chairman of Island Def Jam Music, recently told *The Steve Harvey Morning Show* audience that it takes about $2 million to $4 million to break an artist, including all of the marketing. Reid also encouraged artists to build your "buzz" and create a fan base for your music, stating, "it's a very different meeting with a label when you have created some local buzz and people are talking about you." For purposes of our discussion, marketing is defined by six easy points:

- A means to communicate about your music or services offered for the purposes of encouraging someone to purchase or use the music
- The process of planning and executing a marketing plan, including the conception, pricing, promotion, and distribution of ideas, goods, and services to satisfy the music listener
- The business of advertising, promoting, and selling your music and product to the public and distributors
- A technique used to attract and persuade consumers to buy your album or product
- Finding out what customers want, then setting out to meet their needs, provided it can be done at a profit, including market research, deciding on products and prices, advertising, promoting, distributing, and selling
- The process of organizing and directing all of the label or production company's activities that relate to determining the market demand and converting the customer's buying power into an effective demand for an artist's CD or label's product and bringing that service to the customer

These definitions are textbook and will aid in basic understanding of general marketing principles. However, for purposes of this book, we zoom in on some of the music industry's top execs to tell us firsthand about marketing.

DISCUSSION ON KEY POINTS

COMMUNICATING ABOUT YOUR MUSIC

First, when we talk about "a means to communicate about your music or services offered for the purposes of encouraging someone to purchase or use the music," we are talking about creating the proper marketing that communicates the vision of your music and captures the essence of you as an artist. The communication should not go out to the masses without clarity and specific focus on the targeted consumer. For example, if you are a gospel artist, you should advertise on GospelFlava.com and in *Gospel Today* and *Black Gospel Promo*. Similarly, as an urban artist, you should advertise in *Ebony*, *Jet*, *Billboard*, *VIBE*, and/or *Essence* magazine to reach your target consumer. Likewise, if your genre is specifically hip-hop, you should consider an advertising or communication in the *Source* magazine or *XXL*.

DEVELOPING THE MARKETING PLAN

Rhone will quickly tell you that her training in business school and common sense gathered from thirty years in the music industry combined to make it clear to her that a label must have a marketing plan to break an urban artist. Indeed, luck plays a role, but a game plan is critical to have the entire team aware of the direction of the project.

The second point, the process of planning and executing a marketing plan, including the conception, pricing, promotion, and distribution of ideas, goods, and services meant to satisfy the music listener, is critical. As stated in earlier chapters, the business plan should be well thought out and include pricing of the targeted market, cost of promotion, and distribution. For example, if you know you plan to purchase ads on BET, include this in the marketing plan. Additionally, a marketing plan is useless without the budget to actually execute it. Keep in mind, if you are solely an artist, there are plenty of companies that specialize in writing marketing plans, so as always, do your research.

Advertising Your Urban Music

In our third point above, we describe marketing as "the business of advertising, promoting, and selling your music and product to the public and distributors." We zoom in on advertising because it is such a critical element to breaking an urban artist. Proper advertising will build buzz and create major interest in a new urban project. Advertising is costly, but to make a great record without advertising is as useless as writing a marketing plan with no budget to implement it. You must figure out a way to advertise and spread the word about your product. Keep in mind that you are not expected to spend forty thousand dollars to buy a full-page ad in *USA Today*, but you can look locally for creative ways to advertise and keep your budget. Consider flyers, banners, e-blasts, urban websites, posters, radio advertising, a MySpace account, and any way possible to promote your new project or music.

Persuasion of the Customer in Marketing

Over the years, it has been widely reported that Berry Gordy would ask his staff at Motown one question: "If you had a dollar, and you had to buy a sandwich or this record, which one would you choose?" If the staff member chose the sandwich, then Gordy knew the record did not push or persuade a consumer to drop down the ten bucks then or $19.99 today for a Motown CD.

In marketing your album, you have to realize that once you have a marketing plan for advertising, promotion, and buzz, you are not through. There is an element of persuasion involved in convincing an urban music listener to walk into a record store and buy your CD or to download your hot new single on iTunes. There is no formula for what will persuade a consumer. However, most label execs will tell you buzz, interest, and great music are the key. If you get buzz going, drum up street interest, and back that up with solid advertising, gradually the consumer will become persuaded to buy an album, whether someone told them it was a great album or they heard it on the radio and read about it in press reviews. The platinum success of the *American Idol* singers (Ruben Studdard, Fantasia, etc.) is a direct result of the power of persuasion television has in convincing the public-at-large that these artists were bona fide stars. The same can be true of you as an artist or any artist you sign to your label, if the marketing plan is solid and executed well.

FINDING OUT CONSUMERS' NEEDS—AND MEETING THEM

In the early 1990s, Kedar Massenburg, while describing his artists D'Angelo and Erykah Badu, coined the term "neo-soul." The two artists went on to sell over 20 million records, and Massenburg set off a wave of copycat neo-soul artists and record labels worldwide. What is more interesting is that Massenburg cleverly surveyed the American landscape and realized the soulful music of the 1960s Motown heyday was still alive; however, it was being hooked and sample by rap artists, not being produced and released by singers. He knew if he could find soulful crooners, like D'Angelo and Badu, he could reinvigorate a soulful music sound that still had an audience. Kojo Bentil, right-hand partner to Massenburg, and a dear friend in the industry, explained to me once that "we saw an area of music that consumers loved, and we followed through with a game plan." In essence, he found the consumers need and met their demands for soul music. Whatever type of artist you are in urban or gospel music, you have to make sure you study your demographic: don't copy what's out there (there can only be one Kirk Franklin, Diddy, or Whitney Houston) but rather meet the demands with cutting-edge marketing.

DIRECT ALL OF LABEL OR PRODUCTION COMPANY'S ACTIVITIES

I often watch artists sign with small labels that lack direction for their artists or themselves. Phillana Williams, an executive with Def Jam's marketing and manager of super-hot R&B artist Ciara, says, "Some major labels are throwing out acts without major marketing, and the artists will fail."

It is still common for a label to sign an artist on talent alone, giving no thought to mobilizing an entire staff and actually breaking the artist in the marketplace. Thus, in this last point, it is important to make sure the artist and label, well-known or independent, sit down and devise a plan that works to maximize the marketing, promotion, and distribution of the artist to the end consumer. In regards to Ciara's multiplatinum success, Williams notes that they "worked for years on Ciara's marketing." The last thing you want to happen is to have a great record but a confused label that doesn't know how to promote your album or break you as an artist. Urban artists have dealt with this problem for years. Williams, in her job at Def Jam, says that she will often sit down with an artist, his management company, and her team and spend the time necessary to make sure all wheels are turning in the same direction.

CLOSING TIPS

MARKETING URBAN MUSIC

Again, as stated above, if you talk to a variety of people you will get a variety of answers on marketing in urban music. However, I think all will agree that marketing is a key means to communicate about your music and encourage consumers to buy your product, whether over the Internet or at a local record store. And, as stated, there must be a well-thought-out marketing plan to execute. Marketing is the most important part of promoting and selling your music and image. And once you figure out what the consumers want, like L. A. Reid, or Sylvia Rhone, or Kedar Massenburg have done, you can hopefully deliver a winning urban music product.

CHAPTER 24

Making the Video

"Where would the music industry be without music videos? The video changed the landscape for artists."
—BILL DUKE, AWARD-WINNING FILM AND VIDEO DIRECTOR

On August 1, 1981, a little network with three letters—*MTV*—stormed across American households. Two years later, in 1983, a groundswell was led by a fourteen-minute Michael Jackson video called "Thriller," The result was a nation of young adults chanting, "I want my MTV!" This evolution changed the entire landscape of the music industry, and the marketing of albums and CDs has never been the same. Sean Johnson, a former ten-year industry veteran with MTV, who now runs BETJ, once told me, "Videos changed the face of the music industry forever, and prior to the Internet explosion, an artist had to make a good video to help his marketing and exposure."

As a result of this evolution, many industry experts feel that without a good video, it is extremely hard and near impossible to break a record in the mainstream market. Urban music videos can range from small-budget productions to multi-million-dollar epics. For example, it was reported that Michael Jackson's video for "Remember the Time," featuring Eddie Murphy, supermodel Iman, and Magic Johnson as guests, cost well over $1 million. TLC's "Waterfalls" video, directed by F. Gary Gray, very nearly surpassed the $1 million figure; at the time, Gray told BET that TLC was the top-selling girl group in history and it was therefore important to deliver a video that would go down as one of the best of all time. (Destiny's Child has since eclipsed the record sales of TLC.)

Despite a huge budget, the outlets to air these videos are somewhat limited. BET, Fuse, BET Gospel, MTV Video Countdown, VH1, and a few less well-known players have tried to air as many videos as possible, but airtime is still limited. In this chapter, we will discuss music videos and the impact on the music industry as a whole and the growing presence of videos in urban and gospel music.

MAKING THE VIDEO

A music video is usually a three-to-five-minute visualization of a song that includes visual and audio performances by the recording artist. As an artist, you hope the video will secure airplay on TV and increase your record sales. And, if it does not get airplay on TV, with DVDs, Blockbuster, and other major chains as well as YouTube, you hope the availability of a video will enhance the marketing and sales of your CD. A couple of years ago Usher and Alicia Keys's video for "My Boo" helped propel both of their albums to multiplatinum status.

Many record labels believe the creation, marketing, and broadcasting of a music video is a critical component to the success of a new CD in urban music and gospel music. In gospel music, it is common to shoot the video or DVD while recording the album. For example, Richard Smallwood once recorded his album at a popular church in Detroit. Verity Records, his label, arranged for a camera crew and filmed *Healing: Live in Detroit*, which included behind-the-scenes interviews and footage on a DVD. While a music video is usually no longer than five minutes, gospel artists often tape an entire two-hour video or DVD and sell it at churches and department stores, among other outlets.

A top-selling gospel video or DVD is considered successful at ten thousand units sold. Meanwhile, an urban artist like Usher can sell 2 million videos and be a top-rented concert video at Blockbuster. Video performances alone have led to some new artists becoming superstars, and explains former Def Jam marketing executive Johnnie Walker, "established artists have used music videos to expand their popularity." Michael Jackson saw *Thriller* sell 50 million albums, led by super-hot videos for "Billie Jean," "Beat It," and "Thriller" (not to mention the countless days of MTV running "24 hours of MJ videos").

Historically, a top video or TV exposure on MTV can lead directly to top record sales. For example, in 1999, MTV aired the weekly video "Diary of DMX" and helped the top rapper sell over 10 million records. And, recently, R. Kelly decided to use a series of videos to promote his "Trapped in the Closet" video. The album soared up the charts, and Kelly, despite legal woes and various lawsuits, still maintained his position as a top seller on the urban charts.

THE DIRECTORS

If you are making a video as a gospel or urban artist, the choice of director can be key. You can't just hire the latest and greatest director. Instead, find a producer or video director who can capture the essence of your art and the message you hope to convey with your music. A common criticism of gospel videos is that they lack a true, carefully thought-out concept or treatment prior to filming. Thus, the video fails to accomplish the main goal: exploiting the artist to the highest possible level and increasing CD sales.

On the urban side, MTV recently honored video director and pioneer Hype Williams, who has directed the likes of Diddy, Busta Rhymes, Missy Elliott, and Janet Jackson and in major videos. Williams, Nzinga Stewart, and Gray are three of the top urban video directors of all time. Williams sees each music video assignment as an opportunity to express the artist's vision, which may not necessarily be his own. "My personal opinion doesn't matter. I want every [video to be] the visual equivalent to what that song means to the artist," he explained in a *Source* magazine interview some years ago. "I make sure that each video is tailor-made and brings out the individual."

Gray is not as active in the music video scene as much, having moved on to big feature films like *Set It Off*, *The Italian Job*, and Vin Diesel's *A Man Apart*. In describing his videos and film, Gray says, "I really don't think about it in terms of color. I just have a different point of view. I had to sharpen my instincts in different ways, and I didn't go the typical route."

A video delivered to a network with the stamp of Williams or Gray assures playing time and a serious look by the viewers who know their work. But keep in mind, these directors are also extremely expensive, and, unless a label really believes you are the next big thing, it may be difficult to budget and accommodate for a director of their magnitude.

Nevertheless, it is important to know the top directors, their work, and those who have paved the way and set the landscape for the hundreds of the videos you see on the air today.

RECORDING CONTRACT LANGUAGE

In a standard music contract, there is usually a section toward the end of the agreement that deals with music videos. This section usually provides that in exchange for advancing the upfront costs for production the label will own the video rights. A standard contract clause for videos will provide that the artist must reimburse the record company for the cost of making the video and can only recoup 50 percent of the artist's royalty. A standard passage might read:

Section 18. <u>Music Videos.</u>

Music Videos, as they are distinguished from other audiovisual recordings under this Agreement, are governed by the following provisions:

(a) You and Company hereby guarantee the production of one video for each Record delivered under this Agreement. Company hereby retains the right to request additional videos for any record produced under the Agreement.

(b) Company shall have the right to require you to perform at such times and places as Company designates for the production of films or videotapes featuring your performances of Compositions embodied on Master Recordings recorded hereunder. Company shall be the exclusive owner throughout the world and in perpetuity of such Videos and all rights therein, including all copyrights and renewals of copyrights, and shall have all of the rights with respect thereto which are set forth in the paragraph above, including without limitation, the right (but not the obligation) to use and exploit such Videos in any and all forms from technology now discovered or hereinafter invented.

(c) As to the exploitation of the Videos by Company's licensees, Company shall credit your account with fifty (50%) percent of Company's net receipts attributable to the Videos. ("Net receipts" shall mean all amounts received by Company, less any amount which Company pays in connection with the exploitation of the videos, specifically payments to publishers, shipping and duplication costs, and third-party distribution fees.)

Notice that in this language, the record company controls and retains most of the rights. The artist grants these rights but earns only "net" and half of those monies collected from the video promotion. This means the label can run up a tab in video costs and only pay the artist on the "net," which could be nothing under industry standard accounting practices. The success of music videos in both promotional and commercial markets is the main reason record labels in urban music will demand video rights like those above from artists. The language in recording contracts reflects this.

Typical definitions of video recordings in recording agreements contain no limitations on time or length. By definition, the artist could not perform in "films or videotapes of live concerts, full-length feature films or documentaries, or film television programs in which an artist visually performs only a single song" without violating the recording contract.

The record company retains the ability to refuse consent or condition its approval on its right to distribute the film. This brings to mind the film *Mahogany*, featuring Diana Ross and produced by Motown founder Berry Gordy. One wonders if as part of Ross's contract, Motown had the right to feature her in the movie and push her music and its albums along the way. This type of deal poses a problem for an artist who is actively seeking film appearances. If you can, as an artist, work hard to specifically restrict the definition of a video recording and what rights the label is retaining.

Also, a label might refuse to allow commercial exploitation of a music video without its prior consent, which is why you, as the artist, would want the language to reflect a need for mutual approval at the slightest, or leave the decision up to the artist alone, at best. Admittedly, because of the strong resistance of some record companies, a new artist will encounter difficulties in obtaining the right to approve commercial uses of music videos. For example, based on the general deals we have seen over the years, a major label like Verity will insist it keep some, if not all, control of the video rights, if only to squeeze a little more cash from the artist.

Even in those cases where the record companies agree to limit their rights in audiovisual performances of sound recordings, they insist on "retaining the exclusive control over the video exploitation rights for promotional purposes and for home video sales." The successful WOW Video series is an example where the labels will feature its artists' videos on a compilation video.

Lastly, most recording contracts will provide that the record companies are permitted to use recordings in audiovisual form. As an artist you will also be restricted from appearing in audiovisual media for other companies. And, with the iPod explosion and in preparation for future technology, the record labels now include language that provides for their control of the release of material in any "technology hereinafter discovered," to encapsulate all future media.

Some of the major negotiation issues involved in the production and exploitation of rights in and to a music video include (1) the right for the label to produce the music video; (2) creative controls in the production of the music video (e.g., selection of musical compositions, producer, director); (3) copyright ownership of the music video, which gives the label the power to re-license it for something like a WOW Gospel video compilation; (4) financing and recoupment by the label of production costs of the music video; and (5) the right to exploit the music video for promotional uses and commercial uses.

With the direct-to-video market soaring into the billions, many artists want to record a live concert appearance and sell it the following month at a Best Buy, Blockbuster, or other retail chain. However, as stated above, the label will retain control of these rights in hopes of recovering its costs for marketing and promoting the album or CD. For an artist, the key is to tie the two products together so that both the label and the artist can reap the benefits of the DVD, like Snoop Dogg's label did with the *Snoop Live at Daytona Beach Unplugged* concert video. The tie-in allows the artist to make the video he or she desires but also allows for the record label to recoup some of its expenses in making the album and cross-promote the album in a concert format.

Unlike hip-hop and R&B, gospel music has not seen overwhelming success; to date, no great video has propelled an artist to a top-selling record. Most of the gospel labels will only spend approximately fifty to one hundred thousand dollars to make a decent contemporary gospel album, so the thought of spending major money on videos and DVDs is unheard of in this genre.

But again, with technology advancing at such a rapid pace, gospel artists can see the rewards of streaming video and direct point-to-point consumer connections with less costly videos.

CLOSING TIPS

By the end of 1983, music video programming was proliferating at a frantic pace throughout the United States, and music-video clips such as those derived from Michael Jackson's *Thriller* album were significantly contributing to the economic resurgence of the record business. Although music videos were previously considered by record companies and recording artists as mere promotional devices, used to enhance record sales, their exploding popularity created new, burgeoning commercial markets for these works in their own right.

Accordingly, record companies began expanding the music video provisions in recording artist agreements to tie up all commercial exploitation rights in music videos. By early 1986, almost all major record companies, which had initially distributed music videos as marketing tools free of charge, were charging broadcasters, video pools, and other exhibitors and users for access to their music video catalogs. In today's market, YouTube has record-label executives and top TV brass scrambling in confusion as millions of videos air daily on the Internet. But, while we look for clarity and the legal rights of all concerned, because of the potential revenues to be derived from home video, broadcast, video jukebox, theatrical, and other existing and future markets for music videos, the various rights in and to such music videos have become critical issues in negotiations between recording artists, record companies, and the various other parties involved in the production and exploitation of such music videos.

After the Christmas retail season of 2005, it was reported that Apple had sold over 11 million iPods. Thus, the ability to sell videos, downloads, streaming clips, and other technology, makes today's music videos a multibillion-dollar industry. With direct access to consumers now via the Internet, an artist can make and sell a video quite profitably with a diminishing need for record labels. The key is to understand video rights and how to make the video and enjoy the profits. Or as Gray says, "think, decide, and, execute."

CHAPTER 25

Touring and Merchandising

"For an urban artist to successfully tour, they must have a good stage show."
—GARY BONGIOVANNI, EDITOR IN
CHIEF, *POLLSTAR* MAGAZINE

Four years ago, the Artist Formerly Known as Prince, who later returned as the artist known as Prince, had the most successful tour of 2004, grossing $87.4 million in ticket sales. Prince is one of a short list of urban stars who understands the importance of touring and giving your loyal fans a great show. Says *Pollstar* editor-in-chief Gary Bongiovanni, "When a fan goes to a Prince concert, they know they are going to see something interesting and exciting, and it makes the fan come back for another show in the future." Repeat business, great word of mouth, and fan excitement are all key factors in understanding the billion-dollar world of touring and merchandising. In this chapter, we take a brief look at touring and merchandising in urban music.

KEY CONSIDERATIONS IN TOURING AND MERCHANDISING

- Status of the touring industry today
- Building your tour team
- Touring as a new artist
- Superstar tours
- Urban merchandising

STATUS OF THE TOURING INDUSTRY TODAY

To break an album, one school of thought says that you must go out on the road and tour. A tour can be as small as a one-week tour through several local bars and lounges or as large as two years spanning the country and around the world, depending on the artist and the life of the record. In urban and gospel music, there have been several notables multi-city tours, specialty-themed concerts, and festivals. These include "Power 99"; the landmark Al Walsh gospel "Tour of Life"; the popular hip-hop "Up in Smoke Tour"; the Yolanda Adams–and–Shirley Caesar-led "Sistas in the Spirit"; and the "Budweiser Superfest," which was sponsored by the top black promoter of all time, Alan Haymon. All made history as successful tours.

Gary Bongiovanni explains: "An urban artist has to do a dynamic live show that leaves people satisfied and wanting to repeat the experience again." He gave an example of Bruce Springsteen as an artist that gives fans that experience. "His audiences feel like they've seen a great show and had the kind of experience they want to repeat."

In 2005, U.S. tours grossed $3.1 billion, which was an increase from $2.8 billion in 2004. In 2005, over 36 million tickets were sold for tours in 2005, with average ticket prices hovering around fifty-seven dollars. *Pollstar* is a leading industry resource for concert information. Every year, they release information on the top tours in the United States, although their website (www.pollstar.com) provides a lot of other information about tour dates, ticket sales, industry contact information, and trade news.

Jeremiah "Ice" Younossi is one of the industry stars in the urban music touring scene. He recently left Emmel Communications, the booking division of Violator Management, where he was involved in tours and international concerts for artists such as 50 Cent, Busta Rhymes, Missy Elliott, and G-Unit. He now has his own company, called "A List," and has put together large club tours for Mobb Deep and many others. He offers input on several ways to define the word *tour*.

According to Younossi, a tour can be anything from a few consecutive shows to a major world tour. Tour packaging can be initiated through a collaboration of one or more of the following: a promoter, manager, agent, label, or even the artists themselves, directly through personal relationships with other artists.

Younossi also explained that popular new artists (both signed and unsigned) usually open or support larger acts, as they are not yet capable of selling tickets across the board. I have also found that newer urban acts with a strong "mixtape" distribution and/or radio buzz can usually support their own solo tour if directed to the right cities, venues, and days of week.

On December 30, 2005, *Pollstar* published its year-end data on tour ticket sales for 2005 in an article entitled "Stones Score 2005's Top Tour" and compiled this list of the top artists. The Rolling Stones tour was number one, grossing $162 million with an average ticket price of about $134. According to *Pollstar*, these six groups were the top urban tours of 2006.

Rank	Artist	Total Gross
1.	Eminem/50 Cent	$21.6 million
2.	Destiny's Child	$17.7 million
3.	Scream tour	$9.8 million
4.	Alicia Keys	$8.5 million
5.	Kanye West	$8.1 million
6.	Erykah Badu & Friends	$6.2 million

Eminem and 50 Cent were a part of the Anger Management Tour in 2005, a twenty-date tour that also featured Lil Jon & the East Side Boyz, G-Unit, D12, Obie Trice, and Stat Quo. Bongiovanni explains that while Eminem and 50 Cent can sell millions of records at the one-time Tower Records store, it is difficult sometimes for urban artist to sell out concert venues, unless they have really honed their touring skills as artists. But, Younossi explains the legwork that 50 Cent did to build a successful tour. "50 Cent, for example, started his G-Unit movement having no label, TV, or mainstream radio support and was able to launch the 'Mix Tape Tour' in which he toured small urban clubs all over the country," recalls Younossi.

"This club tour gave 50 Cent the confidence and practice performing in front of his fans and was the foundation for his amazing live-music touring career today."

Bongiovanni states that the Anger Management Tour was very successfully done by Eminem and 50 Cent, but many artists who "are capable of selling huge numbers of records sometimes have [limited] drawing ability as a live act. . . . You see very few urban rap hip-hop tours out there because sometimes the stage show has to really give fans something they want." He warns: "You have to spend four to five years working the local clubs and small venues to really develop a good stage show, whoever you are in any genre . . . there are a lot of acts who can do a great video, but when you see them live, they are not as good."

Bongiovanni explains that typically an urban tour will pile up a lot of artists, like the five or six artists pulled together for the "Up in Smoke" and "Scream" tours. It is important to note that on the "Up in Smoke" tour, Dr. Dre, Snoop, and other artists on the tour were highly praised for putting together a tour that featured props, different stage sets, and some heavy investment in giving the fans a full blowout of effects to go along with the smooth raps. They also found a way for all of the artists to coincide with the various managers, business folks, and backup teams. Reportedly, they banned unnecessary entourages and organized a united-front security to avoid any incidents.

R. Kelly also saw a successful tour in 2006. His tour did about $8.3 million in ticket sales, even though he and Jay-Z could not work out a tour that probably could have doubled or tripled that amount. As of mid-2007, the parties were engaged in a heated lawsuit over a failed united tour.

In any event, touring is a critical key for an artist to understand. With a solid set of headliners, good venues, and the right pricing, touring can be a great way for an artist to make money and can often provide more financial support for an artist than advances and royalties from a record deal.

BUILDING YOUR TOUR TEAM

To put together a solid tour, you need a solid group of professionals to help you manage your business and to help your star shine as brightly as it can. Your team can help you book gigs, keep you on schedule, collect monies on your behalf, and deal with any problems that should happen to come up while you are on the road.

PERSONAL MANAGER

Even if you are not on tour, you should have a manager. As we know from Chapter Three, industry managers like Benny Medina, Michael Elder, Shakim Compere, and Jeff Robinson act as liaisons between their artists and the rest of the outside world. Managers can help you make sure that you are always ready for whatever obstacles come up along the path. For touring, and even the occasional shows and events, your manager will work closely with your booking agent (discussed later) to make sure that all of your concerts are in order. Your manager will also make sure that your tour itinerary is carried out, and in the absence of a road manager, your manager will take many of the on-the-road responsibilities of a road manager, including transportation issues, managing road crews, booking accommodations, supervising promoters, and other duties on the road.

ROAD MANAGER AND ROAD TEAMS: KEEP IT SMALL

If you are about to embark on a major tour, you might want to consider hiring a road manager as an addition to your team. A road manager takes care of all of the logistics required in a tour. They book, confirm, and manage all of your transportation needs, including, if necessary, a bus and trucks for gear and stage sets, airline tickets, and hotel reservations, and they help keep your entourage in tow. Road managers also collect money for performances after concerts and make sure that is it properly deposited, unless your celebrity and tour are large enough to support a tour accountant.

The road manager will sometimes have a team of people working with him. Most industry experts agree: "Keep it small." Says Rod Hutcherson, who manages gospel musician and producer Melvin Crispell and his wife and artist Tunesha Crispell, and whose company Synergy, out of New York, handles a number of acts and touring artists for gospel, urban and Broadway plays: "A lot of times people don't understand, this is *business*, don't bring a lot of people on the road . . . it only creates problems in the long run." Hutcherson explained that the more people you bring, the more you cut into your profits and the more headaches you have in dealing with hangers-on, who really have no purpose.

Younossi points out that large entourages increase the potential for major problems on the road, and very often an artist will take the blame for crew members that are inexperienced and irresponsible. His advice: "Bring along people you can trust and those that can honestly have some control over what the artist is doing at any given time."

BOOKING AGENT: AN IMPORTANT PLAYER IN TOURING

For coordinating a tour, there is nothing more essential than a booking agent. In many states, especially in New York and California, anyone who acts as an employment agent (which applies to booking agents) must have a license. Some cities may also require a booking agent to have a license. Needless to say, you should always make sure that your newest team member has the necessary credentials to perform her duties before you officially hire her.

Younossi also suggests that you find someone who is "genuinely interested in developing your career and someone that understands your music and where you come from—i.e., your story. . . . There are so many agents that book carelessly and selfishly. This often ends up hurting the artist and significantly reducing the life of their touring career." He adds, "Your booking agent should want to build your value in the market over a period of time."

Booking agents book your tour and work very closely with your managers. Your booking agent will also coordinate deals with promoters. For your team, you will want a booking agent who knows how to read people and will only get you deals with promoters who will follow through and not run off with your money. Younossi reminds, "It is also important to look for someone with experience and someone that can bring forth many different types of opportunities, ideally worldwide."

If you are just getting started in the industry, it will be necessary for your booking agent to make a hard sell to promoters. Needless to say, once you become a superstar, promoters will come to you.

Along with your manager, your booking agent will work on your itinerary. Your itinerary is your schedule of tour dates. Your booking agent needs to be able to coordinate an efficient itinerary to ensure that you make your dates on time and that you are not bouncing back and forth across the country instead of taking a direct route strategically from city to city.

Image and branding are also important considerations for your booking agent and manager. If you are starting as an opening act, it is important that your audience is similar to the audience of the headliner so that your music will appeal to the headliner's crowd and so that you can expand your audience and fan base. Also, does the venue match the image that you are trying to portray? Selecting the right venues will also be a part of your booking agent's job.

Your booking agent and manager will also coordinate ticket sales. The timing of ticket sales can be a crucial factor in tour management. Some venues only need walk-up sales, like a show at a bar or lounge where people might regularly come to the venue or that is the venue's primary source of business. However, larger tours and arena tours require advanced ticket sales, with timing of ticket release important. Pricing is also an important factor. As we have seen from 2005's top ticket sales, major artists can ask for over one hundred dollars per ticket. Pricing can be a slippery slope, and your pricing should reflect your audience's ability and willingness to pay in combination with covering your costs and expenses plus a reasonable expectation of what you want to bring home at the end of the tour. Your booking agent and manager can help strategically plan the right ticket price for each venue.

Oftentimes, promoters will make a deposit for an artist to appear. This advance is usually about 50 percent of the total price as calculated about thirty days before the concert. The agent will then hold the deposit and pay you following the performance.

TOURING AS A NEW ARTIST

Most new artists will have a hard time getting gigs at venues much larger than local watering holes, and in the gospel realm, local churches. However, starting small can be a great way to get a buzz going. You may have a hard time getting paid at first, but eventually you should be able to start making some money and building your brand and ability to make further investments in promoting yourself.

If you have a record deal, you must tour to build buzz for the record and ultimately sales and visibility. I recall Flava Unit, headed by Queen Latifah and Shakim Compere, organizing incredible tours for artists like Naughty by Nature and Zhané.

You also will need the marketing that comes with touring, radio and press. You will want your fans to be able to put their hands on your album once they have fallen in love with your performance—and vice-versa. As a new artist on a label, you will probably only be able to headline clubs with about one hundred to fifteen hundred seats, if you are lucky. Alternatively, you can also be an opening act on a big tour. Becoming an opener can depend a lot on the influence of your manager, especially if your sales are not phenomenal. If you are a new hip-hop or R&B artist, and have a younger target audience, you will want to try to tour during the summer months when young fans have fewer school obligations and more availability to go to shows.

For your newbie gigs, you can usually get about $250 to $1,500 per night from clubs or as an opener. However, if you are unable to get to that point right away, you will be in the position of either having to play for free or even having to pay to play. Paying might also include pre-selling tickets to your concert to your fans directly. Or, an intermediate step to getting paid directly is a "split" where you take portion of the door and the remaining portion goes to the venue. The artist portion is also split amongst all of the other artists performing that night.

PROMOTERS AND SUPERSTAR TOURS

Getting paid is much more complicated when it comes to superstar touring. In most cases, superstars do not get paid a flat fee but a guarantee against a portion of net profits or gross receipts from a show. The big promoters in the urban and gospel music scene are Alan Haymon (Alan Haymon Enterprises/SFX), Al Walsh (ALW Entertainment), and Bill Washington (Dimensions Unlimited). Al Walsh has sat on numerous panels with me and often tells me that "everyone can get paid and make a decent living if the artist recognizes his position in the marketplace and does his or her part to make sure the show is successful, the promoter is successful, and that the audience leaves feeling that they got their money's worth."

Most of these promoters will tell you that all monies received are split with the promoter who booked the show for you. A guarantee is like an advance: It is a guarantee of the minimum amount of money the superstar artist will be paid if the tour does not make a profit. If your tour is profitable, your guarantee will be deducted from your profits. Guarantees for major artists can be anywhere from about $25,000 to $250,000 for arena shows. Most splits with promoters are anywhere from 85/15 to 90/10. The artist will get 85 to 90 percent of net profits and the promoter gets 10 to 15 percent.

Net profits are calculated out of gross receipts minus all expenses. Expenses can cover anything from advertising, rental fees for the venue and equipment, and stage crew to insurance, security, ticket printing, catering, and limousines. Any perks you get while on the road, as well as any other expenses you can think of, will come out of your gross receipts. Make sure that you and your managers scrutinize expense invoices from promoters to ensure that they are accurate and that your promoter is not skimming off the top of your expenses.

Superstar tours can present a lot of complicated agreements and payment arrangements, along with an elaborate promotional scheme to match your tour. Once you have reached the superstar status and you have surrounded yourself with a superstar support team, they will help you with the tools and information you need to put on a stellar tour.

URBAN MERCHANDISING

A few years ago, I went on a speaking tour with Dr. Jackie McCullough, a phenomenal minister, author, speaker, teacher, and artist in the gospel industry. Her following was unlike any other I had ever seen. She tours city to city, spreading the Gospel and packing churches, hotels, and even stadiums throughout the United States and overseas.

A very smart businesswoman, she understands that it is not a compromise of the ministry if she also creates helpful marketing for her supporters, fans, and consumers. Thus, she makes CDs, tapes, DVDs, books, and other paraphernalia to sell at her speaking engagements. On some occasions, she sees hundreds of items sold at the tables in the lobby area of the venue where she speaks.

Merchandising is a very important part of the urban and gospel music scene, if done properly. Once an artist reaches a certain level of success, it is important to find merchandising companies that can print items bearing the brand, logo, image, or selling points of the artist. Sometimes the record label will agree to sell you items at wholesale rate or a bulk rate, and the artist can sell these at the venue where he is performing.

It was reported that years ago the New Kids on the Block grossed over $100 million just in merchandising income. Boyz II Men, in their heyday, also sold millions of dollars in merchandising, including T-shirts, hats, and CDs. Signed photos and other items featuring an artist's signature or trademark also do well at concerts and engagements, if marketed properly and authentic.

CLOSING TIPS

A lot of artists focus on record sales and making a video. However, touring should be the real focus. An artist with a good touring schedule can survive year-round, even when there is no record in the market. Says R&B artist Ciara's manager, Phillana Williams, "touring can be very profitable if the artist and manager learn how to do it right." A road team must consist of people that can both manage and lead, as the artist will often look to this core group for guidance and support.

CHAPTER 26

Technology and the Internet: A Brief Overview of Popular Urban and Gospel Internet Sites

"The Internet has totally changed the game in the music industry."
—PIERRE REDDING, PRESIDENT OF TOP
GOSPEL WEBSITE GOSPELCITY.COM

The Internet and companies like Napster and services like iTunes have changed the face of the music industry. Web surfers can quickly and easily find news about their favorite artists, order CDs, download digital music, and even discover new artists. As an artist, the Internet provides a vital promotional resource.

A lot of major companies in the music biz host websites, like BET.com, MTV.com, and Billboard.com. But there are many informational websites out there that are a lot more specialized toward urban music. Informational and news websites often act as online magazines, and oftentimes are even sponsored by magazines that also produce print publications. In this chapter, we will discuss some of the different informational websites that are available for both gospel and hip-hop resources. We will also discuss several social networking sites and digital music stores that are available on the web.

KEY TYPES OF ORGANIZATIONS, CONVENTIONS, AND CONFERENCES

◆ Gospel news and informational websites
◆ Hip-hop and R&B news and informational websites
◆ Social networking websites
◆ Selling digital music

GOSPEL NEWS AND INFORMATIONAL WEBSITES
GOSPELFLAVA.COM

GospelFlava.com is a website that was established in 1997. GospelFlava.com shares industry information, provides interviews of gospel artists new and old, and publishes information and reviews on upcoming new releases. The mission and vision of GospelFlava is "to lift up Jesus Christ by supporting gospel music, the gospel-music industry, gospel artists, and their ministries." The GospelFlava website typically receives about 1.5 million hits per month, which translates to about 95,000 visitors and about 220,000 page views per month.

You can find GospelFlava.com at www.gospelflava.com.
E-mail: mailbag@gospelflava.com.

GospelCity.com

GospelCity is another leading online resource for information about gospel music. Featuring gospel news, reviews, articles, insights, and even contests, GospelCity.com leads gospel fans to the industry's latest trends and influential ministries. GospelCity.com also provides users with a chance to voice their own opinions and share their experiences. GospelCity.com offers a message board and blogs for site users to read and participate in. GospelCity.com has about 24.5 million hits per month and about 160,000 unique users per month.

You can find GospelCity.com at www.gospelcity.com.

E-mail: info@gospelcity.com

GospelToday

GospelToday is a gospel magazine as well as an online publication. GospelToday is a lifestyle magazine, not just a magazine about gospel music. The magazine features articles about the holistic Christian lifestyle, including health, fashion, travel, fitness, spirituality, music, and entertainment. According to founder Teresa Hairston, GospelToday's mission is to "Inform: clearly identify, define, and present current information about a subject. Inspire: Provide relevant testimonials from person(s) considered an expert (experimentally or educationally) on a subject. Educate: Provide information regarding new and pertinent developments, events, or programs in the Christian community. Empower: Present advice/assistance relative to an area of discussion, providing relevant and accessible sources of information."

You can find GospelToday online at www.gospeltoday.com.

HIP-HOP AND R&B NEWS AND INFORMATIONAL WEBSITES

AllHipHop

AllHipHop.com is valuable resource. The website features daily news, interviews, reviews, multimedia, and other content. A unique feature of AllHipHop.com is its "Rumors" section, which publishes gossip that is buzzing through the hip-hop world. Also a fast-growing community, AllHipHop.com features an "Ill Community" message board with a list of active members. AllHipHop.com was founded by "Grouchy" Greg Watkins and Chuck "Jigsaw" Creekmur in 1998. In addition to the website, AllHipHop.com offers a daily news alert service to its members, a mix of music industry tastemakers and hip-hop lovers, via two-way pagers, cell phones, and e-mail.

You can find AllHipHop.com at www.allhiphop.com.

HipHopGame

HipHopGame is another online resource for hip-hop music news. HipHopGame offers audio and video clips of songs from the hottest artists, CD reviews, and mix tapes for download. HipHopGame also provides a glimpse at some of the latest fashions and offers them for sale. HipHopGame has worked tirelessly to bring hip-hop news, audio, and features to its visitors since 1998. HipHopGame receives about seventy thousand unique visitors each month. In 2000, HipHopGame received the Encyclopedia Britannica Award for the "Best Hip-Hop Website." HipHopGame has helped to launch several new artists, such as underground favorite Immortal Technique.

You can find HipHopGame at www.hiphopgame.com.

DAVEY D's HIP-HOP CORNER

Davey D's Hip-Hop Corner is one of the oldest and largest hip-hop websites. Davey D is a hip-hop historian, journalist, deejay, and community activist. Davey D has been active in hip-hop since 1977, when he started as an emcee in the Bronx. In 2002, Davey D launched a newsletter called HHPN (Hip-Hop Political Newsletter). Davey D's Hip-Hop Corner includes a history of hip-hop, hip-hop news and articles, commentaries, album reviews, quizzes, photos, and even political news. The website also has a collection of interviews with some of the biggest names in hip-hop and features Hard Knock Radio.

You can find Davey D's Hip-Hop Corner at www.daveyd.com.

SOCIAL NETWORKING SITES

Social networking sites have become one of the trendiest new ways to promote an artist. Today, these sites are a primary tools of communication for young adults, who log on to these websites to share information about themselves, connect with new friends, and reconnect with old ones. But more than just being an online place to meet up with buddies, social networking sites provide one of the broadest audiences on which to launch an online marketing campaign for a new artist. Not only can you reach out to fans, but you can reach out to new ears and let network users find you as well.

MYSPACE.COM

MySpace.com is the hottest online social networking site. MySpace.com has over 100 million registered users, the largest membership for a site of its kind. MySpace is aptly named as it allows users to create their own private online communities and personal webpages where they can share photos, journals, and interests with their friends and members of their networks. But aside from building their profiles and viewing the profiles of their friends, users can check out MySpace Music. MySpace Music features music clips, video clips, and information about artists. Users can also check out the profiles of artists. MySpace has become such a renowned source for music and entertainment information for young adults that now artists and even movie producers use their MySpace addresses to promote their projects. Artists can sign up on MySpace.com and create their own profiles and contact other users and let them know about their music and even send out notifications about upcoming events, concerts, and shows.

For any artist or record company trying to break into the industry today, creating a MySpace page is a must.

Check out MySpace at www.myspace.com.

BLACKPLANET.COM

Blackplanet.com is another social networking website that allows members to meet new people and express themselves. BlackPlanet is a leading social networking website for African Americans. Like MySpace, members can create their own profiles called a "Personal Page." Members can post pictures, design their pages, and using HTML can even place music on their pages. With over 14 million members, BlackPlanet offers artists an ideal opportunity to create another Internet presence and connect with new fans. Blackplanet.com will allow an artist to search through members and contact them to let them know about their projects and upcoming shows. BlackPlanet has a diverse membership body, so it is an ideal opportunity for hip-hop or gospel artists to promote their music and spread their word.

Check out BlackPlanet at www.blackplanet.com.

GARAGEBAND.COM

GarageBand.com is not exactly a social networking site, but it does allow artists to share their music with website users. While it sounds like it might be a more rock-oriented website, GarageBand.com provides hip-hop and rap sections and allows artists to create a "band profile" and offers free MP3 hosting. Members can also review the music posted by artists. Unlike some of the other social-networking sites, where users join primarily for social purposes rather than exclusively looking for new music, GarageBand.com provides artists with members who are looking for music, not just making new friends. Every day, GarageBand.com is working on ways to enhance their services. GarageBand.com will also be releasing a new service, iLike.[34] iLike will be a service to help users organize their music, share their music tastes, and discover new music through their network of friends.

Check out GarageBand.com at www.garageband.com.

SELLING DIGITAL MUSIC

In today's music industry, as a part of having a web presence, you must also have digital music available for your fans. If you have a large budget set aside for your promotions, especially online promotion, hire a web designer. Try to seek out a web designer who can help set up an online marketplace that offers digital downloads for a fee. This is still a newer feature for individual artists or small record companies, but you can certainly inquire into what the costs might be.

If you are unable to afford the services of a website designer, there are many websites out there and software that will help you host your MP3s and sell them. Companies like PayLoadz will link up directly with your website or with online auctions to help you sell your music. Other companies, like BroadJam.com, will use their websites to host your music and provide you with a web address to direct your fans so that they can buy and download your music. Companies like Indie911 will help you sell your music through other retailers like iTunes, Napster, and Jamster, although some of their services require a monthly fee. Easybe offers 1-2-

---

[34] www.ilike.com

3 Music Store, which is a software program that helps you set up an online music store of your own.

Just remember when you are selling music online that you still need to pay the copyright owners. Having a website for purposes of selling music is not a free ticket to exploit the rights of other copyright owners without proper payment. There are a litany of lawsuits out there for illegal copyright infringement by websites downloading illegally or improperly selling or distributing music that does not below to the proprietor of the website.

CLOSING TIPS

Regardless of what method you choose for selling your music, creating MP3s and making them available online should be an essential part of your marketing plan. The music industry is rapidly growing and changing with the technological advances that become available, so it is important to stay on the cutting edge—it could help you make it big. Also, realize with the Internet that the entire means of distribution and reaching the consumer has changed. Somewhere in the near future, an artist may not need a distributor at all, as the Internet continues to develop and consumers become more familiar with downloading *legally*!

CHAPTER 27

Organizations, Conferences, and Conventions in Urban and Gospel Music

The music industry is full of resources for musicians and artists. Aside from your team (your personal manager, your booking agent, your attorney, and your business manager), record companies, record distributors and retailers, and all of the other resources out there that make the development of music their mission, there are organizations, conferences, and conventions out there to help budding artists succeed.

Organizations, conferences, and conventions provide opportunities for people involved in the music industry to get together, to get to know one another, to provide tips, suggestions, and strategies with one another, and even share their music.

KEY TYPES OF ORGANIZATIONS, CONVENTIONS, AND CONFERENCES

+ Conferences, retreats, and conventions
+ Organizations & awards shows
+ Hip-hop and R&B organizations and conferences

CONFERENCES, RETREATS, AND CONVENTIONS

THE BOBBY JONES INTERNATIONAL GOSPEL INDUSTRY RETREAT

The International Gospel Industry Retreat is a biannual event with a mission of teaching new artists to develop business skills to help them thrive in the gospel music industry, as well as to foster the growth of gospel music.[35] The IGIR was founded by Dr. Bobby Jones and Vickie Winans in 1997. At the retreat, artist-participants can learn anything about the industry, from composing music to contract negotiations. Recording industry executives are also invited to the retreat to share their knowledge and participate in the seminars. At the May 2006 retreat, the theme was "Setting the Stage for Academic Success and Opportunities in Performing Arts" and included the following "information stations": The Gospel Recording Executives; Attorneys Specializing in Gospel Music; National Recording Artist; New Artist; Christian Mime'; Christian Comedians; Hip-Hop Gospel; Gospel Artist Managers, Promoters, Public Relations, and Media; Theatrical Production; Christian Songwriters; and Christian Instrumentalist.

---

[35] www.gospelindustryretreat.com/template_layout_1.htm

The retreat also features a gospel artist showcase, which is taped and later aired on the Word Network, previously including artists such as Kim Burrell, Bobby Perry & R.A.I.N., and LYRIC Sings. Dr. Bobby Jones has held the retreat for nearly twenty years, and it has become one of the most successful gospel industry retreats ever.

To contact the International Gospel Industry Retreat:

International Gospel Industry Retreat
5145 Roxborough Drive
Hermitage, TN 37076
Phone: (615) 232-2560
Fax: (615) 232-2561

Or

International Gospel Industry Retreat
10097 Cleary Blvd., Suite 284
Plantation, FL 33324
Phone: (945) 494-7596
Fax: (954) 382-1126
E-mail: info@gospelindustryretreat.com
Website: www.gospelindustryretreat.com

THE GOSPEL MUSIC WORKSHOP CONVENTION

The Gospel Music Workshop of America was founded by Reverend James Cleveland in 1967.[36] The GMWA started as a small circle of gifted writers, singers, and instrumentalists in that Rev. Cleveland gathered together in Philadelphia with the hopes of nurturing young talent and developing gospel music, to which he had devoted himself and his life. Today, the GMWA continues Rev. Cleveland's mission and thrives with more than 185 chapters in the United States, Europe, the Caribbean, and Asia. The first GMWA convention was held in Detroit in 1968 at the King Solomon Baptist Church, where three thousand delegates attended. Each convention is held on the second Sunday in August annually and attracts nearly fifteen thousand registrants. Thousands of local gospel lovers also wander to the convention to attend workshops and musical services during the week.

To contact the GWMA:
GMWA, Inc
3908 West Warren
Detroit, MI 48208
Phone: (313) 898-6900
E-mail: manager@gmwanational.org
Website: www.gmwanational.org

---

[36] www.gmwanational.org/about.htm

SHIRLEY CAESAR OUTREACH MINISTRY

Each year, Shirley Caesar sponsors the Outreach Ministry Conference, which provides an opportunity to gospel artists to perform and for artists and industry professionals alike to participate in workshops, services, and seminars. The recent Thirty-Fourth Annual Conference featured Evangelist Kimberly Ray, Bishop George Bloomer, Apostle Richard D. Henton, A7, and Tye Tribett. Carolyn Sanders, top administrator and manager for Dr. Caesar, explained that the conference is a good event for those seeking to learn more about the gospel industry.

To contact Shirley Caesar Outreach Ministry:

Shirley Caesar Outreach Ministry
P.O. Box 3336
Durham, NC 27702
Phone: (919) 683-1161
Website: www.shirleycaesar.com

Or

Mount Calvary Word of Faith
3100 Sanderford Road
Raleigh, NC 27601

URBAN IMPACT SUMMIT

The Urban IMPACT Summit was created in 2005 by our legal team. Our mission at the Urban IMPACT Summit is to "Educate, Embrace, Empower." The Urban IMPACT Summit takes place at the Foxwoods Resort in Mashantucket, Connecticut, and other East Coast sites and is one of the largest gospel conferences in the Northeast. The Urban IMPACT Summit offers many panel discussions on topics ranging from artist development, church and ministry, and African American political issues to financial planning advice. Some of the speakers that have attended the panel discussions include Kurtis Blow, Afrika Bambaataa, and Armstrong Williams. The summit also offers a New Artist Showcase with Dr. Bobby Jones, in which gospel artists from all over the country come and perform with Dr. Bobby Jones, the shows later aired on the Word Network. Gospel and hip-hop artists have also been invited to perform live at the summit at the Club BB King at Foxwoods. The summit also features a concert each evening featuring performances from artists like Shirley Caesar and Dottie Peoples. In 2006, the Urban IMPACT Summit also featured the We Got Nex Teen Summit, sponsored by the Urban IMPACT Summit and Feel So Good Entertainment. The We Got Nex Teen Summit "provides a platform for change starting with the youth being the leader and catalyst for change."[37] The We Got Nex Teen Summit identifies with the youth and engages, inspires, and empowers them to "take positive action with their lives."

---

[37] www.urbanimpactsummit.com/wegotnex3/about.htm

To contact the Urban IMPACT Summit:
Urban IMPACT Summit
JW Consulting, LLC
251 Long Ridge Road
Stamford, CT 06902
Phone: (203) 588-1843
Website: www.urbanimpactsummit.com

ORGANIZATIONS AND AWARDS SHOWS

THE NATIONAL ACADEMY OF RECORDING ARTS AND SCIENCES, INC.

The National Academy of Recording Arts and Sciences (NARAS) was founded in 1957 when the Hollywood Beautification Committee asked five of the top record executives in LA to recommend music artists that deserved stars on Hollywood Boulevard.[38] Paul Weston of Columbia Records, Lloyd Dunn of Capitol Records, Sonny Burke of Decca Records, Jesse Kaye of MGM Records, and Dennis Farnon of RCA Victor Records looked at the request as an opportunity to put together an association of professionals in the recording industry that would "reward artistic creativity, foster better relationships among members of the industry, and obtain world recognition." NARAS was born at the Brown Derby restaurant in that same year. Since 1959, NARAS has sponsored the Grammy Awards annually. Neil Portnow is the current president, and has made the organization one of the most credible music industry associations dedicated to helping artists and uplifting the music industry as a whole. The Grammys are the only peer-presented awards ceremony that rewards artistic achievement, technical proficiency, and overall excellence in the recording industry with no regard for album sales or chart positioning.

NARAS established the Grammy Foundation in 1989 with a mission to cultivate an awareness, appreciation, and advancement of recorded music of the past and the future. The Grammy Foundation works with NARAS to bring national attention to important issues such as the value and impact of music and arts education and the urgency of preserving our rich cultural legacy.

Anyone wishing to support the Grammys, even if they are not a member of the recording industry, can join NARAS at their website: www.grammy.com/Recording_Academy/Member_Services/.

To Contact NARAS or the Grammy Foundation:
The Recording Academy
3402 Pico Blvd.
Santa Monica, CA 90405
Phone: (310) 392-3777
Fax: (310) 399-3090

---

[38] www.grammy.com/Recording_Academy/History/

The Grammy Foundation
3402 Pico Blvd.
Santa Monica, CA 90405
Phone: (310) 392-3777
Fax: (310) 392-2188
Phone (Toll Free): 1-877-GRAMMY-ED
E-mail: grammyfoundation@grammy.com
Website: www.grammy.com

STELLAR AWARDS GOSPEL MUSIC ACADEMY

Every year, the Stellar Awards Gospel Music Academy puts on the Stellar Gospel Music Awards. The first Stellar Awards show was in 1984 at the Arie Crown Theater in Chicago. The Stellar Awards are sponsored and produced by Central City Productions Inc. in Chicago and its producers Don Jackson and Barbara Wilson. Since its inception, the Stellar Awards has become the premier gospel awards show to recognize gospel artists. SAGMA, the Stellar Awards Gospel Music Academy, was created in 2000. SAGMA is a voting body of industry professionals. You can become an associate member of SAGMA and apply online at the Stellar Awards website (see the address below). Vickie Winans, Israel Houghton, and Donnie McClurkin hosted the 2006 ceremony, and Mary Mary, BeBe Winans, Kurt Carr, and Dr. Charles Hayes & the Warriors were amongst the 2006 nominees.

To contact the Stellar Awards:
Central City Production
212 E. Ohio
Suite 300
Chicago, IL 60611
Website: www.thestellarawards.com

BLACK ENTERTAINMENT AND SPORTS LAWYERS ASSOCIATION

The Black Entertainment Lawyers Association (BELA) was formed in 1980. However, in 1986, the association was renamed to reflect opportunities in the sports industry to its current name: the Black Entertainment and Sports Lawyers Association (BESLA). The goal of BESLA is to support a more diversified, expert, and informed group of entertainment and sports industry professionals. To achieve this goal, BESLA provides networking opportunities for lawyers and industry professionals as well as resources for identifying talented professional individuals. BESLA also provides Mandatory Continuing Legal Education (MCLE) accredited programs for members. BESLA even offers scholarships for law students aspiring to become entertainment and sports attorneys.

At the First Annual Black Music Association Conference in Philadelphia, a group of distinguished African American attorneys got together to discuss the future of African American attorneys in the entertainment industry. They determined that there was and continues to be a need to establish a learning and networking environment for African American attorneys in the entertainment industry: Together, they devised BESLA, an organization that provides attorneys "an opportunity to share and exchange information, refer business, learn of industry opportunities, sharpen their skills, and support each other in the highly competitive field of entertainment."[39] Today, there are over six hundred members of BESLA.

BESLA sponsors the Annual BESLA Conference, at which members of BESLA come together to network and participate in some of many offerings the conference provides for continuing education. The 2006 Annual BESLA Conference focused on the changing entertainment marketplace (entitled Content & Commerce: Creative Solutions for a Digital Marketplace), and Antonio L. A. Reid of Def Jam, recipient of the BESLA Lifetime Achievement Award, was one of the featured speakers.

To contact BESLA:
Black Entertainment and Sports Lawyers Association, Inc.
P.O. Box 441485
Fort Washington, MD 20749-1485
Phone: (301) 248-1818
E-mail: beslamailbox@aol.com
Website: www.besla.org

HIP-HOP AND R&B ORGANIZATIONS AND CONFERENCES

VIBE MAGAZINE'S MUSICFEST AND MUSIC AWARDS

VIBE is the leading urban music and lifestyle magazine. It's only natural that they would take their passion for urban music off the printed page and bring it directly to the people. In 2005, *VIBE* presented MusicFest, which featured performances from artists like Kanye West, Ludacris, 112, Lauryn Hill, and Sean "P. Diddy" Combs as the master of ceremonies.[40] MusicFest also featured an Expo, which included an urban fashion show, a video-game demonstration, live performances from MusicFest participants, and information from industry executives about getting in and staying afloat in the music biz.[41]

In 2005, *VIBE* also presented the Third Annual VIBE Awards on UPN.[42] Some of the nominees included 50 Cent, Destiny's Child, John Legend, and Mariah Carey, who walked away with four awards.

To contact *VIBE*:

---

[39] www.besla.org/history.aspx

[40] www.vibe.com/musicfest/index.htm

[41] www.vibe.com/musicfest/expo.htm

[42] www.vibe.com/awards2005/index.htm

VIBE
215 Lexington Avenue
New York, NY 10016
Phone: (212) 448-7300
Fax: (212) 448-7400
Website: www.vibe.com

BILLBOARD R&B HIP-HOP CONFERENCE

Billboard is a leader in music-industry publications and is the most trusted resource for chart ratings. Each year, *Billboard* sponsors many music industry conferences and events, including a dance-music conference, a Latin-music conference, and a summit on the increasing importance of ringtones to the music industry. The *Billboard* R&B Hip-Hop Conference provides an opportunity for members of the R&B and hip-hop industry to network, learn, and show off their talent. The conference features speakers, panels, workshops, an artist showcase, and an awards show.[43] The conference has hosted over seven hundred industry attendees, including agents, artists, managers, producers, press, and record executives. The conference's We Hear the Future Showcase and Competition provides new artists an opportunity to be heard by major record executives, but it does come with a steep entrance fee, i.e., upwards of five thousand dollars.[44] The 2006 awards show featured nominees including Jamie Foxx, Ludacris, Alicia Keys, Black Eyed Peas, and Mary J. Blige.

To contact the *Billboard* R&B Hip-Hop Conference:
General Information
Michele Jacangelo, director of conferences and special events
Phone: (646) 654-4660
E-mail: bbevents@billboard.com

Registrations & Group Discounts:
Erin Parker, events registration manager
Phone: (646) 654-4843
E-mail: eparker@billboard.com
Website: www.billboardevents.com/billboardevents/rb/2005/index.jsp

---

[43] www.billboardevents.com/billboardevents/rb/2005/index.jsp

[44] www.billboardevents.com/billboardevents/rb/2005/showcase.jsp

CHAPTER 28

A Few Closing Thoughts, Thank-Yous, and Shout-Outs!

"A lot of people are in love with the glamor [of the music business], but do you really love music . . . Do you study music, listen to music all day and all night, and eat, sleep, and breathe music? The people that win are usually the people that do . . ."

—LISA ELLIS, PRESIDENT, SONY URBAN MUSIC

"The music industry is a huge business now, where very young people make enormous amounts of money, and have to deal with an almost superhuman position and try to absorb that kind of adulation and recognition and fame, and adoration and money. It's a very abnormal situation, and they're trying to make it normal, 'cause it's not normal, so we have a lot of casualties as a result of that."

—MUSIC LEGEND QUINCY JONES

About two years ago, Kanye West told *Rolling Stone* magazine that one of his main goals early on as an artist was to have his album achieve gold- and platinum-level sales. But later, his desire was "to have songs that are respected across the board, to have some sort of influence on the culture, and to change the sound of music and to inspire up-and-coming artists to go against the grain." Indeed, with his 2007 *Graduation* album release selling over a million copies in just days, it is clear West has made his mark across all color lines and has influenced a nation of music lovers. And, of course, West is known to stand true to his principles, despite any backlash from the critics or public.

In writing this book, my hope was to create a book that was respected across music genres of urban music, including hip-hop, gospel, and R&B; and inform and also change the everyday thinking of thousands of artists and songwriters who knock down the doors of this *business of urban music* hoping to gain fame, glory, and wealth with little regard for the business. As stated so eloquently in the above contrasting quotes of Sony's Lisa Ellis and Quincy Jones from recent interviews, the hype surrounding the music industry—with its seductive traits of power, wealth, and fame—has made it one that is almost surreal. Many brothers and sisters are therefore making a deal with the devil to sing gospel music, selling their soul to break into R&B, and lacing their lyrics with misogyny and self-hate to *keep in real* in selling hip-hop. But, in the end, we will all be casualties if we do not understand the history of *urban music, black music, R&B*, or whatever you call it at the time, and comprehend the business implications of the documents we sign when passing through today's gatekeepers: labels, production companies, and publishers. We have this multibillion-dollar industry created on the backs of the likes of Jean

Riggins, LeBaron Taylor, Denise Brown, Kevin Evans, Lionel Ridenhour, Brian Jackson, Ron Sweeney, Hiriam Hicks, Andre Harrell, Al Hobbs, Sharon Heyward, Mona Scott, and Jackie Rhinehart, to name just a few, who created the fame, wealth, and adulation swirling around your 50 Cents, Ashantis, Brandys, Kanyes, Ciaras, Chris Browns, and Beyoncés.

Remember, just fifty years ago, white-owned labels were putting out black music with white artists on the cover. Then, in the 1960s, the Motown era brought us Diana Ross & the Supremes on the *Ed Sullivan Show*. Thereafter, black music or *urban music* was here to stay. The question is: Will we, this generation, maintain the dignity, integrity, character, grace, and social consciousness that initial pioneers like Sammy Davis, Jr., Aretha Franklin, Marvin Gaye, James Brown, Al Green, James Cleveland, and Minnie Ripperton possessed? Will this generation make sure we have more than ten artists making *real* money in hip-hop and more than five *gospel superstars*? And, will we realize *urban* music must find a true appreciation for our R&B icons such as Freddie Jackson, Chaka Khan, Patti Labelle, Roberta Flack, and Peabo Bryson? Understanding the *business* of urban music and the industry as a whole can only help empower more artists, producers, songwriters, engineers, executives, and labels in the music industry and our communities as a whole.

And, indeed, I know there are some who would have wanted me to write a more legal, dry, and boring book filled with hundreds of cases, citations, case notes, and law-journal articles. However, for this first step, I wanted to make sure we covered the basics first, recognized the pioneers, and identified the business principles that must guide one if they are entering the music industry.

Lastly, as I stated over 200 pages ago, the examples I used are merely examples, and do not in anyway overlook the fact that we have dozens of brilliant artists, executives, and musicians in the urban industry, who due to space limitations were not included in this first edition.

But I cannot overlook the thank you's due to so many students, staff members, and friends who helped me in the past five to six years as we pulled together the title, the chapter outlines, and the research. Of course, my wife, Cristi, and our four children, Jordan, Joi, James, and Zion, must be mentioned in the opening thank-you shout-outs as they sacrificed the long weekends and nights while Dad pulled out the laptop and wrote a fourth, fifth, and sixth revision of the book. Secondly, I want to thank my parents, Delores and James Sr., as well as my godparents, Gail and Mac, who have always pushed me to soar. Lastly, I must mention my staff and assistants: Rachel, Dana, Lori, Deborah, Erika, Christina, Brice, Terrence, Chanelle, Kathy, Vanessa, Lauren, Jennifer, and Duke, among many others; and of course, my longtime business partner, Richard Byrd, who forced me to take that horrible photo that adorns the jacket of this book. And, at Billboard Books, I want to thank Victoria, Nicole, Brian, and of course, my editors, Ross Plotkin and Bob Nirkind—who pushed me harder than a lonely law professor. And, to Bill Krasilovsky, a mentor and friend of fifteen years, I thank you for your initial guidance and suggestions. Similar to Bill is my dear law professor, Mr. Spencer Boyer, who told me one day I could have the privilege of a career in the music business as an attorney.

And, to my legal brethren (and sisters), Matt Middleton, Ward White, Ed Woods, Charles King, Reggie Osse, James McMillian, Darrell Miller, Adrienne Howard, Sean Johnson, Paul Butler, Heather Cunningham, Garrett Johnson, Londell McMillian, and the BESLA brothers and sisters, please continue to do what you do in holding down the urban-music industry until the next set of movers and shakers come through and take the baton and run with it. I am proud of all of you!

Remember, as I often say to each of you, we're all branches on a big tree. Some of our branches get a little more visibility because we have well-known clients or law practices that are a little more high-profile and that gain a little more notoriety. However, our branches are still merely a limbs on the tree; and without our roots and pioneers—like Leroy Bobbitt, Virgil Roberts, Amy Goldson, C. Lamont Smith, Louise West, Gregory Reed, Michael Ashburne, Bill Strickland, Dwight Ellis, Denis Kellman, Kendall Minter, Fred Brown, and Fletcher "Flash" Wiley, to name just a few—the tree would tumble to the ground and the branches would all fall to the wayside.

I shared most of what I could, given deadlines and space limitations in the chapters of this book; but I am sure each of you have that and much more to share, and would encourage you to do so. Just whatever you do, please don't divide and conquer—there are so many deals to do together and everyone can win, even if you're not best friends at the end of the day. Please figure out a way to empower more artists and yourself in the process. There is enough work in the urban industry for all of us to do well, if we support each other, share the knowledge, and put our clients before ourselves.

Okay, before this turns into soapbox opera, let's get back to the purpose of our book. Throughout the first twenty-seven chapters, we talked extensively about the music business and the cash that flows through the various entities. As a closing reminder, I have included a chart that will give many of you who are unfamiliar with the industry a visual understanding of how the industry works when you sign a deal with a record label and/or its sister companies, and the potential for multiple levels of debt to the various entities.

Until urban music artists understand the business, the digital age, and step out on faith in this age of internet distribution, they will never reap the full business benefit and revenue associated with the millions of records sold each year by urban artists.

Take a look at the next page, and remember, do not let yourself become one of the casualties caused by lack of knowledge in this thing we call this *business of urban music*.

Cash Flow Trail

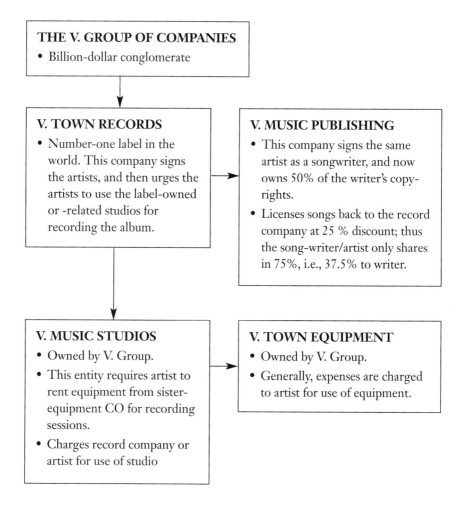

THE V. GROUP OF COMPANIES
- Billion-dollar conglomerate

V. TOWN RECORDS
- Number-one label in the world. This company signs the artists, and then urges the artists to use the label-owned or -related studios for recording the album.

V. MUSIC PUBLISHING
- This company signs the same artist as a songwriter, and now owns 50% of the writer's copyrights.
- Licenses songs back to the record company at 25 % discount; thus the song-writer/artist only shares in 75%, i.e., 37.5% to writer.

V. MUSIC STUDIOS
- Owned by V. Group.
- This entity requires artist to rent equipment from sister-equipment CO for recording sessions.
- Charges record company or artist for use of studio

V. TOWN EQUIPMENT
- Owned by V. Group.
- Generally, expenses are charged to artist for use of equipment.

In the illustration above, for example purposes only, an artist like Fred Hammond would hypothetically sign with V. Town Records first. He would then sign his publishing company with sister-company V. Music Publishing; and V. Music Publishing would share in his income as a songwriter. When it came time to record the album, Hammond might be asked to use V. Music Studios in NYC owned by V. Town Records, and rent or use equipment from V. Town Equipment to finish the album in the studio. At the end of the day, the V. Group keeps all of the money flowing throughout its circle of companies, whether the artist is gospel or R&B or hip-hop; and the artist ends up paying for everything. And, in many cases, unless prevented, the V. Group will cross-collateralize or dip into any pot of money to pay off the artist debt from his recording. So if album is released and does not sell well, V. Town Records will look to recoup its debt from the income collected from the songs before paying the artist/songwriter.

And *that* is *This Business of Urban Music*! See ya next time.

Valuable Resources

The Music Publishers Association is a great place for experienced and novice publishers to share ideas and expertise. Founded in 1895, the MPA is the oldest music trade organization in the United States. It prides itself on fostering communication among publishers, dealers, music educators, and all ultimate users of music (see www.mpa.org).

The MPA is nonprofit and should be of interest to publishers in every genre of music, but especially those who use and publish print music—gospel publishers, this means you! The MPA serves the industry through its cooperation with other organizations, such as the American Choral Directors Association, the American Music Center, the American Music Conference, the American Symphony Orchestra League, the Church Music Publishers Association, the International Confederation of Music Publishers, the International Federation of Serious Music Publishers, the Music Library Association, the Major Orchestra Librarians Association, the National Association for Music Education, the National Orchestra Association, the Music Teachers National Association, and the Retail Print Music Dealers Association.

Music Publishers Association members meet once a month throughout the year in New York and address the music industry's important issues. They support and advance compliance with the copyright law and work to combat copyright infringement and to protect intellectual property. The members of the association are also kept informed of the new laws, decisions, and regulations affecting the music industry.

These are some publishing companies that either specialize in, or have large departments for, urban and hip-hop music.

Almo/Irving Music
360 North La Cienega Blvd.
Los Angeles, CA 90048
(310) 289-3500

BMG Music
8750 Wilshire Blvd.
Beverly Hills, CA 90211
(310) 358-4700

1540 Broadway, 39th Floor
New York, NY 10036
(212) 930-4000

Cherry Lane
6 East 32nd St., 11th Floor
New York, NY 10016
(212) 561-3000

5757 Wilshire Blvd., Suite 401
Los Angeles, CA 90036
(323) 904-4510

Chrysalis Music
8500 Melrose Ave, Suite 207
Los Angeles, CA 90069
(310) 652-0066

1204 16th Ave. South
Nashville, TN 37212
(615) 327-4797

DreamWorks Music
331 North Maple Dr., Suite 300
Beverly Hills, CA 90210
(310) 288-7722

EMI Music
2700 Colorado Ave., Suite 100
Santa Monica, CA 90404
(310) 828-1087

1290 Sixth Ave., 42nd Floor
New York, NY 10104
(212) 830-2000

Famous Music
10635 Santa Monica Blvd.
Los Angeles, CA 90025
(310) 441-1300

1633 Broadway, 11th Floor
New York, NY 10019
(212) 654-7418

Hitco Music
500 Bishop St. NW, Suite A-5
Atlanta, GA 30318
(404) 352-5911

Peer Music
810 Seventh Ave., 10th Floor
New York, NY 10019
(212) 265-3910

Key Publishing Terminology

If you are going to be a publisher, you need to be hip to the lingo of the music industry. Below are some commonly used terms. Get to know these and you won't be caught off guard at your next meeting. Please note that this is in no way an exhaustive list of all of the music industry terms, but it should be helpful to you in understanding the publishing world.

Administration: The supervising of the music publisher's financial and copyright matters regarding one or more songs or an entire catalog. The administrator does not necessarily own a share of the copyright and usually gets paid a percentage of the royalties.

Advance: The usually non-refundable payment in advance of royalties to be earned in the future. This is a number that is calculated by the earning potential of the person who receives the advance.

A&R (artists and repertoire): The department in a record company that selects and deals with new artists, songs and records.

Assignment of copyright: The transfer of ownership of a copyright from one party to another, which must be in writing to be effective. Songwriters will assign their copyright to you, as their publisher.

Audio Visual Index (AVI): A database containing title and production information for cue sheets, which are available from a performing rights organization.

Audiovisual work: Film, television, music video, or any other visual production.

Audit clause: A critical clause in an agreement between a songwriter and a publisher that allows the songwriter the right to have access to the publisher's books and records so that the songwriter can determine the validity of the publisher's accounting practices

Author: Composer, lyricist, record producer, choreographer, artist, photographer, writer, or anyone else who creates intellectual property.

Blanket license: For an annual fee, radio and television stations, public broadcasters, restaurants, and others can acquire a "blanket license" from a performing rights organization. This license gives them the right to perform every piece of music contained in the respective repertoire as often as they wish during the term of the license. The royalties are then split between the writers whose music was performed.

Bootlegging: Also known as pirating, it is the unauthorized recording and selling of a song.

Catalog: The collection of songs owned by a publisher or a songwriter.

Composers: People who create music compositions.

Controlled composition: A composition written or co-written by the recording artist under an exclusive recording agreement. Typically, the recording company will pay 75 percent of the minimum statutory rate on only ten to twelve cuts per CD and two cuts per single, regardless of the actual number of sides or length of the compositions.

Copyright royalty judges: A panel of three judges that are employees of the Library of Congress that determine rates and terms for copyright statutory licenses and make determinations on distribution of statutory license royalties collected by the Copyright Office.

Derivative work: A work derived from another work, such as a translation or alternate version.

Direct license: A license obtained by a music user directly from the copyright owner allowing the user to publicly perform the licensed work.

Exclusive rights: The right of a copyright owner to exclusively authorize recording, performance, dramatization, or other uses of his works.

Exclusive songwriter agreement: A contract between a publisher and a songwriter in which the songwriter assigns all songs written during the term of the contract to the publisher in return for a percentage of royalty income and advances paid by the publisher to the songwriter.

Favored nations clause: A general term commonly used in the entertainment industry to protect one's established salary or royalty rate and to assure no one gets paid more than another participant on a deal, i.e., an album with various writers or producers or a compilation album featuring several artists. You want assurance that your client is paid the exact same as everyone else, but never lesser.

Feature work: A performance that constitutes the main focus of audience attention at the time of the performance on television. It is also the sole sound broadcast at the time of the performance on the radio.

Infringement: A violation of the exclusive rights granted by the copyright law to a copyright owner.

Jukebox licensing office: A Nashville-based organization representing ASCAP, BMI, and SESAC in the licensing of coin-operated phonorecord players (jukeboxes).

Lead sheet: A handwritten version on paper of a newly written song.

Logs: Schedules prepared by radio and television stations for performance rights and uses as a basis for payment to writers and publishers.

Master: A completed recording of a song from which multiple copies are manufactured.

Nonexclusive rights: Songwriters and publishers have the right to license their music directly to music users; therefore, performance rights organizations do not have exclusive rights.

Per-program license: A license that bases its fee on revenues from only those programs using music licensed by that organization. It is used instead of a blanket license.

Phonorecord: A term used in the Copyright Act to describe the material object in which sounds, other than those on a soundtrack of an audiovisual work, are fixed and from which they can be reproduced. This includes CDs, cassettes, and LPs.

Piracy: See *Bootlegging*

Print music: Written music that comes in five varieties: sheet music, folio, arrangements for a particular musical instrument, concert edition, and method book.

Print rights: The exclusive right to print sheet music, folios, band parts, and instrumental arrangements.

Publication: Offering to distribute phonorecords to a group of persons for purposes of further distribution, public performance, or public display constitutes publication. This does not include public performance of a song.

Public domain: Work that has no copyright protection and because of this belongs to everyone. When a work is in the public domain it means it is available for unrestricted use by anyone. Permission and payment are not required for use.

Recapture of rights: The right granted to an author and some of his successors, under certain conditions and certain limitations, to recapture rights to a copyright previously granted to a publisher or other grantee.

Sampling: When sound bites are removed from a master recording and placed within the context of another composition. Unauthorized sampling could be held to be a copyright infringement.

Songwriters: People who write the lyrics and/or music to songs.

Split publishing: When the publishing rights in a song are held by more than one publisher. Each of the several publishers is called a co-publisher.

Statutory damages: Monetary damages obtainable by a copyright owner of a work for its infringement. If actual damages and profits attributable to the infringement would be greater than statutory damages, the copyright owner can choose to seek those instead.

Video buyout: An agreement by which the user agrees to pay the licensor a flat fee for the use of a song, with no increase based on sales of videocassettes/discs.

Video rollover: An agreement by which the user agrees to pay the licensor a continuing fee; every time a specific sales point has been reached, the fee is paid again.